Improving
Human Resource
Effectiveness

Improving Human Resource Effectiveness

An Annotated Bibliography of Behavioral Science Contributions

L. L. Cummings

J. L. Kellogg Distinguished Professor of Organizational Behavior
Kellogg Graduate School of Management
Northwestern University

Foundation
Berea, Ohio 44017

CONTENTS

PREFACE

The purpose of this book is to present a review, an abstraction, and an analysis of the literature of human resource effectiveness utilizing a behavioral approach to the definition and/or solution of selected problems in managing the human resources of an organization.

The review is not intended to be exhaustive of all literature in organizational behavior of relevance to human resource management. Rather, the review is selective in three respects. First, it focuses on those studies and accounts of experience that utilize a behavioral paradigm in presenting descriptions of research and drawing prescriptions for practice. The term "behavioral paradigm" is defined broadly to allow inclusion of any study or prescription utilizing an analysis of the antecedents and consequences of a behavior or attitude within a functional perspective. The basic framework is defined as including several *independent variables* (antecedents or causes of an outcome) and several *dependent variables* (results produced by the independent variables; effects or consequences resulting from changes in the independent variables). The specific independent variables included were selected by two criteria: a) sufficient literature was available to assure a meaningful review and analysis, and b) the variables needed to be susceptible to managerial action or change in most organizational environments. The dependent variables were selected to reflect major categories of managerial and organizational human resource symptoms, problems, and opportunities for improved performance and productivity.

The second factor limiting the focus of the book was the author's attempt to include studies reporting data and offering prescriptions of relevance to normal, noninstitutionalized, adult human populations. Thus, no attempt is made to exhaust all the materials dealing with the mentally ill or with subhuman samples.

Thirdly, only those studies thought to be illustrative of the typical research design, the typical implementation procedure or the modal prescriptive assertions are included. In other words, the review is illustrative, hopefully representative, but certainly not exhaustive.

A listing of the sources reviewed is presented in the Glossary on page 332. The review encompassed the period from 1946 through the first quarter of 1980. The vast majority of the sources are post-1960, however. Only historically significant atricles prior to 1960 are referenced.

A number of persons and organizations have been instrumental in achieving this project. Each deserves important credit and my sincere gratitude. One institution and one person stand out. The Foundation of the American Society for Personnel Administration provided the initial funding for the project through a research grant. Mrs. Ruth Dresen provided important editorial, organizing, and secretarial competence throughout the project. Beyond these two, a number of institutions and persons contributed to the project. I wish to thank the following: The Research Fund of the School of Business, University of Wisconsin-Madison; The Graduate School Research Committee, University of Wisconsin-Madison; Dr. Chris Berger; Dr. Robert Mathis, Ms. Jane Nordling, Mr. Peter Sherer, Mr. Dan Sprague, Dr. M. Susan Taylor, and Mr. Theodore Weinberger.

The American Society for Personnel Administration (ASPA) has provided encouragement for this project since its inception. Several individuals associated with ASPA have been particularly helpful. I wish to thank Catherine Bower, Fred Crandell, Clyde Benedict, Bob Berra, Virgil Hanson and Len Brice.

INTRODUCTION

IMPROVING HUMAN RESOURCE EFFECTIVENESS

In researching the literature on behavioral contributions to management, each source was classified according to a scheme of independent variables, dependent variables, or overview articles as follows:

Independent Variables	*Dependent Variables*
Feedback	Absenteeism
Goals	Drug Use and Alcoholism
Interaction	Performance Quality
Money	Safety
Praise	Satisfaction
Productivity:	Turnover
Concepts and Measurement	*Overview Articles*
Punishment	
Schedules and Expectancy	
Task Design	
Time Off Work	
Work Schedules	

Independent variables are those factors which can be brought under managerial control and which are thought to have an impact upon one or more dependent variables. These variables are frequently described as the causes of organizational performance, employee behavior, and employee satisfaction. The key assumption for the purposes of this book is that these variables can be brought under the intentional, systematic human control. Ultimately, of course, this is a question of fact. One of the purposes of this work is to assess the degree to which systematic changes have been attempted in these independent variables and to discover what results have been produced through such changes.

The results produced when independent variables are systematically changed are referred to as *dependent* variables. Their variations and fluctuations are assumed to be dependent upon variations in the independent variables. They are frequently described as the effects produced by the independent variables. From organizational and employee perspectives, these dependent variables represent the outcomes desired, the results to be achieved, and frequently the focus of problems.

The references abstracted and reviewed in the following pages include three different approaches:

1. Some define an independent variable using a general behavioral orientation,

2. Most relate variations in one or more independent variables to one or more dependent variables, and

3. Several review the evidence on the causes of variations in one or more dependent variables and offer suggestions for integration of current knowledge.

Each source was classified according to type of article as indicated below:

Applied	*Integrative*
Descriptive	*Prescriptive*
Empirical	*Theoretical*

These themes are intended to guide the reader toward those types of articles that will maximize the efficiency and effectiveness of his/her search. Each article has been categorized into one or more themes. Where multiple themes have been assigned, duplicate abstracts are presented to aid the use of the material.

Each theme is defined as follows:

Applied

Articles classified as applied report on *actual application* of an independent variable or the solution of a problem centering on one of the dependent variables in *real, naturally occurring situations*. The article frequently reports sufficient detail to replicate the application. However, fewer of the application articles will report sophisticated implementation methodologies or evaluation designs.

Descriptive

Articles classified as descriptive report the *results achieved* by an application without detail concerning the nature of the application and the processes through which it was implemented. The article's purpose is not to advocate a position or technique but to present a balanced description of the results achieved.

Empirical

Articles classified as empirical serve the primary purpose of *reporting original data* from a research investigation. Their purpose is to add to our store of fundamental knowledge by providing new evidence. Only as a secondary theme do they report the implementation and results of an application.

Integrative

Articles classified as integrative serve to *review and synthesize* the literature on one or more of the independent or dependent variables. They may also offer, as a *secondary purpose*, suggestions for advancing the literature via research or theory and for applying the findings reviewed.

Prescriptive

Articles classified as prescriptive advocate a *specific position or technique*. Their main focus is on "selling" or arguing for this technique as a solution to an important management problem. Some articles so classified will also offer data and theory to support their prescriptions.

Theoretical

Articles classified as theoretical develop a *systematic propositional framework* for analysis of a topic. Some of these articles also will present empirical findings in support of the theory posited. Some also will suggest possible applied implementations of the theory.

A matrix of the abstracted articles is presented by focus and type beginning on page 324 in the Summary Section. This allows for a composite, visual review of the material researched.

An abstracted bibliography followed by a commentary is presented for each variable. Finally, an overview or summary is presented to assess the state of our present knowledge and research in the area of behavioral management and the implications that management can draw to enhance organizational effectiveness through a behavioral policy.

Independent Variables

Independent Variable

FEEDBACK

Type of Article	No. of Articles
Applied	10
Descriptive	11
Empirical	34
Integrative	4
Prescriptive	20
Theoretical	1

APPLIED

Migliore, R. H., "Improving Worker Productivity Through Communicating Knowledge of Work Results," *Management of Personnel Quarterly*, Summer 1970, Vol. 9, No. 2, 26–32.

Two experimental studies were conducted using knowledge of results as a technique for improving employee productivity in a unionized production department of a mass production manufacturing plant. Study 1 was made in the Press Department on the third shift during a two-year period. The study was divided into three stages: control (no K-O-R in effect), preliminary (K-O-R introduced), and full-scale implementation (sophisticated K-O-R methods in effect). Five methods were used for presenting knowledge of results: 1) department efficiency was daily charted on a graph for all to see, 2) a form posted on the bulletin board informing workers about actual production and efficiency compared to the standard for each production line, 3) informal contact with individuals by the supervisors, 4) formal meetings were held with the trainees in skilled labor, and 5) performance statistics were discussed in monthly meetings.

Results: Significant production improvement was seen after the introduction of K-O-R. All quantitative measures improved.

Study II was conducted in the same plant but in a different department and only one means of presenting K-O-R was used. K-O-R was given the workers by means of posting a revised copy of the daily production report on the bulletin board.

Results: Although the study did not provide evidence of a high degree of improvement in performance, the results were in the hypothesized direction. The significant difference in the results of the two studies indicates that the daily form posted on the bulletin board is important but it must be backed up with other methods of presenting K-O-R to be most effective.

Dodd, William E. and Pesei, Michael L., "Managing Morale Through Survey Feedback," *Business Horizons,* June 1977, Vol. 20, No. 3, 36–45.

The authors contend that opinion survey feedback can be used by trained supervisors for improving employee morale. Application of behavioral modification (interaction modeling) techniques to supervisory training is advocated to teach supervisors to respond more effectively to employee concerns during opinion survey feedback meetings. The procedure for interaction modeling involves the following: a model demonstrating the specific behavior to be learned, an opportunity to practice the behavior, reinforcement from instructor or peers for the behavior, and an opportunity to transfer the behavior to the actual situation. Managers who are trained in specific feedback skill through interaction modeling techniques in a defined morale improvement system tend to be more successful at this enterprise than colleagues left to their own resources.

Seligman, Clive and Darley, John M., "Feedback as a Means of Decreasing Residential Energy Consumption," *Journal of Applied Psychology,* August 1977, Vol. 62, No. 4, 363–368.

The present study tested the hypothesis that providing immediate feedback to homeowners concerning their daily use of electricity would be effective in reducing electric consumption. In the 29 physically identical three-bedroom homes used in the study, central air conditioning is the largest single source of electricity usage during the summer. Accordingly, it was possible to predict the household's expected electric consumption in terms of the average daily outdoor temperature. Feedback was expressed as a percentage of actual consumption over predicted consumption, and it was displayed to the homeowners four times a week for approximately one month. The results confirmed the hypothesis. Before feedback began, the feedback and control groups were consuming electricity at approximately equal rates. During the feedback period, the feedback group used 10.5 percent less electricity. The effectiveness of the feedback procedure is discussed in terms of its cuing, motivational, and commitment functions.

Kirby, Peter G., "Productivity Increases Through Feedback Systems," *Personnel Journal,* October 1977, Vol. 56, No. 10, 512–515.

The author presents a practical approach for improving worker productivity in organizations by establishing feedback systems. The feedback system described is one where information regarding the results generated by employees is related back to them. This information was used by employees to compare their performance with that of a measurable standard. A case history involving a manufacturing plant demonstrates the efficacy of the feedback system. Management established goals for each operating unit which were then made known to employees by use of chalkboards in the production area. At the end of each shift, the quantity produced was posted next to the goal. This approach resulted in productivity increases, more employee suggestions to improve productivity, and fewer grievances.

The author further prescribes a four-step model for establishing a feedback system. The steps include: specifying the behavior where improvement is desired, recording the actual performance, providing positive reinforcement when desired performance occurs, and the evaluation of process.

Andrasik, Frank; McNamara, J. Regis and Abbott, David M., "Policy Control: A Low Resource Intervention for Improving Staff Behavior," *Journal of Organizational Behavior Management*, 1978, Vol. 1, 125–133.

This investigation, centering on staff employed in a forensic psychiatry setting, was initiated in an attempt to increase staff adherence to an important program function. During a baseline period, it was discovered that staff compliance with the program function was only 4.2 percent. Minimal revision of administrative policy increased staff compliance to 80.5 percent. The effects of this revision, which involved no additional consequation other than information feedback, were attributed to cuing, shaping, and feedback functions. Additional results and implications of these findings were discussed.

Emmert, Gerald D., "Measuring the Impact of Group Performance Feedback Versus Individual Performance Feedback in an Industrial Setting," *Journal of Organizational Behavior Management*, 1978, Vol. 1, 134–141.

This study represents efforts of first-line supervisors to affect a performance increase within a manufacturing area of a production facility. Effects of group feedback versus individual feedback were measured on four separate crews totaling 32 hourly employees. Feedback was provided graphically on the basis of a daily crew average during the first intervention. Individual feedback graphs were used during the second intervention. The data shows a performance increase during group feedback, and a more dramatic increase during the use of individualized feedback. Several complications were identified which may interfere with the pure application of the principles of behavior management employed in many industrial settings.

Sulzer-Azaroff, Beth, "Behavioral Ecology and Accident Prevention," *Journal of Organizational Behavior Management,* 1978, Vol. 2, 11–44.

Many laboratory accidents could readily be avoided by carefully arranging the physical environment to reduce potential hazards. Effective, nonintrusive, economical, safety strategies are apt to be broadly utilized. The purpose of this study was to identify and analyze the ecological impact of a simple, nonintrusive, cost-efficient system to reduce hazards in a university laboratory research facility. The system involved periodic inspections by safety officers who provided written feedback about and suggestions for ameliorating hazards. The procedure was replicated across 30 laboratories. An initial building inspection indicated the presence of various mechanical, chemical, and electrical hazards. Hazardous conditions were defined and listed on an observation sheet containing a generic laboratory map. Observed hazards were noted and their locations indicated on the form. A conservative assessment system provided evidence of the reliability of observation. An across-subjects-multiple-baseline experimental design was used with laboratories assigned to either an early, middle, or late feedback condition. Results showed a marked improvement in safety conditions during the feedback phase, indicating that it was possible to produce a sharp reduction in hazardous conditions in a research laboratory facility by means of a simple, nonintrusive, economical feedback system. The ecological assessment indicated a general increase in safety-related activities by the members of the Institute.

Eldridge, L.; Lemasters, S. and Szypot, B., "A Performance Feedback Intervention to Reduce Waste: Performance Data and Participant Responses," *Journal of Organizational Behavior Management,* Summer 1978, 1, 4, 258–266.

A performance feedback system was designed to reduce waste for the target department in this company. Initially, performance feedback principles were explained to the supervisors, a goal was set and a feedback sheet was designed to calculate piece yield for each of the 23 employees in the department. The supervisors praised, both verbally and on notes, on the piece yield forms for improved performance. This was followed by a meeting every two weeks to talk about individual piece yield graphs. Once a month the supervisors' manager talked to the whole group about improvements in piece yield and finally the industrial engineer dropped by about three times per week to talk with each person in the group and to praise good piece yield performance. The goal was reached four weeks after reinforcement was introduced. Meeting the goal was worth $105,000 in reduced waste the first year. The increase in productivity helped make it possible to eliminate the second shift. To obtain the employees' subjective evaluations of the program, open-ended interviews were conducted. Results indicated an overall neutral to positive reaction to the system. Benefits derived from the system included increased productivity and clarification of the quality standards. The desired performance change was attained at minimal cost to the company by use of the feedback system and the process seemed to improve the quality of working life for the employees.

McNees, Patrick; Gilliam, Sharon W.; Schnelle, John F. and Risley, Todd, "Controlling Employee Theft Through Time and Product Identification," *Journal of Organizational Behavior Management*, Winter 1979, 2, 2, 113–119.

It is estimated that employee theft constitutes 75 percent of all retail theft or approximately $3.6 billion per year. While in most situations it is difficult to determine whether employees or customers are responsible for retail theft, in some cases customer theft is impossible, so employees are known to be responsible. The present study utilized a situation in which all theft could be attributed to employees to evaluate the effects of providing time and product specific theft feedback. In a snack bar where theft was occurring when the business was closed, the effect on employee theft was evaluated by placing signs by the time clock that described, for four types of merchandise, what, when and how much was stolen. After the signs were posted, the average rate of stealing for these four types of merchandise dropped from 13 items per five days to one item per five days, thus eliminating almost all employee theft. The theft rates remained low for as long as three weeks after the feedback was discontinued, implying that these procedures may have long-term effects. Public feedback thus appears to be an effective strategy in situations where employee theft is known to be a problem.

Ford, John E., "A Classification System for Feedback Procedures," *Journal of Organizational Behavior Management*, Summer 1980, 2, 2, 183–191.

This paper suggests a classification system for organizing feedback literature and identifies a number of dimensions along which feedback procedures may be analyzed. Data are presented as evidence of the utility of the classification system.

Nine mental retardation professionals participated in the six-month study. All had post-secondary education ranging from five to seven years, but all had similar responsibilities in performing management and quality control functions within organizational divisions of a large, residential facility for mentally retarded persons.

An examination of goal development within habilitation plans of individual facility residents had revealed weaknesses in goal statement writing and interrelationship goals. The vast majority failed to include appropriate conditions, observable and measurable behaviors, and/or appropriate criteria for accomplishment. The participants were trained in these areas and subsequently assigned to either a no feedback, monthly feedback or weekly feedback condition. Results support the performance maintenance characteristic of feedback. The delivery of both monthly and weekly feedback yielded high and stable performance levels, while the performance of individuals receiving no feedback was highly variable and gradually decreased over time. In terms of cost effectiveness, the average performance of individuals receiving weekly feedback was 2.3 percent higher than that of those receiving monthly feedback. However, the cost of the weekly feedback procedures was double that of the monthly feedback procedure.

DESCRIPTIVE

Brown, I. D., "An Asymmetrical Transfer Effect in Research on Knowledge of Performance," *Journal of Applied Psychology*, 1966, Vol. 50, No. 2, 118–120.

Gibbs and Brown (1955) reported that the motivational aspect of knowledge of results had a significant effect upon performance of a repetitive monotonous task, aside from its informative and rewarding aspects. In an experiment with 12 Ss, output on document copying was 25 percent higher when it was displayed on a digital counter than when the counter was covered. Chapanis (1964) duplicated the main features of the experiment by testing 16 Ss on the task of punching teletype tape and found there was no significant advantage in displaying output. The present note demonstrates that the discrepancy between these findings results from a difference between the experimental designs used. The two-way asymmetrical transfer effects produced by Gibbs and Brown's design, in which Group I had condition K then NK, Group II had NK then K, show that knowledge of results may have a significant effect only when the task has previously been performed without it. The importance of other variables for future investigation of this topic are also briefly discussed.

Thornton, G. C., "The Relationship Between Supervisory and Self-Appraisals of Executive Performance," *Personnel Psychology*, Winter 1968, Vol. 21, No. 4, 441–455.

This study investigates the relationship between supervisory perceptions and incumbent self-perceptions of the performance of executive personnel. Supervisory ratings and self ratings on 20 performance variables were obtained for the top executives of a large manufacturing corporation. A measure of promotability was used as the criterion and analysis of variance and correlation analyses were carried out to attain the objectives.

The major conclusions of the study were: 1) executives tended to rate themselves higher than they were rated by their supervisors, 2) disagreement in the relationship of the two sets of ratings was found in several areas, 3) executives who tended to overrate themselves were found to be the ones who were considered least promotable on the basis of a criterion measure of success in the organization.

Deci, E. L., "The Effects of Contingent and Noncontingent Rewards and Controls on Intrinsic Motivation," *Organizational Behavior and Human Performance*, 1972, Vol. 8, 217–229.

Theories of management and work motivation distinguish between two kinds of rewards—extrinsic and intrinsic. Extrinsic rewards are ones such as money and verbal reinforcement which are mediated outside of the person, whereas intrinsic rewards are mediated within the person. We say a person is intrinsically motivated to perform an activity if there is no apparent reward except the activity itself or the feelings which result from the activity. All of the theories of work motivation which consider both kinds of rewards assume that the effects of the two are additive. This paper examines that assumption by reviewing a program of research which investigated the effects of external rewards and controls on intrinsic motivation. It was reported that a person's intrinsic motivation to perform an activity decreased when he received contingent monetary payments, threats of punishment for poor performance, or negative feedback about his performance. Noncontingent monetary payments left intrinsic motivation unchanged, and verbal reinforcements appeared to enhance intrinsic motivation. A cognitive evaluation theory was presented to explain these results, and the theory and results were discussed in relation to management.

Fletcher, Clive and Williams, Richard, "The Influence of Performance Feedback in Appraisal Interviews," *Journal of Occupational Psychology*, June 1976, Vol. 49, No. 2, 75–84.

This investigation attempts to resolve issues relating to the effects of discussing an individual's strengths and weaknesses in job performance during appraisal interviews. Interviews were conducted in a government department under varying degrees of performance feedback. Both positive and negative, positive only, negative only and none at all were compared on a number of variables indicating the effectiveness of the appraisal (individual's perception of own performance rating from interview as compared to recorded performance rating, the effects of post-interview performance, the extent to which the interview was perceived as an encouraging experience, and the appraisee's overall feelings about appraisal). Measurement of these variables were accomplished by mailed questionnaires. The results indicate that interviews perceived as containing a balanced review of the individual's strengths and weaknesses in performance achieved the greatest positive effect overall, while those containing no feedback whatsoever achieved relatively little.

Baird, Lloyd S., "Feedback: A Determinant of the Relationship Between Performance and Satisfaction," *Academy of Management Proceedings 1976*, 70–73.

The research investigated the extent to which feedback and the nature of the task affects the relationship between performance and satisfaction. One hundred and three students (subjects) were randomly assigned to a task either low or high in the dimensions of identity, variety, and autonomy (part of a mathematical exercise and a complete in-basket exercise, respectively). Subjects of both tasks were divided into either a feedback group (goals were set and assessors' ratings were returned to participant) and a no-feedback group. Performance in the mathematical exercise was determined by both the number of problems attempted and those solved. In the in-basket exercise, performance was determined by time-limit responses and the assessors scoring on response quality. Satisfaction with the task was measured by a seven-point Likert scale on five items (i.e., "I found the task enjoyable"). Also, satisfaction with performance was measured by the same Likert format on items. It was found that the relationship was highest in stimulating tasks (high) when feedback was given. Feedback did affect the correlations between performance and satisfaction—individuals received more satisfaction from performance when they were provided with feedback. The correlations were higher in the stimulating (high) than nonstimulating task (low).

Kao, Henry S. R., "Effects of Intermittency of Feedback on a Compensatory Tracking Task," *Perceptual and Motor Skills*, December 1976, Vol. 43, 1339–1345.

Target intermittency in tracking has been studied as frequency of target presentation of various time intervals. Task efficiency increased as a function of increased frequency of target display in open-loop tracking tasks, where the steady state of presentation resulted in the best performance. The present study examined effects of feedback intermittency in compensatory tracking as a major source of disruption of the motor-sensory feedback process in the closed-loop tracking system. Feedback intermittency is defined as the feedback of momentary sampling of the difference between target movements and the operator's control motion for specific time lengths before being displayed to him in a continuous tracking task. The task was operationalized through instructing the subjects to track random waves of 9.76 cpm at various amounts of feedback intermittency displayed on the Offner Dynograph Recorder as computer outputs. Seven magnitudes (0.0, 0.2, 0.4, 0.6, 0.8, 1.0, and 1.5 sec.) were used to represent various levels of feedback intermittency. Task efficiency decreased as a function of increased magnitudes of intermittency. Results are discussed relative to the difference between target intermittence and feedback intermittency and their effects of different tracking tasks. The magnitude of task error increased with the increasing levels of intermittency. The findings also establish the concept of feedback intermittency as a disturbing factor in compensatory tracking in degrading the operator's performance.

Seligman, Clive and Darley, John M., "Feedback as a Means of Decreasing Residential Energy Consumption," *Journal of Applied Psychology*, August 1977, Vol. 62, No. 4, 363–368.

The present study tested the hypothesis that providing immediate feedback to homeowners concerning their daily use of electricity would be effective in reducing electric consumption. In the 29 physically identical three-bedroom homes used in the study, central air conditioning is the largest single source of electricity usage during the summer. Accordingly, it was possible to predict the household's expected electric consumption in terms of the average daily outdoor temperature. Feedback was expressed as a percentage of actual consumption over predicted consumption, and it was displayed to the homeowners four times a week for approximately one month. The results confirmed the hypothesis. Before feedback began, the feedback and control groups were consuming electricity at approximately equal rates. During the feedback period, the feedback group used 10.5 percent less electricity. The effectiveness of the feedback procedure is discussed in terms of its cuing, motivational, and commitment functions.

McCarthy, M., "Decreasing the Incidence of High Bobbins in a Textile Spinning Department Through a Group Feedback Procedure," *Journal of Organizational Behavior Management*, 1978, Vol. 1, No. 2, 150–154.

This case study reports the management of employees' behavior in a textile operation that resulted in improved performance quality. A "high bobbin" is the consequence of a doffer not pushing all the way down on a spindle. This causes tangles, resulting in waste, lower wind efficiency, and lost man-hours clearing tangles. Baseline data on the incidence of high bobbins were collected and then the ABAB reversal design was employed. In phase one, a feedback graph of the baseline data was posted in the spinning department showing the number of high bobbins on each of four shifts. Revised data were posted daily. Also, supervisors were instructed to reinforce their doffers verbally whenever an improvement was made. In phase two, feedback and reinforcement were removed, while in phase three they were restored. High bobbins decreased dramatically during phase one. Removal of feedback and reinforcement resulted in an increase in high bobbins. When feedback and reinforcement were restored there was again a decrease in the number of high bobbins.

Quilitch, H. Robert, "Using a Simple Feedback Procedure to Reinforce the Submission of Written Suggestions by Mental Health Employees," *Journal of Organizational Behavior Management*, 1978, Vol. 1, 155–163.

Suggestion systems have traditionally used cash awards to encourage employees to submit their ideas for solving organizational problems. The system created for use in this mental health setting used feedback, not cash, to encourage employees' participation. A suggestion system manager simply posted each submitted suggestion publicly, along with her answer, within two days of its receipt. The 80 employees of this facility submitted 76 suggestions over the 32 weeks of this study, drawing attention to and successfully solving many problems pertaining to personnel practices, environmental conditions, and client care.

Lamal, P. A. and Benfield, A., "The Effect of Self-Monitoring on Job Tardiness and Percentage of Time Spent Working," *Journal of Organizational Behavior Management,* Winter 1978, 1, 2, 142–149.

The purpose of this study was to improve actual working time of an adult male draftsman who was habitually late for work and spent a good deal of time during the day "goofing off". A self report system was set up for him to indicate arrival time and actual hours worked each day. A multiple baseline design was used with interventions on day 11 and day 16. Results showed that self-monitoring reliably decreased the two behaviors and a follow-up 11 weeks later indicated the gains were maintained. The fact that the subject's behaviors changed so dramatically with the onset of self-monitoring lends plausibility to the interpretation that the behavior changes were the result of perceived potential aversive consequences for failure to meet acceptable levels of performance.

Kim, J. S. and Schuler, R. S., "The Nature of the Task as a Moderator of the Relationship Between Extrinsic Feedback and Employee Responses," *Academy of Management Journal,* 1979, Vol. 22, No. 1, 157–162.

Previous research investigating the relationships between extrinsic feedback and employee responses indicates inconsistent results. On the one hand, researchers have reported that extrinsic feedback has a positive relationship with employee responses such as work satisfaction (Kim, 1975) and intrinsic motivation (Arnold, 1976). On the other hand, researchers report no relationship, and in one study (Kim, 1975) a negative relationship with fellow employee satisfaction was found. The authors attribute inconsistent findings to be the result of the task as a moderator and hence hypothesize: The level of employee responses in nonstimulating tasks with high extrinsic feedback will be higher than the level with low extrinsic feedback, whereas in stimulating tasks the level of employee responses with high extrinsic feedback will be equal to the level with low extrinsic feedback. Using a sample of 272 employees of a large midwestern public utility, the effects of high and low extrinsic feedback, with tasks as a moderator, on work satisfaction, supervision satisfaction, co-worker satisfaction, and internal motivation. As predicted, task moderated the relationship between feedback and employee responses.

EMPIRICAL

Chapanis, A., "Knowledge of Performance as an Incentive in Repetitive, Monotonous Tasks," *Journal of Applied Psychology,* 1964, Vol. 48, No. 4, 263–267.

This experiment tried to isolate the purely motivational effect of knowledge of performance from its informational and rewarding aspects. The subjects (Ss) worked an hour a day, for 24 days, punching random digits into a teletype tape. They were told they were programming a computer and efforts were made to lend credibility to this fiction. Sixteen male undergraduate students were assigned to one of four groups. Ss in one group received no information about their output. In two other groups, the Ss could see a counter which tallied every stroke on the perforator and could, if they so chose, determine their daily work output. In the fourth group, Ss were required to write down their output at the end of 15, 30, and 45 minutes "for accounting purposes only". No significant differences were discovered among the four groups. Suggestions are offered to account for the discrepancy between the results of this experiment and those of a similar experiment reported by Gibbs and Brown in 1955.

Johnson, E. M. and Payne, M. C., Jr., "Vigilance: Effects of Frequency of Knowledge of Results," *Journal of Applied Psychology*, 1966, Vol. 50, No. 1, 33–34.

For an hour Ss observed an oscilloscope on which eight signals appeared per 15 minutes which they were to report. Knowledge of results was given after 0, 25, 50, 75, or 100 percent of the signals. Significant differences occurred between the number of targets detected by the 0 and 25 percent groups, the 25 and 50 percent groups, but none between the 50, 75, and 100 percent groups. The vigilance decrement was not significantly affected by frequency of KR.

Locke, E. A., "Motivational Effects of Knowledge of Results: Knowledge or Goal-Setting?", *Journal of Applied Psychology*, 1967, Vol. 51, No. 4, 324–329.

Research on knowledge of results (KR) has generally not controlled for motivational effects resulting from differential goal-setting. The present experiment was carried out to separate the effects of KR and goal-setting using a 2 × 2 fixed-model design; the variables were KR versus no KR and specific hard goals versus "do-best" goals. The goals (manipulated by instructions) were representative of the goals typically assigned (explicitly or implicitly) to KR and No KR Ss in previous studies, respectively. No difference was found between KR and No KR groups, but a significant goal effect was found in favor of Ss given specific hard goals. The results indicated that effects previously attributed to differential KR were actually due to different levels of motivation produced by the different goals.

Burke, R. J. and Wilcox, D. S., "Characteristics of Effective Employee Performance Review and Development Interviews," *Personnel Psychology*, 1969, Vol. 22, 291–305.

Four performance review (and development) feedback variables (subordinate participation, constructive supervisor, problem-solving, mutual goal-setting) were positively correlated with the subjects: a) satisfaction with the performance review, b) desire to improve performance, and c) self-report of active job performance improvement. Subjects were 300 female telephone operators.

Zajonc, R. B. and Brickman, P., "Expectancy and Feedback as Independent Factors in Task Performance," *Journal of Personality and Social Psychology*, February 1969, Vol. 11, No. 2, 148–156.

The analysis of the reciprocal effects of expectancy and performance requires that task feedback be made independent of both initial expectancies and actual performance, a condition not met in level-of-aspiration studies. The analysis also requires that some meaningful measure of actual performance be retained, a condition not met in the arbitrary tasks employed in dissonance studies. The present study realized such requirements by using a reaction-time task to explore the independent effects of performance expectancy, feedback, and expectancy changes on performance. After 30 trials of base-line performance subjects (120 males) either stated performance expectancies (being classified into high-expectancy and low-expectancy groups) or did not give expectancies. Following additional trials without feedback, subjects in each expectancy condition either continued without feedback or received success or failure feedback.

Major conclusions were that stating expectancies is a sufficient condition for performance enhancement in the absence of feedback; higher expectancies resulted in greater improvement than lower expectancies. Subjects who resisted lowering their expectancies after failure showed more subsequent improvement than those who lowered their expectancies sharply. Stating expectancies moderated differential reactions to success versus failure, but the crucial dissonance theory prediction, that low expectancy subjects would show a performance decrement under success, was not supported for the reaction-time task.

Mischel, W.; Grusec, J. and Masters, J. D., "Effects of Expected Delay Time on the Subjective Value of Rewards and Punishments," *Journal of Personality and Social Psychology*, April 1969, Vol. 11, No. 4, 363–373.

Four experiments examined how the length of anticipated temporal delay periods preceding the occurrence of rewards and punishments affects their subjective value for both children and adults. Subjects were confronted with a series of rewards or punishments which were presented as occurring immediately or after specified delay periods of up to several weeks in duration. In each set, subjects indicated their preferences for outcomes of objectivity equal value that differed only in the amount of expected time delay before their occurrence.

As predicted, as the anticipated delay interval for attainment of a reward increased, the subjective value of the reward decreased for both children and adults. In contrast, the length of anticipated delay time did not affect the subjective value of punishments. Any anticipated delay, however, *regardless of duration*, consistently did affect the aversiveness of punishments for adults, but not for children. Adults preferred immediate punishments to more delayed ones, regardless of specific time intervals; children's evaluations of punishments were not influenced systematically by any future temporal considerations. The overall results help clarify how future time may come to guide behavior.

Hundal, P. S., "Knowledge of Performance as an Incentive in Repetitive Industrial Work," *Journal of Applied Psychology*, June 1969, Vol. 53, No. 3, 224–226.

This study was designed to assess the purely motivational effects of knowledge of performance in a repetitive industrial task. The Ss were low paid workers with a few years (one to five) experience on the job. The experimental task was to grind a metallic piece to a specified size and shape. Experimental conditions were imposed a week before starting the experiment. The workers adjusted readily since the experimental conditions did not interfere with the work. Eighteen male workers were divided randomly into three groups. The Ss in Group A received no information about their output; Ss in Group B were allowed a rough estimate of their output; Ss in Group C were given accurate information about their output and could check it further by referring to a figure displayed before them. Results show increased output with increases in degree of knowledge of performance.

Clarke, D. E., "The Effects of Simulated Feedback and Motivation on Persistence at a Task," *Organizational Behavior and Human Performance*, 1972, Vol. 8, 340–346.

Simulated normative feedback and the motivational variables of achievement and affiliation were examined in relation to persistence and subjective probability of success at an insolvable figure-tracing task. Forty twelfth-grade students were assigned randomly to feedback or nonfeedback groups. Analyses of variance indicated that: a) feedback was highly significant in promoting persistence behavior, b) subjects with high achievement and low affiliation motivation persisted longest and exhibited highest probabilities of success, and c) subjects with high achievement and high affiliation motivation persisted least and exhibited lowest probabilities of success. The effects of supervision on motivation and persistence at occupational tasks were discussed.

Prather, D. C.; Berry, G. A. and Jones, G. L., "The Training of a Perceptual Skill by Either Rewarding or Aversive Feedback Compared on Efficiency, Transfer, and Stress," *Journal of Applied Psychology*, 1972, Vol. 56, No. 6, 514–516.

Forty male students at the United States Air Force Academy were trained on a range-estimation task. The Ss were randomly assigned to either Group RFB, those given feedback by their actual range plus a verbal reinforcer if they were within a given range, or Group SFB, those given feedback by their actual range plus a 60 volt electric shock if they were outside the given range. The learning curves showed no differences in the groups during training. After training to asymptote, there was no significant differences on the transfer variable, but Group SFB's performance was superior under stress ($p<.05$). The results were discussed in reference to the possibility of training resistance to stress.

Williges, R. C. and North, R. A., "Knowledge of Results and Decision-Making Performance in Visual Monitoring," *Organizational Behavior and Human Performance*, 1972, Vol. 8, 44–57.

Two experiments were conducted to investigate the role of knowledge-of-results (KR) on decision-making performance in a simple visual monitoring task in which subjects were required to detect periodic, long-duration brightness changes and ignore short duration changes. Both experiments demonstrated the characteristic decrease in percent of signals detected over the watch period when KR was not given. In addition, the results of each study were analyzed in terms of the Theory of Signal Detectability.

Experiment I resulted in significant changes in log β and d' when cumulative total events KR and cumulative detect response KR were provided. Experiment II factorially compared the effects of cumulative total events KR, correct detection KR, and false alarm KR. Correct detection KR was effective in increasing d' over the monitoring session. The implications of the results of each study were discussed in terms of a decision-making point-of-view. It was concluded that the role of KR on decision performance is complex and depends upon the specific type of KR presented.

Kritzer, R., "The Use of Videotape in Behavioral Change," *Public Personnel Management*, July-August 1974, Vol. 3, No. 4, 325–331.

An experiment was performed with 26 randomly selected students divided into three experimental groups. Two instruments were used for this study. A questionnaire was administered to measure how well the subjects perceived themselves on certain constructs (aggression, apathy, and decision-making) within a group situation. The second instrument used was the Fiedler LPC scale which measures attitudes. Experimental Group I was given the two instruments at the pretest. Next followed a discussion which was videotaped. Next they received a lecture and a discussion which was held on process observation skills. The two instruments were then given again as a post-test. Experimental Group II was given the pretest, unstructured discussion, process observation lecture and discussion, and post-test of the two instruments. Experimental Group III was given the pretest, unstructured 30-minute discussion which was videotaped, no process observation lecture, discussion about the videotaping session and subject participation, and the post-test.

Results: Experimental Group I, which participated in the process observation seminar and also in the videotaping, experienced a delay change in self-perception. Experimental Group II, which had the process observation seminar without the videotape, experienced no significant change. In Experimental Group III, which only had the videotape experience, immediate significant changes occurred. No significant change occurred between the pre and post tests of the control group. The immediate feedback of the videotape is a powerful tool for assisting a participant toward behavioral change through self-perception.

Greller, M. M. and Herold, D. M. "Sources of Feedback: A Preliminary Investigation," *Organizational Behavior and Human Performance,* 1975, Vol. 13, No. 2, 244–256.

Five sources of feedback (the formal organization, supervisor, co-workers, the task, one's own self) were investigated for their "informativeness" as providers of information about what the job requirements are (referent) and the extent to which they were met (feedback). Findings indicate that there is a greater reliance on intrinsic sources (sources psychologically "closer" to the individual) than on more external sources for feedback information, this reliance being reduced for referent information. These findings are discussed in terms of job description items which indicate that various characteristics of the external sources are associated with a reduced reliance on intrinsic sources. Implications for future research and organizational life are discussed.

Nebeker, D. M.; Dockstader, S. L. and Vickers, R. R., "A Comparison of the Effects of Individual and Team Performance Feedback Upon Subsequent Performance," Navy Personnel Research and Development Center, May 1975.

This study sought to determine the effects of a performance feedback presented to subjects acting singly or as members of a team. The experimental questions addressed were whether being identified as a team member enhances performance and whether individual performance in groups is affected by variation in the amount and specificity of the feedback provided.

The results indicated that subjects who were a part of a team, and felt so, did not perform at significantly higher levels than nonteam members when the effects of feedback were controlled. It was also found that any sort of feedback resulted in increased performance. Increasing the amount or specificity of the feedback provided had no additive effect.

Catano, Victor M., "Improvement in Workers' Performance Through Feedback of Information on System Performance," *Perceptual and Motor Skills,* April 1976, Vol. 42, No. 2, 487–490.

Two groups of helicopter technicians (N = 196) filled out data forms after completing maintenance and repairs as routine procedure. When information was given to the experimental group stating what changes (i.e., changes in supply sources) had been made in the system (inventory) as a result of data collected from the forms, the mean error-rate fell significantly from 58.2 to 46.5 percent. The experimental group had a significantly lower average error-rate (24.6 percent) than the control group (50.6 percent). The control group's performance was not different from pre-experimental levels. Results indicate that feedback in the form of information concerning system performance affected the level of group performance and further suggest that individuals are not only influenced by feedback about their own performance but also by what is happening at the end of the system.

Fletcher, Clive and Williams, Richard, "The Influence of Performance Feedback in Appraisal Interviews," *Journal of Occupational Psychology*, June 1976, Vol. 49, No. 2, 75–84.

This investigation attempts to resolve issues relating to the effects of discussing an individual's strengths and weaknesses in job performance during appraisal interviews. Interviews were conducted in a government department under varying degrees of performance feedback. Both positive and negative, positive only, negative only and none at all were compared on a number of variables indicating the effectiveness of the appraisal (individuals perception of own performance rating from interview as compared to recorded performance rating, the effects on post-interview performance, the extent to which the interview was perceived as an encouraging experience, and the appraisee's overall feelings about appraisal). Measurement of these variables were accomplished by mailed questionnaires. The results indicate that interviews perceived as containing a balanced review of the individual's strengths and weaknesses in performance achieved the greatest positive effect overall, while those containing no feedback whatsoever achieved relatively little.

Schmitt, Neal; Coyle, Bryan and King, Larry, "Feedback and Task Predictability as Determinants of Performance in Multiple Cue Probability Learning Tasks," *Organizational Behavior and Human Performance*, August 1976, Vol. 16, No. 2, 388–402.

Several studies conducted within the last decade have suggested that outcome feedback is less than optional feedback in a multiple cue probability learning situation. Some of these studies have neglected one or more of the following: a no-feedback control group, analysis of the several different types of feedback, assessment of feedback over time, and the effect of feedback on tasks of different levels. Two 2 (outcome feedback) × 2 (cue utilization feedback) × 2 (task information) × 3 (trial blocks) experiments were conducted.

It was found that outcome feedback resulted in significantly less consistency, and task information resulted in significantly better matching. Cue utilization feedback enhanced achievement and matching only in combination with task information and only in high predictability tasks. Further research on feedback should focus on feedback and task difficulty interactions as well as the effects of delay of feedback.

Henderson, William T. and Wen, Shih-Sung, "Effects of Immediate Pos-

five items (i.e., "I found the task enjoyable"). Also, satisfaction with performance was measured by the same Likert format on items. It was found that the relationship was highest in stimulating tasks (high) when feedback was given. Feedback did affect the correlations between performance and satisfaction—individuals received more satisfaction from performance when they were provided with feedback. The correlations were higher in the stimulating (high) than nonstimulating task (low).

Schmitt, Neil; Coyle, Bryan W. and Saari, Bruce B., "Types of Task Information Feedback in Multiple-Cue Probability Learning," *Organizational Behavior and Human Performance*, April 1977, Vol. 18, No. 2, 316–328.

While it is documented that task information or task information plus subjects' own cue utilization coefficients are superior to outcome feedback in multiple-cue probability learning studies, no attention has been directed to an evaluation of the different possible types of task information it is possible to give subjects when the task involves dimensions of information that are highly intercorrelated. In the present study, subjects' achievement, consistency, and matching were evaluated in a 2 (outcome feedback versus no outcome feedback) × 4 (no task information, beta weights, B; zero-order correlations, "r"; or beta weights times correlations, Br) × 4 (trial blocks) design in which the task involved using cues whose B, r, and Br values indicated different strategies of combination.

Results indicate that 1) outcome feedback produces lower consistency but slightly better matching than no outcome feedback, 2) no task information produces matching superior to that of the three treatment groups, and 3) the matching performance of Br conditions is significantly inferior to that of the B and r conditions. Though performance differences among B, r, and Br groups were significant, they were very small in correlational terms. It is suggested that future research might focus on the social as opposed to statistical implications for task information feedback and the form in which the feedback is presented.

Andrasik, Frank; McNamara, J. Regis and Abbott, David M., "Policy Control: A Low Resource Intervention for Improving Staff Behavior," *Journal of Organizational Behavior Management*, 1978, Vol. 1, 125–133.

This investigation, centering on staff employed in a forensic psychiatry setting, was initiated in an attempt to increase staff adherence to an important program function. During a baseline period, it was discovered that staff compliance with the program function was only 4.2 percent. Minimal revision of administrative policy increased staff compliance to 80.5 percent. The effects of this revision, which involved no additional consequation other than information feedback, were attributed to cuing, shaping, and feedback functions. Additional results and implications of these findings were discussed.

Becker, Lawrence J., "Joint Effect of Feedback and Goal-Setting on Performance: A Field Study of Residential Energy Conservation," *Journal of Applied Psychology*, 1978, Vol. 63, No. 4, 428–433.

The facilitating motivational effect of feedback on performance has been attributed by some to difficult goals set in response to feedback. In the present article, the effect was attributed to the presence of both a difficult goal and feedback about performance in relation to that goal. Eighty families were asked to set a goal to reduce their residential electricity consumption for several weeks during the summer, half of them by 20 percent (a difficult goal) and half by two percent (an easy goal). Within each of these groups, half of the families were given feedback three times a week about their consumption. Twenty more families served as a control. As predicted, the 20 percent feedback group conserved the most (13 to 15.1 percent) and was the only one that consumed significantly less electricity than the control. It was concluded that improved performance was a result of the joint effect of feedback and goal-setting. The implications of the present research for a national residential conservation strategy are discussed.

Emmert, Gerald D., "Measuring the Impact of Group Performance Feedback Versus Individual Performance Feedback in an Industrial Setting," *Journal of Organizational Behavior Management*, 1978, Vol. 1, 134–141.

The following represents efforts of first-line supervisors to affect a performance increase within a manufacturing area of a production facility. Effects of group feedback versus individual feedback were measured on four separate crews totaling 32 hourly employees. Feedback was provided graphically on the basis of a daily crew average during the first intervention. Individual feedback graphs were used during the second intervention. The data shows a performance increase during group feedback, and a more dramatic increase during the use of individualized feedback. Several complications were identified which may interfere with the pure application of the principles of behavior management employed in many industrial settings.

Frederiksen, L. W., "Behavioral Reorganization of a Professional Service System," *Journal of Organizational Behavior Management*, 1978, Vol. 2, No. 1, 1–9.

The service delivery behavior of professional staff was altered with a systems level reorganization of an outpatient mental health clinic. Service delivery problems were specified and analyzed. Solutions were developed in the form of an intervention, which involved *rescheduling workloads*, increasing individual staff member's responsibility for specific patients, and installing a *feedback system*. Following this, patient drop-out rates decreased, average interval between appointments decreased, and latency to first appointment was reduced. These improvements achieved organizational (service delivery) goals without observable negative side effects or major costs.

Komaki, Judi; Barwick, Kenneth D. and Scott, Lawrence R., "A Behavioral Approach to Occupational Safety: Pinpointing and Reinforcing Safe Performance in a Food Manufacturing Plant," *Journal of Applied Psychology*, 1978, Vol. 63, No. 4, 434–445.

The behavior analysis approach was used to improve worker safety in two departments in a food manufacturing plant. Desired safety practices were identified, permitting construction of observational codes suitable for observing workers' on-the-job performance over a 25-week period of time. The intervention consisted of an explanation and visual presentation of the desired behaviors (with a goal being set) as well as frequent, low-cost reinforcement in the form of feedback. A within-subject (multiple baseline) design was used. Employees in the two departments substantially improved their safety performance from 70 percent and 78 percent to 96 percent and 99 percent, respectively, after the staggered introduction of the program. During the reversal phase, performance returned to baseline (71 percent and 72 percent). It was concluded that the intervention, particularly the frequent feedback, was effective in improving safety performance. Not only did employees react favorably to the program, but the company was later able to maintain the program with a continuing decline in the injury frequency rate. The results suggest that behaviorally defining and positively reinforcing safe practices is a viable approach to occupational accident reduction.

Runnion, Alex; Johnson, Twila and McWhorter, John, "The Effects of Feedback and Reinforcement on Truck Turnaround Time in Materials Transportation," *Journal of Organizational Behavior Management*, 1978, Vol. 1, 110–117.

The length of time which trucks spent at each mill while transporting goods between 58 plant locations of a textile company was reduced with the introduction of a feedback plus reinforcement system. The average truck turnaround time was reduced from a baseline average of 67 minutes to an average of 38.2 minutes. This level was maintained even though the frequency of feedback was reduced substantially. The project demonstrated the use of periodic feedback to improve and maintain improved performance of workers across many locations in a large textile company.

Strang, Harold R.; Lawrence, Edith C., and Fowler, Patrick C., "Effects of Assigned Goal Level and Knowledge of Results on Arithmetic Computation: A Laboratory Study," *Journal of Applied Psychology*, 1978, Vol. 63, No. 4, 446–450.

The present study examined the effects of knowledge of results (KR) and assigned goals on arithmetic computation. Female university students (n = 100) either received or did not receive explicit KR while under easy or challenging goal assignment. A control group (n = 50) received neither KR nor goal assignment. Subjects receiving KR under challenging goal assignment significantly increased their computational speed at no apparent cost in accuracy. These findings are congruous with the 1977 findings of Erez. With the minimizing of implicit KR in the no-KR groups in the present study, challenging goal assignment in itself had no noticeable effect on computational speed and led to a significant increase in errors. It is suggested that feedback may be a necessary complement to assigned goals in facilitating performance.

Sulzer-Azaroff, Beth, "Behavioral Ecology and Accident Prevention," *Journal of Organizational Behavior Management*, 1978, Vol. 2, 11–44.

Many laboratory accidents could readily be avoided by carefully arranging the physical environment to reduce potential hazards. Effective, nonintrusive, economical, safety strategies are apt to be broadly utilized. The purpose of this study was to identify and analyze the ecological impact of a simple, nonintrusive, cost-efficient system to reduce hazards in a university laboratory research facility. The system involved periodic inspections by safety officers, who provided written feedback about, and suggestions for, ameliorating hazards. The procedure was replicated across 30 laboratories. An initial building inspection indicated the presence of various mechanical, chemical, and electrical hazards. Hazardous conditions were defined and listed on an observation sheet, containing a generic laboratory map. Observed hazards were noted and their locations indicated on the form. A conservative assessment system provided evidence of the reliability of observation. An across-subjects-multiple-baseline experimental design was used with laboratories assigned to either an early, middle, or late feedback condition. Results showed a marked improvement in safety conditions during the feedback phase, indicating that it was possible to produce a sharp reduction in hazardous conditions in a research laboratory facility by means of a simple, nonintrusive economical feedback system. The ecological assessment indicated a general increase in safety-related activities by the members of the Institute.

Quilitch, H. Robert, "Using a Simple Feedback Procedure to Reinforce the Submission of Written Suggestions by Mental Health Employees," *Journal of Organizational Behavior Management*, 1978, Vol. 1, 155–163.

Suggestion systems have traditionally used cash awards to encourage employees to submit their ideas for solving organizational problems. The system created for use in this mental health setting used feedback, not cash, to encourage employees' participation. A suggestion system manager simply posted each submitted suggestion publicly, along with her answer, within two days of its receipt. The 80 employees of this facility submitted 76 suggestions over the 32 weeks of this study, drawing attention to and successfully solving many problems pertaining to personnel practices, environmental conditions, and client care.

Kim, J. S. and Schuler, R. S., "The Nature of the Task as a Moderator of the Relationship Between Extrinsic Feedback and Employee Responses," *Academy of Management Journal*, 1979, Vol. 22, No. 1, 157–162.

Previous research investigating the relationships between extrinsic feedback and employee responses indicates inconsistent results. On the one hand, researchers have reported that extrinsic feedback has a positive relationship with employee responses such as work satisfaction (Kim, 1975) and intrinsic motivation (Arnold, 1976). On the other hand, researchers report no relationship, and in one study (Kim, 1975) a negative relationship with fellow employee satisfaction was found. The authors attribute inconsistent findings to be the result of the task as a moderator and hence hypothesize that: The level of employee responses in nonstimulating tasks with high extrinsic feedback will be higher than the level with low extrinsic feedback, whereas in stimulating tasks the level of employee responses with high extrinsic feedback will be equal to the level with low extrinsic feedback. Using a sample of 272 employees of a large midwestern public utility, the effects of high and low extrinsic feedback, with tasks as a moderator, on work satisfaction, supervision satisfaction, co-worker satisfaction, and internal motivation. As predicted, task moderated the relationship between feedback and employee responses.

Fisher, Cynthia D., "Transmission of Positive and Negative Feedback to Subordinates: A Laboratory Investigation," *Journal of Applied Psychology*, October 1979, Vol. 64, No. 5, 533–540.

A literature review revealed that while employees often say that their superior is the most valuable interpersonal source of feedback, the evidence suggests that superiors are often poor sources of performance feedback. A laboratory study was performed to discover if and when delay and upward distortion of feedback occurred. It was expected that superiors of low performing subordinates would wait longer in giving feedback as well as rate subordinates higher than those superiors with moderately high performing subordinates. Superiors of low performers were also expected to believe that their subordinates would react unfavorably to the feedback and like them less than superiors with moderately high performers. A 2 × 2 design was used with the factors of moderately high versus moderately low subordinate performance and feedback versus no feedback. The subjects were 168 college students who served as superiors to a subordinate who was a confederate. Subjects monitored and rated their subordinates' performance with those in the feedback condition providing feedback at a time of their choosing. All the hypotheses were supported except for the delay hypothesis. The author's overall conclusion was that the level of subordinate performance does affect superiors' behavior with respect to giving feedback to their subordinates. The results are discussed in terms of their implications for performance appraisals in organizations.

Conlon, Edward J., "Feedback About Personal and Organizational Outcomes and Its Effect on Persistence of Planned Behavioral Changes," *Academy of Management Journal,* June 1980, Vol. 23, No. 2, 267–286.

This research examines the problem of creating persistent changes in work behavior through planned intervention techniques. It also examines the relationship between the presence and content of feedback about differentially valued outcomes and the decision to persist at a novel task performance strategy. In a task involving 70 undergraduates, who were asked to produce edited manuscript copy and were paid money for both quality and quantity, the author concludes that confirming and disconfirming feedback about the expected outcomes of a behavior affects the decision to persist only when the outcomes are valued. Conlon also concludes that it is the content of feedback, not its presence, that affects behavior and belief. The research is an attempt to formulate a decision-making framework useful for developing research on the adoption and persistence of new behavior in planned change contexts.

INTEGRATIVE

Brethower, K. K. S., "Performance Indicators as Feedback in Business Settings," a dissertation, 1973, The University of Michigan.

This study investigates the extent to which one operant conditioning technique, feedback, can be used by managers in business. Feedback as defined by Olds, as performance information which is 1) external, 2) displayed in some way over time, 3) related to some parameter of the response, and 4) response modifying or maintaining over time. Performance data were gathered by managers and used to determine whether a performance indicator system which met requirements No. 1, 2, and 3 above could be administered by managers in such a way that it would fulfill requirement No. 4 and thus qualify as feedback.

Five studies were carried out in two field settings, a petrochemical company and an air freight forwarding company. The behaviors investigated were length of time to handle telephone inquiries, making callbacks on schedule, and delays in telephone answering. The findings from the five studies are as follows: 1) Performance indicator systems can be administered by business managers to fulfill the requirements of feedback. 2) Effects of feedback on performance in business settings have been shown to be extensive. Three conditions that appeared to play a role in the success of the feedback systems existed in all five studies: *valued performance, perceived control,* and *small groups.* These studies indicate that employees can improve their job performance if managed by properly administered feedback. They further support the idea that managers can administer feedback systems such that they initially modify and subsequently maintain performance.

Aplin, J. C., Jr., and Thompson, D. E., "Feedback: Key to Survey-Based

Change," *Public Personnel Management*, November-December 1974, Vol. 3, No. 6, 524–530.

This article examines the feedback process in detail. Initially, consideration is given to feedback objectives. The distinction between content objectives (relating to the survey itself and analysis of information contained within the data) and process objectives (pertain to the interpersonal process of the meeting) are emphasized. A six-phase model of feedback meetings is developed and used to illustrate how feedback leader skills can be improved. The phases discussed are: contracting, validity testing, problem identification and analysis, problem-solving and closure.

Nadler, David A., "The Effects of Feedback on Task Group Behavior: A Review of the Experimental Research," *Organizational Behavior and Human Performance*, June 1979, Vol. 23, No. 1, 309–338.

This examination of literature leads to a proposal of three specific models of the effects of different types of feedback data and, on another level, a general model of group feedback effects. The research suggests that different factors may influence the cuing effects of feedback from the motivational effects of feedback and, when individual performance becomes highly confounded with group performance, individuals may be incorrectly cued by group level feedback. Feedback is also seen as leading to affective and cognitive outcomes and is termed a potential for leading to behavioral outcomes.

Ilgen, Daniel R.; Fisher, Cynthia D. and Taylor, M. Susan, "Consequences of Individual Feedback on Behavior in Organizations," *Journal of Applied Psychology*, August 1979, Vol. 64, No. 4, 349–371.

This review focuses upon the multi-dimensional nature of feedback as a stimulus and addresses the process by which feedback influences behavior. The study is a review of literature with emphasis on the effect of feedback on the behavior of individuals in performance oriented organizations. The authors note a large body of experimental research exists relating one or two dimensions of feedback to a given response, but little exists with respect to the intermediate psychological processes triggered by the feedback. The study concludes, one of the most critical deficiencies of our understanding is in the area of perceptions of feedback which, they say, is frequently misperceived.

PRESCRIPTIVE

Anderson, J., "Giving and Receiving Feedback," *Personnel Administration*, March-April 1968, Vol. 31, No. 2, 21–27.

Feedback has no purpose unless it is useful to the employee. The author prescribes three criteria of "useful" feedback: 1) The worker must be able to understand the feedback, i.e., it must be specific rather than general; it should include recent examples of behavior. 2) The feedback must be presented in such a way as to gain acceptance with the worker. 3) The recipient needs to be able to do something with it; i.e., concrete as opposed to abstract criticism and suggestions should be given.

Weatherbee, H. Y., "Steering Marginal Performers to Solid Ground," *Personnel*, July-August 1969, Vol. 46, No. 4, 34–43.

The marginal performer can be found in almost any kind of organization. They may be underqualified or overqualified for the positions they hold; there are all sorts of variations, but the marginal employee is a drag on the efficiency of any operation and on group performance. Typically, operating managers ignore the problem as long as possible and then resort to one of two standard solutions: they manipulate the workforce to transfer the employee out of their own bailiwicks or they get rid of him entirely by firing him. It is as difficult to generalize about how to handle a marginal employee as it is to generalize what a marginal employee is. Each case will be special and should be handled specially, but there are some guidelines both to identify and to cope with the marginal employee that are described in this article.

Heller, F. A., "GFA Applied to Training and Learning Situations," *Journal of Management Studies*, October 1970, Vol. 7, No. 3, 335–346.

This article describes Group Feedback Analysis (GFA) as a method of teaching while a previous article analyzed its use for the purpose of obtaining accurate field research information. Three steps are necessary: 1) information gathering, 2) analysis, and 3) feedback of results and critical evaluation. As a method of teaching, GFA usually produces considerable interest and insight into the subtleties of apparently simple problems. It also increases an awareness of differences in attitudes and judgments between people. The method is flexible and enables a teacher to move from facts to theory and back again to facts. However, it does not lead to the enunciation of rigid principles since almost any result can be shown to produce deviations from the average even in small groups. The approach is *analytic rather than descriptive* and has been used with various groups of managers up to Board level. There are limitations. The most serious is that the method can only be used to teach those subjects for which a practical class exercise of short field investigation can be devised. This throws a considerable burden on the ingenuity of the teacher.

Rummler, G. A., "Human Performance Problems and Their Solutions," *Human Resource Management*, Winter 1972, Vol. 11, No. 4, 2–10.

For the most part, human performance deficiencies can be classified as deficiencies of knowledge, which result from an employee's not knowing what, how, or when to do it; or as deficiencies of execution, which result from an employee's failing to perform because of factors in the work environment; or as some combination of the two. This D/k-D/e framework can be used to analyze existing problems and to predict problems that might occur if changes in procedures or changes in emphasis on some performance variable are being considered. The value of this framework for viewing people-related performance problems is that: 1) It requires a closer look at the problem. It forces specification of exactly what is desired and how what is desired is different from what we are currently getting. In so doing, a systematic examination is made of the variables that influence performance—the consequences, feedback, and barriers to performance. 2) It provides real and specific solutions. The solutions are not just grand abstractions but rather are specific and derived from looking directly at the performance problem. The implementation of these solutions is frequently within the domain and authority of management.

Hall, Douglas T.; Alexander, Michael O.; Goodale, James G. and Livingstone, J. Leslie, "How to Make Personnel Decisions More Productive," *Personnel*, May-June 1976, Vol. 53, No. 3, 10–20.

This article presents a method by which managers can receive information and feedback regarding changes in employee performance (human resource accounting, HRA). The authors view problems such as job enrichment as investments which must be evaluated in terms of certain benefits (i.e., reduction in the cost of turnover). Moreover, employees' perceived work environment can be monitored through periodic attitude surveys, thus shortening the feedback cycle for management. Management can then make necessary adjustments if efforts to enrich jobs fail to alter employee perceptions of their work without performance degradation or loss of satisfaction. The authors suggest that resistance to installing behavior information systems can be overcome by first diagnosing whether the organization feels a need for behavioral accounting information and then letting the users design the system.

Nisberg, Jay N., "Performance Improvement Without Training," *Personnel Journal*, December 1976, Vol. 55, No. 12, 613–615.

The author contends that deficiencies in job performance are frequently a function of poor execution by employees rather than inadequate knowledge. Three causes are identified and corrective measures are offered. First, inadequate feedback, the failure to provide workers with information about the results of their labor can be rectified by making progress reports known. Second, task interference, the lack of adequate materials or the presence of competing tasks can be corrected by job engineering changes. Finally punishment, that which is grueling, difficult or exhausting in performing the task can be remedied by altering incentives.

Dodd, William E. and Pesei, Michael L., "Managing Morale through Survey Feedback," *Business Horizons*, June 1977, Vol. 20, No. 3, 36–45.

The authors contend that opinion survey feedback can be used by trained supervisors for improving employee morale. Application of behavioral modification (interaction modeling) techniques to supervisory training is advocated to teach supervisors to respond more effectively to employee concerns during opinion survey feedback meetings. The procedure for interaction modeling involves the following: a model demonstrating the specific behavior to be learned, an opportunity to practice the behavior, reinforcement from instructor or peers for the behavior, and an opportunity to transfer the behavior to the actual situation. Managers who are trained in specific feedback skill through interaction modeling techniques in a defined morale improvement system tend to be more successful at this enterprise than colleagues left to their own resources.

Kirby, Peter G., "Productivity Increases Through Feedback Systems," *Personnel Journal*, October 1977, Vol. 56, No. 10, 512–515.

The author presents a practical approach for improving worker productivity in organizations by establishing feedback systems. The feedback system described is one where information regarding the results generated by employees is related back to them. This information was used by employees to compare their performance with that of a measurable standard. A case history involving a manufacturing plant demonstrates the efficacy of the feedback system. Management established goals for each operating unit which were then made known to employees by use of chalkboards in the production area. At the end of each shift, the quantity produced was posted next to the goal. This approach resulted in productivity increases, more employee suggestions to improve productivity, and fewer grievances.

The author further prescribes a four-step model for establishing a feedback system. The steps include: specifying the behavior where improvement is desired, recording the actual performance, providing positive reinforcement when desired performance occurs, and the evaluation of process.

Kreitner, Robert, "People are Systems Too: Filling the Feedback Vacuum," *Business Horizons*, December 1977, Vol. 20, No. 6, 54–58.

The author identifies three types of feedback which can be employed by managers for supporting high quality job performance: informational feedback (e.g., account default data fed back to salespersons who make credit decisions); corrective feedback (evaluative and judgmental); and reinforcing feedback (praise or material gain for an appropriate behavior). Based on behavioral research, four rules are mentioned as useful concerning feedback. First, feedback must be specifically related to performance. Second, feedback should be reserved for only the important aspects of performance. Third, feedback should be given as soon as possible. Fourth, feedback should be given for improvement of performance or progress in the right direction.

Andrasik, Frank; McNamara, J. Regis and Abbott, David M., "Policy Control: A Low Resource Intervention for Improving Staff Behavior," *Journal of Organizational Behavior Management*, 1978, Vol. 1, 125–133.

This investigation, centering on staff employed in a forensic psychiatry setting, was initiated in an attempt to increase staff adherence to an important program function. During a baseline period, it was discovered that staff compliance with the program function was only 4.2 percent. Minimal revision of administrative policy increased staff compliance to 80.5 percent. The effects of this revision, which involved no additional consequation other than information feedback, were attributed to cuing, shaping, and feedback functions. Additional results and implications of these findings were discussed.

Becker, Lawrence J., "Joint Effect of Feedback and Goal-Setting on Performance: A Field Study of Residential Energy Conservation," *Journal of Applied Psychology*, 1978, Vol. 63, No. 4, 428–433.

The facilitating motivational effect of feedback on performance has been attributed by some to difficult goals set in response to feedback. In the present article, the effect was attributed to the presence of both a difficult goal and feedback about performance in relation to that goal. Eighty families were asked to set a goal to reduce their residential electricity consumption for several weeks during the summer, half of them by 20 percent (a difficult goal) and half by two percent (an easy goal). Within each of these groups, half of the families were given feedback three times a week about their consumption. Twenty more families served as a control. As predicted, the 20 percent feedback group conserved the most (13-15.1 percent) and was the only one that consumed significantly less electricity than the control. It was concluded that improved performance was a result of the joint effect of feedback and goal-setting. The implications of the present research for a national residential conservation strategy are discussed.

Emmert, Gerald D., "Measuring the Impact of Group Performance Feedback Versus Individual Performance Feedback in an Industrial Setting," *Journal of Organizational Behavior Management*, 1978, Vol. 1, 134–141.

The following represents efforts of first-line supervisors to affect a performance increase within a manufacturing area of a production facility. Effects of group feedback versus individual feedback were measured on four separate crews totaling 32 hourly employees. Feedback was provided graphically on the basis of a daily crew average during the first intervention. Individual feedback graphs were used during the second intervention. The data shows a performance increase during group feedback, and a more dramatic increase during the use of individualized feedback. Several complications were identified which may interfere with the pure application of the principles of behavior management employed in many industrial settings.

Frederiksen, L. W., "Behavioral Reorganization of a Professional Service System," *Journal of Organizational Behavior Management*, 1978, Vol. 2, No. 1, 1–9.

The service delivery behavior of professional staff was altered with a systems level reorganization of an outpatient mental health clinic. Service delivery problems were specified and analyzed. Solutions were developed in the form of an intervention, which involved *rescheduling workloads*, increasing individual staff member's responsibility for specific patients, and installing a *feedback system*. Following this, patient drop-out rates decreased, average interval between appointments decreased, and latency to first appointment was reduced. These improvements achieved organizational (service delivery) goals without observable negative side effects or major costs.

Komaki, Judi; Barwick, Kenneth D. and Scott, Lawrence R., "A Behavioral Approach to Occupational Safety: Pinpointing and Reinforcing Safe Performance in a Food Manufacturing Plant," *Journal of Applied Psychology*, 1978, Vol. 63, No. 4, 434–445.

The behavior analysis approach was used to improve worker safety in two departments in a food manufacturing plant. Desired safety practices were identified, permitting construction of observational codes suitable for observing workers' on-the-job performance over a 25-week period of time. The intervention consisted of an explanation and visual presentation of the desired behaviors (with a goal being set) as well as frequent, low-cost reinforcement in the form of feedback. A within-subject (multiple baseline) design was used. Employees in the two departments substantially improved their safety performance from 70 percent and 78 percent to 96 percent and 99 percent, respectively, after the staggered introduction of the program. During the reversal phase, performance returned to baseline (71 percent and 72 percent). It was concluded that the intervention, particularly the frequent feedback, was effective in improving safety performance. Not only did employees react favorably to the program, but the company was later able to maintain the program with a continuing decline in the injury frequency rate. The results suggest that behaviorally defining and positively reinforcing safe practices is a viable approach to occupational accident reduction.

Runnion, Alex; Johnson, Twila and McWhorter, John, "The Effects of Feedback and Reinforcement on Truck Turnaround Time in Materials Transportation," *Journal of Organizational Behavior Management*, 1978, Vol. 1, 110–117.

The length of time which trucks spent at each mill while transporting goods between 58 plant locations of a textile company was reduced with the introduction of a feedback plus reinforcement system. The average truck turn-around time was reduced from a baseline average of 67 minutes to an average of 38.2 minutes. This level was maintained even though the frequency of feedback was reduced substantially. The project demonstrated the use of periodic feedback to improve and maintain improved performance of workers across many locations in a large textile company.

Strang, Harold R.; Lawrence, Edith C. and Fowler, Patrick C., "Effects of Assigned Goal Level and Knowledge of Results on Arithmetic Computation: A Laboratory Study," *Journal of Applied Psychology*, 1978, Vol. 63, No. 4, 446–450.

The present study examined the effects of knowledge of results (KR) and assigned goals on arithmetic computation. Female university students (n = 100) either received or did not receive explicit KR while under easy or challenging goal assignment. A control group (n = 50) received neither KR nor goal assignment. Subjects receiving KR under challenging goal assignment significantly increased their computational speed at no apparent cost in accuracy. These findings are congruous with the 1977 findings of Erez. With the minimizing of implicit KR in the no-KR groups in the present study, challenging goal assignment in itself had no noticeable effect on computational speed and led to a significant increase in errors. It is suggested that feedback may be a necessary complement to assigned goals in facilitating performance.

Sulzer-Azaroff, Beth, "Behavioral Ecology and Accident Prevention," *Journal of Organizational Behavior Management*, 1978, Vol. 2, 11–44.

Many laboratory accidents could readily be avoided by carefully arranging the physical environment to reduce potential hazards. Effective, nonintrusive, economical, safety strategies are apt to be broadly utilized. The purpose of this study was to identify and analyze the ecological impact of a simple, nonintrusive, cost-efficient system to reduce hazards in a university laboratory research facility. The system involved periodic inspections by safety officers, who provided written feedback about, and suggestions for, ameliorating hazards. The procedure was replicated across 30 laboratories. An initial building inspection indicated the presence of various mechanical, chemical, and electrical hazards. Hazardous conditions were defined and listed on an observation-sheet, containing a generic laboratory map. Observed hazards were noted and their locations indicated on the form. A conservative assessment system provided evidence of the reliability of observation. An across-subjects-multiple-baseline experimental design was used with laboratories assigned to either an early, middle, or late feedback condition. Results showed a marked improvement in safety conditions during the feedback phase, indicating that it was possible to produce a sharp reduction in hazardous conditions in a research laboratory facility by means of a simple, non-intrusive economical feedback system. The ecological assessment indicated a general increase in safety related activities by the members of the Institute.

Quilitch, H. Robert, "Using a Simple Feedback Procedure to Reinforce the Submission of Written Suggestions by Mental Health Employees," *Journal of Organizational Behavior Management*, 1978, Vol. 1, 155–163.

Suggestion systems have traditionally used cash awards to encourage employees to submit their ideas for solving organizational problems. The system created for use in this mental health setting used feedback, not cash, to encourage employees' participation. A suggestion system manager simply posted each submitted suggestion publicly, along with her answer, within two days of its receipt. The 80 employees of this facility submitted 76 suggestions over the 32 weeks of this study, drawing attention to and successfully solving many problems pertaining to personnel practices, environmental conditions, and client care.

Greenlaw, Paul S., "Suggestion Systems: An Old Approach To A New Problem," *Personnel Administrator*, January 1980, Vol. 25, No. 1, 49–54.

There have been many strategies to attack the problem of double digit inflation, declining productivity and the massive energy problems. The purpose of this article is to "look backward" 100 years to an old and familiar personnel management technique that could effectively deal with these problems. This technique is the "suggestion system" devised in 1880 by the York & Towne Company. It is on the assumption that people are generally selfish (i.e., won't do something without expecting a reward) that the two premises of this article are based. The focuses are "how organizations can reward employees to help keep up with double digit inflation while simultaneously stimulating employees to come up with energy saving ideas profitable to the firm." Several reward mechanisms are then examined with emphasis on the "suggestion system". It is found that one mechanism, "compensation increases," fails to keep employees up with "tax inflation". Employee benefits may help employees cope with inflation but there is little evidence that they increase productivity. On the other hand, psychic rewards may increase productivity, but probably don't help alleviate inflation at all. It's hard to fill a gas tank with "Good job, Smitty". The suggestion system involves paying an individual directly for the adoption of his or her idea which saves the firm money. The individual would receive 10 to 20 percent of the first year's net savings realized. The following suggestions were given for increasing the viability of the suggestion system: promoting current systems, increasing awards, giving energy awards, and government stimulation of energy saving suggestions.

Alpander, Guvenc G., "Training First-Line Supervisors to Criticize Constructively," *Personnel Journal*, March 1980, Vol. 59, No. 3, 216–221.

In investigating the problem of communicating poor performance to the employee, this study proposed two goals: 1) To delineate the extent to which first-line supervisors are comfortable in criticizing their subordinates' performance, and 2) to design and implement a training module on how to criticize constructively. Results of a pre-test questionnaire which included a Likert-type scale and covered 240 first-line supervisors from six different organizations showed that those functions pertaining to negative employee performance or use of discipline produced reactions of discomfort or indifference on the part of the supervisors. Certain avoidance techniques in conducting negative performance interviews employed by supervisors were pointed out. A training program/workshop to assist supervisors in overcoming their uneasiness in conducting appraisal sessions and taking disciplinary action as a means of learning how to criticize constructively was conducted. The post-test indicated that the average change in feelings for the 200 supervisors was from being uncomfortable to being rather comfortable or at least indifferent. They could accept these responsibilities and perform them well and know how to handle them. In summary, this training/workshop approach to critical appraisal interviews seems to be effective and should definitely be included in supervisory training programs.

THEORETICAL

Powers, W. T., "Feedback: Beyond Behaviorism," *Science*, 1973, Vol. 179, 351–356.

The author intended to show in this article how a new theoretical approach to behavior can be developed simply by paying attention to feedback effects. A control system model of behavior, properly organized for its environment, is advocated by the author and is one in which he feels will produce whatever output is required to achieve a constant sensed result, even in the presence of unpredictable disturbances. A control-system model of the brain provides a physical explanation for the existence of goals, and shows that behavior is the control of input and not output.

A systematic investigation of controlled quantities can reveal an organism's structure of control systems. When controlled quantities are discovered, the related stimulus-response laws become trivially predictable. Variability of behavior all but disappears once controlled quantities are known. Behavior itself is seen in terms of this model to be self-determined in a specific and highly significant sense that calls into serious doubt the ultimate feasibility of operant conditioning of human beings by other human beings.

Commentary

FEEDBACK

Feedback or knowledge of results (KOR) is an effective management technique which can improve employee productivity and satisfaction, modify behavior, affect morale, and increase motivation to perform even repetitive, monotonous tasks.

Several studies have given us some insights into results that may be expected when using feedback to improve performance or productivity. For example, experiments in a mass-production manufacturing plant used five methods for presenting knowledge of results to employees:

1. Department efficiency was charted daily on a graph for all to see.

2. A form posted on the bulletin board informed workers about actual production and efficiency compared to the standard for each production line.

3. Informal contact with individuals by supervisors.

4. Formal meetings with trainees in skilled labor training program.

5. Performance data were discussed in monthly meetings.

Using these methods improved production significantly. When one of the methods was used alone—daily charting—it was found that, though important, it must be backed up with the other methods used for maximum results (Migliore, 1970).

Another case study used objectives coupled with measurement as a feedback device, posting the objective for each operating unit and entering the quantity produced next to the goal. This method produced productivity increases, employee suggestions to improve productivity, and fewer employee grievances. This research produced a four-step model for establishing an effective feedback system. The elements proposed are:

1. Specify the behavior where improvement is desired,

2. Record the actual performance,

3. Provide positive reinforcement when desired performance occurs, and

4. Monitor and evaluate the process over time (Kirby, 1977).

In researching the effect of feedback on individual or team performance, results showed that there were no significant differences in performance between individual or team members when the effects of a feedback were controlled, thus testifying to the effectiveness of feedback as a managerial tool.

Other experiments show that knowledge of results may have its greatest effect only when a task has previously been performed without this feedback (Brown, 1966); that output increases according to degree of increase in knowledge of performance (Hundal, 1969); and that individuals are not only influenced by feedback about their own performance but also by feedback concerning the consequences of their performance for the work of others (Catano, 1976).

Another aspect of controlled feedback frequently includes explicit attempts at behavioral modification. It is evident from Kritzer's (1974) experiments that feedback is a powerful tool for assisting a member toward positive behavioral change through self-perception. In other behavioral modification studies, five studies of performance as a function of feedback revealed three conditions that seemed to be crucial to the success of the feedback systems studied: 1) performance had to be valued by the performer, 2) the performer had to believe that s/he exercised personal control, and 3) feedback worked best in small groups. It was clearly evident that job performance could be improved with properly administered feedback and that managers can modify and/or maintain performance through a controlled feedback system (Brethower, 1973).

Interaction modeling is another behavioral technique utilizing feedback to improve management skills. Managers trained in this technique in a morale improvement program tended to exhibit more improvement on the job than those without training (Dodd and Pesei, 1977). These authors developed four rules for a successful feedback system based on behavioral approaches:

1. Feedback must be specifically related to performance,

2. Feedback should be reserved for only the important aspects of performance,

3. Feedback should be given as soon as possible after performance, and

4. Feedback should be given only for improvements in performance.

Intrinsic motivation to perform a task is strongly influenced by the type of feedback received. Negative feedback has been found to decrease intrinsic motivation and positive feedback has resulted in greater satisfaction from high performance (Baird, 1976). Baird also found that the effects previously believed to be due to knowledge of results were actually attributable to the different levels of motivation produced by different goals. Motivation toward achievement and affiliation, in conjunction with feedback, were tested in another experiment. Results indicated that:

1. The use of feedback was significant in promoting persistence at a task, and

2. The correlations between feedback and persistence are highest for those with high achievement and low affiliation motivation.

In any human resource system, it is necessary to diagnose human error. In studies of deficiencies of human performance, results seem to indicate that performance decrements are due to deficiencies of knowledge about the nature of the task and/or deficiencies of execution due to factors in the work environment. Analysis via a deficient knowledge/deficient environment framework allows solving people-related performance problems. Rummler (1972) has offered specific prescriptions for managerial action using their framework. Other studies have indicated that deficiencies in job performance are due to poor execution by employees in addition to inadequate knowledge concerning the nature of the task. Poor execution has been attributed to inadequate feedback, task interference, and difficult and exhausting tasks. Many of these causes can be corrected by providing progress reports, engineering job changes, and altering incentives to compensate for task difficulty. Clearly, more research is needed to clarify the complexity of the findings and to more clearly define actions that can be taken to solve performance decrements.

In considering all the intricacies of the application of feedback systems, there seems to be gaps in the research in several areas. More research on the interactive effects of feedback and task difficulty is indicated. In addition, the effects of delays of feedback need more systematic study. A focus on the social system impacts of performance feedback is needed in understanding the effects of knowledge of performance. That is, it is important for us to begin to understand the differential effects of performance feedback on individuals and groups.

However, using the available literature as a base, there is sufficient, reliable evidence available to design a reasonable system that would be effective for certain types of organizations and tasks. The intentional development and implementation of performance-based feedback systems is one of the more useful managerial tools developed by behavioral scientists working within a reinforcement paradigm.

Independent Variable

GOALS

Type of Article	No. of Articles
Applied	3
Descriptive	13
Empirical	31
Integrative	5
Prescriptive	9
Theoretical	7

APPLIED

Latham, G. P. and Kinne, S. B. III, "Improving Job Performance Through Training in Goal-Setting," *Journal of Applied Psychology*, 1974, Vol. 59, No. 2, 187–191.

This article examined the generality of goal-setting theory through an investigation of employee behavior in a natural work environment. Twenty pulpwood logging operations were matched and randomly assigned to either a one day training program in goal-setting or a control group. Measures of production, turnover, absenteeism, and injuries were collected for 12 consecutive weeks. Analysis of variance indicated that goal-setting can lead to an increase in production and a decrease in absenteeism.

Latham, G. P. and Yukl, G. A., "Assigned Versus Participative Goal Setting with Educated and Uneducated Woods Workers," *Journal of Applied Psychology*, June 1975, Vol. 60, No. 3, 229–302.

A field experiment was conducted to compare assigned goal-setting, participative goal-setting, and a "do your best" condition. The experiment was conducted separately for two samples of logging crews that differed in level of education. For the uneducated sample, the participative condition had higher productivity than the assigned and "do your best" conditions. In addition, goal difficulty and goal attainment were significantly higher in the participative condition than in the assigned condition. No significant differences among conditions were found for the educated sample, although this may have been due to problems in implementation of the goal-setting program with this sample.

Campbell, Donald J. and Ilgen, Daniel R., "Additive Effects of Task Difficulty and Goal-Setting on Subsequent Task Performance," *Journal of Applied Psychology*, June 1976, Vol. 61, No. 3, 319–324.

The present study was designed to investigate the relative contribution of goal-setting and task difficulty to performance on chess problems. Employing a 3 × 3 factorial design, 82 chessplaying undergraduates attempted to solve either an easy, moderately difficult, or difficult chess problem after accepting either an easy, moderately difficult, or difficult goal. Task difficulty was operationalized as the number of moves needed to achieve checkmate (1, 2, 3) for each chess problem from a distributed packet (10 problems). Goal-setting was manipulated in the instructions by telling the subject that he should "try to solve at least 20 percent (50 percent or 80 percent)" of the 10 chess problems provided. After feedback was provided on the first problems another packet of chess problems was distributed with instructions specifying the same goal setting level the subject had had before. The packets contained an equal number of 1, 2, and 3 move problems to be completed in 20 minutes. Performance was measured by the number of problems solved correctly overall. The results showed that both goals and task difficulty contributed additively and did not interact with task performance. Those subjects who had experience on the difficult tasks outperformed those with experience with the easy task. Performance with respect to goal-setting was a monotonically increasing function of goal difficulty. The results suggest that effects on task performance were attributable to task knowledge and motivation through goal-setting.

DESCRIPTIVE

Conley, W. D. and Miller, F. W., "MBO, Pay, and Productivity," *Personnel*, January-February 1973, Vol. 50, No. 1, 21–25.

Honeywell Information Systems disclose what they feel to be the keys to the productivity challenge: goal-setting (MBO) and compensation. Honeywell's interpretation of MBO: involves the three-step sequence of 1) agreeing on objectives, 2) putting the goals down on paper, and 3) the periodic review. Honeywell's concept of compensation: based on the conviction that only with unequal compensation can an organization have any hope of preserving and improving its productivity gains. Managers are given maximum flexibility in rewarding performance.

Brady, R. H., "MBO Goes to Work in the Public Sector," *Harvard Business Review*, March-April 1973, Vol. 51, No. 2, 65–74.

An application of MBO in the public sector is reported—the U.S. Department of HEW. Major MBO goals: a) to identify clear, measurable objectives, b) to monitor progress toward objectives, c) to evaluate results. HEW instituted a six-stage objective-setting procedure, implementing the program and an ongoing review process was put into effect. Problems in application: the primary constraint to the success of MBO at HEW has been an attitude required of them by such a system is either a) not consistent with their roles, or b) not as effective a way to manage as some other approach. Benefits/results of HEW's application of MBO: 1) during the fiscal year 1972, the FDA determined that it would attempt to increase by 50 percent the number of import products inspected. It accomplished this goal through MBO, 2) in fiscal year 1971, an objective of a program run by the Social and Rehabilitation Service was to train and place 35,000 welfare recipients in meaningful jobs. It accomplished this goal after the first full year of MBO in operation.

Schultz, G. P. and McKersie, R. B., "Participation-Achievement-Reward Systems (PAR)," *Journal of Management Studies*, May 1973, Vol. 10, No. 2, 141–161.

The PAR approach, its benefits and the factors which determine its feasibility, are discussed in this article. A case study of an oil company is presented, which provides insights into the process of determining whether or not a PAR approach is feasible. A crucial step in the application of the PAR approach is the development of a system to measure achievement. This study explored in depth the measurement problems of the three different operations of the oil company, being especially interested in seeing what adaptations could meet the standards set forth for a good measure. The conclusions of the study make clear that good employee relations are critical to any application of PAR. The authors emphasize that a PAR system will only work when management is ready to exert real leadership. Some weaknesses of the PAR approach are listed as: too much attention may be focused on labor savings and too little on other areas where savings should be made; the approach may occasionally produce inequitable effort-earnings relationships.

Ronan, W. W.; Latham, G. P. and Kinne, S. B. III, "Effects of Goal-Setting and Supervision on Worker Behavior in an Industrial Setting," *Journal of Applied Psychology*, 1973, Vol. 58, No. 3, 302–307.

The effects of goal-setting by supervisors on four performance criteria were investigated. A factor analysis of a questionnaire administered to 292 pulpwood producers indicated that goal-setting is correlated with high productivity and a low number of injuries only when it is accompanied by supervision. Goal-setting without immediate supervision was related to employee turnover. Supervision alone did not correlate with any performance criterion. No relationship was found between the two job behaviors and absenteeism. The factor analysis results pertaining to productivity were partially corroborated in a second study involving data collected from 892 additional producers.

Fay, P. P. and Beach, D. N., "Management by Objectives Evaluated," *Personnel Journal*, October 1974, Vol. 53, No. 10, 767–769.

This reports a study designed to fill the void of systematically controlled MBO research. Subjects: a division of a major manufacturing company. Procedure: an MBO program was implemented. Plant managers were trained in an MBO system which emphasized the definition and delineation of job responsibilities, establishment of the effectiveness of the performance of the job responsibilities, and development of meaningful, measurable and integrated goals. Two years following MBO implementation, a "Coaching Practices Survey" (CPS) was administered. CPS consists of 45 questions dealing with nine types of managerial activity (i.e., responsibilities and goals, delegation, knowledge of performance, motivation). Results demonstrate a consistent relationship existing between the mean of the combined CPS scales and degree of MBO usage. These results supported the conclusion that use of MBO leads to increased managerial activity as measured by the CPS.

Steers, R. M., "Task-Goal Attributes, n Achievement, and Supervisory Performance," *Organizational Behavior and Human Performance*, 1975, Vol. 13, No. 3, 392–403.

This investigation analyzes the relationship between employees' task goals and supervisory performance as moderated by n Achievement among a sample of first-level supervisors working under a formalized goal-setting program. Before need strength levels were taken into account, little consistent relationship was found between the five task-goal attributes and performance. After dividing the subjects into high and low n Ach groups, however, it was found that performance was significantly related to increases in feedback and in goal specificity for high n Ach subjects, and to participation in goal-setting for low n Ach subjects. Goal difficulty and peer competition were found to be unrelated to performance for both groups. These results are then compared to other studies on the topic and it is concluded that individual difference factors, like n Achievement, must be taken into account in any comprehensive theory of goal-setting in organizations.

Steers, Richard M., "Factors Affecting Job Attitudes in a Goal-Setting Environment," *Academy of Management Journal*, March 1976, Vol. 19, No. 1, 6–16.

The relationship between variations in employees' task-goal attributes, individual need strengths, and two job attitudes was studied. The task-goal attributes included are: employee participation in goal-setting; feedback on goal effort; peer competition on goal attainment; goal difficulty; and goal specificity. The subjects in the study were female supervisors employed by a major public utility. Task-goal attributes were measured by a questionnaire (Steers, 1973) designed to measure subject perceptions of variations in goal-setting environment. The two job attitudes, job involvement and job satisfaction, were measured by questionnnaires (Lodahl and Keymen, 1965, and Hackman and Lawler, 1971, respectively).

Job involvement and satisfaction were found to be related to the amount of participation allowed in goal-setting; goal difficulty; and goal specificity; satisfaction was also related to feedback. Neither attitude was related to peer competition. The findings support the contention that variations in a goal-setting environment can play an important role in the determination of job attitudes.

Ivancevich, John M., "Effects of Goal-Setting on Performance and Job Satisfaction," *Journal of Applied Psychology*, October 1976, Vol. 61, No. 5, 605–612.

A field experiment was conducted to compare participative, assigned and no training goal setting with regard to subordinate performance and job satisfaction. A group of 37 sales personnel managers were trained in participative goal-setting. Another group of 41 sales personnel managers were given training in assigned goal-setting. A third group of 44 sales personnel served as a comparison unit. A goal-setting training program using role playing, case analysis, group discussion and lecture was used to illustrate participative goal-setting for the participative group. For the assigned goal-setting, goals were set via assignment by a superior. Measures of four performance and two satisfaction criteria were collected at four data points: baseline (before training), and six months, nine months, and 12 months after training. Performance was measured by a market potential index which took into account total weekly retail sales volume as a function of potential weekly sales volume. Satisfaction of sales personnel was measured by two scales of the JDI (work and supervision).

Analysis of variance and Duncan's multiple range test results indicate that for at least nine months, both the participative and assigned goal-setting participants were more effective than no goal-setting in improving performance and satisfaction. The improvements, however, were generally not found 12 months after training. Participative goal-setting was not superior to assigned goal-setting with regard to performance. However, assigned goal-setting was more effective with regard to satisfaction. He believes this was a function of the particular setting.

Hall, Douglas T. and Foster, Lawrence W., "A Psychological Success Cycle and Goal-Setting: Goals, Performance, and Attitudes," *Academy of Management Journal*, June 1977, Vol. 20, No. 2, 282–290.

Based upon a model of the causes and effects of psychological success, the following series of relationships was predicted for participants (students, N = 61) in a simulated management exercise: goals→ efforts→ performance→ psychological success→ self-esteem→ involvement→ later goals. Two measurements were taken and the relationships were tested with path analysis and cross-lagged correlations. Goals (strength of a person's intentions to perform well) and effort (time and energy spent on the course) were measured by a three-item scale. Performance (net profit) was measured after each of the eight simulated quarters in the exercise. Psychological success (how successful a person feels in the exercise), self-esteem (respondent's image of himself as a player) and involvement (importance of the exercise to the person) were operationalized by various scale items, semantic differential items and an adaptation of the Ledahl and Keyner (1965) scale, respectively. Measurement of all the components in the model, except performance (measured every simulated quarter) was done twice: (third (t_1) and sixth (t_2) quarters). Except for effort→ performance significant relationships indicated support for a cyclical model of career goal development. Correlational causal analyses indicated that good performance leads to increased involvement. Goals were related to effort and effort to psychological success. Also, results support the hypothesized role of involvement as a feedback link between outcome (performance and self-esteem) and inputs (goals). Performance and self-esteem were not related to later goals, while involvement showed a strong relationship.

Ivancevich, John M., "Different Goal-Setting Treatments and Their Effects on Performance and Job Satisfaction," *Academy of Management Journal*, September 1977, Vol. 20, No. 3, 406–419.

A field experiment was conducted to compare participative, assigned and no training goal-setting supervisory groups with regard to subordinate performance and job satisfaction. A group of 58 skilled technicians and eight supervisors in a medium-sized equipment and parts manufacturing organization were trained in participative goal-setting. Another 59 technicians and nine supervisors were given assigned goal-setting training. Sixty-two (62) technicians and 11 supervisors were instructed to "do your best" (no training). A goal-setting training program using role playing, case analysis, group discussion and lecture prepared the two goal-setting groups. The participation program stressed participation between the superior and subordinates in setting goals. In the assigned program, the supervisor was trained in assigning challenging goals. The performance criterion included unexcused absenteeism, service complaints, cost of performance and incidence of work-related accidents. Indexes or rations were devised to measure the performance criterion. Job satisfaction was measured by the "satisfaction with work" and "satisfaction with supervision" scales of the JDI. Performance and satisfaction measures were collected at four data points: baseline (before training) and six months, nine months, and 12 months after training.

Results indicated the participation and assigned goal-setting employees performed better on the indexes of service complaints, cost of performance and safety than that of the no training employees. No significant difference existed between the trained employee groups and the no trained employees with regard to unexcused absenteeism. Both trained groups of employees were more satisfied with work and supervisors than the no training group of employees. The assigned goal-setting group revealed better performance improvement and less service complaints than the participation group but the opposite was true with regard to safety. No differences were found with regard to unexcused absences or job satisfaction between the two trained groups of employees. However, improvements in performance and satisfaction began to dissipate six to nine months after training.

Ivancevich, John M. and McMahon, J. Timothy, "A Study of Task-Goal Attributes, Higher Order Need Strength, and Performance," *Academy of Management Journal*, December 1977, Vol. 20, No. 4, 552–563.

This study attempted to determine how six task-goal attributes are related to various effort and quantitative performance measures. The subjects were 141 skilled maintenance technicians in a manufacturing organization. The six task-goal attributes, challenge of goals, goal clarity, goal-setting involvement, goal feedback, goal committment and goal acceptance, were derived through subject completion of a 34-item questionnaire measuring perception of task-goal attributes. Effort toward quantity (i.e., "working hard to do a lot of work") and effort toward quality (i.e., taking pride in doing excellent work) was measured by supervisory evaluation of subjects on four Likert-Scale items (two each). Four quantitative performance measures were also measured. Absenteeism (percentage of hours absent to total hours), service complaints (employee satisfaction with technicians work), safety (time off the job-related accident), cost of performance (repair job cost) were the quantitative performance measures.

The initial analyses found little consistent relationship between the task-goal attributes and performance measures. When higher-order need strength (i.e., "the chance to work at your own pace") as measured by nine questions answered on a seven-point scale, was introduced as a moderator, the relations between the task-goal attributes and performance measures became clearer. Technicians with high higher-order need strengths indicated that goal challenge, feedback, and clarity were related to effort toward quality and improved unexcused absenteeism, service complaints and safety. The findings indicate that individual differences in the strength of higher-order needs moderated the task-goal attribute-performance relationship.

Wexley, K. N. and Nemeroff, W. F., "Effectiveness of Positive Reinforcement and Goal-Setting as Methods of Management Development," Working Paper, University of Akron, Akron, Ohio, 1–16.

Two managerial training programs were evaluated. One program involved role playing together with delayed appraisal sessions and assigned goal-setting. The other program involved role playing with delayed appraisal sessions, assigned goal-setting, and immediate reinforcement via telecoaching. Measures of managerial behavior and subordinate satisfaction were collected 60 days after the completion of training. The results indicated that the training programs were statistically more effective than a control group in improving the consideration and integration skills of managers and reducing the absenteeism of their subordinates, although the programs were not statistically different from each other. The success of both treatments was accomplished without any undesired reduction in the managers' general level of initiating structure or production emphasis. The program involving delayed appraisal sessions and assigned goal-setting was most effective in increasing subordinate work satisfaction.

Umstot, D. D.; Mitchell, T. R. and Bell, C. H., "Goal-Setting and Job Enrichment: An Integrated Approach to Job Design," *Academy of Management Review*, 1978, Vol. 3, No. 4, 867–879.

This article reviews the empirical literature relating task goals and job enrichment to performance outcomes. The interaction of job characteristics, individual differences, and organizational characteristics is also reviewed, and an integrated model presented that explains the relationships. The authors point out that available research suggests that most of the interactive effects of goal-setting and job enrichment are positive and job design should, therefore, integrate these techniques. Combining job enrichment and goal-setting should improve job satisfaction and productivity, two dominant concerns of managers, which have often been viewed as incompatible.

EMPIRICAL

Locke, E. A., "The Relationship of Intentions to Level of Performance," *Journal of Applied Psychology*, 1966, Vol. 50, No. 1, 60–66.

Three laboratory experiments are reported which stem from Ryan's approach to motivation. The fundamental unit is the "intention". The experiments examined the relationship between intended level of achievement and actual level of performance. Experiment I: Ss (paid summer school volunteers) were divided at random into three groups; assigned a different "standard of achievement" to beat on each trial. The task involved listing objects or things that could be described by a given adjective. Levels of intended achievement were taken to be standards of success. Conclusion: Ss in the "easy" group, whose task was to beat a standard of four, actually beat it comparatively less often than did the Ss in the "medium" and "hard" groups, whose standards were higher. Two more experiments were performed which were similar to the first experiment but with slight task variation. A significant linear relationship was obtained in all three experiments: the higher the level of intention, the higher the level of performance. The findings held both between and within Ss and across different tasks. The implications for the explanation of behavior are discussed.

Locke, E. A. and Bryan, J. F., "Cognitive Aspects of Psychomotor Performance: The Effects of Performance Goals on Level of Performance," *Journal of Applied Psychology*, 1966, Vol. 50, No. 4, 289–291.

An experiment stemming from Mace's work on the effects of performance standards on level of performance is reported. Ss: 29 paid male volunteers from the University of Maryland. Methods: Ss task was to manipulate a set of controls on the Complex Coordination apparatus in order to illuminate a pattern of green lights to match a pre-fixed pattern of illuminated red lights. At the finish of the experiment, Ss were given a questionnaire asking them: a) whether or not they had tried to reach the goals, and b) how many of the patterns they had been able to memorize. This was checked by an actual written recall test. Results: It was found that Ss given specific (but difficult) standards performed at a higher level on a complex psychomotor task than Ss told to "do their best," thus replicating Mace's findings with a computation task. In contrast to Mace's study where performance goals worked by prolonging effort during the latter part of the work periods, standards intensified effort at all stages of the work periods in the present case.

Bryan, J. F. and Locke, E. A., "Goal-Setting as a Means of Increasing Motivation," *Journal of Applied Psychology*, 1967, Vol. 51, No. 3, 274–277.

On the basis of differences in performance in relation to maximal ability and differences in attitude ratings on an addition task, a low-motivation and a high-motivation group were selected for two retests on the same task. The low-motivation group was given specific goals to reach, and the high-motivation group was told to do their best on each trial of each retest. By the end of the second retest, the group given specific goals had "caught" the "do-best" group both in terms of favorable attitudes toward the task. The results suggested that specific goals can be used to motivate Ss who bring a low degree of motivation to the task situation.

Locke, E. A. and Bryan, J. F., "Performance Goals as Determinants of Level of Performance and Boredom," *Journal of Applied Psychology*, 1967, Vol. 51, No. 2, 120–130.

Six experiments (two pilot studies and four main experiments) are reported dealing with the relationship of performance goals to level of performance and degree of boredom or interest in the task. Tasks used included simple addition, perceptual speed, and psychomotor coordination. Trial times ranged from two minutes to two hours. In the two pilot studies post-experimental goal descriptions were significantly related to performance level, and Ss indicated that trying for a specific goal or score was the major source of task interest. In the four main experiments a specific hard goal led to a higher level of performance and more task interest than a goal of "do your best". There was no consistent relationship between changes in boredom or interest and changes in performance within the experimental groups.

Locke, E. A.; Bryan, J. F. and Kendall, L. M., "Goals and Intentions as Mediators of the Effects of Monetary Incentives on Behavior," *Journal of Applied Psychology*, 1968, Vol. 52, No. 2, 104–121.

Based on the assumption that goals and intentions are the most immediate determinants of an individual's behavior, it was hypothesized that monetary incentives would affect task performance only through or by means of their effects on the individual's goals or intentions. Five experiments were performed to explore this hypothesis. Two dealt with the relationship of performance goals to level of performance (output) on a task as a function of incentive condition. Three experiments examined the relationship of behavioral intentions to task choice as a function of incentive. In all five studies, significant relationships were obtained between performance goals or behavioral intentions and behavior. However, when goal or intention level was controlled, there was no effect of monetary incentive on behavior. In the three choice studies where incentives did have an initial effect on choice, these choice differences were accompanied by equivalent differences in intentions. When the latter were partialled out, the original incentive effect was vitiated. The data were interpreted as supporting the hypothesis.

Locke, E. A. and Bryan, J. F., "The Directing Function of Goals in Task Performance," *Organizational Behavior and Human Performance*, 1969, Vol. 4, 35–42.

Two studies are reported which deal with the directing function of goals in task performance. Experiment I: Ss (49 people) worked an addition task for 20 two-minute trials. On one-half of the trials, they were told to maximize the number correct; on the other half of the trials, they were told to minimize the number of errors. Conclusion: Ss made fewer errors when they were trying to minimize errors than when they were trying to maximize the number correct.

Experiment II: Ss were 20 male, undergraduate, paid volunteers. The task was driving a station wagon around a course. Five different aspects of driving performance were monitored. A control group drove the same course receiving no explicit directions.* Conclusions: The experimental findings emphasize the role of goals in regulating the relative amount of improvement individuals will show on different task parameters over time.

Locke, E. A.; Cartledge, N. and Kneer, C.S., "Studies of the Relationship Between Satisfaction, Goal-Setting, and Performance," *Organizational Behavior and Human Performance*, 1970, Vol. 5, 135–158.

Previous research and theory has indicated that a) goals and intentions are the most immediate motivational determinants of task performance;

---

*Postexperimental interviews with the subjects indicated that all of them were trying for their assigned goals. In fact, 100 percent of the experimental subjects changed their performance in the direction of their goals on each trip.

b) external incentives affect behavior through their effects on goals; and c) emotional (affective) reactions are the result of value judgments. The present research was concerned primarily with the problem of how evaluations and emotions lead to goal-setting. It was argued that being dissatisfied with one's past performance generates the desire (and goal) to change one's performance, whereas satisfaction with one's performance produces the desire (and goal) to repeat or maintain one's previous performance level. Five experiments were reported in which: a) satisfaction was predicted from value judgments; b) goal-setting was predicted from satisfaction; and c) performance was predicted from goals. In nearly all cases the correlations were both high and/or significant. It was found, however, that in some cases the level of performance that yielded satisfaction in the past was not necessarily that which produced it in the future. In these cases it was the individual's anticipated (rather than past) satisfaction that best predicted subsequent goal-setting. The relationship of the present theory to other theories of task motivation is discussed briefly (e.g., Dulany; Miller, Galanter, and Pribram; Porter and Lawler; Ryan; and Vroom).

Pritchard, R. D. and Curts, M.I., "The Influence of Goal-Setting and Financial Incentives on Task Performance," *Organizational Behavior and Human Performance*, 1973, Vol. 10, 175–183.

Locke and his colleagues have argued that financial incentives have no effect on behavior outside of their effects on goal-setting. The present study attempted to test this hypothesis with a design that called for the use of larger incentives and for separating the effects of incentives and goal-setting. The subjects were 81 male and female students who signed up for the introductory psychology course at Purdue University. A perceptual-motor task was used which required subjects to sort index cards into stacks according to the information contained on the card. They were told that the task was a type of information sorting task. Each card contained data from one person: sex, education, and income level. Thus 12 configurations of information were possible. The subject's task was to read the card and place it on the one of 12 piles which correspond to that pattern of information. With this type of task, performance could vary along both dimensions of quantity and quality. One of five experimental manipulations were given: goal-setting—no incentive; goal-setting—50¢ incentive; etc. The Ss gave verbal commitment to a goal, after which they were given the incentive manipulation. Each subject had two trials. The study results indicated that both incentives and goal-setting have positive effects on performance and that the Locke predictions are only supported when the incentive is small.

Mobley, W. H., "The Link Between MBO and Merit Compensation," *Personnel Journal*, June 1974, Vol. 53, No. 6, 423–427.

On the basis of a brief review of some of the arguments for and against linking MBO to merit compensation it was suggested that in many situations the positive arguments may outweigh the negative arguments. The results of the study reported here serve to reinforce that conclusion. Most managers in this study, 625 middle-top level managers of a large corporation thought that goal attainment should have some to considerable bearing on merit compensation; believe the advance determination of the importance of goals and mutual understanding of goal difficulty are generally possible; and attempt to link goal attainment to merit compensation. The extent to which MBO is perceived, desired, and/or used with subordinates as a basis for merit compensation is positively associated with perceptions of the worth of MBO, role clarity, and feel for accomplishment; and enhancement of subordinate development and performance. Strengthening the MBO-merit compensation link would appear to be well worth considering.

Hamner, W. C. and Harnett, D. L., "Goal-Setting, Performance and Satisfaction in an Interdependent Task," *Organizational Behavior and Human Performance*, October 1974, Vol. 12, No. 2, 217–229.

This study was designed to determine the effect that goals have on performance and the effect that performance has on reported levels of satisfaction in a comparatively structured task. Subjects were 160 male undergraduate students. Procedure: The subjects participated in an interdependent bargaining task in which a buyer and a seller must reach agreement on the price and quantity of a fictitious commodity which is to be exchanged between them. Variables: Variables measured were 1) performance level (amount of money earned by each subject in the experiment); 2) goal set (amount of money each subject expected to earn); 3) performance satisfaction (determined by a satisfaction with earnings questionnaire); 4) perceived earnings of significance to others (determined by a post-experimental questionnaire to estimate the earnings of their bargaining partners); 5) goal performance discrepancy (degree to which the performance level achieved differed from the goal set). Results: Results of the study found that subjects who exceed their goals performed better, on the average, than those subjects whose performance did not exceed their goals. The results demonstrate a strong similarity between the effect of goal-setting behavior in an independently structured task and a competitively structured task which is consistent with Locke's theory that the higher the intended level of achievement, the higher the levels of performance.

Kim, Jay S. and Hamner, W. Clay, "Effects of Performance Feedback and Goal-Setting on Productivity and Satisfaction in an Organizational Setting," *Journal of Applied Psychology*, February 1976, Vol. 61, No. 1, 48–57.

A quasi-experimental design (N = 113) was employed to investigate the effect of evaluative and nonevaluative feedback and goal-setting performance and satisfaction in a large telephone company. Three experimental groups of blue-collar, unionized employees received either extrinsic feedback (receiving information from the foreman on weekly goal attainment), intrinsic feedback (workers would rate themselves) or extrinsic and intrinsic feedback in addition to goal-setting, while a fourth group received only goal-setting instructions. Goals were set by the management staff without employee participation and were based on three objective performance measures: cost performance (dollar expenditures); absenteeism (eight-hour shifts spent away from the job); safety (point value system for various accidents) and one subjective measure, service (foreman's rating on quality). Satisfaction was measured by using the JDI.

The results show that it is possible for goal-setting alone to enhance performance without a formal knowledge-of-results program, and thus yield external validity for Locke's theory of goal-setting. However, when evaluative and nonevaluative feedback was added to a goal-setting program, performance was generally enhanced beyond that found in the goal-setting-only group. Results also show that extrinsic feedback is not superior to intrinsic feedback although in the area of cost performance the combination of the two resulted in higher performance. The greatest amount of improvement on the subjective rating scale occurred in the external feedback condition. In the area of satisfaction, goal-setting alone enhanced employee's satisfaction as much as feedback. No significant shift in absenteeism was recorded.

Steers, Richard M., "Factors Affecting Job Attitudes in a Goal-Setting Environment," *Academy of Management Journal*, March 1976, Vol. 19, No. 1, 6–16.

The relationship between variations in employee's task-goal attributes, individual need strengths, and two job attitudes was studied. The task-goal attributes included are: employee participation in goal-setting; feedback on goal effort; peer competition on goal attainment; goal difficulty; and goal specificity. The subjects in the study were female supervisors employed by a major public utility. Task-goal attributes were measured by a questionnaire (Steers, 1973) designed to measure subject perceptions of variations in goal-setting environment. The two job attitudes, job involvement and job satisfaction, were measured by questionnaires (Lodahl and Keymen, 1965, and Hackman and Lawler, 1971, respectively).

Job involvement and satisfaction were found to be related to the amount of participation allowed in goal-setting, goal difficulty, and goal specificity; satisfaction was also related to feedback. Neither attitude was related to peer competition. The findings support the contention that variations in a goal-setting environment can play an important role in the determination of job attitudes.

Latham, Gary P. and Yukl, Gary A., "Effects of Assigned and Participative Goal-Setting on Performance and Job Satisfaction," *Journal of Applied Psychology*, April 1976, Vol. 61, No. 2, 166–171.

The job performance of typists (N = 41) under participative or assigned goal-setting was evaluated over a 10-week period. In the participative goal-setting condition, weekly goals were set jointly by the typists and supervisors. In the assigned condition, the weekly goals were set by the supervisor alone ("difficult but attainable"). Performance was measured by the weighted sum of the lines typed during the week divided by the number of hours worked. Job satisfaction was measured by a two-item questionnaire administered before the study began and during the final week of the goal-setting. Goal attainment was measured as the percentage of weeks in which the performance of a typist was equal to or better than the goal.

Results indicated significant productivity improvement occurred in both goal setting conditions during the second five weeks of goal-setting. There was no significant difference between conditions with respect to goal difficulty or frequency of goal attainment. Job satisfaction declined slightly in both goal-setting conditions. Conclusions reached in the study suggest that the amount of subordinate participation in goal-setting is not as important as the actual setting of the goal itself, assuming that the goal is accepted by the subordinate.

Lopes, Lola L., "Individual Strategies in Goal-Setting," *Organizational Behavior and Human Performance*, April 1976, Vol. 15, No. 2, 268–277.

Information integration theory was applied in a study of long-term behavior in a goal-setting task. Goal-setting was conceptualized as a process of series integration in which the goal on any one trial is a weighted average of previous successes and failures. Six subjects performed a computer controlled maze-running task, received score feedback, and predicted their score for the next trial. The data of all six subjects supported the serial integration model, but with individual differences in the number of preceding trials to which the subject attended. In addition, the data of two subjects suggested that they also attended to immediate rate of progress on the task.

Campbell, Donald J. and Ilgen, Daniel R., "Additive Effects of Task Difficulty and Goal-Setting on Subsequent Task Performance," *Journal of Applied Psychology*, June 1976, Vol. 61, No. 3, 319–324.

The present study was designed to investigate the relative contribution of goal setting and task difficulty to performance on chess problems. Employing a 3 × 3 factorial design, 82 chessplaying undergraduates attempted to solve either an easy, moderately difficult, or difficult chess problem, after accepting either an easy, moderately difficult, or difficult goal. Task difficulty was operationalized as the number of moves needed to achieve checkmate (1, 2, 3) for each chess problem from a distributed packet (10 problems). Goal setting was manipulated in the instructions by telling the subject that he should "try to solve at least 20 percent (50 percent or 80 percent)" of the 10 chess problems provided. After feedback was provided on the first problems, another packet of chess problems was distributed with instructions specifying the same goal-setting level the subject had had before. The packets contained an equal number of one, two, and three move problems to be completed in 20 minutes. The results showed that both goals and task difficulty contributed additively and did not interact with task performance. Those subjects who had experience on the difficult tasks outperformed those with experience with the easy task. Performance with respect to goal-setting was a monotonically increasing function of goal difficulty. The results suggest that effects on task performance were attributable to task knowledge and motivation through goal-setting.

Ivancevich, John M., "Effects of Goal-Setting on Performance and Job Satisfaction," *Journal of Applied Psychology*, October 1976, Vol. 61, No. 5, 605–612.

A field experiment was conducted to compare participative, assigned and no training goal setting with regard to subordinate performance and job satisfaction. A group of 37 sales personnel managers were trained in participative goal-setting. Another group of 41 sales personnel managers were given training in assigned goal-setting. A third group of 44 sales personnel served as a comparison unit. A goal-setting training program using role playing, case analysis, group discussion and lecture was used to illustrate participative goal-setting for the participative group. For the assigned goal-setting goals were set via assignment by a superior. Measures of four performance and two satisfaction criteria were collected at four data points: baseline (before training), and six months, nine months, and 12 months after training. Performance was measured by a market potential index which took into account total weekly retail sales volume as a function of potential weekly sales volume. Satisfaction of sales personnel was measured by two scales of the JDI (work and supervision).

Analysis of variance and Duncan's multiple range test results indicate that for at least nine months, both the participative and assigned goal-setting participants were more effective than no goal-setting in improving performance and satisfaction. The improvements, however, were generally not found 12 months after training. Participative goal-setting was not superior to assigned goal-setting with regard to performance. However, assigned goal-setting was more effective with regard to satisfaction. He believes this was a function of the particular setting.

Terborg, James R., "The Motivational Components of Goal-Setting," *Journal of Applied Psychology*, October 1976, Vol. 61, No. 5, 613–621.

The relationships among goal-setting, monetary incentives, two indexes of motivation (i.e., effort and direction of behavior), and performance were examined in an experimental simulation. Sixty subjects (male and female) were hired to a one-week job consisting of working on programmed texts (PTs) designed to teach introductory principles of electricity. Subjects were required to study the PTs and pass short tests (75 percent correct) on each section. Goal-setting was determined by the degree to which their responses during interviews represented performance goals with regard to test score and speed of completion. A three-point scale was used to code responses. Monetary incentive was manipulated by the different methods pay used (average $2.00 per hour)—either hourly (not contingent on speed in completing text) or contingent on speed. Effort (i.e., how hard a person tries) was measured by time-lapse photography and coded with reference to visual contact with PTs. Direction of behavior (appropriate behaviors while working through the material) was measured by a 23-item questionnaire which listed various activities judged to be appropriate. The performance variable included indexes for speed of performance (total number of minutes to complete PTs) and percentage correct on a 55-item comprehensive test (test score goal setting item).

The general pattern of the results suggested that goal-setting and monetary incentives were related independently to measures of motivation and performance. Incentives, however, had no impact on whether or not subjects set performance goals. The importance of identifying the processes surrounding the effects of stated task goals and monetary incentives on performance is discussed.

Frost, Peter I and Mahoney, Thomas A., "Goal-Setting and the Task Process: An Interactive Influence on Individual Performance," *Organizational Behavior and Human Performance*, December 1976, Vol. 17, No. 2, 328–350.

Goal performance relationships investigated in this laboratory study were based on a model of individual performance as influenced by the specificity and difficulty of goals assigned and by the frequency of performance intervals allocated for task completion. The form of these relationships was considered to be shaped by the prescriptiveness of the task process involved. Task process was found to differentiate the form of some goal-performance characteristics: pacing the individual improved performance on a repetitive task (fixed process), but had no significant effect on a problem-solving task (non-prescribed, variable process); focusing effort through a specific goal improved performance on a problem-solving task, but had no significant influence on repetitive task performance.

A post hoc separation of the 240 subjects in the experimental group into low and high task interest categories showed on analysis that high interest subjects outperformed low interest subjects on each task. The findings suggest a differential locus of interest, being externally induced in a repetitive task and intrinsic to a problem-solving task.

Ivancevich, John M., "Different Goal-Setting Treatments and Their Effects on Performance and Job Satisfaction," *Academy of Management Journal*, September 1977, Vol. 20, No. 3, 406–419.

A field experiment was conducted to compare participative, assigned and no training goal-setting supervisory groups with regard to subordinate performance and job satisfaction. A group of 58 skilled technicians and eight supervisors in a medium sized equipment and parts manufacturing organization were trained in participative goal-setting. Another 59 technicians and nine supervisors were given assigned goal-setting training. Sixty-two (62) technicians and 11 supervisors were instructed to "do your best" (no training). A goal-setting training program using role playing, case analysis, group discussion and lecture prepared the two goal-setting groups. The participation program stressed participation between the superior and subordinates in setting goals. In the assigned program, the supervisor was trained in assigning challenging goals. The performance criterion included unexcused absenteeism, service complaints, cost of performance and incidence of work related accidents. Indexes or ratios were devised to measure the performance criterion. Job satisfaction was measured by the "satisfaction with work" and "satisfaction with supervision" scales of the JDI. Performance and satisfaction measures were collected at four data points: baseline (before training) and six months, nine months, and 12 months after training.

Results indicated the participation and assigned goal-setting employees performed better on the indexes of service complaints, cost of performance and safety than that of the no-training employees. No significant difference existed between the trained employee groups and the no-trained employees with regard to unexcused absenteeism. Both trained groups of employees were more satisfied with work and supervisors than the no training group of employees. The assigned goal-setting group revealed better performance improvement and less service complaints than the participation group but the opposite was true with regard to safety. No differences were found with regard to unexcused absences or job satisfaction between the two trained groups of employees. However, improvements in performance and satisfaction began to dissipate six to nine months after training.

The initial analyses found little consistent relationship between the task-goal attributes and performance measures. When higher-order need strength (i.e., "the chance to work at your own pace") as measured by nine questions answered on a seven-point scale, was introduced as a moderator, the relations between the task-goal attributes and performance measures became clearer. Technicians with high higher-order need strengths indicated that goal challenge, feedback, and clarity were related to effort toward quantity and unexcused absenteeism. Technicians with low higher-order need strength reported that goal acceptance was related to effort toward quality and improved unexcused absenteeism, service complaints and safety. The findings indicate that individual differences in the strength of higher-order needs moderated the task-goal attribute-performance relationship.

White, Sam E.; Mitchell, Terence R. and Bell Jr., Cecil H., "Goal-Setting, Evaluation Apprehension, and Social Cues as Determinants of Job

Performance and Job Satisfaction in a Simulated Organization," *Journal of Applied Psychology*, December 1977, Vol. 62, No. 6, 665–673.

A simulated organizational setting involving a routine clerical task was the experimental context for the research. One hundred and four subjects (business students) were randomly assigned in a factorial design including two levels of goal-setting (either as assigned production goal or no goal), two levels of evaluation apprehension, and three types of social cues (positive, neutral, and negative) to investigate the effects of the independent variables on employee productivity and job satisfaction. The task involved card sorting based on some fictitious biographical information. Goal-setting was manipulated by telling the subject to set his production goal at 750 cards per hour as opposed to no assigned goal. Social cues were established by pairing subjects with confederates who verbalized either positive, neutral or negative comments about the task and work environment. Productivity was measured by the number of cards sorted per minute. Job satisfaction was assessed by a questionnaire consisting of various scales of the JDI (work scale) and JDS (general satisfaction scale).

The results showed that people with assigned goals produced more than people without assigned goals, people with high evaluation apprehension produced more than people with low evaluation apprehension, and people receiving positive social cues produced more than people receiving negative social cues. The independent variables had no main effect on overall job satisfaction. The implications of the results are that goal-setting does have an independent motivating effect on task performance but also that evaluation apprehension and social cues contribute to increased performance.

Erez, Marian, "Feedback: A Necessary Condition for the Goal-Setting Performance Relationship," *Journal of Applied Psychology*, October 1977, Vol. 62, No. 5, 624–627.

The study focused on feedback as a necessary condition for goals to affect performance. It was predicted that feedback and goals would be interactively related to performance. This prediction complements the findings of Locke that knowledge alone is not a sufficient condition for effective performance. It was also hypothesized that feedback would facilitate the display of individual differences in goal setting and hence the goal-setting performance relationship. The subjects (N = 86) were two groups of undergraduates who participated in a task in which lists of numbers were quickly checked for discrepancies. After performing the task the first time (10 minute period), the experimental group were given information of their performance in relation to group (10 percent, 25 percent, 50 percent, 90 percent) percentiles. The control group received no feedback on performance. A questionnaire designed to assess subjects' intentions or self-set goals for the second period. The questionnaire was a five-point scale, similar to the levels of feedback (10 percent, 25 percent, etc.).

Results supported the hypotheses by indicating that the individual differences in self-set goals were significantly higher in the feedback group (N = 38) than in the no-feedback group (N = 48), and that it was in the feedback condition that the relationship between goals and performance (4 = .60) was significantly higher than in the no-feedback condition (4 = .01). The author concludes that knowledge of score has a significant effect on goal-setting and that it is a necessary condition for goals to affect performance.

Ivancevich, John M. and McMahon, J. Timothy, "A Study of Task-Goal Attributes, Higher Order Need Strength, and Performance," *Academy of Management Journal*, December 1977, Vol. 20, No. 4, 552–563.

This study attempted to determine how six task-goal attributes are related to various effort and quantitative performance measures. The subjects were 141 skilled maintenance technicians in a manufacturing organization. The six task-goal attributes—challenge of goals, goal clarity, goal setting involvement, goal feedback, goal committment and goal acceptance—were derived through subject completion of a 34-item questionnaire measuring perception of task-goal attributes. Effort toward quantity (i.e., "working hard to do a lot of work") and effort toward quality (i.e., taking pride in doing excellent work) was measured by supervisory evaluation of subjects on four Likert-Scale items (two each). Four quantitative performance measures were also measured. Absenteeism (percentage of hours absent to total hours), service complaints (employee satisfaction with technicians work), safety (time off the job-related accident), cost of performance (repair job cost) were the quantitative performance measures.

Becker, Lawrence J., "Joint Effect of Feedback and Goal-Setting on Performance: A Field Study of Residential Energy Conservation," *Journal of Applied Psychology*, 1978, Vol. 63, No. 4, 428–433.

The facilitating motivational effect of feedback on performance has been attributed by some to difficult goals set in response to feedback. In the present article the effect was attributed to the presence of both a difficult goal and feedback about performance in relation to that goal. Eighty families were asked to set a goal to reduce their residential electricity consumption for several weeks during the summer, half of them by 20 percent (a difficult goal) and half by two percent (an easy goal). Within each of these groups, half of the families were given feedback three times a week about their consumption. Twenty more families served as a control. As predicted, the 20 percent-feedback group conserved the most (13-15.1 percent) and was the only one that consumed significantly less electricity than the control. It was concluded that improved performance was a result of the joint effect of feedback and goal-setting. The implications of the present research for a national residential conservation strategy are discussed.

Latham, G. P.; Mitchell, T. R. and Dosset, D. L., "Importance of Participative Goal-Setting and Anticipated Rewards on Goal Difficulty and Job Performance," *Journal of Applied Psychology*, 1978, Vol. 63, No. 2, 163–171.

This article presents a two-stage field experiment to assess the impact of participative goal-setting and anticipated rewards on goal difficulty and job performance. In the first stage, engineers/scientists (n = 76), either participated in the setting of or were assigned specific behavioral goals during their performance appraisals. Also, they were put into three types of anticipated reward conditions: private recognition, public recognition, and monetary bonus. The dependent variable was goal difficulty. Participative goal-setting resulted in more difficult goals being set than was the case when the goals were assigned. Perceptions of goal difficulty, however, were not significantly different in the two goal-setting conditions. The second part of the experiment used data (n = 132) collected six months later on actual job performance. The 2 × 3 design of the first stage of the experiment was expanded to a 3 × 3 by adding a "do your best" goal condition. The analysis of the performance data revealed main effects for both goal-setting and anticipated rewards. Only participative goal-setting led to significantly higher performance than the "do your best" group and a control group. There was no significant difference between the performance of the latter two conditions despite the fact that the individual in the "do your best" group received knowledge of results.

Strang, Harold R.; Lawrence, Edith C. and Fowler, Patrick C., "Effects of Assigned Goal Level and Knowledge of Results of Arithmetic Computation: A Laboratory Study," *Journal of Applied Psychology*, 1978, Vol. 63, No. 4, 446–450.

The present study examined the effects of knowledge of results (KR) and assigned goals on arithmetic computation. Female university students (n = 100) either received or did not receive explicit KR while under easy or challenging goal assignment. A control group (n = 50) received neither KR nor goal assignment. Subjects receiving KR under challenging goal assignment significantly increased their computational speed at no apparent cost in accuracy. These findings are congruous with the 1977 findings of Erez. With the minimizing of implicity KR in the no-KR groups in the present study, challenging goal assigment in itself had no noticeable effect on computational speed and led to a significant increase in errors. It is suggested that feedback may be a necessary complement to assigned goals in facilitating performance.

Terborg, James R. and Miller, Howard E., "Motivation, Behavior, and Performance: A Closer Examination of Goal-Setting and Monetary Incentives," *Journal of Applied Psychology*, 1978, Vol. 63, No. 1, 29–39.

Some experimenters often test predictions from theories of motivation using performance outcomes as dependent variables. We argue that observable behaviors that are likely to be affected by motivation manipulations should be used in combination with performance outcomes. Such procedures would be sensitive to differential effects of manipulations on various behaviors and would allow for investigation of relationships among behaviors and performance outcomes. For this experiment, 60 males were hired to work individually on a two-hour construction task. Subjects were assigned to one of two pay conditions (piece-rate versus hourly) and one of three goal-crossed conditions (no goal, quantity, or quality) resulting in a 2 × 3 crossed analysis of variance design. Dependent variables included three measures of effort, three measures of direction of behavior, and both quantity and quality performance. Method of payment affected quantity performance and effort. Goal-setting affected quantity and quality performance and direction of behavior. Implications for designing and testing work motivation systems are discussed.

Yukl, Gary A. and Latham, Gary P., "Interrelationships Among Employee Participation, Individual Differences, Goal Difficulty, Goal Acceptance, Goal Instrumentality, and Performance," *Personnel Psychology*, 1978, Vol. 31, No. 2, 305–323.

A field study was conducted with 41 female typists in a large corporation to test an explanatory model of goal-setting. Weekly productivity goals were either assigned by the supervisors or were set jointly with a typist. Goals were set for 10 consecutive weeks. A correlational analysis of the data indicated that difficult goals led to higher performance. Higher performance led to higher absolute goals for the subsequent week, but smaller improvement goals. Persons with a high need for achievement and an internal control orientation set higher goals. Goal-setting led to greater overall performance improvement for employees who had high self esteem or who perceived goal attainment to be instrumental for getting extrinsic rewards. Hypothesized relationships involving goal acceptance were not supported, which may have been due to a lack of validity for the goal acceptance measure.

Latham, G. P. and Saar, L. M., "The Effects of Holding Goal Difficulty Constant on Assigned and Participatively Set Goals," *Academy of Management Journal*, 1979, Vol. 22, No. 1, 163–168.

The authors point to three field experiments (Latham and Yukl, 1975; Latham and Yukl, 1976; Latham, Mitchell, and Dosset, 1978) which suggest that employee participation in goal-setting is important to the extent that it leads to higher goals being set than when a manager sets goals unilaterally. The present study was designed to test this assumption by holding goal difficulty constant between two goal-setting conditions, assigned and participative, and a "do your best" condition. College students (n = 60) were randomly assigned to a condition. Results found that 1) more ideas were generated in both the assigned and participative groups in comparison to the "do your best" group. This indicates that setting a specific goal leads to higher performance on a brainstorming task than does a philosophy of trying to do one's best; 2) holding goal difficulty constant resulted in a significantly higher number of ideas being generated in the participative condition as compared to the assigned condition.

Latham, Gary P. and Saar, Lise M., "Importance of Supportive Relationships in Goal-Setting," *Journal of Applied Psychology*, April 1979, Vol 64, No. 2, 151–156.

The importance of supportive behavior by an authority figure when setting goals was lasting. Ninety students were randomly assigned to a supportive or nonsupportive condition and to one of three goal-setting conditions. Goal difficulty was held constant. Supportive behavior resulted in higher goals being set than nonsupportive behavior. Participatively set goals led to better performance than assigned goals. Participation seems important in that it increases understanding of task requirements. Supportiveness appears to be important primarily because it gives both subordinates and supervisors the confidence to set high goals, which in turn lead to high levels of performance.

Dossett, Dennis L.; Latham, Gary P. and Mitchell, Terence R., "Effects of Assigned versus Participatively Set Goals, Knowledge of Results, and Individual Differences on Employee Behavior When Goal Difficulty is Held Constant," *Journal of Applied Psychology*, June 1979, Vol. 64, No. 3, 291–298.

Female clerical personnel were randomly assigned to participative, assigned and "do best" goal conditions on a clerical test. Specific goals led to higher performance than did the "do best" goals. And, with goal difficulty held constant, there was no significant difference between the assigned and participative conditions on performance or goal acceptance. No main or interaction effects were found for knowledge of results or for individual difference measures with performance or goal acceptance. There was a positive linear relationship between goal difficulty and performance in the participative condition only. The authors say that assigned goals that are difficult and challenging can lead to efficient performance, and the time saved by deleting the participation process could be substantial.

Dossett, Dennis L.; Latham, Gary P. and Saar, Lise M., "The Impact of Goal-Setting on Survey Returns," *Academy of Management Journal*, September 1980, Vol 23, No. 3, 561–566.

This study was conducted within a theoretical framework that can be used to explain the impact of organizational deadlines on employee behavior in an industrial setting. The sample consisted of 401 male employees ages 25 to 65 in an international company in the northwestern U.S. Questionnaires were given to each employee, some requested return within two days, another group within five days and the last group "as soon as possible". Degrees of anonymity and authority were manipulated by a cover letter. When the cover letter was signed by a supervisor (not the researcher) there was a greater effort to comply with instructions. The authors conclude that the results extend the generalizability of the goal-setting theory regarding time limits. Setting specific hard goals affects the speed of return; a hard goal can lead to surveys being returned with more frequency than "as soon as possible". Also, goal-setting did not appear to affect the percentage of returns. But supervisory (authority) presence appeared to be a key to goal acceptance.

INTEGRATIVE

Hersey, P. and Kellner, C. A., "A Behavioral Approach to Training the Sales Force," *Training and Development Journal*, November 1968, Vol. 22, No. 11, 2–9.

The author examines ideas from the behavioral sciences and develops a framework to apply a new approach to sales management philosophy and manpower development. A portrait of today's salesman: less susceptible to group interaction; highly individual in his work habits; morale is very important to his overall effectiveness; and motivation must be self-sustaining. The authors foresee the most hope in the organization that provides a climate in which the sales force have a sense of working for themselves, through achieving their personal goals by the achievement of company goals. Goal-setting and management-by-objectives are what is prescribed to meet these ends. However, whether or not MBO will actually prove to be an improvement over previous motivational methods will depend in the final analysis on the "review and revision" procedures. The real success is the continuing dialogue and feedback which these new concepts encourage.

Locke, Edwin A., "The Ubiquity of the Technique of Goal-Setting in Theories of and Approaches to Employee Motivation," *Academy of Management Review*, 1978, Vol. 3, No. 3, 594–601.

Goal-setting is recognized, explicitly or implicitly, by virtually every major theory of work motivation. It was recognized explicitly by advocates of Scientific Management and of Management by Objectives. Ignored in early versions of Human Relations and expectancy (VIE) theory, it now is more openly acknowledged. Cognitive Growth and Organizational Behavior Modification deny the significance of goal-setting in theory, but not when they are put into practice. The ubiquity of goal-setting in these theories stems from the general recognition that rational human action is goal directed.

Pate, Larry E., "Cognitive Versus Reinforcement Views of Intrinsic Motivation," *Academy of Management Review*, 1978, Vol. 3, No. 3, 505–514.

The research of Deci and associates regarding the effective of extrinsic rewards on intrinsic motivation has stimulated controversy among cognitive and reinforcement theorists. Theoretical roots of cognitive and reinforcement theories are traced, and the controversy over Deci's research is examined, particularly with regard to Scott's recent critique (1975). Implications of these discrepant positions and potential areas of research and application in work organizations are discussed.

Umstot, D. D.; Mitchell, T. R. and Bell, C. H., "Goal-Setting and Job Enrichment: An Integrated Approach to Job Design," *Academy of Management Review*, 1978, Vol. 3, No. 4, 867–879.

This article reviews the empirical literature relating task goals and job enrichment to performance outcomes. The interaction of job characteristics, individual differences, and organizational characteristics is also reviewed, and an integrated model presented that explains the relationships. The authors point out that available research suggests that most of the interactive effects of goal-setting and job enrichment are positive and job design should, therefore, integrate these techniques. Combining job enrichment and goal-setting should improve job satisfaction and productivity, two dominant concerns of managers, which have often been viewed as incompatible.

Guzzo, Richard A., "Types of Rewards, Cognitions, and Work Motivation," *Academy of Management Review*, 1979, Vol. 4, No. 1, 75–86.

Work rewards often are conceptualized as being of two types: intrinsic and extrinsic. Further, cognitions associated with different types of rewards typically are conceived of in terms derived from attribution theory. A review of the grounds used to dichotomize reward types reveals they are inadequate for distinguishing types of rewards and a review of existing data on the nature of cognitions associated with work rewards indicates the attributional perspective to be deficient. Alternative approaches to the definition of types of work rewards and variants of cognitions mediating the relationship between work rewards and motivation are discussed.

PRESCRIPTIVE

Sterner, F. M., "Do You Motivate or Manipulate?", *Personal Journal*, March 1970, Vol. 15, No. 3, 29–33.

Sterner describes some sample situations with the intent of distinguishing for the reader between motivation and manipulation. He prescribes how to effectively motivate: 1) talk to employees about their objectives and ambitions; 2) encourage an MBO approach; 3) provide recognition when deserved; 4) help people to develop competence which leads to top performance; and 5) share company information with subordinates.

Zimmerer, T. W., "Increasing Productivity Among Marginal Employees," *Industrial Management*, January 1973, Vol. 15, No. 1, 1–3.

The marginal worker is one whom the system has failed to get involved or motivated. This motivational breakdown can be repaired through implementation of mutually reinforcing programs of management by objectives and self-rating appraisal systems. The marginal employee who has poor performance due to failure to understand his role is unmotivated by the present techniques. This linking of MBO and performance appraisals brings solidarity between top management's plans or goals and individual success on the job. The employee can subsequently perceive his goal achievement as being a function of participation within a prescribed pattern of behavior. This pattern of behavior rewards the employee with recognition and success and, when combined with similar patterns of behavior of other employees, forms a system of activities directed toward completion of objectives at all levels of the organization.

Hand, H. H. and Hollingsworth, A. T., "Tailoring MBO to Hospitals," *Business Horizons*, February 1975, Vol. 18, No. 1, 45–52.

This article is concerned with the general problem of the administration of a hospital wage system and specifically concerned with the problems of employee productivity and turnover. MBO is suggested as a method by which administrators can best use their budgets to maximize utilization and retention of the hospital's human assets. The first part of the article deals with the effect of pay on employee turnover and productivity. The latter portion of the article deals with establishing an MBO Program. Ideally, the program should be initiated when both the executive director and board of directors establish support for the program and clearly define the mission of the hospital. The executive director should arrange meetings with directors of various agencies. This process should be continued through the hospital organization until all employees have taken part in the objectives-setting process. The program recommended is designed to decrease costs, improve patient care, and involve a system of specific checklists (feedback) to measure various aspects of quality care. The authors conclude with the reminder that a major problem in MBO is implementation of the program. Commitment to the precepts of MBO is perhaps the single most critical factor in improving a wage administration program in hospitals.

Becker, Lawrence J., "Joint Effect of Feedback and Goal-Setting on Performance: A Field Study of Residential Energy Conservation," *Journal of Applied Psychology*, 1978, Vol. 63, No. 4, 428–433.

The facilitating motivational effect of feedback on performance has been attributed by some to difficult goals set in response to feedback. In the present article, the effect was attributed to the presence of both a difficult goal and feedback about performance in relation to that goal. Eighty families were asked to set a goal to reduce their residential electricity consumption for several weeks during the summer, half of them by 20 percent (a difficult goal) and half by two percent (an easy goal). Within each of these groups, half of the families were given feedback three times a week about their consumption. Twenty more families served as a control. As predicted, the 20 percent feedback group conserved the most (13-15.1 percent) and was the only one that consumed significantly less electricity than the control. It was concluded that improved performance was a result of the joint effect of feedback and goal-setting. The implications of the present research for a national residential conservation strategy are discussed.

Locke, Edwin A., "The Ubiquity of the Technique of Goal-Setting in Theories of and Approaches to Employee Motivation," *Academy of Management Review*, 1978, Vol. 3, No. 3, 594–601.

Goal-setting is recognized, explicitly or implicitly, by virtually every major theory of work motivation. It was recognized explicitly by advocates of Scientific Management and of Management by Objectives. Ignored in early versions of human relations and expectancy theory (VIE), it now is more openly acknowledged. Cognitive growth and organizational behavior modification deny the significance of goal setting in theory, but not when they are put into practice. The ubiquity of goal-setting in these theories stems from the general recognition that rational human action is goal directed.

Strang, Harold R.; Lawrence, Edith C. and Fowler, Patrick C., "Effects of Assigned Goal Level and Knowledge of Results on Arithmetic Computation: A Laboratory Study," *Journal of Applied Psychology*, 1978, Vol. 63, No. 4, 446–450.

The present study examined the effects of knowledge of results (KR) and assigned goals on arithmetic computation. Female university students (n = 100) either received or did not receive explicit KR while under easy or challenging goal assignment. A control group (n = 50) received neither KR nor goal assignment. Subjects receiving KR under challenging goal assignment significantly increased their computational speed at no apparent cost in accuracy. These findings are congruous with the 1977 findings of Erez. With the minimizing of implicit KR in the no-KR groups in the present study, challenging goal assignment in itself had no noticeable effect on computational speed and led to a significant increase in errors. It is suggested that feedback may be a necessary complement to assigned goals in facilitating performance.

Terborg, James R. and Miller, Howard E., "Motivation, Behavior, and

Performance: A Closer Examination of Goal-Setting and Monetary Incentives," *Journal of Applied Psychology*, 1978, Vol. 63, No. 1, 29–39.

Some experimenters often test predictions from theories of motivation using performance outcomes as dependent variables. We argue that observable behaviors that are likely to be affected by motivation manipulations should be used in combination with performance outcomes. Such procedures would be sensitive to differential effects of manipulations on various behaviors and would allow for investigation of relationships among behaviors and performance outcomes. For this experiment, 60 males were hired to work individually on a two-hour construction task. Subjects were assigned to one of two pay conditions (piece-rate versus hourly) and one of three goal-setting conditions (no goal, quantity, or quality) resulting in a 2 x 3 crossed analysis of variance design. Dependent variables included three measures of effort, three measures of direction of behavior, and both quantity and quality performance. Method of payment affected quantity performance and effort. Goal-setting affected quantity and quality performance and direction of behavior. Implications for designing and testing work motivation systems are discussed.

Muczyk, Jan P., "Dynamics and Hazards of MBO Application," *Personnel Administrator*, May 1979, Vol. 24, No. 5, 51–61.

Muczyk says the vast appeal of Management By Objectives is due to its seductive properties: almost anyone can use it, it is offered as a solution to just about any problem an organization faces. But Muczyk calls MBO a gross oversimplification of the management process and states that it is further flawed because reports on its effectiveness are often based on inflated (unreliable) self-reporting systems. The author details specific weaknesses and actual failures in applied cases. The failures will continue, the author concludes, so long as consultants are selling MBO as a "canned" approach. MBO must be melded with appropriate OD techniques of thorough data base needs analysis of technical, managerial and human subsystems and an array of diagnostic methods.

Kaye, Beverly L., "How You Can Help Employees Formulate Their Career Goals," *Personnel Journal*, May 1980, Vol. 59, No. 6, 368–372 and 402.

The author offers the benefit of her experience as a human resource professional in developing and attaining specific career goals and outlines a detailed step-by-step approach which links both organizational realities and individual preference. Goal selection and goal formulation are covered topics as well as how to build an "Action Goal Statement" which includes the following considerations: 1) Specificity of career goals/statements, 2) Time-frame (target dates strengthen the goal statement by providing milestones or benchmarks), 3) Attainability (within a specified time period), 4) Measurability (sequences of desired outcomes along the way), 5) Visibility (sharing career goals with mentors and others in the organization will prove helpful), and 6) Relevance (Is this career goal relevant to the employee's needs and to those of the organization now and in the future?). When the goal-setting process is completed, employees will have identified, written, and selectively chosen goals which are appropriate and meaningful, both for themselves and for the organization.

THEORETICAL

Chung, K. H., "Toward a General Theory of Motivation and Performance," *California Management Review*, Spring 1969, Vol. 11, No. 3, 81–88.

The two approaches to motivational study—partial theory (analyzes particular systems) and general theory (analyzes general features of human motivation and performance)—are not necessarily exclusive but, in fact, complement each other. The primary purpose of this article is to explore the possibilities of developing a general theory which would include a broad class of determinants of performance. Without a change to this direction in the near future, the richness of empirical data in partial theories may destroy the systematic construction of a general theory of motivation and performance. A general theory model is structured on a three stage model. The first stage involves ability and motivation as major determinants of job performance. The second stage specifies the major variables of motivation and describes their interaction. The third stage is primarily concerned with motivational factors that constitute each major variable of motivation and are brought together in a unidimensional theory of performance. A broad class of determinants of performance are taken into consideration in this comprehensive scheme without restricting the study to a limited amount of motivational variables, assuming other variables are constant.

Hall, Douglas T. and Foster, Lawrence W., "A Psychological Success Cycle and Goal-Setting: Goals, Performance, and Attitudes," *Academy of Management Journal*, June 1977, Vol. 20, No. 2, 282–290.

Based upon a model of the causes and effects of psychological success, the following series of relationships was predicted for participants (students, $N = 61$) in a simulated management exercise: goals→ efforts→ performance→ psychological success→ self-esteem→ involvement→ later goals. Two measurements were taken and the relationships were tested with path analysis and cross-lagged correlations. Goals (strength of a person's intentions to perform well) and effort (time and energy spent on the course) were measured by a three-item scale. Performance (net profit) was measured after each of the eight simulated quarters in the exercise. Psychological success (how successful a person feels in the exercise), self-esteem (respondent's image of himself as a player) and involvement (importance of the exercise to the person) were operationalized by various scale items, semantic differential items and an adaptation of the Ledahl and Keyner (1965) scale, respectively. Measurement of all the components in the model, except performance (measured every simulated quarter) was done twice: (Third (t_1) and sixth (t_2) quarters). Except for effort→ performance, significant relationships indicated support for a cyclical model of career goal development. Correlational causal analyses indicated that good performance leads to increased involvement. Goals were related to effort and effort to psychological success. Also, results support the hypothesized role of involvement as a feedback link between outcome (performance and self-esteem) and inputs (goals). Performance and self-esteem were not related to later goals, while involvement showed a strong relationship.

Pate, Larry E., "Cognitive Versus Reinforcement Views of Intrinsic Motivation," *Academy of Management Review*, 1978, Vol. 3, No. 3, 505–514.

The research of Deci and associates regarding the effects of extrinsic rewards on intrinsic motivation has stimulated controversy among cognitive and reinforcement theorists. Theoretical roots of cognitive and reinforcement theories are traced, and the controversy over Deci's research is examined, particularly with regard to Scott's recent critique (1975). Implications of these discrepant positions and potential areas of research and application in work organizations are discussed.

Guzzo, Richard A., "Types of Rewards, Cognitions, and Work Motivation," *Academy of Management Review*, 1979, Vol. 4, No. 1, 75–86.

Work rewards often are conceptualized as being of two types: intrinsic and extrinsic. Further, cognitions associated with different types of rewards typically are conceived of in terms derived from attribution theory. A review of the grounds used to dichotomize reward types reveals they are inadequate for distinguishing types of rewards and a review of existing data on the nature of cognitions associated with work rewards indicates the attributional perspective to be deficient. Alternative approaches to the definition of types of work rewards and variants of cognitions mediating the relationship between work rewards and motivation are discussed.

Wofford, J. C., "A Goal-Energy-Effort Requirement Model of Work Motivation," *Academy of Management Review*, April 1979, Vol. 4, No. 2, 193–201.

A model of work motivation is presented in this study. The work of Locke has been included in a modified conceptualization of his goal construct. A schematic representation of the model includes: 1) Task Goal Level; 2) Task Goal Specificity; 3) Task Goal Commitment; 4) Energy

Potential; and 5) Perceived Effort Required. Essential measurement of motivational constructs are discussed, suggesting that self-report measures can be developed for each of the constructs in the model. In summary, the author states the GEER model lends itself to either laboratory or field research testing and should be the basis for much fruitful study. Areas in need of additional research suggested by the model are indicated.

Klinger, Donald E., "Does Your MBO Program Include Clear Performance Contracts?" *Personnel Administrator*, May 1979, Vol. 24, No. 5, 65–68.

Klinger's premise is that performance improves if the goals are clear and agreeable to the individual concerned. MBO has not been an unqualified success. Reasons include uncertainty of decision-making, conflicting objectives and other intervening variables. Research into the effects of contract-setting on employee productivity has often ignored research in related aspects of psychology, in particular educational psychology, which has developed a large body of research related to how human behavior is acquired and changed. Klinger notes the trend in psychotherapy has been toward an increasing reliance on client-centered therapy rather than therapist-centered. The research supports the belief that self-contracting results in improved performance. Improved clarity and agreeability of contract performance will further complement MBO's basic sound theory, the author suggests.

Chacko, Thomas I.; Stone, Thomas H. and Brief, Arthur P., "Participation in Goal-Setting Programs: An Attributional Analysis," *Academy of Management Review*, July 1979, Vol. 4, No. 3, 433–438.

This article offers a conceptual framework to aid researchers interested in examining the multiple dimensions of goal-oriented programs such as MBO. In particular, through the use of attribution theory, explanations will be offered regarding the affects of the participation component of goal-setting programs. Participation is defined as being concerned with goal-setting in superior subordinate relationships. Previous research on goal-setting has concentrated on the "assigned" versus "participative" or high versus low or no dichotomy and this paper accepts this dichotomy. Participation in this narrow sense is the focus of this paper. It is felt that attribution theory is a useful tool which will provide insights into the goal-setting process.

Some research has pointed out that causes for performance outcomes are generally ascribed to: 1) level of ability; 2) amount of effort expended; 3) level of difficulty of the task; and 4) amount of luck or chance factors experienced. A "Theory of Reasons" covers one's performance outcomes to various causes. The attributional analysis framework suggests we should also examine the effect of goal-setting on perception of causal factors and the consequences of causal attributions. In summary, attribution literature suggests that a) individuals attempt to determine the causes for their performance outcomes, and b) these causal factors may be associated with affective reactions. Thus attribution theory suggests that future research in the goal-setting area should look at individual's perceptions of causes of their success or failure.

Commentary

GOALS

Goals/goal-setting processes within an organization were found to be related to performance measures, motivation, and job satisfaction. In addition, the effects of goals on dependent variables have been found to interact with feedback and compensation. The total organizational environment must be considered in examining the effects of goals. Within this context, the current literature is beginning to point the way toward principles to guide the establishment of successful goal achievement programs. Both individual and organization-wide goal-setting seem to have an impact on the satisfaction and performance levels of employees at all levels—top management, white-collar, or blue-collar workers. The literature highlighted below points to the important considerations in designing and implementing an effective goal-setting program.

HIGHLIGHTS OF CURRENT RESEARCH

Establish Effective Goals

A stream of research by Locke and his colleagues gives us important insights as to the likely effects of goal-setting. In one study, Locke (1966) finds that "the higher the level of intention, the higher the level of performance," indicating the necessity for establishing effective goals to encourage employees to "reach" and grow in their performance. This finding was supported in further studies by Locke & Bryan (1966, 1967) when subjects given specific (but difficult) standards performed at a higher level than subjects told only to "do their best". This finding has been generally supported in studies by Hamner & Harnett (1974) and Latham & Yukl (1975).

In the Locke and Bryan experiments (1966, 1967) subjects indicated that trying for a specific goal or score was the major source of task interest. It would seem relevant, therefore, to emphasize goal-setting in repetitive-type tasks to enhance employee interest in higher performance levels (through achieving assigned or set goals) and to encourage unmotivated employees (Bryan & Locke, 1967). In a study of high and low task interest categories (Frost & Mahoney, 1976), high interest subjects outperformed low interest subjects, suggesting a differential locus of motivation, externally oriented in a repetitive (low interest) task and internally oriented in a problem-solving task. More research on the impact of motivational orientation on the goal-setting performance relationship would be valuable.

Consider Variations in Environment

Monetary incentives, compensation levels, performance measurement, and review processes are all important aspects of the organizational climate which influence goal-setting programs. In earlier research by Locke, Bryan & Kendall (1968), the relationship between monetary incentives and task performance (goal achievement) was explored. After five studies examining these relationships, results indicated significant correlations between performance goals or behavioral intentions and behavior. The authors felt that their general hypothesis was supported— i.e., monetary incentives affect task performance *only* through their effects on the individual's goals or intentions. A later test of this hypothesis (Pritchard & Curts, 1973) revealed that *both* incentives and goal-setting have positive effects on performance and that the Locke, et al. predictions held true *only* when the incentives were small. In yet another study, Terborg (1976) found that goal-setting and monetary incentives were *independently* related to measures of motivation and performance and that incentives had no impact on whether or not subjects set performance goals. More research on this aspect of goal-setting seems indicated to clarify the impact of monetary incentives and goal-setting on goal achievement and performance.

Several studies of Management by Objectives (MBO) and Participation Achievement Reward (PAR) programs point to the importance of taking a systems approach to understanding the effects of goals on performance. Several principles and guidelines emerge from this research:

a) The extent to which MBO (goal achievement) is used as a basis for merit compensation is positively associated with perceptions of worth of MBO, role clarity, feelings of accomplishment, and enhancement of subordinate development and performance (Mobley, June 1974).

b) Goal setting (via MBO) and compensation prove effective by giving managers maximum flexibility in rewarding performance (Conley & Miller, 1973).

c) Implementing an MBO program and following up with a management "Coaching Practices Survey" measurement reveals a consistent relationship between the mean of the survey and usage of MBO, indicating that MBO leads to increased managerial activity (Fay & Beach, 1974) and, assumedly, leading to closer supervision and more effective goal setting/goal achievement.

d) Using MBO in the public sector (HEW) was successful in establishing a six-stage objective-setting procedure and review process to assist in obtaining goals (Brady, 1973).

e) In a study by Hersey & Kellner (1968), a program for salesmen produced success in an organization where the sales force has a sense of working for themselves—achieving their personal goals by achieving company goals. This was implemented through a review and revision procedure (MBO and goal-setting) along with a continuing dialogue and feedback provision.

f) Good employee relations, achievement measurement, and knowledgeable leadership are essential components for a Participation Achievement Reward (PAR) system as reported in a study by Schultz & McKersie (1973).

Strengthening the goal achievement/compensation link, effective management "coaching" (leadership), and measurement and review processes seem to be essential ingredients for successful applications of goal-setting programs. In regard to leadership, a related study (Ronan, Latham & Kinne, 1973) indicates goal-setting is correlated with high productivity only when accompanied by close supervision and that goal-setting without close supervision was positively related to employee turnover. This finding emphasizes the need for knowledgeable, effective management to insure successful goal-setting practices.

ADDITIONAL INFLUENCING FACTORS

In addition to consideration of variations in environment, other important factors impacting on the effectiveness of goal-setting must be recognized. Research has been done on feedback, participation, performance, satisfaction, and individual differences which all impact on successful goal-setting.

In a study by Steers (1976), job involvement and satisfaction were related to the amount of participation allowed in goal-setting, goal difficulty, and goal specificity; satisfaction also was found to be related to feedback. Another study (Erez, 1977) found that feedback (knowledge of score) has a significant effect on goal-setting and is a necessary component for goals to positively affect performance.

Two studies by Ivancevich (1976, 1977) indicate that after a supervisory goal-setting training program, both participative and assigned goal-setting were more effective in improving performance and satisfaction than no goal-setting, although improvements dissipated nine to 12 months after training. A participative goal-setting condition (as opposed to an assigned or a "do your best" condition) achieved higher productivity. Likewise, goal difficulty and goal attainment were significantly higher under participative goal-setting in a field study by Latham & Yukl (1975). In a further study (1976), these authors found that significant productivity improvement occurred in both participative and assigned goal-setting and that the amount of participation was found not to be as important as the actual goal-setting itself—assuming the goal was accepted by the employee. Campbell & Ilgen (1976) found that goals and task difficulty contribute additively and do not interact in impacting upon task performance, and that the effects on task performance were attributable to task knowledge and motivation through goal-setting.

In a study by Locke, Cartledge & Knerr (1970) of how evaluations and emotions lead to goal-setting, high correlations were found suggesting that:

a) Satisfaction can be predicted from value judgments,

b) Goal-setting can be predicted from satisfaction, and

c) Performance can be predicted from goals.

Findings also indicated that the level of performance yielding satisfaction in the past is not necessarily sufficient to yield future satisfaction; yet the individual's anticipated satisfaction best predicts goal-setting. This line of research generally supports the earlier Locke study (1966) indicating the importance of establishing effective goals to encourage employee growth and development.

CONCLUSIONS

Much of the literature on goals/goal-setting has been of an empirical or descriptive nature. Factors affecting goal-setting and performance have been investigated. It is evident that it is important to establish specific, difficult goals—and goals that employees accept; that variations in organizational environments impact on goal-setting and the effects of goal-setting; and that certain factors such as feedback, participation, satisfaction, performance, and individual differences must be considered in utilizing goal-setting as a motivational tool.

A promising beginning has been made toward establishing tested guidelines or parameters for a goal-setting theory. The generality of a goal-setting theory has been examined by Latham & Kinne (1974) and results consistently indicate that goal-setting can lead to an increase in production and a decrease in absenteeism and that goal-setting has an independent motivating effect on task performance.

Independent Variable

INTERACTION

Type of Article	No. of Articles
Applied	4
Descriptive	11
Empirical	13
Integrative	2
Prescriptive	5
Theoretical	4

APPLIED

Burnaska, Robert F., "The Effects of Behavior Modeling Training Upon Managers' Behaviors and Employees' Perceptions," *Personnel Psychology*, Summer 1976, Vol. 24, No. 2, 329–335.

Sixty-two experienced middle-level managers at General Electric were given Interpersonal Skills Training (behavior modeling) to determine whether it improved their interpersonal skills with employees, could be expected to last over time, and if employees could perceive changes in their managers' overall behavior. Training consisted of videotape observation of situations which included behavioral objectives (discussion of work assignments, recognizing the "average" employee, and discussion of performance problems). The measurement of managerial behavior was done by trained judges who evaluated the managers' handling of the situation on four seven-point Likert-type scales: Maintained Employee's Self-Esteem; Established Open and Clear Communication; Maintained Control of the Situation; and Accomplished Objective of the Discussion. Employee perceptions were measured on a 51 item seven-point Likert-type questionnaire that asked them about their relationship with their manager and how he behaved with them. Results (ANOVA) reveal that the trained managers performed better than the untrained managers, that the ratings taken after four months were higher than those taken immediately after training, and that trained managers performed equally well in Discussing a Performance Problem or Giving a Work Assignment but relatively poor on Giving Recognition to an Average Employee (still better than untrained). Employee perception of their managers' overall behavior modeling improves managers' interpersonal skills and practice over time further enhances these skills.

Byham, William C.; Adams, Diane and Kiggins, Ann, "Transfer of Modeling to the Job," *Personnel Psychology*, Summer 1976, Vol. 29, No. 2, 345–349.

Company supervisors participated in a training program (Interaction Management) designed to help them handle interactions with subordinates. The training, based on positive modeling (movies) and skill practice, attempted to effect transfer of newly acquired skills to the job setting by having higher management positively reinforce successful interaction behavior. Examples of training modules included the following: Improving Employee Performance; Teaching an Employee a New Job, and Improving Work Habits. A study was conducted to find out whether training was being transferred to the job. Subordinates' perceptions of their supervisors' handling of interactions were ascertained through structured interview and used as the criterion of training transfer success. A pre-post comparison yielded positive results for most of module areas in question. This study provides evidence of the effectiveness of modeling methodology in supervisory training.

Note: The first author published another article in *Personnel Journal*, (May 1977), which is similar in content.

Moses, Joseph L. and Ritchie, Richard J., "Supervisory Relationships Training: A Behavioral Evaluation of A Behavior Modeling Program," *Personnel Psychology*, Summer 1976, Vol. 29, No. 2, 337–343.

A study was conducted to determine whether line supervisors who underwent Supervisory Relationships Training (SRT) would interact more effectively with their subordinates than a control group. SRT involves behavior modeling of effective supervisory behaviors. As rated by a group of behavioral assessors, the trained supervisors resolved a series of simulated problem discussions (relating to absenteeism, discrimination and theft) in a much more effective manner than the untrained supervisors. The authors report that the SRT supervisors were able to utilize skills specifically learned in the training program and generalize these skills to a novel situation such as confronting an employee with a suspected theft. Behavior modeling is supported as an effective means for supervisors to develop their interaction skills.

Smith, Preston E., "Management Modeling Training To Improve Morale and Customer Satisfaction," *Personnel Psychology*, Summer 1976, Vol. 29, No. 2, 351–359.

Two studies were conducted to determine the effects of behavior modeling training for IBM branch managers on employee morale (first study) and customer satisfaction and sales. In the first study, managers in the trained group received live modeling of important learning points for survey feedback (e.g., soliciting employees feelings) before and after office meeting where opinion survey results were presented to employees. The control group did not receive training. Assessment of the training program's effectiveness was determined by a meeting effectiveness questionnaire and changes in employee opinion survey results. The results indicate that the trained group rated the feedback as much more effective than the control group and that employees of the trained group had a higher morale index than the control group. In the second study, modeling training was used in an attempt to improve managers communication skills and future branch office customer satisfaction and sales quotas. Matched groups of managers were assigned to the following: The Traditional Training Group (trained to read and interpret information from reports); The Modeling Training Group (trained in modeling communication skills); The Modeling Plus Team-Building Group (trained in skills and met as subgroup) and the control group. Managers written answers to verbatim customer comments indicate significant communication skill improvement only for the Modeling and Modeling Plus Team-Building Groups. Customer satisfaction, as measured by random surveying, was correlated with communication effectiveness. A direct positive relationship was present (v = .743) between communication skills after training and later levels of customer satisfaction. The change in actual quota sold from one year to the next showed improvement for only the Modeling Plus Team-Building Group. Decline in quota sales were reported for the other three groups.

The author concluded that behavior modeling programs improve manager communication skills which impact on employees morale and customer satisfaction. Outside influences (e.g., prices) may account for sales performance improvement in only one of the groups.

DESCRIPTIVE

Kipnis, D. and Cosentino, J., "Use of Leadership Powers in Industry," *Journal of Applied Psychology*, 1969, Vol. 53, No. 6, 460–466.

This study investigated a) the range of corrective powers available to military and industrial supervisors when correcting subordinates behavior, and b) the factors influencing the supervisors use of these powers. Method: An open-ended questionnaire was administered to a sample of 184 supervisors from five different companies. The questionnnaire asked each supervisor to describe an incident that occurred within the past year in which a subordinate's behavior was below average. Other information was also asked concerning subordinates. The actions taken by the supervisors were coded according to a classification system used in the naval study upon which this investigation is based. Kinds of problems presented by subordinates were classified as those of attitude, discipline, work, and appearance. Corrective actions taken by supervisors were in the form of: verbal, increased supervision, situational change, penalty, refer, written warning, man fired. Results: Both situational and personal factors (number of employees supervised, years of experience as a supervisor, and the nature of the problem presented by the subordinate) were found to influence the supervisor's choice of corrective power. Military supervisors relied more on direct attempts to change subordinates' behavior through reliance upon extra instruction, direct punishment, and changes in the task environment of subordinates. Industrial supervisors relied more on their persuasive powers.

Zdep, S. M., "Intra Group Reinforcement and Its Effects of Leadership Behavior," *Organizational Behavior and Human Performance*, 1969, Vol. 4, 284–298.

Four-person problem-solving groups were constructed on the basis of participant California Psychological Inventory Leadership scale scores. Each group had a target person with either a high or low leadership score and three other participants with intermediate leadership scores. Half of the groups received "private" reinforcement while the discussion was in progress. This reinforcement consisted of rewarding target person leadership behaviors and punishing non-target persons for these same behaviors. The results revealed that high Leadership scale scorers talked a great deal in group discussion and low scorers talked very little. Those who participated more were rated as better leaders by the group. Participation levels were further increased for high scorers by reinforcement, but not for low scorers. As participation increased, so did subsequent group leadership ratings for high scorers. When low scorers failed to respond to reinforcement, they were rated as poorer leaders than low scorers not receiving reinforcement. Reinforcement effects were found to be stable, while morale and satisfaction with the group product were not lowered. Implications of this method of group reinforcement for leadership training were considered.

Weitzel, W.; Mahoney, T. A. and Crandall, N. F., "A Supervisory View of Unit Effectiveness," *California Management Review*, Summer 1971, Vol. 13, No. 4, 37–42.

This research suggests that the "man-in-the-middle" supervisor holds priorities more akin to those of managers than of employees. The supervisor, in fact, assigns less priority to human relations variables than does his superior. The supervisor tends to perceive human relations variables as instrumental in achieving productivity, not as ends in themselves. Assuming that supervisory values reflect assessment of the instrumental worth of these values, achievements in these human relations dimensions are useful in achieving long-run productive performance. The authors' findings suggest that supervisors, at least, tend to view the human relations dimensions of organizations as having only instrumental value. The supervisor does not appear to have been affected much by the numerous arguments concerning the appropriate ends of business organizations.

Evans, M. G., "Extensions of a Path-Goal Theory of Motivation," *Journal of Applied Psychology*, 1974, Vol. 59, No. 2, 172–178.

This article extends and replicates the Evans' hypothesis concerning the way in which the behavior of the superior affects the subordinate's perceptions of expectancies and instrumentalities in the path-goal theory of motivation. Of the three moderators (the subordinate's position in a web of role relationships, and the supervisor's upward influence) hypothesized, only the first was found to moderate the superior-subordinate relationship as predicted. Results for the other two moderators were equivocal. Additional implications of the path-goal model were explored, that is, the role of motivation as: a) an intervening variable between supervisory behavior and subordinate behavior and b) as a moderator in the behavior/satisfaction relationship.

Nebeker, D. M. and Mitchell, T. R., "Leader Behavior: An Expectancy Theory Approach," *Organizational Behavior and Human Performance*, 1974, Vol. 11, 355–367.

Expectancy theory has found increasing use in the study of such variables as worker effort, performance, and satisfaction. This paper suggests some mathematical modifications of expectancy theory which extend its use to the prediction of leader behavior. Data from a field study of naval aviation maintenance crews and a field study of public works maintenance shop supervisors found that a leader's actual behavior could be predicted from the theory. These results suggest that expectancy theory not only has the ability to account for leader behavior in a real life setting, but also helps us to understand the antecedents of such behavior.

Kavanagh, M. J., "Expected Supervisory Behavior, Interpersonal Trust and Environmental Preferences," *Organizational Behavior and Human Performance*, February 1975, Vol. 13, 17–30.

Preferences regarding "ideal" supervisory behavior, organizational climate, and measures of interpersonal trust were collected from two samples, college students and industrial managers, to test four hypotheses derived from a dyadic model of the behavioral requirements of a leader's role. The results indicated: a) the popular hypothesis arguing for higher preferences for freedom and self-actualization opportunities in the work role was not supported completely by these leadership preference results; b) being employed affected the preferences for "ideal" leadership; c) preference for organizational climate was related to the pattern of leadership behaviors preferred; and d) the relationships between interpersonal trust and preferences for leader behavior appear more complex than anticipated in this paper.

Burnaska, Robert F., "The Effects of Behavior Modeling Training Upon Managers' Behaviors and Employees' Perceptions," *Personnel Psychology*, Summer 1976, Vol. 24, No. 2, 329–335.

Sixty-two experienced middle-level managers at General Electric were given Interpersonal Skills Training (behavior modeling) to determine whether it improved their interpersonal skills with employees, could be expected to last over time, and if employees could perceive changes in their managers' overall behavior. Training consisted of videotape observation of situations which included behavioral objectives (discussion of work assignments, recognizing the "average" employee, and discussion of performance problems). The measurement of managerial behavior was done by trained judges who evaluated the managers' handling of the situation on four seven-point Likert-type scales: Maintained Employee's Self-Esteem; Established Open and Clear Communication; Maintained Control of the Situation; and Accomplished Objective of the Discussion. Employee perceptions were measured on a 51 item seven-point Likert-type questionnaire that asked them about their relationship with their manager and how he behaved with them. Results (ANOVA) revealed that the trained managers performed better than the untrained managers, that the ratings taken after four months were higher than those taken immediately after training, and that trained managers performed equally well in Discussing a Performance Problem or Giving a Work Assignment but relatively poor on Giving Recognition to an Average Employee (still better than untrained). Employee perception of their managers' overall behavior modeling improves managers' interpersonal skills and practice over time further enhances these skills.

Byham, William C.; Adams, Diane and Kiggins, Ann, "Transfer of Modeling to the Job," *Personnel Psychology*, Summer 1976, Vol. 29, No. 2, 345–349.

Company supervisors participated in a training program (Interaction Management) designed to help them handle interactions with subordinates. The training, based on positive modeling (movies) and skill practice, attempted to effect transfer of newly acquired skills to the job setting by having higher management positively reinforce successful interaction behavior. Examples of training modules included the following: Improving Employee Performance; Teaching an Employee a New Job, and Improving Work Habits. A study was conducted to find out whether training was being transferred to the job. Subordinates' perceptions of their supervisors' handling of interactions were ascertained through structured interview and used as the criterion of training transfer success. A pre-post comparison yielded positive results for most of module areas in question. This study provides evidence of the effectiveness of modeling methodology in supervisory training.

Note: The first author published another article in *Personnel Journal,* (May 1977), which is similar in content.

Moses, Joseph L. and Ritchie, Richard J., "Supervisory Relationships Training: A Behavioral Evaluation of A Behavior Modeling Program," *Personnel Psychology,* Summer 1976, Vol. 29, No. 2, 337–343.

A study was conducted to determine whether line supervisors who underwent Supervisory Relationships Training (SRT) would interact more effectively with their subordinates than a control group. SRT involves behavior modeling of effective supervisory behaviors. As rated by a group of behavioral assessors, the trained supervisors resolved a series of simulated problem discussions (relating to absenteeism, discrimination and theft) in a much more effective manner than the untrained supervisors. The authors report that the SRT supervisors were able to utilize skills specifically learned in the training program and generalize these skills to a novel situation such as confronting an employee with a suspected theft. Behavior modeling is supported as an effective means for supervisors to develop their interaction skills.

Smith, Preston E., "Management Modeling Training To Improve Morale and Customer Satisfaction," *Personnel Psychology,* Summer 1976, Vol. 29, No. 2, 351–359.

Two studies were conducted to determine the effects of behavior modeling training for IBM branch managers on employee morale (first study) and customer satisfaction and sales. In the first study, managers in the trained group received live modeling of important learning points for survey feedback (e.g., soliciting employees feelings) before and after office meeting where opinion survey results were presented to employees. The control group did not receive training. Assessment of the training program's effectiveness was determined by a meeting effectiveness questionnaire and changes in employee opinion survey results. The results indicate that trained group rated the feedback as much more effective than the control group and that employees of the trained group had a higher morale index than the control group. In the second study, modeling training was used in an attempt to improve managers communication skills and future branch office customer satisfaction and sales quotas. Matched groups of managers were assigned to the following: The Traditional Training Group (trained to read and interpret information from reports); The Modeling Training Group (trained in modeling communication skills); The Modeling Plus Team-Building Group (trained in skills and met as subgroup) and the control group. Managers written answers to verbatim customer comments indicate significant communication skill improvement only for the Modeling and Modeling Plus Team-Building Groups. Customer satisfaction as measured by random surveying, was correlated with communication effectiveness. A direct positive relationship was present (v = .743) between communication skills after training and later levels of customer satisfaction. The change in actual quota sold from one year to the next showed improvement for only the Modeling Plus Team-Building Group. Decline in quota sales were reported for the other three groups.

The author concluded that behavior modeling programs improve manager communication skills which impact on employees morale and customer satisfaction. Outside influences (e.g., prices) may account for sales performance improvement in only one of the groups.

Vinson, Earl; Kulisch, W. Anthony and Beatty, Richard W., "Incentive Systems and Task Types as OD Intervention Targets," *Academy of Management Proceedings*, 1977, 363–367.

This study explores the interaction effects of incentive systems and task types on group performance. The incentive systems are promotive (person's behavior is beneficial to partner) and contrient (exert contrary effects upon one another) and the task types are unitary (necessary for individual to complete all phases of the job) and divisible (division of labor is feasible). The subjects were 240 students (80 three-person groups) who participated in a card-sorting task in which vouchers (redeemable for monetary reward on the basis of a random drawing) could be earned. Amount of reward was determined by group output. Interdependence was manipulated by either giving a subject a separate stack of cards (unitary) or making it necessary for group members to pass cards to each other (divisible). Results indicate that performance tends to be higher in divisible/contrient groups than divisible/promotive groups. No significant difference exists between unitary/contrient and unitary/promotive groups. The results suggest that OD interventions for groups performing divisible tasks can influence group productivity by modifying the incentive systems for the group.

EMPIRICAL

Klaus, D. J. and Glaser, R., "Reinforcement Determinants of Team Proficiency," *Organizational Behavior and Human Performance*, 1970, Vol. 5, 33–67.

The proficiency of working teams having well-defined structures and member assignments can be considered as a function of the occurrence of reinforcement for the group as a whole following each team response. Findings from a series of seven studies suggest that increments and decrements in team performance are predictable from a knowledge of reinforcement contingencies and team structures and may be attributed to the differential effects of group reinforcement on individual team members. Both "series" teams, requiring specified contributions from all members, and "parallel" teams, those containing redundant members, were studied. The effects of characteristic entering performance, supplementary feedback during team training and the simulation of team conditions during the training of individuals also was investigated. Some implications of the research and the underlying model are identified with respect to the broader context of social behavior.

Oldham, Greg R., "The Motivational Strategies Used by Supervisors: Relationships to Effectiveness Indicators," *Organizational Behavior and Human Performance*, February 1976, Vol. 15, No. 1, 66–68.

This article introduces a new set of activities that a supervisor might use to heighten subordinate work motivation and performance. These activities, entitled "Motivational Strategies," consist of six separate dimensions: Personally Rewarding (i.e., pat on the back), Personally Punishing (i.e., verbal criticism), Setting Goals (i.e., instruction to subordinate to increase sales by a certain percent), Designing Feedback Systems (i.e., adding previous data to a report for comparison purposes), Placing Personnel (i.e., assigning subordinate to a task that is challenging), and Designing Job Systems (i.e., developing a subordinate's existing job so that it is more challenging).

Research involving individuals employed in 10 retail chain-stores was conducted to determine the relationhip between the "motivational strategies" and job effectiveness. Data was collected by administering questionnaires (Likert-type scales) to subordinates, middle managers, and store managers concerning the motivational strategies of the middle manager. Effectiveness (i.e., how effective was each middle manager in getting his subordinates to work hard and well; and the productivity of his subordinates) was also measured by a Likert-type questionnaire. Results show highly significant, positive relationships among five of the proposed strategies of motivation were good predictors of a middle manager's rated effectiveness in his subordinates as well as being predictive of the effectiveness of a subordinate performing his job. The author warns against causal inferences with regard to strategy and effectiveness.

Burnaska, Robert F., "The Effects of Behavior Modeling Training Upon Managers' Behaviors and Employee's Perceptions," *Personnel Psychology*, Summer 1976, Vol. 24, No. 2, 329–335.

Sixty-two experienced middle-level managers at General Electric were given Interpersonal Skills Training (behavior modeling) to determine whether it improved their interpersonal skills with employees, could be expected to last over time, and if employees could perceive changes in their managers' overall behavior. Training consisted of videotape observation of situations which included behavioral objectives (discussion of work assignments, recognizing the "average" employee, and discussion of performance problems). The measurement of managerial behavior was done by trained judges who evaluated the managers' handling of the situation on four seven-point Likert-type scales: Maintained Employee's Self-Esteem; Established Open and Clear Communication; Maintained

Control of the Situation; and Accomplished Objective of the Discussion. Employee perceptions were measured on a 51 item seven-point Likert-type questionnaire that asked them about their relationship with their manager and how he behaved with them. Results (ANOVA) reveal that the trained managers performed better than the untrained managers, that the ratings taken after four months were higher than those taken immediately after training, and that trained managers performed equally well in Discussing a Performance Problem or Giving a Work Assignment but relatively poor on Giving Recognition to an Average Employee (still better than untrained). Employee perception of their managers' overall behavior modeling improves managers' interpersonal skills and practice over time further enhances these skills.

Moses, Joseph L. and Ritchie, Richard J., "Supervisory Relationships Training: A Behavioral Evaluation of A Behavior Modeling Program," *Personnel Psychology*, Summer 1976, Vol. 29, No. 2, 337–343.

A study was conducted to determine whether line supervisors who underwent Supervisory Relationships Training (SRT) would interact more effectively with their subordinates than a control group. SRT involves behavior modeling of effective supervisory behaviors. As rated by a group of behavioral assessors, the trained supervisors resolved a series of simulated problem discussions (relating to absenteeism, discrimination and theft) in a much more effective manner than the untrained supervisors. The authors report that the SRT supervisors were able to utilize skills specifically learned in the training program and generalize these skills to a novel situation such as confronting an employee with a suspected theft. Behavior modeling is supported as an effective means for supervisors to develop their interaction skills.

Smith, Preston E., "Management Modeling Training To Improve Morale and Customer Satisfaction," *Personnel Psychology*, Summer 1976, Vol. 29, No. 2, 351–359.

Two studies were conducted to determine the effects of behavior modeling training for IBM branch managers on employee morale (first study) and customer satisfaction and sales. In the first study managers in the trained group received live modeling of important learning points for survey feedback (e.g., soliciting employees feelings) before and after office meeting where opinion survey results were presented to employees. The control group did not receive training. Assessment of the training program's effectiveness was determined by a meeting effectiveness questionnaire and changes in employee opinion survey results. The results indicate that trained group rated the feedback as much more effective than the control group and that employees of the trained group had a higher morale index than the control group. In the second study, modeling training was used in an attempt to improve managers communication skills and future branch office customer satisfaction and sales quotas. Matched groups of managers were assigned to the following: The Traditional Training Group (trained to read and interpret information from reports); The Modeling Training Group (trained in modeling communication skills); The Modeling Plus Team-Building Group (trained in skills and met as subgroup) and the control group. Managers written answers to verbatim customer comments indicate significant communication skill improvement only for the Modeling and Modeling Plus Team-Building Groups. Customer satisfaction as measured by random surveying, was correlated with communication effectiveness. A direct positive relationship was present (v = .743) between communication skills after training and later levels of customer satisfaction. The change in actual quota sold from one year to the next showed improvement for only the Modeling Plus Team-Building Group. Decline in quota sales were reported for the other three groups.

The author concluded that behavior modeling programs improve manager communication skills which impact on employees morale and customer satisfaction. Outside influences (e.g., prices) may account for sales performance improvement in only one of the groups.

Hackman, Richard J.; Brousseau, Kenneth R. and Weiss, Janet A., "The Interaction of Task Design and Group Performance Strategies in Determining Group Effectiveness," *Organizational Behavior and Human Performance*, August 1976, Vol. 16, No. 2, 350–365.

Norms controlling how members deal with performance strategies were altered experimentally in small task-oriented groups. The basic task required assembly of small electrical components. In one task condition (equal information) all task-relevant information was provided to each group member; in another (unequal information) it was spread unevenly among members, requiring exchange of information for optimum group performance. In the unequal information condition, an intervention inducing explicit discussion of task performance strategies improved group performance. In the equal information condition, effectiveness was increased by an intervention that reinforced existing norms against explicit discussion of performance strategies. Spontaneous discussion of strategy did not take place in control groups for either task condition, and control groups were lowest in performance effectiveness. Measures of interaction process and of member reactions to the group were affected substantially by the experimental interventions.

Keller, Robert T. and Szilagyi, Andrew D., "Employee Reactions to Leader Reward Behavior," *Academy of Management Journal*, December 1976, Vol. 19, No. 4, 619–627.

A study was conducted investigating relationships between positive and punitive leader rewards and employee role conflict and ambiguity, expectancies, and job satisfaction. Leader reward behavior (e.g., merit pay increases, recognition, advancement in the organization or reprimand, dismissal, or withholding of pay) was measured by a 22-item questionnaire designed to determine whether a subordinate perceives that rewards or outcomes (positive or punishment) he receives through his supervisor reflected his performance or accomplishments on the job (Sims and Szilagyi, 1976). Satisfaction was defined as the degree to which an individual's desires, expectations, and needs are fulfilled by his employment in the organization. This variable was measured by the JDI. The data show that positive leader rewards are related to job satisfaction. The authors conclude that positive rewards are more powerful than negative rewards for the explanation of behavior in organizations.

Schuler, Randall S. and Kim, Jay S., "Interactive Effects of Participation in Decision-Making, The Goal-Setting Process and Feedback on Employee Satisfaction and Performance," *The Academy of Management Proceedings*, 1976, 114–117.

A 2 × 2 × 2 factorial design was employed to investigate the nature of the interactive effects of participation in decision-making, the goal-setting process, and feedback from goal attainment on employee satisfaction and performance. White-collar workers (409) in a large public utility company were the subjects. Participation in decision-making was measured by a five-item Likert-scale questionnaire (i.e., to what extent are you able to decide how to do your job?) Goal-setting was determined by having subjects rate the frequency of the goal-setting meetings they have with their supervisors. Feedback was measured by items relating to the perceived relationship between goal attainment and their performance evaluation and goal attainment and merit pay. A median split was performed on individual scores on the three measures. The results indicated that when participation in decision-making was low, the goal-setting process was highly related to employee satisfaction with work and satisfaction with peers (as measured by scales from the JDI). On the other hand, when the degree of the goal-setting process was low, participation in the decision-making was important in increasing the employee's satisfaction with the supervisor. Only participation and merit pay feedback had significant main effects with performance (peer rating). There were no significant interactions with performance. The findings of this study seem to imply that employee participation and goal-setting significantly influence higher performance and job satisfaction.

Barrow, Jeffrey C., "Worker Performance and Task Complexity as Causal Determinants of Leader Behavior Style and Flexibility," *Journal of Applied Psychology*, August 1977, Vol. 61, No. 4, 433–440.

The effects of differing worker performance levels and task complexity on leader behavior style and flexibility were investigated. Utilizing a simulated leadership situation, data were collected on the leader behaviors of 12 subjects. Results indicate that task-emphasis (initiating-structure) leader behaviors were caused by the complexity of the task, not by the performance level of the workers. Supportive-consideration, punitive-performance emphasis, and autocratic leader behaviors were caused by how well the workers performed and were not significantly influenced by task-complexity differences; and increasing performance levels of workers caused a leader to become more supportive-consideration oriented, whereas decreasing performance levels resulted in heavier use of punitive-performance emphasis and autocratic behaviors.

McFillen, James M., "The Effects of Supervisory Power and Subordinate Performance upon the Perceptions and Behaviors of a Supervisor," *Academy of Management Proceedings*, 1977, 91–96.

Ninety male undergraduate subjects were assigned to supervisory roles in which they possessed either reward power (reward subordinates up to 50¢), penalty power (penalize up to 50¢) or both (either reward or penalize up to 50¢). Preprogrammed performance indicated to each subject that he was engaged in supervising two "successful" and two "unsuccessful" subordinates. The subordinate's performance on an audio balance task was continually being monitored (feedback) by the subject. At the end of the task each subject rated his subordinate on a seven-point Likert scale questionnaire with regard to overall performance and satisfaction. This measure was used in conjunction with the incentive allocation in representing the dependent variable. Subordinate performance was found to have a significant affect upon a subject's evaluating, reinforcing, and monitoring subordinates. Supervisory power was found to have a significant affect upon a subject's perception of subordinate's work quality and upon reinforcing behavior. This study suggests that the type of power possessed by a supervisor does not consistently affect his perceptions or behaviors in regard to his subordinates but is guided by the nature of subordinate performance.

Kabanoff, Boris and O'Brian, Gordon E., "The Effects of Task Type and Cooperation Upon Group Products and Performance," *Organizational Behavior and Human Performance*, April 1979, Vol. 23, No. 2, 163–181.

Few studies have been able to show how differences in task organizaton influence group productivity. This study investigates systematically the direct and interactive effects of task type and group structure on the characteristics of group products and selected performance dimensions. For this study, a 2 × 2 × 3 factorial design with two levels of coordination, two levels of collaboration, and three levels of task type was used. For the first two factors, the absence of that type of cooperation constituted the first level of each factor, and its presence the second. The third factor was a repeated measures factor with three types of task representing each level—production, problem-solving, and discussion. Results of the study covered: 1) effect of task type on product characteristics; 2) effect of structure on product dimensions; 3) interactions between task type and structure; and 4) group structure and product length. The authors state major conclusions of the study appear to be: 1) group tasks do make a difference to group output, but so does group structure; and

2) for these types of tasks the major effect of group structure is upon product length, which is in turn a significant correlate of performance measures.

Kabanoff, Boris and O'Brien, Gordon E., "Cooperation Structure and the Relationship of Leader and Member Ability to Group Performance," *Journal of Applied Psychology*, October 1979, Vol. 64, No. 5, 526–532.

This study experimentally examined the moderating effect of cooperation structure on a group's ability/productivity relationship, and provided an opportunity to examine the importance of a group's task organization and subordinates' ability on the relationship between leader ability and leader effectiveness. Another goal was the provision of information on the relative influence of group structures and group ability on task performance on the affect of different cooperative patterns on group performance. The study varied the creative ability of leaders and subordinates in 48 three-person groups. Groups were required to carry out a creative verbal task while working under one of four possible forms of cooperation structure. Each structure varied in the amount of two types of cooperation—collaboration and coordination. Collaboration reflects the degree to which group members must work simultaneously with one another on each aspect of the task. Coordination depends on the extent to which different group members have different subtasks arranged in an order of precedence to perform. Both the form of cooperation and the level of group ability had a significant affect on group creativity. Coordinated groups were significantly more productive than coacting groups. Groups with high ability leaders or subordinates were more productive than those with low ability leaders and subordinates. Collaborating groups were the least productive. There was a significant two-way interaction between collaboration and leader ability because group leader ability did not have a significant affect on the performance of collaborative groups. The results are discussed in terms of the constraints different group structures place on leaders' effectiveness and of the relevance of these findings to theories of leader performance. The results also provide further evidence of the importance of group structure in determining productivity.

Mitchell, Terence R. and Wood, Robert E., "Supervisor's Responses to Subordinate Poor Performance: A Test of an Attributional Model," *Organizational Behavior and Human Performance*, February 1980, Vol. 25, No. 1, 123–138.

This paper describes the use of an attribution model to help leaders deal with poor performers and provides an empirical test of some of its propositions. Hypotheses derived from the model were tested via two experiments with 23 nursing supervisors from two different hospitals. Materials used, manipulations, and measures of each experiment were covered in detail. Results of the experiments were described in relation to manipulation checks, causal attributions, responses to poor performance, attributions and responses, and bias toward internal responses. Summary of the findings were: 1) in their evaluation of nurses involved in an incident of poor performance, supervisors attributed causality more to the internal factors than external factors regardless of surrounding circumstances; 2) this bias toward internal attributions was increased when the work history of the nurse was poor and when the outcome was serious; 3) the behaviors chosen as responses to the poor performance were related to the attributions and surrounding circumstances. The more internal the attribution, the more the response was directed at the nurse. Results of the experiments indicated theoretical support for the study.

Attribution, whether directly manipulated or influenced through cues of consistency, distinctiveness, and consensus, was a more powerful predictor of intended response than the seriousness of the outcome. Some practical implications suggested by the data are: 1) to the degree that attributions serve as a mediator of poor performance—leader response relationships, difference in perception of causes of poor performance may lead to inaccurate appraisals and conflict, and 2) supervisors make attributions and responses partly as a function of the seriousness of the outcome. This can lead to serious negative consequences. To change behavior, we must focus on the behavior, not the outcome.

INTEGRATIVE

Wofford, J. C., "Behavior Styles and Performance Effectiveness," *Personnel Psychology*, Winter 1967, Vol. 20, No. 4, 461–495.

The purpose of this paper is to provide an approach to the classification, description, and measurement of human behavior which should be useful in personnel psychology. The approach attempts to avoid many of the pitfalls inherent in the use of abstract personality trait constructs. It suggests a basis for measurement that appears to be more reliable and more valid for the personnel field. On the basis of this approach to understanding behavior, a framework for the description of job goals, activities, and situational factors was proposed. By closely relating the job description to this approach, one has a solid foundation for clearly and accurately determining man requirements for each job. Previous research regarding the most effective behavior patterns for managerial and sales jobs was reviewed. This research was easily interpreted in the light of the behavior pattern framework and seems to provide a basis for establishing hypotheses concerning the most effective behavioral styles for managerial and sales jobs. The framework presented here appears to have unveiled the intense need that is apparent for the construction of behavior description measurement instruments which can be used in the personnel field.

Ferris, G. R., Beehr, T. A., and Gilmore, D. C., "Social Facilitation: A Review and Alternative Conceptual Model," *Academy of Management Review*, 1978, Vol. 3, No. 2, 338–347.

Zajunc (1965) reviewed the social facilitation literature, proposing that the mere presence of others during task performance has arousal properties which facilitate the emission of dominant responses. Contrary to this, Cottrell found that expected evaluation, rather than the mere presence of others, is necessary for the facilitation of dominant responses. This contradiction, plus numerous other weaknesses to Zajunc's proposition, indicate a need for a more cognitive model, constructed in an expectance framework. Recommendations are made regarding directions of future research for testing the model.

PRESCRIPTIVE

Pistolese, C., "Behaviorally-Based Supervisory Development," *Training and Development Journal*, January 1970, Vol. 24, No. 1, 36–38.

This article presents a procedural model to aid supervisors in applying behavioral principles. The model is suggested as an approach that can be used by the training director as is, or which can be modified to conform to the organizational restrictions that may already exist. Ten points are included in the checklist for program development. In concluding, the author touches on the merits of this approach: it focuses directly on end results; it involves all levels of management in designing the program objectives and thus ensures management's endorsement of the program; it allows supervisors to choose their own behavioral goals and thus increase their motivation to participate; it sets the stage for all levels of management to come to an agreement, or at least an understanding of approved supervisory behaviors. Finally, since performance objectives will be measurable and observable, it is possible to make an objective evaluation of the effectiveness of the program.

Warren, M. W., "Performance Management: A Substitute for Supervision," *Management Review*, October 1972, Vol. 61, No. 10, 28–32, 41–42.

This article tells of the Questor Corporation's experiences with "performance management"—one basic approach to employee relations which is tailored to fit each individual facility. Performance management is based on five assumptions: 1) expectations, 2) skill, 3) feedback, 4) resources, and 5) reinforcement. Questor sees their most profitable discovery as being positive reinforcement and has begun programs at various facilities using reinforcement techniques. The following are some of the approaches that Questor has used in applying its five assumptions of employee relations to individual operations: Tactic No. 1: team approach; Tactic No. 2; analytical trouble shooting; Tactic No. 3; motivational needs; Tactic No. 4: creating a climate for advancement; Tactic No. 5: measurable standards of performance.

Clary, T. C., "Motivation Through Positive Stroking," *Personnel Administration*, March-April 1973, Vol. 2, No. 2, 113–117.

A "stroke", be it physical or verbal, is the basic motivation for human survival and enjoyment of life. Stroking can be a positive thing or it can be negative, involving forms of discipline and punishment to which many people are more accustomed. Stroking is being more and more commonly used to initiate performance change. One person cannot motivate another person, they can only set the climate. A number of varying positive stroking techniques are discussed, including their pros and cons. Goals for a consciously planned stroking program are outlined: a) to establish or strengthen a desired behavior, stroking must be increased; b) to eliminate undesired behavior, eliminate negative stroking; c) for a behavior to survive, it must be reinforced either from an external source or from the event itself; d) more conditional stroking may be given at the outset of the program.

Van Fleet, D. D., "Toward Identifying Critical Elements in a Behavioral Description of Leadership," *Public Personnel Management*, January–February 1974, Vol. 3, No. 1, 70–82.

One of the major problems in studies of leadership and managerial effectiveness is a lack of an operational definition. Campbell, Dunnette, Lawler, and Weick call for the use of the critical incident technique with a variety of subject/organizations to develop such a definition. This study, which involved nearly 50 subjects from over 25 different organizations, consisted of collecting, condensing, "testing" for criticality, and categorizing a fairly large number of such incidents. A "Behavioral Description of Leadership" was then developed. While this description may not be "the" operational definition which is being sought, it does represent yet one more step toward such a definition. Hopefully, other researchers will begin to pool results so that an operational definition will be forthcoming.

Rosenbaum, Bernard L., "New Uses for Behavior Modeling," *Personnel Administrator*, July 1978, Vol. 23, No. 7, 27–28.

Behavior modeling, a training technique which teaches employees to interact more effectively with their co-workers, is discussed in this article. Although based solidly in theory, behavior modeling avoids teaching theory. Instead it teaches ways to successfully deal with problems which are frequently encountered in a prescribed setting. The training programs described are tailor-made for the corporation in which they'll be given, often utilizing personnel from the specific company in video-tapes which illustrate the skills being taught. The modular format for the training gives participants a chance to try out technqiues so they may discuss them at the next meeting. The author sees behavior modeling as a highly effective tool with wide application to the field of management.

THEORETICAL

Evans, Martin G., "The Effects of Supervisory Behavior on the Path-Goal Relationship," *Organizational Behavior and Human Performance,* 1970, Vol. 5, 277–298.

This paper attempts to extend the understanding of leadership behavior by examining the impact of a leader's behavior (in terms of initiation of structure and consideration) on the subordinates' path-goal instrumentalities. Data relevant to the theoretical scheme are presented for two organizations. In both, support is gained for the theory—although in one organization a set of positive results emerges while in the second there is a consistent failure to support hypothesized relationships.

Kerr, Steven; Schriesheim, Chester A.; Murphy, Charles J. and Stogdill, Ralph M., "Toward a Contingency Theory of Leadership Based Upon the Consideration and Initiating Structure Literature," *Organizational Behavior and Human Performance,* 1974, Vol. 12, No. 1, 62–82.

The Ohio State Leadership Studies have been criticized on grounds that they lack a conceptual base and fail to take situational variables into account. This article reviews the published literature involving the leader behavior dimensions "Consideration" and "Initiating Structure" for the purpose of developing some situational propositions of leader effectiveness. Among the variables found by researchers to significantly moderate relationships between leader behavior predictors and satisfaction and performance criteria are the following: subordinate need for information, job level, subordinate expectations of leader behavior, perceived organizational independence, leader's similarity of attitudes and behavior to managerial style of higher management, leader upward influence, and characteristics of the task, including pressure and provision of intrinsic satisfaction. The article concludes by presenting 10 situational propositions, and linking them to form two general postulates of leadership effectiveness.

Mahwinney, Thomas C., and Ford, Jeffrey D., "The Path Goal Theory of Leader Effectiveness: An Operant Interpretation," *Academy of Management Review,* July 1977, Vol. 2, No. 3, 398–411.

Concepts and terms of the "operant paradigm", based on the empirical law of effect, are suggested as alternatives to the hypothetical path-goal motivation construct which provides the major premise of the path-goal theory of leadership. Hypotheses in the path-goal theory may be explained by acognitive arguments as well. The resulting interpretation supports the basic propositions comprising the path-goal theory without supporting the validity of the motivational model. The operant interpretation of leader effectiveness has several features which recommend its use: It is based on a set of empirically derived generalizations; it shows that the assumption of high powered mental activities on the part of subordinates need not be postulated to explain their behavior; having explained behavior as an observable activity (what subordinates and leaders actually do, determined by other observable environmental events), remedial action by leaders is more clearly defined; using the logic of matching law, leader importance and organizational influence in determining subordinate performance, can be predicted; and the matching law and correlation-based law of effect predict reciprocally caused leader-follower behaviors.

Ferris, G. R., Beehr, T. A., and Gilmore, D. C., "Social Facilitation: A Review and Alternative Conceptual Model," *Academy of Management Review*, 1978, Vol. 3, No. 2, 338–347.

Zajunc (1965) reviewed the social facilitation literature, proposing that the mere presence of others during task performance has arousal properties which facilitate the emission of dominant responses. Contrary to this, Cottrell found that expected evaluation, rather than the mere presence of others, is necessary for the facilitation of dominant responses. This contradiction, plus numerous other weaknesses to Zajunc's proposition, indicate a need for a more cognitive approach. The authors present as a plausible alternative a more cognitive model, constructed in an expectancy framework. Recommendations are made regarding directions of future research for testing the model.

Commentary

INTERACTION

LEADER/SUBORDINATE RELATIONS

"Mutual or reciprocal action or influence . . . a measure of how much the effect of one statistical variable upon another is determined by the values of one or more other variables." *Webster's Third New International Dictionary*, Unabridged, 1971.

For interaction, Webster's definition suggests a mutuality of interests that, unfortunately, does not always exist in an organizational hierarchy. However, designing systems to seek such outcomes can reap rich rewards in both performance and productivity. In reviewing the current literature utilizing a reinforcement paradigm to study the effects of interaction in an organization, we find a multiplicity of suggested modes through which interaction is thought to influence our dependent variables. One is introduced to various methods and theories for effective managerial-subordinate interaction, e.g., behavior modeling, use of various supervisory power tactics, performance management, stroking, operant interpretations of the path-goal theory of leadership, and the well-known consideration and initiating structure dimensions of leadership. We learn that the kind and extent of interaction is important and, as with other organizational variables studied, it is found that interaction effectiveness is a major organizational need and that interactions are even more complex than anticipated, impacting in many ways on our dependent variables.

BEHAVIOR MODELING

Several studies have investigated behavior modeling training programs to improve managerial interpersonal/interaction skills. But what *is* it? At GE an Interpersonal Skills Training Program (behavior modeling) consisted of videotape observations of situations which included behavioral objectives (discussion of work assignments, recognizing the "average" employee, and discussion of performance problems), followed by a measurement system to obtain progress results. In another company, behavior modeling was termed "Interaction Management" and was designed to handle interactions with subordinates. Training was based on movies and skill practice and then transferred to the job setting. In another setting, Supervisory Relationships Training (SRT) involved behavior modeling of effective supervisory behaviors via a series of simulated problem discussions and applying these learned skills to actual problems.

In the application of behavior modeling to industry, it has been found that managers trained via behavior modeling perform better than untrained and that behavior modeling improves employees' perceptions of their managers' interpersonal skills. Furthermore, it has been shown that practice over time further enhances these skills. In two studies (Byham, Adams & Kiggins, 1976; Moses & Ritchie, 1976), the effectiveness of behavior modeling as a means for improving specific supervisory interaction skills has been demonstrated. In a study to determine the effects of behavior modeling on employee morale and customer satisfaction, results indicated that employees of a trained group had a higher morale index than a control group, and produced a positive relationship between communication skills after training and later levels of customer satisfaction (Smith, 1976).

SUPERVISORY POWER/EFFECTIVENESS

Situational and personal factors influence a supervisor's choice of the means of exercising his/her power. In a study of military and industrial leadership power (Kipnis, Cosentino, 1969), it was found that military leaders relied on direct attempts to change subordinate behavior through instruction, direct punishment, and changes in the task environment, while industrial supervisors relied more on their persuasive powers. More recently, it has been found that mechanisms of expressing supervisory power have a significant effect on supervisors' perceptions of subordinate work quality and reinforcing behavior (McFillen, 1977).

"Ideal" supervisory behavior is illusory and many complex factors must be considered. A path-goal theory of motivation and expectancy theory have been used to assess how the behavior of supervisors affects subordinates' perceptions of the relation among effort, performance, and rewards. This approach has also been used to make prescriptions concerning how to account for leader behavior in real life situations (Evans, 1974; Nebeker & Mitchell, 1974). Leadership behaviors indicating initiating structure and consideration were examined in the light of their impact on subordinate path-goal instrumentalities in a study by Evans (1970). He found these behaviors to influence several satisfaction and performance criteria. Several factors have been found which influence the effectiveness of a leader's structuring and considerate behavior:

1. Subordinate need for information.

2. Job level.

3. Subordinate expectations of leader behavior.

4. Perceived organizational independence.

5. Leader's similarity of style to higher management.

6. Leader upward influence.

7. Characteristics of tasks (including pressure and provision of intrinsic satisfaction.

PERFORMANCE MANAGEMENT

One company has worked out a basic approach to employee relations which they term "performance management". In a study of this approach (Warren, 1972), it was found that five basic components were included:

1. Expectations

2. Skill

3. Feedback

4. Resources

5. Reinforcement

The company sees their most profitable discovery as being positive reinforcement and has begun programs at various facilities using reinforcement techniques. Their tactical approach in applying the five assumptions of employee relations included:

1. Team approach

2. Analytical trouble shooting

3. Assessing motivational needs

4. Creating a climate for advancement

5. Measurable standards of performance

This approach was found to be flexible and could be tailored to each individual operation.

In a study by McFillen (1977) it was found that subordinate performance and type of leadership mutually interact; that employee performance was found to have a significant effect on the supervisor's evaluation, reinforcement, and monitoring of that employee; and that supervisory power has a significant effect on the perception of employee work quality and reinforcing behavior. Thus this study suggests that the type of power possessed by a supervisor does not consistently affect his perceptions or behaviors of his subordinates but is guided by the nature of subordinate performance. Therefore, it would seem employee performance and supervisory reinforcement can be mutually fulfilling.

STROKING

Finally, stroking ("pat on the back," "you're doing a great job") is a technique that is being used to initiate performance change—to establish or strengthen desired behavior, to eliminate undesired behavior by eliminating negative stroking, and to reinforce continued desired behavior (Clary, 1973). It is one of the reinforcement techniques that required good rapport between manager and subordinate to be effective—a manager who is sincere, straightforward, and honest with subordinates and appreciates their accomplishments—and effectively articulates that appreciation.

In the literature we have learned about some of the effects of various approaches to good leader-subordinate relations (interaction). We know that leader-subordinate relations have many intervening moderators but the emphasis in the literature here seems to be on "accentuating the positive". Considerations for a workable framework are available in the literature so that methods can be devised which are effective for a specific organization in creating positive behavior patterns for good leader-subordinate relations and top performance. Further testing of the methods proposed and examination of the effects of the moderators is needed to more fully understand the best procedures to establish for attaining good leader-subordinate relations.

Independent Variable

MONEY

Type of Article	No. of Articles
Applied	8
Descriptive	12
Empirical	23
Integrative	18
Prescriptive	26
Theoretical	6

APPLIED

Rothe, H. F. and Nye, C. T., "Output Rates Among Machine Operators: II. Consistency Related to Methods of Pay," *Journal of Applied Psychology*, 1959, Vol. 43, No. 6, 417–420.

Investigation of magnitude and variability of performance (quantity) under an incentive system. Cautionary note: 1) incentive system not defined or described; 2) study took place during a period of increasing unemployment which was quite severe, in an area of limited alternative employment opportunities for employees. Method: longitudinal survey. Sample: Approximately 40 male machine operators. Conclusion: a) "incentives" were effective in keeping quantity of performance at approximately 125 percent of the managerially set standard; b) variance in performance was greater between individuals than intra-individually (over time).

Grove, B. A., "Attendance Reward Plan Pays," *Personnel Journal*, February 1968, Vol. 47, No. 2, 119–120.

Two attendance incentive periods per year were established beginning January 1 and July 1. One hundred dollars or 40 hours straight time pay (whichever is greater) for perfect attendance. Fifty dollars or 20 hours straight time pay (whichever is greater) for perfect attendance except for up to three occurrences of either tardiness or leaving early or a combination of these two totaling no more than three occurrences; or perfect attendance except for one day's absence-no tardiness or leaving early. There was a 34 percent decrease in absenteeism.

Rothe, H. F., "Output Rates Among Welders: Productivity and Consistency Following Removal of a Financial Incentive System," *Journal of Applied Psychology*, 1970, Vol. 54, No. 6, 549–551.

Production data for a group of welders were analyzed for 48 weeks following the removal of a financial incentive system, and an accompanying loss of take-home pay. Productivity dropped immediately and then began to climb. Two previously stated hypotheses relative to the effectiveness of incentives were examined. One hypothesis concerning the ratios of the ranges of intra-versus interindividual differences was not supported. The second hypothesis concerning the week-to-week consistency of productivity was supported. As productivity increased over a period of time, the consistency of productivity also increased.

Scheflen, K. C.; Lawler, E. E. III and Hackman, J. R., "Long-Term Impact of Employee Participation in the Development of Pay Incentive Plans," *Journal of Applied Psychology*, 1971, Vol. 55, No. 3, 182–186.

In an earlier study Lawler and Hackman examined the effects of worker participation in the development of pay incentive plans. In the original study, three work groups developed their own incentive plans to reward high attendance, and identical plans were then imposed by company management in two other work groups. A significant increase in attendance was found during the first 16 weeks following implementation of the plans only in the groups where the plans were participatively developed. Data reported in the present study cover a 12-week period beginning one year after the original plans had been installed. After the data reported in the earlier study had been collected, the incentive plans were discontinued by company management in two of the three participative groups. The present results show that attendance dropped below pretreatment levels in these two groups, and that attendance continued high in the third participative group. An increase in attendance was found after one year in those groups where incentive plans had been imposed by company management.

Woska, W. J., "Sick Leave Incentive Plans-A Benefit to Consider," *Public Personnel Review*, January 1972, Vol. 33, No. 1, 21–24.

Sick leave incentive plans involve reducing sick leave usage through a varied assortment of incentive plans such as additional pay, time off, sick leave time converted to paid up insurance, etc. The most prevalent argument against sick leave incentive plans is the additional cost to provide for what many contend is a benefit on top of a benefit. The city of Sacramento's sick leave program was investigated and discussed. The city considered a number of different incentive plans before finally adopting one, which was devised to fulfill three objectives: 1) to serve as an incentive to the employee to save his sick leave in the event of an accident or injury; 2) to serve as a deterrent to sick leave misuse; 3) to modify the inequity between the careful and careless user of the benefits. The plan proved to be effective in subsequently reducing the number of sick days used by employees when comparing the 1969-70 statistics to the three previous years.

McManis, D. L. and Dick, W. G., "Monetary Incentives in Today's Industrial Setting," *Personnel Journal,* May 1973, Vol. 52, No. 5, 387–392.

Reviews the role of incentives in manufacturing the labor union's influence. Tests the productivity of wage incentives in a rather stable industry—the corrugated shipping industry—where such stability would help hold constant many variables. The original study covered the application of monetary incentives to the reduction of waste, the application of monetary incentives to the increase of productivity and the interaction between two plans. The "before and after" study of one plant considers only the effect of monetary incentives on productivity. Three separate tests were employed: 1) 15 of 18 operations clearly support the theory that monetary incentives can be used to induce workers to increase their productivity; 2) a statistically significant increase in average monthly efficiency, and 3) statistically significant increase in output. Each test clearly supported the theory that monetary incentives can be effective in increasing productivity in many firms today. However, a monetary incentive plan should not be expected to compensate for poor management practices or an inadequate pay scale. They do remain a very powerful management tool—one that should not be overlooked by modern management.

Sasser, W. E. and Pettway, S. H., "Case of Big Mac's Pay Plans," *Harvard Business Review,* July-August 1974, Vol. 52, No. 4, 30–48.

Between 1963-1972, McDonalds tried several compensation plans: 1963—a managers' bonus was a function of his sales increase over the previous year; 1964-1966—bonuses were awarded purely on the basis of subjective evaluations; 1967-1971—the company tied the base salaries of each unit's manager and first assistant-manager to their ability to meet the QSC (quality, service, cleanliness) standards. It made the quarterly bonus payments depend on a profit contribution. The plan proved unpopular with those on the front line because it mainly rewarded high volume. 1972—unit manager's compensation consisted of his base salary and quarterly bonuses that rewarded his ability to meet predetermined goals. The requirements for a pay plan were reviewed again. A workable plan, it was decided, should possess these elements: 1) manager participation in pay plan design; 2) base salary competitive within the industry; 3) a bonus would be rewarded a manager when someone from his

unit is promoted; 4) a full bonus paid when a manager reaches his predetermined business goals, and 5) a predetermined floor and ceiling would correlate the level of bonus paid with the level of business goal attained.

Panyan, Steven W. and McGregor, Michael, "How to Implement A Proactive Incentive Plan: A Field Study," *Personnel Journal*, September 1976, Vol. 55, No. 9, 460–463.

An incentive plan, designed to reduce absenteeism and sick leave, was initiated in a small city administration. The plan consisted of paying employees a bonus of $10.00 per day for each unused sick leave per year. A pre-post incentive plan comparison indicated a marked drop in mean annual sick leave days between the two periods (1967 to 1970 and 1971 to 1974). The authors emphasize the following considerations for adopting proactive incentive plans: select a target objective which is meaningful and measurable; seek employee suggestions on procedures and incentives; and reserve rewards for exceptional performance.

DESCRIPTIVE

Nealey, S. M., "Determining Worker Preferences Among Employee Benefit Programs," *Journal of Applied Psychology*, 1964, Vol. 48, No. 1, 7–12.

The paired comparison method was applied to measure the preferences of 1133 members of a trade union among a pay raise, a union shop proposal, a vacation plan, a shorter work week, hospital insurance, and a pension increase. Hospital insurance was most preferred while the shorter work week was least preferred. Differences in preference were markedly related to age and seniority, moderately related to physical-clerical job type, marital status, and number of dependent children. Preference for the pay raise was scarcely related to the demographic variables. The preference judgments were highly transitive and allow the six compensation options to be ranked in an ordinal scale.

Zedeck, S. and Smith, P. C., "A Psychophysical Determination of Equitable Payment: A Methodological Study," *Journal of Applied Psychology*, October 1968, Vol. 52, No. 5, 343–347.

The practicality of using psychophysical methods to determine ranges for payment plans was explored. Thresholds of perceived equitable payment (PSE) and the "just meaningful difference" (jmd) of payment were determined by an adaptation of the psychophysical Method of Limits. PSE and jmd were significantly greater for junior executives than for secretaries of an academic institution, whereas the respective Weber ratios, K (the proportionate meaningful additions to the base salary), were not significantly different. There were no significant differences between two secretarial subgroups in jmd and K, but a significant difference in PSE. The limitations and implications of this method, and its relevance to equity theory, were discussed.

Butlar, W. H., "Successful Wage Incentives," *Industrial Management,* May 1969, Vol. 11, No. 5, 13–15.

The author believes that wage incentives are a sound concept and provides proof through a detailed example of a successful wage incentive installation in industry. Suggests the major reason for failure of American industry to achieve maximum benefits from an incentive program can be attributed to poor installation and poor controls; establishes a procedure to avoid these pitfalls through use of Standard Data and other control mechanisms. Lists seven benefits achieved through installation of the sample plan.

Evans, W. A., "Pay for Performance: Fact or Fable," *Personnel Journal,* September 1970, Vol. 49, No. 9, 726–731.

Surveyed the Fortune 500 firms to determine if a) performance was measured "objectively", and b) if pay was contingent upon performance. Methods: mail survey. Sample: Fortune 500 companies (response rate 78 percent). Variables: in addition to other performance questions, the responses were separated by blue collar, clerical, and professional. Conclusions: most companies indicate that a) performance is the primary determinant of compensation (especially for clerical and professional employees), but b) a large percentage of companies do not have a formal appraisal and/or do not actually use performance appraisal devices.

Patton, A., "Why Incentive Plans Fail," *Harvard Business Review,* May-June 1972, Vol. 50, No. 3, 58–66.

Most incentive plans are unproductive for a number of reasons which can be most effectively discussed under three headings: 1) industry characteristics; 2) misused bonus mathematics, and 3) administrative flaws. The incentive-use "spectrum" is presented. At one extreme, almost every large company or industry has an executive incentive plan. At the other end, relatively few incentive plans are found among public utilities, banks, mining companies, railroads, etc. The success or failure of an incentive program and an important factor in the high fail-rate of executive incentive plans is the inhospitable industry environment at the low end of this incentive-use spectrum. Characteristics of companies that exhibit greatest use of incentives: 1) numerous short-term decisions which influence profit are made by individuals at several levels of the organization; 2) decentralized organization is typical; 3) budget variances, market-share data, and economic analysis are the tools for judging performance; 4) companies demand a great deal of their people. Executives involved in companies which are characterized by the above conditions must live with the fact that their jobs are less secure than most. Marginal incentive industries are characterized by 1) a few, long-term decisions which have the most important profit impact; 2) functional organization is typical; 3) sophisticated market and economic research tools for judging performance are not used often, 4) lower executive stress factor. An executive in these industries is rarely fired, due primarily to the difficulty management has in objectively judging an individual's performance. As incentive plans have become increasingly popular, they have been adopted by many companies in industries at the low-use end of the spectrum. The author discusses bonus formulas and how to make them work. In the conclusion, it is reemphasized that the split between the undemanding, familial environment of certain industries and the highly charged environment of other industries is why the will to make an incentive plan work varies so greatly from one industry to the next.

Mustafa, H., "Escalator Pay Plans," *Public Personnel Management*, January-February 1974, Vol. 3, No. 1, 4–9.

It is essential to a sound pay structure that differences between jobs based on levels of responsibility and kinds of duties are reflected in pay levels. The city of Akron, Ohio came to this realization and developed their own escalator pay plan. Recognizing that normal adjustment in the wage scale of city workers was taking place at a slower rate than in industry, the city sought to achieve three principle objectives by the adoption of a Wage Index Increase system to: 1) keep city pay scales competitive and comparable; 2) maintain internal relationships relative to classification and pay plans, and 3) simplify the process of paysetting and make it more rational. In 1966, Akron adopted its "Escalator clause" to provide periodic adjustment to city wages to reflect changes in wages in the Akron area. The effect of each occupational category's percentage increase on the city's overall increase in each of the years the escalator has operated is significant. In evaluation of the plan, it has achieved its objective of allowing Akron's municipal and industrial wages to grow at comparable rates. It has also helped to maintain pay relationships between job categories based on kinds of duties and levels of responsibility. A major criticism of the plan has been that the salary gap between the low-paying jobs and top-level officials has widened.

Schuster, J. R., "Executive Compensation-in the Eyes of the Beholder," *Business Horizons*, April 1974, Vol. 17, No. 2, 79–86.

The purpose of this study was to probe elements of the Porter-Lawler motivational model. The study determines how senior executives in larger corporations feel about the forms of compensation they receive and what they see as the relationship of their compensation to the position that they hold. Questionnaires were distributed to 600 corporate executives, selected from three upper levels of management. Study results show that most participants felt strongly that their positions allowed them to significantly affect their firm's growth and that they did make such a difference. About 66 percent of participants felt that their level of compensation actually depends on their performance and that their compensation changes as their performance changes. Ten forms of compensation are discussed in the article in reference to questionnaire responses. Study results indicated that top executives have different feelings about different types of compensation, there being two major types: 1) those which executives feel should be related to their level of performance, and 2) those which they should receive regardless of performance level. Performance-related compensations hold the greatest opportunities for motivation. Unfortunately, this is the type of compensation that companies have failed to extensively develop, as evidenced by so many executives in the study that reported that performance-related compensations did not actually depend on performance level.

Goode, R. V., "Compensation at the Cafeteria Checkout Line," *Personnel*, November-December 1974, Vol. 51, No. 6, 45–49.

In theory, the cafeteria compensation plan sounds fine; however, different age groups have different preferences and needs and also there is frequently much misunderstanding concerning the long-range benefits. A survey was made among safety, clerical, trades, and professional employees in the state of California. A total cafeteria compensation concept represents a severe downside risk to companies, particularly in the employee benefits area—and the potential gains today are negligible. Few companies offer it, so there is little competitive pressure to justify risk.

Pritchard, Robert D.; Campbell, Kathleen M. and Campbell, Donald J., "Effects of Extrinsic Financial Rewards on Intrinsic Motivation," *Journal of Applied Psychology*, February 1977, Vol. 62, No. 1, 9–15.

Deci's hypothesis that contingent extrinsic reward will decrease intrinsic, motivation was evaluated with a chess-problem task. After observing the amount of time male and female college student subjects spent working on the task in a free period, one group (N = 17) was offered a financial incentive for performing the task while another group (N = 11) was not. One week later, subjects were again observed in a free period and they performed the task again with no financial incentive. Results supported the hypothesis, and data that rule out specific methodological criticisms of this paradigm were presented. The results are discussed in terms of whether extrinsic rewards and motivation interact with intrinsic motivation.

Patten, Thomas H. Jr., "Pay for Performance or Placation?" *Personnel Administrator*, September 1977, Vol. 22, No. 7, 26–29.

In this article, the author examines the merits of "paying for performance" and of "paying for placation". To state the cases both for and against performance pay incentives, Patten draws on research done by Herbert H. Meyer at General Electric Company and Edward E. Lawler III, professor of psychology at the University of Michigan. Meyer maintains that the use of performance incentives will build resentment among employees who feel that they deserve incentive pay but do not receive it. Lawler feels that incentive pay leads to higher motivation and morale among good employees.

The author agrees with Lawler that pay incentives are a good form of employee motivation, but states that further analysis must be done before incentive pay can be effectively implemented. The OD-MBO-RS model (organizational development - management by objectives - rewards system) should be supplemented with goal-setting among managerial, technical and professional persons which incorporates interaction between all facets of the organization. Personnel managers must 1) distinguish between "performance motivation" and "membership motivation"; 2) build appropriate pay plans upon these distinctions; and 3) provide means through which management and professional peers may judge one another's performance. Finally, actual pay decisions must be left in the chain of command so that the total employee is recognized, budget constraints considered, and manager's accountability unchanged.

Field, Robert L. and Voght, Gary A., "Ways to Pay Your Key People Well," *Personnel Administrator*, May 1979, Vol. 24, No. 5, 37–40.

Field and Voght say large amounts of cash paid to key people may not be attractive to stockholders and might not be best for the executive. The authors itemize goals a large or small corporation should adopt as its purpose in executive compensation and, they say, long-term compensation plans are readily available to both the very large and very small companies. A six-step formula is detailed for use in aiding a determination of the compensation alternatives best suited for a given company.

Krogman, Robert, "What Employees Need to Know About Benefit Plans," *Personnel Administrator*, May 1980, Vol. 25, No. 5, 45–57.

Because up to 30 percent of an employee's compensation is in the form of fringe benefits of some kind, the question "Is your company getting the most out of its benefits programs?" must be asked. Many times the answer is probably no. One company, Chicago Title & Trust, found that oftentimes the implementation of simple "explanation programs" resulted in getting more mileage from their company's benefits programs. They cited full, careful explanations of the benefits, employee involvement, and benefits reporting as being essential to the success of their benefits programs. The total impact of their communications effort on behalf of the company's benefits package has served corporate objectives well.

EMPIRICAL

Rothe, H. F. and Nye, C. T., "Output Rates Among Machine Operators: II. Consistency Related to Methods of Pay," *Journal of Applied Psychology*, 1959, Vol. 43, No. 6. 417–420.

Investigation of magnitude and variability of performance (quantity) under an incentive system. Cautionary note: 1) incentive system not defined or described; 2) study took place during a period of increasing unemployment which was quite severe, in an area of limited alternative employment opportunities for employees. Method: longitudinal survey. Sample: approximately 40 male machine operators. Conclusion: a) "incentives" were effective in keeping quantity of performance at approximately 125 percent of the managerially set standard; b) variance in performance was greater between individuals than intra-individually (over time).

Jones, L. V. and Jeffrey, T. E., "A Quantitative Analysis of Expressed Preferences for Compensation Plans," *Journal of Applied Psychology*, August 1964, Vol. 48, No. 4, 201–210.

The method of factorial paired comparisons is employed in two studies designed to evaluate employee preferences for alternative forms of job compensation. Explicitly considered are four compensation features with two levels each; weekly salary versus hourly wage, use or non-use of supervisory merit-ratings, inclusion or exclusion of a piece-incentive plan, and pay increase versus no increase. A 2^4 factorial design provides estimates for the tests of significance on preference scale values associated with each compensation "package," as well as for scale contrasts between the two levels of each separate compensation feature.

Nealey, S. M., "Determining Worker Preferences Among Employee Benefit Programs," *Journal of Applied Psychology*, 1964, Vol. 48, No. 1, 7–12.

The paired comparison method was applied to measure the preference of 1,133 members of a trade union among a pay raise, a union shop proposal, a vacation plan, a shorter work week, hospital insurance, and a pension increase. Hospital insurance was most preferred while the shorter work week was least preferred. Differences in preference was markedly related to age and seniority, moderately related to physical-clerical job type, marital status, and number of dependent children. Preference for the pay raise was scarcely related to the demographic variables. The preference judgments were highly transitive and allow the six compensation options to be ranked in an ordinal scale.

Toppen, J. T., "Effect of Size and Frequency of Money Reinforcement on Human Operant (Work) Behavior," *Perceptual and Motor Skills*, 1965, Vol. 20, 259–269.

Forty (40) college males were assigned by counterbalancing to four equal groups in a 2 × 2 factorial design which involved mean ratios of reinforcement of 1/500 and 1/2500, and magnitudes of monetary payoff of 1¢ and 25¢. The work was that of repetitively pulling a manipulandum against a constant tension spring requiring 25 lb. of force, horizontally, through 5/8 inches. Analysis of variance showed significantly smaller work output for the 1¢ groups and for the 1/2500 ratio groups for the 30 minute work period.

Toppen, J. T., "Money Reinforcement and Human Operant (Work) Behavior: II. Within-Subject Comparisons," *Perceptual and Motor Skills*, 1965, Vol. 20, 1193–1199.

Five groups each of 10 college male Ss were given the same frequency of reinforcement (1/1000): a control group received 10¢ each reinforcement, two groups were given systematically decreasing-sized payment schedules. The last four groups began at the same level as the control group, i.e., of 10¢ for each of the first three payments. The work was that of repetitively pulling a manipulandum against a constant-tension spring requiring 25 lb. of force, horizontally, through a 5/8 inch distance, for one hour, Compared with control group performance over time as predicted. The increasing-magnitude groups were at first inconsistent in performance, but upon repetition of one of the increasing schedules and adding a third, it was found that increasing schedules evoked performances generally higher than those of the control group, although the differences in performance compared with that of the control group were not statistically significant.

Toppen, J. T., "Money Reinforcement and Human Operant (Work) Behavior: III. Piecework-Payment and Time-Payment Comparisons," *Perceptual and Motor Skills*, 1965, Vol. 21, 907–913.

Two groups of 10 college male Ss were given different money reinforcement schedules in single one-hour work periods for each S (following a combination of "pretests" and a questionnaire, used for reasons described). The work was that of repetitively pulling a manipulandum against a constant-tension spring requiring 25 lb. of force, horizontally, through a 5/8 inch distance. The control group was paid at a rate of 10¢ for each 1000 pulls. The tests Ss were paid in advance with instructions that they had the job of working at the machine for one hour, if they wished (though they were required to remain in the room) and were given the maximum rate of pay ($1.50 per hour) which it was anticipated the control Ss might earn. The test Ss were told that their work "may provide information on which to base later studies." As predicted, the control Ss showed markedly greater output (approximately 100 percent greater) than that obtained from Ss paid in advance on a time basis.

Haire, M.; Ghiselli, E. E. and Gordon, M. E., "A Psychological Study of Pay," *Journal of Applied Psychology Monograph*, August 1967, Vol. 51, No. 4, Whole No. 636, Part 2 of 2 Parts, 1–24.

A study in three sections of empirical data on managerial compensation for three groups of managers (N = about 90 for each group): 1) a description of the distributional characteristics of pay over time (about 25 years); 2) the correlation of pay with pay over time and presents statistical analyses to explain the observed relationships; 3) a statistical model of pay capitalizing on the cumulative character of pay (pay at Year n is composed of pay at Year 1 + raises at Years 2, 3,. . . n) and the formulas for the distributional and correlational character of composites. The potential psychological leverage of hitherto little-considered variables stands out—for instance, without increasing the total salary bill, management of the variance of pay over a group in a given year and of the correlation of pay with raises from year to year allows one to deal with the level of aspiration of the individual and his relative standing in the group. The managerial implications of the statistical behavior of pay are discussed in detail.

Smith, R. L.; Lucaccini, L. F. and Epstein, M. H., "Effects of Monetary Rewards and Punishments on Vigilance Performance," *Journal of Applied Psychology*, 1967, Vol. 51, No. 5, 411–416.

In a complex visual vigilance task lasting one hour, Ss in five experimental groups were rewarded for correct detections and punished either for missed targets or for false alarms. Ss in a control group performed the task without possibility of reward or punishment, three levels of monetary incentive were used as rewards. The major results of the study indicated that a) some combinations of reward and punishment facilitated detection performance while others did not, and b) Ss punished for missed targets performed better than Ss punished for false alarms. Implications for vigilance research and theory are discussed.

Lawler, E. E. III, "Effects of Hourly Overpayment on Productivity and Work Quality," *Journal of Personality and Social Psychology*, November 1968, Vol. 10, No. 3, 306–313.

This study focuses upon several predictions of Adams' equity theory that appear to be in disagreement with the assumption that people try to maximize their economic gain and minimize their job inputs. The effects of hourly overpayment on productivity and work quality are considered. Adams' finding that overpayment leads to high productivity was replicated. However, in contrast to the predictions of equity theory, there was a general tendency for the overpaid Ss to do lower quality work, particularly during the last two of the three sessions they worked. An additional group of overpaid Ss was included in the study and, in contrast to the Ss used in Adams' work, they were made to feel overpaid by virtue of circumstance rather than by their own low qualifications. The data from this group suggested that just feeling overpaid is not enough to cause Ss to produce large quantities of work. The significance of this finding for equity and expectancy theory was considered, and it was concluded that much of the data from the overpaid hourly equity studies can be explained without recourse to equity theory.

Rothe, H. F., "Output Rates Among Welders: Productivity and Consistency Following Removal of a Financial Incentive System," *Journal of Applied Psychology*, 1970, Vol. 54, No. 6, 549–551.

Production data for a group of welders were analyzed for 48 weeks following the removal of a financial incentive system, and an accompanying loss of take-home pay. Productivity dropped immediately and then began to climb. Two previously stated hypotheses related to the effectiveness of incentives were examined. One hypothesis concerning the ratios of the ranges of intra versus inter individual differences was not supported. The second hypothesis concerning the week-to-week consistency of productivity was supported. As productivity increased over a period of time, the consistency of productivity also increased.

Deci, E. L., "The Effects of Contingent and Noncontingent Rewards and Controls on Intrinsic Motivation," *Organizational Behavior and Human Performance*, 1972, Vol. 8, 217–220.

Theories of management and work motivation distinguish between two kinds of rewards—extrinsic and intrinsic. Extrinsic rewards are ones such as money and verbal reinforcement which are mediated outside of the person, whereas intrinsic rewards are mediated within the person. We say a person is intrinsically motivated to perform an activity if there is not apparent reward except the activity itself or the feelings which result from the activity. All of the theories of work motivation which consider both kinds of rewards assume that the effects of the two are additive. This paper examines that assumption by reviewing a program of research which investigated the effects of external rewards and controls on intrinsic motivation. It was reported that a person's intrinsic motivation to perform an activity decreased when he received contingent monetary payments, threats of punishment for poor performance, or negative feedback about his performance. Noncontingent monetary payments left intrinsic motivation unchanged, and verbal reinforcements appeared to enhance intrinsic motivation. A cognitive evaluation theory was presented to explain these results, and the theory and results were discussed in relation to management.

Fossum, John A., "Publicity or Secrecy? Pay and Performance Feedback Effects on Satisfaction," *The Academy of Management Proceedings*, 1976, 270–272.

This study involved crossing two pay conditions—publicity and secrecy—with two performance feedback conditions—publicity and no feedback—to examine their relation to pay satisfaction. Forty-one subjects were hired through the want ads to perform a coding task. The pay-performance conditions were the following: public posting of pay and performance, public posting of pay with no performance feedback, private communication of pay and public posting of performance, and private communication of pay without performance feedback. Individuals were paid between $2.25 and $3.75 per hour, depending on their ranked performance level. All pay increments were in 35¢ steps based on merit. Satisfaction was measured by a questionnaire consisting of seven five-item semantic differential scales which measure reactions to satisfaction with the pay and job aspects. The results showed no significant main effects or interactions. In short, pay publicity, performance feedback or congruent pay-performance communication systems made no difference in pay satisfaction. In general, the subjects in this study indicated a preference for equitable pay and performance-linked pay, but expressed rather neutral opinions as to the secrecy-openness issue. These results fail to support Lawler's (1971, 1972) contention that employees generally desire pay publicity in compensation systems.

Chung, Kae H. and Vickery, W. Dean, "Relative Effectiveness and Joint Effects of Three Selected Reinforcements in a Repetitive Task Situation," *Organizational Behavior and Human Performance*, June 1976, Vol. 16, No. 1, 114–142.

The relative effectiveness and joint effects of the three selected reinforcements (incentive-pay rates, IR, partially reinforced bonus, PR, and knowledge of results, KR) were investigated in a repetitive task situation (transferring responses from a standardized answer sheet to another answer sheet). A 2 × 2 × 2 factorial design was utilized to study the independent and interactive effects of IR, PR, and KR on performance. The IR condition included either a piece rate or hourly rate; the PR condition included either no partial bonus or a partial bonus for each completed page (token drawing) and either no KR or KR (comparative information with performance information with performance norms). Performance was based on the number of completed answer sheets. Eighty subjects were randomly assigned to eight experimental groups and were subject to different experimental treatments. The results of variance analysis indicated that the differences in performance between IR and hourly rate (HR) groups, between PR and no PR, and KR and no KR were statistically significant at .05, approximately .05 and .001 levels, respectively. None of the interactive effects were significant at .05 level. The comparison of treatment means showed that the performance under the condition of IR × PR × KR is the most superior and was followed by that of no KR and no PR groups. The high performances of the jointly reinforced groups were attributable more to additive main effects than to interactive effects.

Farr, James L., "Task Characteristics, Reward Contingency, and Intrinsic Motivation," *Organizational Behavior and Human Performance*, August 1976, Vol. 16, No. 2, 294–307.

A factorial laboratory study investigated the affects of task characteristics and reward contingency upon intrinsic task motivation. Task characteristics were varied along the core dimensions suggested by Hackman and Lawler (1971) with three levels used: low, high except for feedback, and high including feedback. Two levels of reward contingency were used: contingent (piece-rate) and noncontingent (hourly). Intrinsic task motivation was measured by the subjects volunteering for a nonrewarded work session and by productivity data. It was hypothesized, following Deci (1972), that contingent pay would lead to decreased intrinsic motivation due to a change in subjects' attribution of the causes of task motivation and performance. Neither the psychological process nor the behavior prediction was supported. Contingent pay did result in higher levels of productivity. It was also hypothesized that the high on core dimensions conditions would lead to higher levels of intrinsic motivation than the low condition. This hypothesis received some support. It was concluded that contingent reward systems combined with tasks designed to be high on the core dimensions appeared to be both extrinsically and intrinsically motivating to task performers.

Greenberg, Jerald and Leventhal, Gerald S., "Equity and the Use of Overreward to Motivate Performance," *Journal of Personality and Social Psychology*, August 1976, Vol. 34, No. 2, 179–190.

Two studies were conducted in which subjects played the role of industrial consultants who distributed bonus pay ($0 to $100) to groups of hypothetical workers (students). The subjects were told either to give workers what they deserved based on performance (maintain equity) or to use the reward to motivate the workers. Subjects who were told to motivate better performance gave higher reward to poor performers than subjects who were told to maintain equity. In some instances, the tendency to over reward poor performers was so strong that subjects who tried to motivate the workers violated the equity norm by giving higher pay to workers with lower inputs. Thus, in study 1, subjects who attempted to raise workers performance gave higher reward to members of failing groups than to members of successful groups. In study 2, male subjects who attempted to motivate better performance gave higher reward to lazy (attributes supplied by experimenter) workers than to well-motivated workers.

Farr, James L., "Incentive Schedules, Productivity, and Satisfaction in Work Groups: A Laboratory Study," *Organizational Behavior and Human Performance*, October 1976, Vol. 17, No. 1, 159–170.

A factorial laboratory study examined the effects of individual incentives and group incentives. The subjects were 144 college students who worked in three-person groups on a card-sorting task. Both individual and group incentives significantly increased task performance. The experimental condition which contained both an individual and group incentive resulted in the highest level of performance, but also resulted in perceptions of the pay system as being unfair. Personal pay satisfaction was not affected by any pay condition. Results also were not in accord with predictions of equity theory concerning both performances and satisfaction. It was concluded that current conceptions of pay inequality may have to be modified to include a distinction between personal pay satisfaction and the perceived fairness of a pay system.

Turnage, Janet J. and Muchinsky, Paul M., "The Effects of Reward Contingency and Participative Decision-Making on Intrinsically and Extrinsically Motivating Tasks," *Academy of Management Journal,* September 1976, Vol. 19, No. 3, 482–488.

The purpose of this study was to address some of the questions raised in Deci's research regarding the additivity of intrinsic and extrinsic rewards in work behavior. The subjects were 80 male undergraduates. The study used a 2 × 2 × 2 factorial design to examine the effect of three variables. The first variable was intrinsically versus extrinsically motivating tasks which were operationalized by the Arthur Point Stencil Design Test and a repetitive card-sorting task, respectively. The second variable, participative decision-making, was manipulated by either allowing the subject to choose their preferred reward (monetary payment or additional experimental credit) or they were given no choice of payment. The third factor was contingency versus noncontingency of payment. Subjects in the contingency condition were told they would be rewarded after successful completion of their task. Subjects in the noncontingency condition were told they would be rewarded for their participation. The dependent variables were intrinsic motivation (the amount of time spent working on tasks in free-time period), experimenter monitored performance time and task interest (as measured on a nine-point scale). Subjects who performed the stencil-design task worked longer during the free-time period and rated the task more interesting than subjects who performed the card-sorting task. Contingently rewarded subjects performed the tasks faster than those under the noncontingency condition. The choice variable was also significant for the card-sorting subjects, with subjects having a choice of reward working slower. The authors conclude that the effects of external rewards and participation on performance and intrinsic motivation are quite different in job decisions and are paid noncontingently, increase intrinsic motivation. But paying workers contingently and allowing them no participation in the job also appears to increase intrinsic motivation while increasing productivity.

London, Manuel and Oldham, Greg R., "Effects of Varying Goal Types and Incentive Systems on Performance and Satisfaction," *Academy of Management Journal,* December 1976, Vol. 19, No. 4, 537–546.

Goals for high and minimum acceptable performance were manipulated under three incentive conditions: piece-rate, fixed rate and no incentive. Subjects were 180 male and female students who participated in a perceptual motor card-sorting task. Goal setting was introduced by having subjects agree to a goal above (10, 25, or 40 percent) and a minimum level below five or 40 percent) previous task performance. The incentive conditions were operationalized by providing one group with one percent per card sorted on each trial (piece-rate), $2.00 for participating regardless of performance (fixed rate), and no pay. Results indicated that the nature of the incentive system and the difficulty of the high performance goal independently affected performance (number of cards sorted). Satisfaction, performance, and the relationship between the two were a function of the level of minimum acceptable performance, attainment and the difficulty of the high performance goal. Performance was found to be significantly higher under piece-rate *and* no pay conditions than fixed rate. This may indicate that goal-setting (regardless of level) results in better performance when no incentive is offered than when a fixed sum is paid. Finally, since the type of incentive system affected performance independently of the impact of goal-setting, the author suggests that goal-setting procedures should not replace financial incentives as means of enhancing performance in organizations.

Pinder, Craig C., "Additivity Versus Nonadditivity of Intrinsic and Extrinsic Incentives: Implications for Work Motivation, Performance, and Attitudes," *Journal of Applied Psychology*, 1976, Vol. 61, No. 6, 693–700.

Male subjects (N = 80) were randomly assigned to either an intrinsically appealing or an intrinsically nonappealing assembly task. Half of the subjects were paid according to a highly salient, continuous, contingent reward schedule, while the other half were paid according to an extremely noncontingent payment schedule. Thus, 20 subjects worked for both intrinsic and extrinsic incentives, 20 for extrinsic only, 20 for intrinsic only, and 20 for minimal incentives of either type. Data on four dependent variables (performance, intrinsic motivation, orientation toward the task, and intrinsic satisfaction) provided convergent support for Deci's hypothesis that intrinsic and extrinsic incentives are not additive in determining attitudes and behavior.

Shapira, Zur, "Expectancy Determinants of Intrinsically Motivated Behavior," *Journal of Personality and Social Psychology*, December 1976, Vol. 34, No. 6, 1235–1244.

An experiment was conducted to contrast and reconcile two cognitive theories of motivation and to investigate the expectancy determinants of intrinsically motivated behavior. Subjects (60 undergraduates) were presented with seven challenging tasks (mechanical spatial-relations puzzles) which varied in their level of difficulty. The subjects were asked to select their most preferred task to work on and then to rank order the remaining tasks on their preference for working on them. Subjects were either told or not told that they would receive $2.50 for successfully accomplishing the task. Subjects who could earn money for a successful completion of the task chose relatively easy tasks (though not the easiest), while subjects who could get no money for performing the task chose rather difficult tasks. The results indicate that when a salient monetary reward was available, people behave largely (though not solely) as predicted by an extrinsically oriented expectancy-valence theory such as Vroom's, whereas when no external reward was available, people's choices and preferences could be most accurately accounted for by an expectancy-valence theory utilizing an intrinsic valence function which relates in a positively accelerated manner to task difficulty.

London, Manuel and Oldham, Greg R., "A Comparison of Group and Individual Incentive Plans," *Academy of Management Journal,* March 1977, Vol. 20, No. 1, 34–41.

The effects of three variations of group incentive plans on goals and performance were compared in the laboratory and contrasted with individual piece-rate and fixed-rate incentive systems. The three group incentive conditions are the following: payment based on the highest performer in the group; payment based on the lowest performer in the group; and payment based on the average performance of the group. Thirty-five (35) pairs of male students served as subjects for a perceptual motor card-sorting task. Piece-rate was operationalized as 1¢ paid for each card sorted over five-minute trials. Fixed rate was operationalized as receiving 50¢ per trial regardless of performance. The results emphasize the importance of both the design of the pay system and the level of a person's performance in the work group. Performance was significantly higher under the high performance piece-rate condition and the individual piece-rate condition than under other incentive systems taken together. The goal and subsequent performance levels were highest and increased most over trials when pay was contingent solely on the subject's own performance (individual piece-rate) and when it was based on the higher performer in a work group (high performance piece-rate). The author concludes that a group incentive system can be effective as an individual system when it is designed properly. However, the effects of the incentive plan may be moderated by another person's performance.

Farr, James L.; Vance, Robert J. and McIntyre, Robert M., "Further Examinations of the Relationship Between Reward Contingency and Intrinsic Motivation," *Organizational Behavior and Human Performance,* October 1977, Vol. 20, No. 1, 31–53.

A series of laboratory studies were conducted to examine the effect of contingent monetary reward on the occurrence of behavior presumably determined by intrinsic task motivation. A general hypothesis that contingent monetary rewards would reduce the frequency of such behaviors was derived from a postulate of cognitive evaluation theory. For all of the studies, intrinsic task motivation was operationally defined as the amount of free time a subject spent working on a task without receiving reward. Study 1 investigated the effects of reward contingency and reward magnitude upon the behavioral measure of intrinsic motivation and upon related attitudinal variables. Study 2 examined the effects of reward contingency and two individual difference variables (self-esteem and perceived locus of control) on intrinsic motivation and attitudinal measures. Although Study 2 showed no significant results, Study 1 demonstrated support for the hypothesis with the behavioral measure of intrinsic motivation, but not with the attitudinal measures. Further examination of behavioral measure of intrinsic motivation suggested that this variable was bimodally distributed in both Studies 1 and 2. A test for normality indicated that the distributions were significally nonnormal and that parametric analyses of mean differences were inappropriate. Study 3 reported the results of the nonparametric reanalyses of Studies 1 and 2 and of data previously published by Deci as supportive of the postulate under examination. Deci's data were also found to be generally bimodal. The nonparametric analyses were nonsignificant for all data sets. Theoretical implications of these results are discussed and future directions for research are suggested.

Terborg, James R. and Miller, Howard E., "Motivation, Behavior, and Performance: A Closer Examination of Goal-Setting and Monetary Incentives," *Journal of Applied Psychology*, 1978, Vol. 63, No. 1, 29–39.

Some experimenters often test predictions from theories of motivation using performance outcomes as dependent variables. We argue that observable behaviors that are likely to be affected by motivation manipulations should be used in combination with performance outcomes. Such procedures would be sensitive to differential effects of manipulations on various behaviors and would allow for investigation of relationships among behaviors and performance outcomes. For this experiment, 60 males were hired to work individually on a two-hour construction task. Subjects were assigned to one of two pay conditions (piece-rate versus hourly) and one of three goal-setting conditions (no goal, quantity, or quality) resulting in a 2 × 3 crossed analysis of variance design. Dependent variables included three measures of effort, three measures of direction of behavior, and both quantity and quality performance. Method of payment affected quantity performance and effort. Goal-setting affected quantity and quality performance and direction of behavior. Implications for designing and testing work motivation systems are discussed.

INTEGRATIVE

Rothe, H. F., "Does Higher Pay Bring Higher Productivity?", *Personnel*, July-August 1960, Vol. 37, No. 4, 20–27.

A review of the literature on motivating people with higher pay is presented. The concept of motivation is broken down in an effort to find what an employer is actually doing when he offers some financial inducement to his employees in hope of raising their productivity. It is summarized that the learning process requires that there be certain conditions present: 1) an intent to learn or motivate, 2) an understanding of what is to be learned, and 3) an incentive that is appropriate to the motive, recognized as being related to the action, and certain of being applied immediately after the correct action has been successfully completed. The author attempts to apply these criteria to various types of financial incentives, i.e. merit increases, negotiated increases, general increases, productivity increases, profit-sharing plans, bonuses and commissions, individual incentive plans and group incentive plans. Analysis of results show that only two types of incentives, individual and group incentive plans, meet all of the specified conditions required for increasing productivity.

Richman, B. M., "Increasing Worker Productivity: How the Soviets Do It," *Personnel*, January-February 1964, Vol. 41, No. 1, 8–21.

The Soviets have three main methods of improving the productivity of their industrial workers: 1) Money. The Soviets clearly use monetary incentives as a key device for motivating workers and rely upon this type of incentive to a greater extent than any other industrial nation. Regarding which kind of incentive is more effective—collective or individual payments—most Soviet sources feel that a combination of both types works best. 2) Worker participation in planning and decision-making. Each enterprise has a "participating body" including elected representation from workers, management, and Party and union officials. The purpose of their meetings is to obtain wide and continuing participation in planning and decision-making. Also existing are technical councils whose members are appointed on the basis of their technical abilities with their focus being product design and modification, improvement of production processes, etc. Most plants also generally have a Council of Rationalizers and Innovators whose major concerns are to initiate proposals for more efficient use of resources and to study new methods and procedures. A council member is paid for an accepted suggestion as well as granted prestige and recognition. 3) Indoctrination through education and mass media of a moral obligation of each worker to behave in accordance with directives of the state.

In concluding, the author notes that despite the great stress placed by the Soviet authorities on indoctrinating workers to gain their cooperation, they seem to recognize that material incentives and not moral stimuli are the most potent motivating force.

von Kaas, H. K., "Workable Wage Incentives: Factors to Bear in Mind," *Personnel*, March-April 1965, Vol. 42, No. 2, 57–65.

Uses a specific company example of experience with a wage incentive plan to point out problems of application which are inherent to some degree in every situation involving wage incentives. Covers the following considerations: 1) inherent limitations of time study and rate-setting, 2) variations in shop methods, 3) variations in operator performance and ability, 4) adequacy of shop services, 5) operator motivation, 6) effectiveness of shop supervision. Concludes that the successful operation of any wage incentive plan requires: 1) a high degree of cooperation between operators, foremen, and time study men, 2) a plan that is technically suited to the type of work being performed, 3) adequate standardization of methods, 4) adequate shop services, particularly tooling, production, and quality control, as well as material handling, 5) the will to produce on the part of operators, 6) a supervisory group that will administer the incentive plan in strict accordance with basic, spelled-out policies, and 7) maintenance and periodic auditing of the rate structure.

Cassell, F. H., "Management Incentive Compensation," *California Management Review*, Summer 1966, Vol. 8, No. 4, 11–20.

Examines the shift of incentive compensation systems from flexibility to rigidity in relation to its effect on three types of managers: lower level line management, upper level line management, and professional staff people. The latter two systems assume that entrepreneurial rather than bureaucratic behavior is desirable and should be rewarded. The decision as to whether enlightened systems of incentive compensation will be instituted is in the hands of business leaders. It would not be realistic to assume they will make early changes as the trends in manpower mix and shifts in importance of organizational units are neither easily observed nor, when observed, quickly understood. We tend to be more bureaucrat than entrepreneur than we are willing to admit; more parochial than broadscaled in outlook than we realize; more addicted to fads and formulas than we should be; more preoccupied with economic man than with the whole man; more interested in immediate results than in experimentation. These attitudes underlie our incentive compensation and pay systems, and they are costly—no one can estimate how much. Change we must if incentive compensation is to have real meaning in the more complex world ahead.

Dunnette, M. D.; Lawler, E. E., III; Weick, K. E. and Opsahl, R. L., "The Role of Financial Compensation in Managerial Motivation," *Organizational Behavior and Human Performance*, 1967, Vol. 2, 175–216.

These four papers are modified versions of papers delivered in a symposium titled "The Role of Financial Compensation in Managerial Motivation" held during the Spring, 1965 meetings of the Midwestern Psychological Association. Dunnette presents an instrumental model of managerial motivation and discusses its implications for research on the motivational effects of compensation. He also reviews research related to preferences (motives) most often found to be salient for managers. Lawler summarizes previous research of the effects of secret salary policies on manager satisfaction and presents results of another recent study showing that policies of pay secrecy have several costs not generally recognized. Secrecy apparently blurs managers' perceptions of what others earn; they overestimate the salaries of peers and of subordinates and this can lead to greater pay dissatisfaction and the belief that job performance is rather unimportant in determining pay. Weick reviews the psychology literature bearing on the effects of insufficient rewards on the intensity of effort. He reviews evidence in support of the relationship, postulates several properties of experimental procedures to explain the effects, and suggests that propositions from frustration or cue-utilization theory may afford the most parsimonious explanation of the relationship. Finally, Opsahl provides an overview of current knowledge about managerial compensation and its effect on managerial job behavior, and suggests areas in need of further intensive research.

Rodney, T. C., "Can Money Motivate Better Job Performance?", *Personnel Administration*, March-April 1967, Vol. 30, No. 2, 23–39.

The purpose of this article is to: 1) examine the Herzberg theory of satisfiers-dissatisfiers to analyze the role which Herzberg assigns to money as a motivator of improved job performance, and 2) to develop the practical implications of that role for day-to-day wage and salary administration applications. According to Herzberg, money can really play two separate and distinct roles in affecting job attitudes. First, when salaries are either too low, or when salary inequities exist as a result of the administrative system in use, money operates as an absolute dissatisfier. Secondly, money which is given in recognition of outstanding performance, in reinforcing the positive "satisfiers" of achievement and recognition, must be viewed in itself, as a "satisfier".

Implications for wage and salary administrators which can be drawn from the Herzberg study are: 1) Such monetary rewards as automatic increases, cost-of-living increases, economic adjustment increases, etc., will only serve to prevent dissatisfaction among employees. Their presence will not motivate increased job productivity. 2) Promotion and merit increases and bonuses which can be directly related to outstanding performance will act to reinforce "satisfiers", achievement and recognition. 3) Wise company managements will clearly distinguish between types of rewards represented by 1) and 2) and will not make the error in believing that monetary rewards are always positive motivators. 4) Distinction between maintenance and motivational monetary rewards must be clearly communicated to affected employees. 5) Better ways must be developed to measure performance in terms of job requirements. 6) Care must be taken to fault poor performers through lack of merit increases.

Stelluto, G. L., "Report on Incentive Pay in Manufacturing Industries," *Monthly Labor Review*, July 1969, Vol. 92, No. 7, 49–53.

Incentive wage plans are, in general, of two major types: 1) piece-rate plans, which tie workers' earnings directly to the number of units produced, and 2) production-bonus plans, which provide extra payments for output in excess of a quota or for the completion of a task in less than standard time. This article supplies empirical data obtained from the Bureau of Labor Statistics' nationwide occupational wage survey providing information on the incidence and methods of incentive wage plans in selected manufacturing industries. It was found that incentive wage plans are most prevalent in industries in which workers are able to exercise substantial control over the pace of output. Few plans are found in industries where manufacturing activities are largely machine-paced. Between the two extremes, the extent of incentive pay practices depends largely on management preference, degree of product standardization, and labor-management relationships.

The proportions of production and related workers paid under incentive wage plans have remained almost unchanged over the past several years for most industries studied. However, a few industries—those manufacturing cigars and certain types of nonelectrical machinery—have experienced substantial declines in the proportions of incentive workers, at least partly due to changes in production techniques.

Bowey, A. M. and Lupton, T., "Productivity Drift and the Make-up of the Pay Packet, Part II," *Journal of Management Studies*, October 1970, Vol. 7, No. 3, 310–334.

In Part I the authors outlined seven selected measurable features—parameters—of a firm to show that altering elements in a pay packet could affect the relationship between the situation of a firm (as measured by the parameters) and the extent of productivity drift. In Part II of the paper, the authors define and describe the seven selected parameters and show how they are related to the make-up of the elements of the pay packet and to productivity drift. They go on to deduce from this 10 equations and inequalities, and show how they may be used to assess the suitability of various alternative arrangements of pay packet elements in a given situation. Also they show how the pay packet can lead to productivity drift and how measurements can be made of a relatively small number of features of an organization to determine the optimum balance of the various elements in the pay packet, given the primary objective is to minimize productivity drift. Two examples of the use of this procedure were worked through. Presently the procedure exposes only 'crude faults' of pay packet but it is anticipated that further refinement will improve this technique.

Nissley, H. R., "Practical Time Study-4: Incentive Systems for Job Shops," *Industrial Management*, June 1971, Vol. 13, No. 6, 7–10.

The author classifies current incentive systems as being of one of two types: 1) simple, non-engineered systems, and 2) stop watch or engineered systems. The first type, non-engineered systems, are not based on conventional time study or predetermined time work measurement. Listed and discussed are among the more common non-engineered incentive plans including: a) the Halsey Plan, b) the Tonnage Plan, c) the Sales-Labor Plan, d) the units shipped plan, and 3) the Ratio Delay System. Although the foregoing plans are simple and inexpensive, in many cases they fail to reward individual effort. The further the incentive gets away from the individual, the less the incentive pull. Hence, for optimum results, most incentive shops go to a plan which is based upon the manual work content in individual jobs; and most of these individual job incentive plans are based upon time study or predetermined measurement of work content. Included in this category are: 1) straight piece work, and 2) the Emerson Efficiency Plan.

The answer to which incentive plan is best for job shop operators depends largely on the caliber of supervision and engineering talent administering it.

Chung, K. H., "Incentive Theory and Research," *Personnel Administration*, January-February 1972, Vol. 35, No. 1, 31–41.

Defines incentives and reviews the various types and their functions. Considers the role of supervision, work group influence, job content, promotional opportunity, and physical environment in relation to incentives, and reviews the literature in these areas. Discusses the methods of incentive application; stresses the importance of matching incentives and needs of employees as well as matching rewards with performance. Concludes that a major task of managers in dealing with human resources is to apply the organizational incentives in such a way not only to induce organizational members to contribute their efforts to the achievement of organizational goals but also to help the members to satisfy their personal goals. This objective is more likely to result in an effective incentive system and allow management to better utilize human resources in the organization.

Patton, A., "Why Incentive Plans Fail," *Harvard Business Review*, May-June 1972, Vol. 50, No. 3, 58–66.

Most incentive plans are unproductive for a number of reasons which can be most effectively discussed under three headings: 1) industry characteristics, 2) misused bonus mathematics, and 3) administrative flaws. The incentive-use "spectrum" is presented. At one extreme, almost every large company or industry has an executive incentive plan. At the other end, relatively few incentive plans are found among public utilities, banks, mining companies, railroads, etc. The success or failure of an incentive program and an important factor in the high fail-rate of executive incentive plans is the inhospitable industry environment at the low end of this incentive use spectrum. Characteristics of companies that exhibit greatest use of incentives: 1) numerous short-term decisions which influence profit are made by individuals at several levels of the organization, 2) decentralization organization is typical, 3) budget variances, market-share data, and economic analysis are the tools for judging performance, 4) companies demand a great deal of their people. Executives involved in companies which are characterized by the above conditions must live with the fact that their jobs are less secure than most. Marginal incentive industries are characterized by: 1) a few, long-term decisions which have the most important profit impact, 2) functional organization is typical, 3) sophisticated market and economic research tools for judging performance are not used often, 4) lower executive stress factor. An executive in these industries is rarely fired, due primarily to the difficulty management has in objectively judging an individual's performance. As incentive plans have become increasing popular, they have been adopted by many companies in industries at the low-use end of the spectrum. The author discusses bonus formulas and how to make them work. In the conclusion, it is reemphasized that the split between the undemanding, familial environment of certain industries and the highly charged environment of other industries is why the will to make an incentive plan work varies so greatly from one industry to the next.

Deci, E. L., "Paying People Doesn't Always Work the Way You Expect It To," *Human Resource Management,* Summer 1973, Vol. 12, No. 2, 28–32.

Research indicates that paying workers doesn't necessarily motivate them and that money is not the only reward workers seek. Money used as a motivator must be contingent on effective performance—i.e., the reward system must be so structured that receiving pay depends on good performance. Intrinsic rewards are valued by employees who become involved in their work and committed to doing it well and can be achieved through strategies of participative management and task design. The author conducted a number of experiments to investigate the question whether intrinsic motivation to do a job remains unaffected by extrinsic rewards. From these experiments the author concludes that intrinsic motivation appears to be affected by two processes; change in locus of causality, and change in feelings of competence and self-determination. Intrinsic motivation decreases when a person's behavior becomes dependent on an extrinsic reward or threat. It also decreases when a person receives negative feedback about his performance on an intrinsically motivated activity. Implications for management are that we must choose between trying to utilize either intrinsic or extrinsic reward systems. The author favors jobs to arouse intrinsic motivation since evidence indicates that intrinsic approaches seem to lead to greater productivity and more satisified workers.

Rue, L. W. and Clark, T. C., "The Cold War on Incentives: U.S.S.R. vs. U.S.," *Public Personnel Management,* January-February 1974, Vol. 3, No. 1, 29–34.

The modern Russian incentive system includes two sources of incentive pay: Wage funds and Material Incentive funds. The size of the Wage fund is determined by central planning authorities and based upon the volume of production actually sold by the enterprise, scientifically determined labor standards per unit of production, and standard wages paid. The incentive payment is directly related to actual performance. The material incentive fund is derived from the profits of the enterprise. It is usually based on factors other than production volume and productivity. Whenever possible, production workers are paid on a piece rate basis.

In comparing Russian incentive systems with the U.S. incentives, their piece rate plan with a higher rate for all pieces above standard is very similar to the "differential day rate" introduced in our country in 1895. The difference in the plans is that in the U.S. plan, once standard was reached, the high rate was paid for all pieces, not just those above a specific standard as in the Russian plan. The Russian incentives for salaried employees are based on a system very similar to management by objectives.

Most U.S. companies take pride in claiming to reward job performance but in fact oftentimes do not support this statement. Frequently pay raises and promotions are based on factors such as seniority, relationships with superiors, etc. It appears that Russia is doing a much better job of rewarding actual performance—placing less emphasis on seniority and chance factors. One reason for this is their tremendous concern for production at all costs and the limited freedom allowed for complaints and grievances. The future predicts Russia's incentive plans losing much of their punch as their standard of living rises. In regards to the question of private ownership per se, many feel that this is the major factor which allows the U.S. to hold an economic edge. However, it is generally thought that while we advocate a free enterprise system, we do not believe it is the real issue in motivating workers.

Dyer, Lee; Schwab, Donald P. and Fossum, John A., "Impacts of Pay on Employee Behaviors and Attitudes: An Update," *Personnel Administrator*, January 1978, Vol. 23, No. 1, 51–57.

Based on a program the authors presented at the Annual Meeting of the American Compensation Association, this article reviews literature on the impacts of pay on worker satisfaction and makes suggestions to lessen pay dissatisfaction. The authors consider the effects of pay on an employee's choice to accept a job, concluding that amount of pay in conjunction with job type is usually the only criteria a job hunter can use to decide to accept or decline a position. Also discussed in the article are the psychological effects of pay on job behavior. Pay impacts more strongly on performance when there is a direct link as through individual or group incentives. Magnitude of pay has little impact on intraorganizational behavior. On the other hand, high voluntary turnover has been linked with employee dissatisfaction, one factor of which is pay dissatisfaction. To summarize, the authors make some comments as to the administrative implications of the issues discussed.

Pate, Larry E., "Cognitive Versus Reinforcement Views of Intrinsic Motivation," *Academy of Management Review*, 1978, Vol. 3, No. 3, 505–514.

The research of Deci and associates regarding the effects of extrinsic rewards on intrinsic motivation has stimulated controversy among cognitive and reinforcement theorists. Theoretical roots of cognitive and reinforcement theories are traced, and the controversy over Deci's research is examined, particularly with regard to Scott's critique (1975). Implications of these discrepant positions and potential areas of research and application in work organizations are discussed.

Guzzo, Richard A., "Types of Rewards, Cognitions, and Work Motivation," *Academy of Management Review*, 1979, Vol. 4, No. 1, 75–86.

Work rewards often are conceptualized as being of two types: intrinsic and extrinsic. Further, cognitions associated with different types of rewards typically are conceived of in terms derived from attribution theory. A review of the grounds used to dichotomize reward types reveals they are inadequate for distinguishing types of rewards and a review of existing data on the nature of cognitions associated with work rewards indicates the attributional perspective to be deficient. Alternative approaches to the definition of types of work rewards and variants of cognitions mediating the relationship between work rewards and motivation are discussed.

Brinks, James T., "Is There Merit in Merit Increases?", *Personnel Administrator*, May 1980, Vol. 25, No. 5, 59–64.

This article details many of the pros and cons of merit increases. It presents three possible approaches to giving merit pay increases; the entire theme for all three approaches is there is a correct salary for each employee that is externally competitive, internally equitable, and reflects the level of responsibility, years of experience, and the individual's sustained performance level. The use of percentages is a traditional approach to merit increases where the midpoint of the range is utilized. In the step progression approach, the annual increase includes both the range change and the step. A relatively new approach described in the literature combines a step-progression guideline up to the going rate for all employees plus a periodic bonus award to distinguish performance.

Tolchinsky, Paul and King, Donald, "Do Goals Mediate the Effects of Incentives on Performance?", *Academy of Management Review*, July 1980, Vol. 5, No. 3, 455–467.

Locke's 1968 proposition that goals mediate the effects of incentives on performance is reviewed to determine the extent to which it is supported by research of eight studies. The authors attempt to integrate the literature and identify individual and situational factors that may mediate the incentive-goal-performance relationship. The article focuses specifically on the research regarding KR, participation and monetary incentives. The literature clearly indicates, they say, that KR is a necessary component of the goal-setting process. But the literature of the last 10 years does not provide an adequate test of Locke's mediation proposition regarding the effects of participation. Tolchinsky and King say that conclusions that can be drawn are consistent with Locke and Schweizer's (1979) larger review of participative-decision-making literature, which has shown assigned and participative goal-setting to be significantly better than "do your best" conditions. Yet there is no clear superiority of participative over assigned goal-setting using either performance or satisfaction criteria. The authors conclude that results presented do not support Locke's claim that money affects performance only if and to the extent that it affects goals and intentions. Rather, the research is more in agreement with the finding that monetary incentives and goal-setting can independently influence performance. The authors conclude that financial incentives remain the least understood of Locke's original external incentives.

PRESCRIPTIVE

Kulberg, R. A., "Relating Maturity Curve Data to Job Level and Performance," *Personnel*, March-April 1964, Vol. 41, No. 2, 45–50.

Because they focus solely on age and experience, maturity curves tend to obscure the all-important criteria of job level and job performance. Traditionally, maturity curves have been based on the fact that salaries tend to rise with increased age and experience. Statisticians select a sample of basically similar persons and collect data on salaries of these persons. This information is then translated into a series of statistical tables from which curves are plotted. The most common method of using these curves has been to plot the salaries of appropriate employees against the curve. The author presents a method whereby the salary administrator can make the most effective use of maturity curve data without losing sight of the fundamental principles of a traditional salary administration program. The system depends on the following assumptions concerning maturity curves and salary ranges: 1) maturity curve summarizes the practical impact of salary administration programs on a large group of basically similar persons, 2) job-oriented salary range represents the salary potential of an individual assigned to a job in that range. Also where there is a natural promotional sequence of jobs which the employee can reasonably aspire to ascend, the ranges applicable to this sequence represent the salary potential of an employee in the sequence. Having made these assumptions, a method was sought to compare the salary potentials of their ranges with the salary expectations described by the curves. If these compared favorably, it could then be assumed that their salary program would provide salary levels that compare favorably to the maturity curves.

Lesieur, F. G. and Puckett, E. S., "The Scanlon Plan Has Proved Itself," *Harvard Business Review*, September-October 1969, Vol. 47, No. 5, 109–118.

The authors—two of the top experts on the Scanlon Plan—examine its "track record" in industry and evaluate its performance. After a discussion of general principles, the authors take three different cases of Scanlon Plan application and analyze the implications for manufacturers in general. Some of the benefits derived from the plan are employee willingness to accept change, performance measurement with employee cooperation and interest, and a positive impact on plant-wide efficiency. The authors conclude that the factor most important to the success of a Scanlon Plan is that everyone in the organization knows management wants to work with employees to improve operations. The message of the Scanlon Plan is simple: operations improvement is an area where management, the union, and employees can get together without strife.

Schuster, J. R., "A Spectrum of Pay for Performance: How to Motivate Employees," *Management of Personnel Quarterly*, Fall 1969, Vol. 8, No. 3, 35–38.

This article reviews some of the controversial research on "pay for performance" and/or "pay as a motivator". Points out that Herzberg and Myers have uncovered dissatisfaction with the *methods used* to distribute pay and *not* the value of pay as a possible motivator. The author suggests different people are motivated by different things and it is important in using pay as a motivator that a causal relationship of performance to pay is understood by the reward-receiver. Other research reports that to the extent that pay is offered in forms responsive to the needs of the individual recipient and is perceived by him as proportional to his actual and/or perceived performance level, it can be a motivator. Blake's grid presentation method is used to illustrate various pay spectrum applications and their probable results. Concludes that managers can make pay become a motivator for individuals who perform for pay if it is directly related to performance and people know that a causal relationship exists. A manager must spend the money he has for pay on individuals contributing most to the organization's objectives and can accomplish this by a four-step process of: 1) evaluation, 2) a "preference survey" to determine valued rewards, 3) provide pay increases for better employees, and 4) communicate relationship between pay and performance.

Winstanley, N. B., "Management 'Incentive' Bonus Plan Realities," *Conference Board Record*, January 1970, Vol. 7, No. 1, 35–89.

The author hypothesized about a number of different reasons why most bonus plans quickly become ineffective: 1) when almost all of those eligible get a bonus, 2) when ineffective amounts are awarded, 3) when performance is inadequately appraised, awards not being well related to individual differences in performance, 4) when bonuses are used to make up salary deficiencies, 5) when bonus schedules are expressed as a percentage of base salary, and 6) when bonus pools are tied to group performance rather than individual performance. Alternative action to customary bonus programs could take the form of: eliminating bonuses— base the company financial reward structure on excellent salary administration, offering extra compensation for extraordinary performance—change to a true plan of extra compensation of extraordinary performance, combining alternatives—bonuses restricted only to outstanding performers and much greater emphasis on the nonfinancial sources of motivation. The author's best bet: to forget bonuses and to concentrate on excellent salary administration.

Schrieber, D. E., "Incentives: Are They Relevant? Obsolete? Misunderstood?", *Personnel Administration*, January-February 1970, Vol. 33, No. 1, 52–57.

Incentive plan systems can be traced back as far as 400 B.C. but despite this long historical evolution of incentive schemes, the effectiveness of such schemes has yet to be clearly demonstrated. To compensate for the lack of effectiveness of financial incentives, growing interest began in the psychological perspective of incentives emerging from an increased understanding of individual and group behavior in organizations. The author suggests an alternative approach to the "incentive" concept, which involves: 1) minimizing factors which contribute to failure of other incentives (inadequate communication, undue complexity of the system), and 2) providing psychological rewards through such areas as job structure and feedback. The implementation of a management system in which a high degree of meaningful employee participation is used to achieve specific measurable objectives involves: communication of objectives and procedures, job design, mutual goal-setting, and continual feedback and coaching.

Gardner, D. M. and Rowland, K. M., "A Self-Tailored Approach to Incentives," *Personnel Journal*, November 1970, Vol. 49, No. 11, 907–917.

This article explores some of the implicit assumptions—ill understood and ill founded—about designing and administering an incentive program for salesmen, points out their fallacies, and suggests some ways in which a typical incentive program for this employee group can be modified and improved. It considers the variables that influence human behavior: 1) physical and social environments, 2) physiological structure, 3) wants and goals, and 4) past experiences. It also considers the personal and environmental factors which affect behavior such as level of aspiration, need for prestige and status, and reference group. Although some generalizations are possible, consideration of these factors make each individual unique. Incentive plans can be used to fit a salesman to the job or to fit a job to the salesman. Not until the latter approach is taken will we be able to encourage salesmen to perform more effectively. If we are cognizant of the complexity of behavior, the task of designing and administering incentives for the sales force is more apt to produce useful results. This discussion also has significance for the design and administration of incentive programs for other similar employee groups.

Schuster, J. R. and Munson, J. B., "Toward a Direct Contribution-Rein-
forcement Pay System," *Management of Personnel Quarterly*,
Spring 1971, Vol. 10, No. 1, 2–5.

To keep the cost of a contingent reward (compensation) system manage-
able, Schuster and Munson suggest that: a) pay be contingent upon performance, b) operate on a fixed interval schedule (approximately one
year), and c) only a part of the merit increase be made permanent for
the year, the remainder must be earned by sustained high performance
the following year.

Wilson, S. R., "The Incentive Approach to Executive Development,"
Business Horizons, April 1972, Vol. 15, No. 2, 15–23.

Executives respond to incentives exactly as machinists and salesmen do,
and their performance can be planned and utilized as scientifically as
any other corporate asset. The author describes an incentive program
that makes it possible to influence results by managing systematically
the controllable factors that shape executive performance. There is no
practical limit to the range of activities or variety of performance objectives that can be achieved by the systematic application of incentives.
The author suggests a sequence of steps for testing the validity of the
approach.

Smith, J. V., "Merit Compensation: The Ideal and the Reality," *Personnel
Journal*, May 1972, Vol. 51, No. 5, 313–316.

A merit compensation program is designed to identify, appraise, and especially reward those employees who are making outstanding contributions. This concept is in the mainstream of the American way of life, yet
why are so many supervisors and workers dissatisfied with a compensation system? The author proposes: 1) the large corporation is not a
highly competitive environment; 2) employees are caught in a highly
structured bureaucratic organization that tends to give the greatest
credit to those who know how to function best in such a system. Basic
elements essential in structuring a program that rewards the deserving
without abusing the many would include: 1) Recognizing that the personnel function is a humanistic social science not capable of determining
cause and effect relationships. Oftentimes, merit compensation systems
are based on questionable premises and are so complex that the line
supervisors do not understand them. 2) In a merit compensation program, a sense of fairness and credibility among employees and supervisors must prevail. 3) If formal evaluations are used, they should be designed tò present an up-beat, positive picture. 4) A compensation
program must be flexible. The immediate supervisor should be responsible for individual merit increases and subject to no one else's control.

Dearden, J., "How to Make Incentive Plans Work," *Harvard Business Review*, July-August 1972, Vol. 50, No. 4, 117–124.

This article describes the various features of bonus systems and examines the advantages and disadvantages of these features. A "bonus plan" is defined as an executive profit-sharing plan. After appraising the management decisions that are critical to the success of company-wide bonus plans, he analyzes some especially thorny problems associated with division-based bonuses. In each case, he shows management how to structure bonus rewards that are both fair to executives and consistent with the short and long-term interests of the organization.

Fein, M., "Restoring the Incentive to Wage Incentive Plans," *Conference Board Record*, November 1972, Vol. 9, No. 11, 17–21.

An approach to increasing productivity in all plants becomes clear by examining why and how wage incentive plans deteriorate over a period of time. The same forces also act to erode productivity in pay-by-time plants, but because the time/work employees have no reasons to try to beat management's systems, it appears that these plants are more effectively controlled by management. Here also, however, the author argues that productivity can be increased substantially by giving employees solid reasons to increase productivity.

Wilson, S. R., "Motivating Managers With Money," *Business Horizons*, April 1973, Vol. 16, No. 2, 37–42.

It is fairly common to have compensation programs which are merely annual bonuses or profit-sharing plans. Seldom is an executive rewarded for actual improvement in performance. The author looks at the situation from two angles: salary administration and incentive bonus administration. First, there must be equality between salary earned and salary received. Second, a company has to establish criteria for evaluating an employee's earned income. The author suggests than an employee's evaluation be based on his observable daily performance, rather than on vague concepts such as his willingness to cooperate or his loyalty to the firm. When a company does award bonuses it should give them for performance that exceeds the daily criteria, and it should pay the bonus immediately.

Mustafa, H., "Escalator Pay Plans," *Public Personnel Management*, January-February 1974, Vol. 3, No. 1, 4–9.

It is essential to a sound pay structure that differences between jobs based on levels of responsibility and kinds of duties are reflected in pay levels. The city of Akron, Ohio came to this realization and developed their own escalator pay plan. Recognizing that normal adjustment in the wage scale of city workers was taking place at a slower rate than in industry, the city sought to achieve three principle objectives by the adoption of a Wage Index Increase system: 1) to keep city pay scales competitive and comparable, 2) to maintain internal relationships relative to classification and pay plans, and 3) to simplify the process of paysetting and make it more rational. In 1966, Akron adopted its "Escalator Clause" to provide periodic adjustment of city wages to reflect changes in wages in the Akron area. The effect of each occupational category's percentage increase on the city's overall increase in each of the years the escalator had operated is significant. In evaluation of the plan, it has achieved its objective of allowing Akron's municipal and industrial wages to grow at comparable rates. It has also helped to maintain pay relationships between job categories based on kinds of duties and levels of responsibility. A major criticism of the plan has been that the salary gap between the low-paying jobs and top-level officials has widened.

Sielaff, T. J., "Modification of Work Behavior," *Personnel Journal*, July 1974, Vol. 53, No. 7, 513–517.

This article reports an experiment in modifying the work behavior of two 22-year-old men working for the same company. After several weeks of work, their poor work behavior became apparent. Verbal reprimands and warnings were administered to no avail. Positive reinforcement techniques of providing praise for on-task behavior also proved fruitless. After several months, a wage-bonus plan was started whereby each S could earn between 60-70¢ extra per hour if they were working at maximum capacity. No improvement in performance occurred. The next course of action to be followed gave the two men the opportunity to compute their wages for one period by choosing one of two systems: 1) existing system with earnings based on hours of work, of 2) a piece-rate system with earnings based on units of work completed. Both men accepted the piece-rate system which brought tremendous results. Productivity per hour increased, earnings per hour increased, and costs per unit declined. The implications to be drawn from this study is that the employer controls behavior through the system that he sets up and through opportunities offered for employee choice.

Goode, R. V., "Complications at the Cafeteria Checkout Line," *Personnel*, November-December 1974, Vol. 51, No. 6, 45–49.

In theory, the cafeteria compensation plan sounds fine; however, different age groups have different preferences and needs and also there is frequently much misunderstanding concerning the long-range benefits. A survey was made among safety, clerical, trades and professional employees in the state of California. A total cafeteria compensation concept represents a severe down-side risk to companies, particularly in the employee benefits area—and the potential gains today are negligible. Few companies offer it, so there is little competitive pressure to justify risk.

Duerr, E. C., "The Effect of Misdirected Employee Behavior," *Personnel Journal*, December 1974, Vol. 53, No. 12, 890–893.

The misdirected incentive is that which causes people to act in a manner directly opposite from the way in which the organization really wants them to act. The fact that they often go unrecognized results in a continuation of poor performance and conflicts among personnel. A number of actual case studies are cited where the misdirected incentives were pinpointed and remedied. Misdirected incentives are considered to arise from three underlying factors: 1) The measurement system. Managers tend to pay the most attention to those things which they know are being measured. 2) The reward systems. The reward systems may similarly serve to encourage counter-productive behavior. For example, if the reporting of new and improved methods would result in problems rather than rewards for the originating unit, the possible new method is not likely to be reported. 3) The personnel practices of the executives. Included here would be such facts as the adverse effects of making subordinates hesitate to bring bad news and the insistence of a key executive on making all decisions himself. Some suggestions are made to help the manager uncover possible undesirable incentives.

Hulme, R. D. and Bevan, R. V., "The Blue-Collar Worker Goes on Salary," *Harvard Business Review*, March-April 1975, Vol. 53, No. 2, 104–112.

Ever since the difference between salaried and hourly workers evolved in the latter part of the 19th century, the reasons for retaining the hourly practice have not really changed. Before that, there were only for-hire workers and entrepreneurs, who believed that if pay were not directly related to work performed, productivity would diminish and result in ineffective utilization of the work force. Then one day an entrepreneur hired an accountant. It seemed appropriate to pay him by the day or week because his output wasn't measurable in hourly units. As more white-collar people were hired, they were paid on the same basis. Now the number of white-collar employees exceeds the blue-collar by about 40 percent. To this day, the presumption of irresponsibility applied to a worker 50 or 100 years ago is in contrast to that belief that salaried people have intuitively responsible attitudes toward their jobs. But even the strongest believers in economic man might accept the fact that the blue-collar worker performs the job not only for money but also for advancement, status, and self-fulfillment, and that these encourage responsibility. A little over-simplified? Perhaps, say the authors, but apparently many people are paid by the hour merely because they always have been. The authors counter a number of specific objections to paying all employees a salary by candidly reviewing the problems and benefits of five companies that have done just that. They then list criteria to determine the practicality of a salary plan for other organizations.

Todd, J. O., " 'Cafeteria Compensation': Making Management Motivators Meaningful," *Personnel Journal*, May 1975, Vol. 54, No. 5, 275–281.

An encouraging recent development in many major companies has been to personalize executive compensations, while keeping each executive's total compensation related to his individual performance. It's called "cafeteria" compensation and it means giving each executive some choices regarding the form of his incentive compensation. Cash bonuses invariably result in tax burdens that reduce their value to executives; whereas if the compensation is taken in another form such as an insurance plan, stock options, estate-planning services, auto expenses, etc., the *net* dollars placed in the executive's hands is greater. This is the object of any reasonable compensation plan. The future for cafeteria compensation looks good, in light of today's tax environment.

Panyan, Steven W. and McGregor, Michael, "How to Implement a Proactive Incentive Plan: A Field Study," *Personnel Journal*, September 1976, Vol. 55, No. 9, 460–463.

An incentive plan, designed to reduce absenteeism and sick leave, was initiated in a small city administration. The plan consisted of paying employees a bonus of $10.00 per day for each unused sick leave per year. A pre-post incentive plan comparison indicated a marked drop in mean annual sick leave days between the two periods (1967 to 1970 and 1971 to 1974). The authors emphasize the following considerations for adopting proactive incentive plans: select a target objective which is meaningful and measureable; seek employee suggestions on procedures and incentives; and reserve rewards for exceptional performance.

Terborg, James R. and Miller, Howard E., "Motivation, Behavior, and Performance: A Closer Examination of Goal-Setting and Monetary Incentives," *Journal of Applied Psychology*, 1978, Vol. 63, No. 1, 29–39.

Some experimenters often test predictions from theories of motivation using performance outcomes as dependent variables. We argue that observable behaviors that are likely to be affected by motivation manipulations should be used in combination with performance outcomes. Such procedures would be sensitive to differential effects of manipulations on various behaviors and would allow for investigation of relationships among behaviors and performance outcomes. For this experiment, 60 males were hired to work individually on a two-hour construction task. Subjects were assigned to one of two pay conditions (no goal, quantity, or quality) resulting in a 2 × 3 crossed analysis of variance design. Dependent variables included three measures of effort, three measures of direction of behavior, and both quantity and quality performance. Method of payment affected quantity performance and effort. Goal-setting affected quantity and quality performance and direction of behavior. Implications for designing and testing work motivation systems are discussed.

Lawler, Edward E. III and Bullock, R. J., "Pay and Organizational Change," *Personnel Administrator*, May 1978, Vol. 23, No. 5, 32–36.

This article discusses factors involved in changing an organization's compensation system based on preliminary results of several longitudinal studies on pay system changes undertaken by the authors. Key decisions in redesigning the compensation system are the aspect of the pay system that is the best starting place and they should be involved in the changes. An analysis of the following situational mediating factors should be undertaken before recommendations for change are made: 1) organization size; 2) quality and type of information; 3) value system of the organization; and 4) technological change. The new pay system can be designed once the important mediating factors have been assessed. The authors' studies have indicated that changes have led to improved attitudes towards pay and higher performance motivation as well as constructive changes in other areas. The compensation system affects and is affected by virtually every other company subsystem with the most important links being performance appraisal, the information system, job design procedures and management style. The advantages and disadvantages of employee participation in pay system design are discussed. The article concludes with two points of caution: redesign takes time and it is important to take a formative view of compensation system changes.

Foster, Ken and Lynn, Karyl V., "Dividing Up the 'Merit' Increase Pie for Top Management," *Personnel Administrator*, May 1978, Vol. 23, No. 5, 42–48.

It is realized that the compensation planner faces formidable problems in establishing an effective and equitable compensation management system. It does not entail simply paying for performance. Major problems of implementation are: 1) identifying the factors that managers (or other employees) and the organization perceive to be legitimate pay determinants; and 2) properly weighting and integrating these factors into an effective compensation management program.

To resolve these issues, a possibly productive approach was presented which would: 1) simulate a real-life salary merit increase; 2) ask the affected employees and the organizational decision-makers to program increases based on the exercise model; 3) capture the pay policies through multiple regression analysis; and 4) develop a pay policy that most effectively represents the perceived needs of the affected employees and the organization. This approach was used in a study using a sample of 56 compensation executives. Results indicated that managers did not base their proposed salary increases on performance alone; they were influenced also by position in salary range and susceptibility to outside inducement. The authors suggest the use of an expanded version of the simulation process described here, other proposed pay-related factors could be tested for their perceived significance to employees and management in determining pay. These inputs can serve as guidelines for a proposed model for appropriate pay increases.

Smith, Charles A., "Lump Sum Increases: A Creditable Change Strategy," *Personnel*, July-August 1979, 59–63.

Giving employees the opportunity to receive salary increases in a lump sum represents a rather significant departure from traditional salary administration concepts. However, companies such as Aetna, American Can, B. F. Goodrich, Clark Equipment, J&L Steel, Times, and Westinghouse have introduced such programs with generally good results. The rationale behind this concept is that 1) lump sums tend to dramatize the amount of the merit increase and perhaps even individual performance, 2) protects an employee's paycheck by allowing purchases not otherwise made, thus having the effect of offsetting erosion by inflation, 3) the lump sum program is consistent with the strong trend toward cash compensation, and 4) it allows employees greater flexibility through personal choice and greater control over personal financial circumstances. Less obvious benefits of the program are that it promotes management's creditability to employees; tends to offset any program changes that may be perceived negatively by employees. Several variations of administering lump sum increases are outlined. A no-strings program had 65 to 90 percent employee participation and a recovery provision program had 40 to 60 percent participation. Increases continue to be made on the basis of performance and position in range so election of an employee to receive a lump sum or some offered variation does not change his level of compensation. There are a few risks involved in such a program but most companies adopting a variation of the lump sum compensation package do it for pragmatic reasons—like taking out an insurance policy. As part of a program of change or strategy, it has been considered an effective tradeoff for discontinuing other traditional forms of compensation.

Piamonte, John S., "In Praise of Monetary Motivation," *Personnel Journal*, September 1979, Vol. 58, No. 9, 597–599.

The author suggests that the traditional view—or "common sense" view—held by most managers (i.e., that productivity of employees is far from what it should be, that employees are not as motivated to produce as they could be, and that offering more dollars can make employees work harder toward organizational goals) is basically sound and would work if it were not for conflicting advice from various experts. The motivation theories of those like Maslow and Herzberg have caused the worth of monetary reward as an incentive to be of less importance—or of no consideration at all. However, the subject of human motivation is an overwhelmingly complex problem which, states the author, will necessitate reopening the debate on the nature of motivation. The development of new motivation theories is suggested. Intrinsic and extrinsic rewards are touched upon but the article demonstrates in depth the factors affecting the use of an important extrinsic reward—money—and relates it to some of the tenets of productivity in today's organizations. In a "truth and consequences" review of the current practices of using money as a motivator in organizations, the author concludes that it is hardly surprising that our remuneration policies fail to exploit the motivational potential of the dollars we pay. The challenge now, says the author, is to undo the damage and develop a compensation scheme which will reinstate money as a respectable incentive, which will integrate it into a total motivational scheme to promote excellence in employees and fairly reward the occurrence of excellence.

Hills, Frederick S., "Pay-for-Performance Dilemma," *Personnel*, September-October 1979, 23–31.

This article reviews the problems inherent in the pay-for-performance theory and indicates two positive avenues open to organizations to eliminate the pay/motivation dilemma: 1) consider updating current notions of pay-for-performance or 2) alter their present compensation programs. Pay-for-performance tends to be viewed as a method of ensuring equity or of rewarding high performance—i.e., as a motivational tool. These views are inaccurate. In covering various aspects of motivation, the author states that given the tendency toward halo effects in management, the pay-for-performance system would seem to have a built-in bias for the high performer and against the low performer. The author analyzes the pay-for-performance programs and offers solutions to help overcome their difficulties. Problems covered include effects of equity in pay, internal wage-structure equity, external pay equity, inflation factors, and the total compensation picture. Problems with administering merit pay systems are assessed and conditions that must be met for a pay-for-performance reward system to work are outlined. In outlining difficulties experienced with administering pay-for-performance programs, several solutions were offered with respect to issues of inflation, market equity, and pay ranges which include: 1) pay range must be large enough to allow for meaningful differences between high and low performers; 2) cost-of-living pay (allowing for inflation) should be distinct and separate from merit pay; and 3) separate pay allocations at two points in time would communicate an organization's desire to reward for performance *and* to maintain equity or real wages.

White, William L. and Becker, James W., "Increasing the Motivational Impact of Employee Benefits," *Personnel*, January-February 1980, 32–37.

In this article, the authors suggest ways to meet the challenge of the ever-increasing rise in benefits as a percentage of total compensation. Over the last 20 years, benefit costs as a percentage of payroll have risen from 22 percent in 1957 to 37 percent in 1977. Factors affecting the rise in absolute cost and the diversity of benefits offered are summarized. In designing an effective benefit program, it is suggested that one avenue to assess the needs and preferences of the employees involved is via a periodic attitude survey to include information on the importance to employees of elements of the program, benefits most in need of improvement, their willingness to contribute toward the cost of new or improved benefits, how understandable the program is (i.e., how it works), the administrative efficiency, and preferences concerning relative proportion of direct compensation to benefit values. Also five steps in installing employee benefits as an effective motivational tool are outlined, their use as a "clincher" in the recruitment process is emphasized, their significance in government-regulated nonprofit institutions and specialized benefits for top executives are covered. The authors suggest that in developing a profile for an effective benefits program one must first understand employees' attitudes, determine the place benefits occupy in the total compensation approach, and finally assess the cost effectiveness of benefits to mesh them with other elements of a compensation package.

THEORETICAL

Jones, L. V. and Jeffrey, T. E., "A Quantitative Analysis of Expressed Preferences for Compensation Plans," *Journal of Applied Psychology*, August 1964, Vol. 48, No. 4, 201–210.

The method of factorial paired comparisons is employed in two studies designed to evaluate employee preferences for alternative forms of job compensation. Explicitly considered are four compensation features with two levels each: weekly salary versus hourly wage, use or nonuse of supervisory merit-ratings, inclusion or exclusion of a piece-incentive plan, and pay increase versus no increase. A 2^4 factorial design provides estimates for and tests of significance on preference scale values associated with each compensation "package", as well as for scale contrasts between the two levels of each separate compensation feature.

Haire, M., Ghiselli, E. E. and Gordon, M. E., "A Psychological Study of Pay," *Journal of Applied Psychology Monograph*, August 1967, Vol. 51, No. 4, Whole No. 636, Part 2 of 2 Parts, 1–24.

A study in three sections of empirical data on managerial compensation for three groups of managers (N = about 90 for each group): 1) a description of the distributional characteristics of pay over time (about 25 years); 2) the correlation of pay with pay over time and presents statistical analyses to explain the observed relationships; 3) a statistical model of pay capitalizing on the cumulative character of pay (pay at Year n is composed of pay at Year 1 + raises at Years 2, 3, ... n) and the formulas for the distributional and correlational character of composites. The potential psychological leverage of hitherto little-considered variables stands out—for instance, without increasing the total salary bill, management of the variance of pay over a group in a given year and of the correlation of pay with raises from year to year allows one to deal with the level of aspiration of the individual and his relative standing in the group. The managerial implications of the statistical behavior of pay are discussed in detail.

Bolle de Bal, M., "The Psycho-Sociology of Wage Incentives," *British Journal of Industrial Relations*, November 1969, Vol. 7, 385–397.

This paper examines the historical function of wage incentives both in its theoretical aspect and in its practical application and defines and examines the practice of stimulation bonuses and participation bonuses. It points out the role of the unions, originally forced into opposition of wage incentives through their traditional role of working against any method of 'intensification' of work and 'exploitation' of the worker, has evolved to become a recognized stabilizing influence and a factor for social peace. The traditional antagonists—employer versus union/employees-now look for negotiation and compromise; necessary compromise. The employer can satisfy union demands in a temporary and conditional way in return for more effort and contribution by employees and the union can accept a compromise of bonuses leaving them free to take action later on integrating the bonuses into the basic pay structure. The current vitality of wage incentives, therefore, seems to be explained by the growing importance of payment by results as a tool of compromise between firms and unions.

Deci, E. L., "The Effects of Contingent and Noncontingent Rewards and Controls on Intrinsic Motivation," *Organizational Behavior and Human Performance*, 1972, Vol. 8, 217–220.

Theories of management and work motivation distinguish between two kinds of rewards—extrinsic and intrinsic. Extrinsic rewards are ones such as money and verbal reinforcement which are mediated outside of the person, whereas intrinsic rewards are mediated within the person. We say a person is intrinsically motivated to perform an activity if there is no apparent reward except the activity itself or the feelings which result from the activity. All of the theories of work motivation which consider both kinds of reward assume that the effects of the two are additive. This paper examines that assumption by reviewing a program of research which investigated the effects of external rewards and controls on intrinsic motivation. It was reported that a person's intrinsic motivation to perform an activity decreased when he received contingent monetary payments, threats of punishment for poor performance, or negative feedback about his performance. Noncontingent monetary payments left intrinsic motivation unchanged, and verbal reinforcements appeared to enhance intrinsic motivation. A cognitive evaluation theory was presented to explain these results, and the theory and results were discussed in relation to management.

Pate, Larry E., "Cognitive Versus Reinforcement Views of Intrinsic Motivation," *Academy of Management Review*, 1978, Vol. 3, No. 3, 505–514.

The research of Deci and associates regarding the effects of extrinsic rewards on intrinsic motivation has stimulated controversy among cognitive and reinforcement theorists. Theoretical roots of cognitive and reinforcement theories are traced, and the controversy over Deci's research is examined, particularly with regard to Scott's recent critique (1975). Implications of these discrepent positions and potential areas of research and application in work organizations are discussed.

Guzzo, Richard A., "Types of Rewards, Cognitions, and Work Motivation," *Academy of Management Review*, 1979, Vol. 4, No. 1, 75–86.

Work rewards often are conceptualized as being of two types: intrinsic and extrinsic. Further, cognitions associated with different types of rewards typically are conceived of in terms derived from attribution theory. A review of the grounds used to dichotomize reward types reveals they are inadequate for distinguishing types of rewards and a review of existing data on the nature of cognitions associated with work rewards indicates the attributional perspective to be deficient. Alternative approaches to the definition of types of work rewards and variants of cognitions mediating the relationship between work rewards and motivation are discussed.

Commentary

MONEY

Money—a measure of value and our medium of exchange—has been said to be the "root of all evil" and it has been known to generate a myriad of problems unless it is properly used. Yet, money is generally regarded as the most frequently used motivational tool in the private sector of the Western world. Here we are considering money as a medium of exchange in return for services, and much research has been done on the impact of money—the payment for services—on the motivation and productivity of the worker. We know that it can increase the motivation to perform and yet, in certain circumstances, can cause dysfunctional and unanticipated effects. Several aspects of the influence of money as compensation on the behavior of employees have been considered in research to date.

Incentive plans—pay over and above a "base" or "maintenance" wage—have been used for various reasons to produce desired or hoped for results. They have been used to reduce employee sick leave, to reduce absenteeism and tardiness, to reduce waste and to increase productivity and efficiency. There seem to be as many variations of types of incentive plans used as there are reasons for their use. We find that the particular design of the pay system is an important consideration as well as the level of a person's performance in the work group. There are certain elements that are necessary to achieve an effective wage incentive plan and consideration must be given to the type of organization, resources available, and desired results. A workable plan has been suggested as including:

1. Cooperation of all members of the organization.

2. Designed for and suited to the type of work.

3. Adequate services and resources must be available to support the plan.

4. Standardization of methods.

5. Management must administer the plan with consistent adherence to set policies.

6. Maintenance and periodic auditing of rate structure (von Kaas, 1965).

Flexibility and consistent review of pay policies and practices to accompany organizational growth and development seems a necessary part of managing a successful wage incentive system. Consistent management, supervision, and administration of the plan is also necessary.

In industry, it is generally agreed that incentive pay should be awarded for performance exceeding an established norm, and that the employer should control the desired results (employee behavior) through the system established and through opportunities offered for employee choice concerning their own effort and performance levels. This may be why incentive pay plans are most prevalent in industries where workers have substantial control over the pace of output since it is under these circumstances that the incentive pay works best as a managerial tool to exert direct influence on output or productivity of the organization.

To ensure success with an incentive plan, it is necessary to consider matching the plan with the needs of the employees as well as matching rewards with performance. Thus, to use money as a motivator for better job performance one must consider how it is applied. Money can be a source of dissatisfaction when salaries are too low or when salary inequities exist as a result of the administration of the pay system; and it can be a source of both satisfaction and performance when it is given in recognition of outstanding performance—in reinforcing the needs for achievement and recognition. Recognition of the importance of distinguishing between base pay and merit pay, therefore, is a necessary factor in administering an incentive plan for enhanced performance.

Also, differentiation between kinds of rewards that bring desired results must be considered. Rewards fall into two categories: 1) extrinsic (e.g., money and verbal reinforcement—mediated outside the person), and 2) intrinsic—mediated within the person. Most theories of work motivation assume the two are additive. However, a study investigating the effects of external rewards and controls on intrinsic motivation found intrinsic motivation to perform decreased when subjects received contingent monetary payments, threats of punishment for poor performance, or negative feedback about his or her performance. Noncontingent monetary payments did not change intrinsic motivation and verbal reinforcement appeared to enhance intrinsic motivation (Deci, 1972).

Further research addressing the question of additivity of intrinsic and extrinsic rewards found that the effects of external rewards on performance and intrinsic motivation are quite different for different jobs. For example, interesting jobs where employees can participate in job decisions and are paid noncontingently were found to increase intrinsic motivation, but paying workers contingently and allowing them no participation in the job also appears to increase motivation while increasing productivity (Turnage and Muchinsky, 1976). Thus, it seems the kind of job is the key factor in influencing intrinsic motivation and/or performance and, more significantly, influencing the effects of pay on motivation.

In another study by Deci (1973), it was found that intrinsic motivation decreases when the person's behavior becomes dependent upon an extrinsic reward or threat and when receiving negative feedback about performance on an intrinsically motivated activity. Deci has argued strongly for intrinsic motivation since evidence indicates intrinsic approaches seem to lead to greater productivity and more satisfied workers and can be achieved through strategies of participative management and task design.

In one study, a negative relationship between reward contingency and intrinsic motivation was found for the behavioral measures of intrinsic motivation but not for the attitudinal measures used. There is need for further testing and clarification regarding the relation between reward contingency and intrinsic motivation (Farr, Vance and McIntyre, 1977).

Several studies highlight results that have been obtained in applying incentives to achieve specific effects. One such study used an incentive pay plan to increase attendance and reduce tardiness. Objectives of the plan were to encourage employees to:

1. Save sick leave for accident or injury,

2. Serve as a deterrent to sick leave misuse, and

3. Modify the inequity between careful and careless uses of benefits.

Results showed a 34 percent decrease in absenteeism after installation of the plan (Woska, 1972). In another study (Panyan & McGregor, 1976) applying an incentive plan to reduce absenteeism and sick leave, experience dictated the following considerations for success:

1. Select a target objective which is meaningful and measurable.

2. Seek employees' suggestions on procedures and incentives.

3. Reserve rewards for exceptional performance.

Several studies have shown that monetary incentives can be used to encourage workers to increase their productivity and output as well as their efficiency (reduction of waste). For example, after trying several variations of plans at McDonalds, it was concluded a workable incentive plan must include:

1. Management participation in the pay plan design,

2. Competitive base salary within the industry,

3. Management should receive a bonus when unit member is promoted,

4. Manager should receive a full bonus when reaching pre-determined business goals, and

5. A pre-determined floor and ceiling would correlate level of bonus paid with level of business goal attained.

This approach illustrates the need for employee involvement, for equity, and for accurate measures (Sasser & Pettway, 1974).

In a study of pay and performance feedback effects on satisfaction, it was revealed employees preferred equitable pay and performance-linked pay (Fossum, 1976). Thus, it is important that incentive plans be structured so rewards are both fair and consistent with the goals of the organization.

Given today's tax structure, "cafeteria" type compensation plans are becoming more popular. In these plans executives are offered a choice among several options and can personalize their pay/benefit system according to their individual needs. Choices are given among such benefits as an insurance plan, stock options, estate planning services, auto expenses, etc. In such programs, companies are able to offer a greater *net* compensation to their executives and at less tax cost (Todd, 1975).

In a statistical and distributional analysis of the total package cost of managerial pay, one study finds that without increasing the total salary bill, by management of variance of pay over a group in a given year plus correlation of pay with raises from year to year, one can deal with the level of aspiration of the individual and his relative standing in the group. This study has implications for management regarding the statistical behavior of pay and how it can be used to advantage (Haire, Ghiselle, and Gordon, 1965).

A survey was made of the *Fortune* 500 firms to determine if performance was measured objectively and if pay was contingent upon performance. Conclusions indicated that most companies agreed:

1. Performance is the primary determinant of compensation, and

2. A large percentage of companies do not have formal appraisal and/ or do not actually use performance appraisal devices (Evans, 1970).

The logical inconsistency of these two findings is disturbing but, apparently, not sufficient to demand managerial attention. Incentives to increase performance and proper measures of performance would seem helpful to growth-oriented corporations.

Some reasons for failures of incentive plans have been contributed to industry characteristics, misused bonus mathematics, administrative flaws, poor installation, or poor controls. It is necessary to establish a control procedure to avoid administrative problems and to adapt the best plan to the type of industry involved (Patton, 1972).

Characteristics of companies exhibiting the greatest use of incentives are those which:

1. Make numerous short-term decisions which influence profit with these being made by individuals at several levels of the organization;

2. Have a decentralized organization;

3. Judge performance through the use of budget variances, market-share data, and economic analysis; and

4. Demand a great deal of their people.

Marginal incentive-use companies are characterized by:

1. A few long-term decisions which have the most important profit impact;

2. A functional organization;

3. Sophisticated market and economic research tools for judging performance are not often used (Patton, 1972).

Some suggested areas of further research would include the relation between insufficient rewards and the intensity of effort; the effect of monetary contingent rewards and negative feedback on intrinsic motivation (these effects have been disputed in the current research), and the development of more accurate ways to measure performance in terms of job requirements.

Independent Variable

PRAISE

Type of Article	No. of Articles
Applied	1
Empirical	1
Prescriptive	4

APPLIED

Dillon, Michael J.; Kent, Harry M. and Mallot, Richard W., "A Supervisory System for Accomplishing Long-Range Projects: An Application to Master's Thesis Research," *Journal of Organizational Behavior Management*, Summer 1980, Vol. 2, No. 3, 213–227.

The article describes a supervisory system that includes an incentive designed to help people maintain a steady rate of work toward the accomplishment of long-range goals. As applied to the supervision of MA degree thesis research, the authors found the presence of the incentive produced a high and steady rate of completion of weekly research tasks. Where there was no incentive, the weekly task completion rate was considerably lower. Twelve of 15 persons and five of seven research tasks showed these results. In this test, the incentive to the participating researchers was a letter of recommendation. The incentive system was supported by requiring 1) written task specification; 2) weekly subgoals or deadlines; 3) weekly monitoring; and 4) weekly feedback.

EMPIRICAL

Catano, Victor M., "Effectiveness of Verbal Praise as a Function of Expertise of its Source," *Perceptual and Motor Skills*, June 1976, Vol. 42, 1283–1286.

Verbal praise was given to 40 undergraduates who worked on a mirror-tracing task by an agent taking the role of experimenter, a member of the subject's peer group, or a peer with expertise on the task. Experimenter's praise improved performance most and peer's praise least; the expert peer's praise was intermediate. Verbal praise (i.e., "Your work looks fine") affected rate of improvement (reduction in tracing errors on the task). The improvement in quality of performance was not at the expense of time needed to complete the task.

PRESCRIPTIVE

Brethower, D. M. and Rummler, G. A., "For Improved Work Performance: Accentuate the Positive," *Personnel*, September-October 1966, Vol. 43, No. 5, 40–49.

This article describes some work situations which call for the application of "behavioral technology." It is the intent of this article to show how applied behavioral technology can and should furnish useful management tools to handle a number of problems in the general areas of on-the-job training, incentive programs, management development, and appraisal systems. Many of the learning concepts are discussed (motivation, nature of reinforcements, and schedules of reinforcement, etc.). In concluding, the author prescribes several things a manager or management can do to realize the optimum effect of a behavior and how it is influenced by its consequences.

Ludwig, S., "The Power of Praise," *International Management*, October 1973, 32–35.

This article tells of the Michigan Bell Telephone Company's application of Skinnerian theories. The Division Traffic Manager, E. Daniel Grady, has been using these theories to boost the quality of performance appraisal reporting, to combat worker absenteeism, and, indirectly, to improve labor negotiations. The author describes Grady's treatment programs and discloses what he feels is the key to success—namely, the application of behavioral technology. The power of praise and of accentuating the positive play a key role in all of Grady's programs.

Bordonaro, Frank P., "The Dilemma Created by Praise," *Business Horizons*, October 1976, Vol. 19, No. 5, 76–81.

The author contends that praise is not always rewarding or accepted because it may not be congruent with an individual's self-concept and expectations. Positive feedback may create a dilemma—the recipient may feel apprehensive if the feedback is linked to new demands which go beyond the person's expectations. The author prescribes using steadily increasing praise (moderate increments) to satisfy the individual's positivity needs without risking a lack of congruence ("gain effects") as derived from experiments by Aronson.

Moore, Lewis, S., "Motivation Through Positive Reinforcement," *Supervisory Management*, October 1976, Vol. 21, No. 10, 2–9.

The author prescribes the utilization of positive reinforcers to motivate employees on their jobs. Three categories of potential reinforcers are delineated: human influences (i.e., recognition, attention, respect, a sense of belonging, and competition); work as its own reward (dependent upon feedback, achievement, independence, and the chance to learn new skills); and money. The author relates that employees who perceive less reward in their work, must be reinforced by management and peer influence or by money. The use of human influences is promoted as the most effective motivator as well as providing the most flexible method of control. However, this category requires the greatest management skill and attention.

Commentary

PRAISE

Praise is a complex behavioral construct and technique to be handled with care. Too little or none as well as too much can produce equally negative results. Thus, this reinforcement must be used judiciously—and generally that means using it contingently. Praising the efforts and performances of others can be effective in sustaining such behaviors. However, used indiscriminately, praise can generate confusion about the meaning and the consequences of desirable and undesirable behaviors.

In one experiment, it was found that praise ("your work looks fine") from a supervisor positively affected rate of improvement of quality of work but that praise from the member's peer group affected performance least (Catano, 1976). Apparently, praise from a superior controller exerts greater influence than from an equal. In other words, the effects produced by the use of praise are not universal. Rather, the consequences are moderated by, at least, the source of the praise. If praise is linked to new demands which go beyond the person's expectations, the employee may feel apprehensive. Using steadily increasing praise in moderate increments has worked out best to satisfy the individual's competence needs without risking a lack of confidence or fear of failure. Therefore, praise, to be rewarding, must be in agreement with an individual's self-concept and expectations (Bordonaro, 1976). Unexpected and unearned praise frequently generates confusion in the eyes of the receiver and can even cause the source of praise to be viewed in insincere or hypercritical.

Positive reinforcers to motivate employees can be categorized as *human influences* (including praise, recognition, attention, respect, a sense of belonging, and competition); *work as its own reward* (feedback, achievement, independence, and learning new skills); and *money* (Moore, 1976). Each has been prescribed as an effective reinforcer available for managerial use. It has been suggested by many that employees who perceive less reward directly from their work must be reinforced for high performance through managerial and peer praise and influence or by money. The use of many forms of direct human influence has been found to be effective as a motivator and method of control but its systematic application requires great management skill. There is evidence, however, indicating that these skills can be acquired through managerial/supervisory training programs. The most effective of these programs utilize some version of the following behavioral analysis procedure to enhance performance through the systematic application of a reinforcer like praise from a boss:

<u>Step No. 1</u> Identify the exact *behavior (s)* (not attitude or feeling) that is to be improved. The key here is to define the behavior(s) in *observable* terms.

<u>Step No. 2</u> Measure this behavior and record these measurements systematically and longitudinally. These measurements are intended to provide a *baseline* for the evaluation to be implemented in Step 4.

<u>Step No. 3</u> Management intervenes (e.g., praises) to reward the desired behavior, or an approximation toward the desired behavior, when it occurs. The principle to be followed is to reward the desired behavior and not to reward, inadvertently, undesired behavior.

<u>Step No. 4</u> Evaluate the intervention by comparing the frequency and/ or quality of the desired behavior against that occurring in the baseline.

PRODUCTIVITY: CONCEPTS AND MEASUREMENT

Type of Article	No. of Articles
Descriptive	10
Empirical	3
Integrative	3
Prescriptive	12
Theoretical	1

DESCRIPTIVE

Rothe, H. F., "Output Rates Among Butter Wrappers: I. Work Curves and Their Stability," *Journal of Applied Psychology*, June 1946, Vol. 30, No. 3, 199–211.

This paper reports an investigation that was made of the problems of patterns, distribution, and stability of rates of output of various employees under various environmental conditions. The present study obtained data on some industrial operators performing a light, repetitive, manual operation. The goal of the author was to determine the pattern of these output data and the stability of their patterning for the operators individually and as a group. Daily individual and group work curves were kept, as well as daily individual and group trend lines.

Findings:

1) Individual work curves may take any different form and do not assume any characteristic, predictable form.

2) Individual daily work curves are specific to the individual and to a lesser extent to the day.

3) Individual trend lines are more highly related among different individual industrial operators than are individual daily work curves.

4) Group trend lines, regardless of method of construction, represent a stable phenomenon.

5) The correlational technique applied to work curves is one that may well be applied more widely in future industrial research on work patterning.

6) Industrial management, in studying the effects of rest periods, music in factories and offices, illumination, etc., by analyzing the effects of these variables upon work curves, would be wise to collect data covering several different operators and several different days in order to establish a "stable" work curve of output.

Rothe, H. F., "Output Rates Among Machine Operators: I. Distribution and Their Reliability," *Journal of Applied Psychology*, October 1947, Vol. 31, No. 5, 484–489.

The data for this study was taken from the books of the Standards Department of the Four Wheel Drive Auto Company. They cover a six-week period and refer to regular employees in the machine shop. Operators were on standards (a standard of perfection has been established for each job), but not incentives. Standard production of the operators was calculated daily and summarized bi-weekly for each operator. Upon examination of the frequency of distributions of the output rates for 130 men, the vast difference between the greatest to least production was noted. The enormousness of these ranges has great significance from both an incentive and a selective point of view. If it is assumed that all of these men were highly motivated to turn out high production, then the value of psychological tests to select only employees with the proper aptitudes is apparent. Then again, if it is assumed that the men had roughly equal aptitudes for the work there is an obvious need for a more effective method of motivating them.

Roth, H. F. and Nye, C. T., "Output Rates Among Coil Winders," *Journal of Applied Psychology*, 1958, Vol. 42, No. 3, 183–186.

As a basis for their study, the authors worked with the previous set forth hypothesis that the output rates of various groups of industrial employees tends to be relatively inconsistent from one period of time to another. In this study, data were taken from the official books of a manufacturing company (27 employees, period of 38 successive weeks) and the week-to-week consistency for a group of employees was determined. There was no financial incentive system in effect. Findings: Inspection of the table showing weekly average output for the year indicates an increase in performance early in the period studied and the group performance later stabilizing. In this situation, where there was no financial incentive system, the intra-individual differences did exceed the inter-individual differences ratio and supported the author's hypothesis: if that is the case, the incentive to work may be considered ineffective.

Rothe, H. F. and Nye, C.T., "Output Rates Among Machine Operators: III. A Nonincentive Situation in Two Levels of Business Activity," *Journal of Applied Psychology*, 1961, Vol. 45, No. 1, 50–54.

Previous studies by these authors had led to some hypotheses relating the consistency of output of industrial operators to the adequacy of the financial incentives in their work situations. This paper presents output data on other groups of industrial operators and relates these data to those hypotheses. Employees were machine operators in a small plant. They were paid an hourly rate—no incentive. The plant had a practice of insisting that all employees reach a certain amount of standard production or be disciplined. Analysis of the data collected indicates that the ratios of the ranges of inter-and intra-individual differences are opposite to what would be expected according to the other hypothesis regarding the effectiveness of incentives. (The relationship of inter-individual ratios exceeding the intra-individual ratios for each year had been hypothesized as indicating effective motivation). The most striking feature of the present study was the skewness of the distributions of output, which has long been hypothesized as indicating "restriction of output".

Sirota, D. and Wolfson, A.D., "Adequate Grievance Channels: Overcoming the Negative Effects of Work Measurement on Employee Morale," *Human Resource Management*, Summer 1972, Vol. 11, No. 2, 22–26.

The article deals with a study done at a large electrical equipment manufacturing company where the morale level of departments with varying levels of openness in grievance channels was examined. Method: Morale was measured through a diagnostic opinion survey administered to the study population of 1200 employees in lower-skill departments. Next, the effect that work measurement and open grievance channels have on morale was measured by means of an opinion survey. Thirdly, the effect of open grievance channels on morale was determined when employees have difficulty meeting work standards. The findings point to the desirability of creating a climate in which employees feel assured that by voicing their complaints about standards, they will be helped rather than hurt. The data indicates that employees who feel free to air their complaints are less antagonistic toward the amount of work expected, toward the company, and toward work measurement. The study demonstrates the importance of early diagnosis of employee attitudes. The fact that the introduction to work measurement had a negative, but controllable impact on attitudes, encouraged and allowed management to modify this program.

Penfield, R. V., "Time Allocation Patterns and Effectiveness of Managers," *Personnel Psychology*, 1974, Vol. 27, 245–255.

The present study provides some empirical information concerning the ways lower-level managers perform their jobs. The study was based on the premise that managers themselves can provide insight into the issue of management effectiveness by describing the way they believe they actually spend their time and the importance each of these functions has to success in their jobs. Ss were 204 first and second-level managers of a public utility company. Data collection was by means of a self-report questionnaire.

Results showed wide difference in time allocations when individual performance profiles were grouped into homogeneous job types on the basis of relative concentration of time spent in the specific activities. It was found that effective performance within any single job type requires different qualification and development programs than would be required by other job type assignments. This study shows a significant difference in the importance that managers with high performance evaluations attach to various managerial activities when compared with managers with low evaluations. These results point to the importance of examining and considering differences of management performance in development and utilization of management skills. This type of approach provides a framework for managerial job descriptions which can serve as a basis for selection, assignment, appraisal, and compensation.

Ely, D. D. and Morse, J. T., "TA and Reinforcement Theory," *Personnel*, March-April 1974, Vol. 51, No. 2, 38–41.

Thorndike's reinforcement theory and Berne's TA are blended to revamp the management training at General Telephone Company of the Southwest. A five-day course was designed for all levels of management. Classes were limited to 10 students. Primary objectives of the course were: 1) student will become aware of his transactions on others and become confident in choosing the most effective transaction strategies; 2) student will be able to modify employees' work behavior by describing the performance in behavioral terms, determining reinforcement given for present behavior and reinforcement necessary for desired behavior. In the course of the five-day training program, students were introduced to TA as a communications theory; students made contracts for changes that they wanted to see in themselves; students worked before a video TV camera in different situations to let the individual see how—in what ego states—he is coming across. To determine the effects of the course on actual on-the-job performance, a study was conducted in one area. All levels of management were represented. During the study time, 96 managers attended the class. The dependent variable was the resignation rate, with the number of employee resignations per month per manager computed for all managers. At the beginning of the study, average resignation rate of employees was .09 as opposed to the resignation rate after the course which dropped to .03.

Johnston, James J.; Duncan, Phillip K.; Monroe, Craig; Stephenson, Hester and Stoerzinger, Albert, "Tactics and Benefits of Behavioral Measurement in Business," *Journal of Organizational Behavior Management*, Spring 1978, Vol. 1, No. 3, 164–178.

The article reviews the application of behavioral measurement tactics in business settings and describes some of the resulting benefits with case history data from two businesses. Attention was called to the overall strategy which must guide the design, implementation, and evaluation of measurement systems in business. First, behavioral data must be *accurate;* second, the measurement system should be *continuous* and routine; third, the measurement system should be both *practical* and *cost-effective.* Tactics of measurement include selecting and defining behaviors (for example, assembly-line performance in a manufacturing plant or service-delivery activities in a public service organization), observing and recording behaviors accurately, display and interpretation (graphic displays of data serve as the central ingredient of a feedback system so employees can review their individual and collective work performance), and quality/accuracy of measurement (it is important that all affected employees have confidence in the measurement system). Behavioral measurements can provide the business person and his or her employees with a precise, continuous picture of how different aspects of the business are functioning, thus allowing problem areas to be rapidly and accurately identified and solutions to be tried and evaluated.

Schneier, Craig Eric and Beatty, Richard W., "Integrating Behaviorally Based and Effectiveness Based Methods," *Personnal Administrator*, July 1979, Vol. 24, No. 7, 65–76.

The first article in a three part series on performance appraisal (PA), the authors discuss PA's objectives, legal requirements, problems and formats. PA, the process of identifying, measuring and developing human performance, should meet five objectives to be fully operational: 1) provide feedback and improve performance; 2) identify employee training needs; 3) identify criteria used to allocate organizational rewards; 4) validate selection techniques to meet Equal Employment Opportunity (EEO) criteria; 5) identify promotable employees. Five types of PA formats are described, compared and evaluated. Human judgment, raters, criteria and PA formats, organizational policy, legal requirements and EEO legislation, and inflexibility can be problems that impair PA system effectiveness. Two solutions to PA problems are briefly discussed.

Schneier, Craig Eric and Beatty, Richard W., "Developing Behaviorally Anchored Rating Scales (BARS)," *Personnel Administrator*, August 1979, Vol. 24, No. 8, 59–68.

This second article in a three part series on performance appraisal discusses the use of Behaviorally Anchored Rating Scales (BARS) to integrate behaviorally-based and effectiveness-based appraisal systems. Management By Objectives (MBO) can fall into the trap of concentrating too heavily on effectiveness or results while ignoring the methods required to achieve objectives. BARS encompasses a systematic procedure for identifying desired behavior which can also facilitate attaining MBO objectives. BARS are developed to specify desired behavior and to judge the performance level certain behaviors indicate. BARS can supply managers attempting to implement MBO with a procedure whereby action plans can be developed in specific terms and MBO programs can be developed with an emphasis on desired behavior as well as results or effectiveness. A seven-step process for developing BARS is discussed. BARS have multiple uses in MBO. Besides their use in the action planning phase, they can aid in the performance review phase, goal-setting phase, and in personnel programs in addition to MBO. Potential problems with BARS are discussed.

EMPIRICAL

Rothe, H.F. and Nye, C. T., "Output Rates Among Machine Operators: III. A Nonincentive Situation in Two Levels of Business Activity," *Journal of Applied Psychology*, 1961, Vol. 45, No. 1, 50–54.

Previous studies by these authors had led to some hypotheses relating the consistency of output of industrial operators to the adequacy of the financial incentives in their work situations. This paper presents output data on other groups of industrial operators and relates these data to those hypotheses. Employees were machine operators in a small plant. They were paid an hourly rate—no incentive. The plant had a practice of insisting that all employees reach a certain amount of standard production or be disciplined. Analysis of the data collected indicates that the ratios of the ranges of inter- and intra-individual differences are opposite to what would be expected according to the other hypothesis regarding the effectiveness of incentives. (The relationship of inter-individual ratios exceeding the intra-individual ratios for each year had been hypothesized as indicating effective motivation.) The most striking feature of the present study was the skewness of the distributions of output, which has long been hypothesized as indicating "restriction of output."

Hise, R.T., "The Effect of Close Supervision on Productivity of Simulated Managerial Decision-Making Groups," *Business Studies*, Fall 1968, 96–104.

This study examines the effects of close supervision on the productivity of groups playing a multivariable, interactive marketing management game developed by the writer. The teams made decisions in the areas of pricing, sales volume forecasting, advertising, sales force deployment, warehouse location, etc. These were intended to simulate the decisions that would normally be made by middle-and top-management personnel. *Methodology:* Two sections, "test" and "control" were divided into teams (six on each team), and competed directly in a simulated national market for five consumer products. The "test" groups were subjected to six types of close supervision.

The following hypotheses were formulated in connection with this study:

1) Test groups subjected to close supervision would exhibit lower productivity.

2) Alienation of team members due to the existence of close supervision.

3) Closely supervised teams would indicate less favorable attitudes toward the game.

4) Less group solidarity.

5) Significant correlation between group solidarity and productivity would occur.

6) Significant correlation between influence, likeability, and worth of ideas and effort to produce would be found.

Findings:

1) Rejected	4) Rejected
2) Rejected	5) and 6) Accepted and correlation found in both areas.
3) Rejected	

Implications:

1) Close supervision may have a positive effect on the productivity of a work group.

2) Close supervision cannot unconditionally be associated with lower productivity.

3) Additional empirical studies need to be conducted on the relationship of close supervision to productivity.

Cherrington, D. J. and Cherrington, J. O., "Participation, Performance, and Appraisal," *Business Horizons*, December 1974, Vol. 17, No. 6, 35–44.

Using performance appraisals to reward performance implies an underlying personal value to the effect that there should be a balance between the contributions of the employee and his level of compensation. This personal value underlies this entire discourse. In return for the compensation an individual receives from the organization, it is appropriate to expect him to make a reliable contribution to the organization. This contribution will be evaluated and will determine in part the magnitude of his reinforcement. Aside from this value is the idea that appropriate reinforcement which is contingent upon certain desired response will increase satisfaction and performance. An empirical study involving 230 undergraduates was carried out to support the preceding statement. As predicted, the highest performance and satisfaction scores were obtained by subjects in conditions where 1) points were given both for the number of items produced and the number estimated, and 2) the groups were forced to accept a high estimate but there was little or no loss of points if the estimate was not reached.

INTEGRATIVE

Wagman, B. L., "An Approach to Measuring the Productivity of Staff Functions," *Public Personnel Management*, September-October 1974, Vol. 3, No. 5, 425–430.

This article is based on a nine-month special program conducted by the author, the purpose of which was to develop reliable, valid, and cost-effective productivity measures to be used to internally evaluate the performance of his department. The article is structured around those variables which form the foundations of productivity measures and their use. 1) *Objectives:* productivity measurement includes program evaluation, i.e., a comparison of objectives with achievements. 2) *Output Measures:* the author defines output measures as specific "achievement" or "performance" measures which are associated with specific objectives. 3) *Input Measures:* reflect the resources consumed in the production of output. The author recommends measuring only the relevant man-hours and fringe benefits in terms of current dollars. 4) *Measures and Change Indices:* the measure of performance of a system will be something like a weighted output minus the cost of input, where the weights are determined by standards of quality. The author sees the necessity of clearly setting forth the interrelatedness of objectives, output measures, and input measures.

Zenger, John, "Increasing Productivity: How Behavioral Scientists Can Help," *Personnel Journal*, October 1976, Vol. 55, No. 10, 513–525.

The author contends that the productivity of an organization can be increased through the application of behavioral science research findings. Such areas as supervisory skills, job design, compensation, and feedback impact on productivity and are subject to modification. Some of the author's recommendations for managers to increase their control over productivity include the following: involving employees in establishing work-unit goals, developing honest communication and open feedback job enrichment, group incentive systems and attitude surveys. Research conducted by various behavioral scientists is offered as support for the implementation of these measures.

Hinrichs, John R., Ph.D., *Practical Management for Productivity*, Van Nostrand Reinhold Company, 1978, 192 pages.

The author examines the role of productivity in achieving economic health and prosperity and argues that it is the human resource considerations—not new capital or new technology—that is the consideration of greatest significance in achieving increased productivity. In pursuit of this point Hinrichs describes, in plain language aimed at working managers, eight technical studies published in 1977 by the Work in America Institute and four new studies not previously published.

In the studies, a variety of private and governmental organizations implemented reward and incentive programs, participative management and job structural changes that in several cases yielded dramatic productivity improvements. The author also attempts to address the irony that in some of the cases several of the new approaches that yielded good results have been abandoned by management.

PRESCRIPTIVE

Lieder, S. L. and Zenger, J. H., "Industrial Engineers and Behavioral Scientists: A Team Approach to Improving Productivity," *Personnel,* July-August 1967, Vol. 44, No. 4, 68–75.

This article looks at two approaches to improve productivity: The conventional industrial engineering approach concerned with the design, improvement, and installation of new systems of men, materials, and machines. The behavioral science approach is advocated at TRW systems, of which one of the authors is a member. At TRW systems, it was felt that the findings of behavioral science could be utilized to implement industrial engineering programs more effectively. Training sessions were initiated and positive results were seen in the various departments. The combining of these two approaches helped to yield precise work standards and even more important is employee acceptance of these standards.

Rosow, J. M., "Productivity and The Blue-Collar Blues," *Personnel,* March-April 1971, Vol. 48, No. 2, 8–16.

The problems that the worker in the lower middle-income bracket faces are looked at: 1) the economic squeeze, a bind that results from an imbalance between wages and budget needs, aggravated by heavy taxes and inflation; 2) poor working conditions; 3) those in the lower middle-income bracket more than others live closely with some serious environmental problems, which combine with certain sociological and personal factors to make home life less than satisfactory. The author predicts ways out of these problems: 1) reorganization of work, 2) opportunities for advancement, 3) incentive systems, 4) supervisory training, 5) occupational health and training, 6) employee thrift plans, and 7) pension systems.

Sirota, D. and Wolfson, A.D., "Work Measurement and Worker Morale," *Business Horizons,* August 1972, Vol. 15, No. 4, 43–48.

A large nonunion electronics manufacturing company increased its productivity dramatically through formal work measurement. However, morale among employees deteriorated seriously. In its search for ways to minimize the negative effects of work measurement and still maintain productivity, management identified two basic inequities in the program. Not all standards for evaluating employee performance were equitable, and the procedure for correcting standards was complex and time consuming. Changes to correct these problems were implemented during a five-month experimental period. Morale improved significantly, but only when the experimental changes were accompanied by changes in managerial assignments. This finding can be interpreted to reflect problems of behavior reversal for managers.

Staats, E. B., "Measuring and Enhancing Federal Productivity," *Sloan Management Review*, Fall 1973, Vol. 15, No. 1, 1–9.

As both Comptroller General of the U.S. and one of the originators of the project on federal government productivity, Mr. Staats is in a unique position from which to view his topic. In this article he presents highlights from the published project report together with his commentary. The analysis covers many of the problems associated with defining and measuring productivity in the federal government. He outlines broad guidelines for successfully measuring federal productivity and examines current attempts to implement them. Some of the major factors which affect federal productivity are also discussed. Unlike so much of the literature about the government which tends to be written by outsiders, this article merits special attention because of the author's present position and background. The proposals and criticisms made reflect what is actually happening in the federal government today.

Polster, H. and Rosen, H. S., "Use of Statistical Analysis for Performance Review," *Personnel Journal*, July 1974, Vol. 53, No. 7, 498–506.

This article relates the experiences of American Greetings Corporation in initiating a program to systematically evaluate and document, on a corporate-wide basis, an individual's ability to handle increased responsibility. The "Potential Evaluation Program" was set up to accurately measure what characteristics contribute to an individual's potential to advance within the organization. The author describes elements of the program. It is felt that a synopsis of organizational trends and individual subordinates' growth can be charted. As a result, the general overall ability of the organization to foster its own growth potential can be measured.

Wagman, B. L., "An Approach to Measuring the Productivity of Staff Functions," *Public Personnel Management*, September-October 1974, Vol. 3, No. 5, 425–430.

This article is based on a nine-month special program conducted by the author, the purpose of which was to develop reliable, valid, and cost-effective productivity measures to be used to internally evaluate the performance of his department. The article is structured around those variables which form the foundations of productivity measures and their use. 1) *Objectives:* productivity measurement includes program evaluation, i.e., a comparison of objectives with achievements. 2) *Output Measures:* the author defines output measures as specific "achievement" or "performance" measures which are associated with specific objectives. 3) *Input Measures:* reflect the resources consumed in the production of output. The author recommends measuring only the relevant man-hours and fringe benefits in terms of current dollars. 4) *Measures and Change Indices:* the measure of performance of a system will be something like a weighted output minus the cost of input, where the weights are determined by standards of quality. The author sees the necessity of clearly setting forth the interrelatedness of objectives, output measures, and input measures.

Purcell, T. V., "How GE Measures Managers in Fair Employment," *Harvard Business Review*, November-December 1974, Vol. 52, No. 6, 99–104.

The General Electric Company is usually considered a leader in providing equal employment opportunity to members of minority groups (notwithstanding a federal action to the contrary now leveled at this and three other corporations and at three unions). Through a reporting system inaugurated in 1968 that accompanies the annual review of managerial performance, and through a penalty-reward policy tied to executive compensation, GE has raised minority employment at all levels by 57 percent. The number of women employed is up by six percent. Higher-level minority employment has climbed nearly 250 percent. This article details the reporting format and its role in the company's attempts to change the behavior of middle managers with respect to fair employment. Finally, the author discusses general issues of measurement, motivation, and application of the format to other areas.

Schaffer, R. H., "Demand Better Results—and Get Them," *Harvard Business Review*, November-December 1974, Vol. 52, No. 6, 91–98.

The author deals with why so few organizations reach their productivity potential. He maintains that managers fail to establish high performance improvement expectations in ways that elicit results. Managers fail because imposing heavy demands entails risks and threatens subordinates. It is safer to ask for less. To avoid facing the facts, a manager may rationalize that his subordinates are doing the best that can be expected; he may place his chips on incentive plans; he may actually establish high goals, but permit his subordinates to escape accountability. Top management needs a few tangible successes in asking for and getting more and the strategy for accomplishing this is: 1) select the goal, 2) specify the minimum expectation for results, 3) communicate your expectations clearly, 4) monitor the project, but delegate responsibility, 5) expand and extend the process.

Patz, A. L., "Performance Appraisal: Useful But Still Resisted," *Harvard Business Review*, May-June 1975, Vol. 53, No. 3, 74–80.

Although top management defines it as strictly a development technique, performance appraisal is infused with goals of salary justification, elimination of low performers, and the correlation of employees behavior with actual results. These purposes are often frustrated by obstacles: difficulties in gathering adequate information in the first place; keeping it up to date; mistrust of the uses to which information is put; and treatment of the evaluation interview itself as a chore. If such impediments exist, why do managers continue to use the process? The author concludes from his cross-section of executives it is because they think that they can help. The question is one of implementation, and this article concludes with a four-point strategy emphasizing manageability and directness: 1) keep the appraisal simple, 2) keep it separate, 3) keep it contained, and 4) keep it participative.

Zenger, John, "Increasing Productivity: How Behavioral Scientists Can Help," *Personnel Journal*, October 1976, Vol. 55, No. 10, 513–525.

The author contends that the productivity of an organization can be increased through the application of behavioral science research findings. Such areas as supervisory skills, job design, compensation, and feedback impact on productivity and are subject to modification. Some of the author's recommendations for managers to increase their control over productivity include the following: involving employees in establishing work-unit goals, developing honest communication and open feedback job enrichment, group incentive systems and attitude surveys. Research conducted by various behavioral scientists is offered as support for the implementation of these measures.

Schulhof, Robert J., "Five Years with a Scanlon Plan," *Personnel Administrator*, June 1979, Vol. 24, No. 6, 55–62.

The report details the long-term effect (five years) on the Rocky Mountain Data Systems company of the Scanlon Plan, a plan that provides a monthly cash bonus based upon improved productivity for all employees in proportion to salary. The subject company has 30 employees, $1 million in annual sales and produces computer analyses of dental x-rays. In support of job-enrichment, Schulhof reports Rocky Mountain experimented with every new management fad published and finally settled on the principle that each worker should make as many decisions as possible about his/her work. Schulhof details the subject company's formula for determining cash bonuses, itemizes the 13 areas in which benefits were realized and seven areas of negatives, or difficulty. The author concludes that the subject company is convinced of its plan's merits and has adopted the philosophy of "sharing the wealth in order to create more."

Schneier, Craig Eric and Beatty, Richard W., "Combining BARS and MBO: Using an Appraisal System to Diagnose Performance Problems," *Personnel Administrator*, September 1979, Vol. 24, No. 9, 51–60.

The third article in a three part series on performance appraisal (PA) explains how BARS and MBO can be integrated by using a case study based on the experience of a large organization. BARS and MBO are integrated on the same format by using measures of effectiveness from MBO to generate behavioral expectations from BARS. In the performance appraisal case study, for each of the objectives chosen, behaviors were specifically identified. The integrated MBO/BARS performance appraisal contains performance objectives and methods of measurement. Considerations for implementing the integrated system are discussed. Integrated MBO/BARS PA systems assist in diagnosing performance problems.

THEORETICAL

Slusher, E. A., "A Systems Look at Performance Appraisal," *Personnel Journal*, February 1975, Vol. 54, No. 2, 114–117.

This article takes a system theory approach in examining the familiar problem of performance appraisal. The Human Resource System is described. It is differentiated from other organization systems by a boundary, implying that those elements not within the system lie in a larger suprasystem or environment. The suprasystem affects the system by providing inputs to the system and accepting outputs from the system. In the HRS, there are three inputs: organizational goals, human talent, and other suprasystem factors. Outputs from HRS are organization performance and human need satisfaction. The human resource system's ability as an open system, to progress toward organizational goals, depends chiefly on the supply of comprehensive feedback from the appraisal subsystem. The appraisal subsystem's feedback contribution can be fully understood by analyzing resource subsystems. Few organizations utilize all the potential feedback interfaces that sound appraisal offers. Moreover, appraisal's full potential can be realized only when it is conceptualized as a multifaceted process rather than simply an annual review session. Most managers can profit from a hard systems look at their appraisal subsystem. It is through careful, continuous appraisal that the organization's human resources are directed toward the organization's goals.

Commentary

PRODUCTIVITY: CONCEPTS AND MEASUREMENT

Various approaches to productivity measurement of an organization and its components have been recommended by researchers. Frameworks for assessing productivity have been applied from several perspectives including behavioral science, industrial engineering, a combination of these two approaches, systems that emphasize individual growth, and open systems approaches.

In measuring the productivity of staff functions in a department of one company (Wagman, 1974), variables were considered which generally form the foundation for a number of industrial approaches to productivity measurement and their use:

1. *Accomplishment:* A comparison of objectives with achievement.

2. *Output Measures:* Goal achievement.

3. *Input Measures:* Human resources used (man-hours plus fringes).

The interrelatedness of these measures should be considered but frequently is not. Thus, a "measure" of organizational productivity would then be the product of:

WEIGHTED OUTPUT   COST OF INPUT   PERFORMANCE
(Determined by standards   − (Man-hours + fringes) =   MEASURES
    of quality)

Most behavioral science approaches to productivity generation and assessment recommend:

1. Involving employees in establishing work-unit goals.

2. Developing honest communication and open feedback;

3. Job enrichment;

4. Establishing group incentive systems; and

5. Conducting attitudinal and/or motivational surveys with feedback and diagnosis of problem areas.

The use of this general approach has been utilized by several behavioral scientists in attempts to enhance human productivity.

Some companies have used a combination of behavioral and industrial engineering approaches to effect precise work standards and obtain employee acceptance of these standards. Following the behavioral principles outlined above allowed the installation of new engineering processes of design improvement and of new systems of men, materials, and machines (Lieder & Zenger, 1967).

A system theory approach to performance appraisal/measurement has been described as the Human Resource System (Slusher, 1975). It has three general components:

1. Organizational goals

2. Human talent

3. Suprasystem or larger environment

and its outputs are:

1. Organizational performance

2. Human need satisfaction.

This author contends that few organizations utilize all the potential feedback interfaces that sound appraisal offers to integrate these components; that appraisal's *full* potential is realized only when conceptualized as a multifaceted process rather than simply as an annual review. It requires careful, continuous appraisal to ensure that the organization's human resources are all directed toward the organization's goals.

Several problems with applications of productivity appraisal or measurement have been identified. An attitude of resistance to assessment is one of the major hurdles to overcome. These sources of resistance are partially a function of the purposes that management proposes for productivity assessment. If the system is infused with goals of salary justification and elimination of low performers, then resistance is likely. Other obstacles seem to be the difficulty in gathering adequate information, keeping it up-to-date, general mistrust of uses to which the information is put, and the treatment of productivity measurement itself as a justifiable outcome without linking such assessments to more systemic outcomes. In other words, unless employees can see desirable outcomes for themselves from productivity assessment and unless such assessments are seen as linked to larger, more inclusive goals, then productivity measurement alone is not likely to enhance human productivity. On the other hand, much of the literature suggests that few organizations reach their productivity potential, partially because managers fail to establish high performance improvement expectations and hold employees accountable for those standards. The performance improvement potential of high expectations and goals has been consistently demonstrated by several of the studies included in the section on goals.

Strategies that have been offered to attain this end generally incorporate some variation on the following steps:

1. Select a goal,

2. Specify expectations for results,

3. Communicate expectations clearly,

4. Monitor progress but delegate responsibility,

5. Expand and extend the process.

Most of the evidence on human resource productivity measurement systems suggests that several general prescriptions, if followed, would enhance human productivity. Such systems should:

1. Keep it simple,

2. Keep it contained (that is, focus on specific outcomes and measures of progress),

3. Keep it participative.

The literature is ripe with prescriptive measures offered for achieving effective productivity and/or appraisal improvements but much is needed in the way of substantive, empirical research to assist with application. Theories and frameworks to guide applications are only beginning to appear in the applied behavioral analysis literature.

Steps are being taken to expand the present research base in order to offer a solid foundation on which organizations can build a more predictable measurement/appraisal system. This future research should be charted in ways that will more clearly define the needed criteria and measures to achieve an organization's full potential for productivity.

Independent Variable

PUNISHMENT

Type of Article	No. of Articles
Descriptive	2
Empirical	2
Integrative	4
Prescriptive	6

DESCRIPTIVE

Mayhew, Gerald L., Enyart, Patience and Cone, John D., "Approaches to Employee Management: Policies and Preferences," *Journal of Organizational Behavior Management*, Winter 1979, 2, 103–111.

A number of studies in the organizational behavior management literature have demonstrated the utility of using positive measures to control problematic employee behaviors traditionally dealt with in a punitive manner. The present study was designed to determine the prevalence of use of different types of both positive and negative consequences in employee management, as well as administrators' and managers' relative preferences for these consequences. Managers and administrators of residential facilities were surveyed for information concerning the types of consequences used to control common personnel problems and their relative preference for various measures. A majority of respondents reported both use and preference for predominantly negative methods of control. The authors proposed several explanations for the continuing reliance on negative methods for controlling employee infractions as well as steps for increasing the use of more positively based management systems.

Harrison, Edward L., APD, "Discipline and the Professional Employee," *Personnel Administrator*, March 1979, Vol. 24, No. 3, 35–38.

Whereas the discipline of the non-professional employee is fairly common in the management literature, the discipline of the professional employee is virtually unheard of. One reason for this condition may be that when professional employees perform unsatisfactorily they are often discharged. The main focus of this article is to get industries to examine the problems and benefits associated with the use of constructive discipline with professional employees. Singled out as an example was the hospital industry. Questionnaires were mailed to 194 hospital personnel directors selected at random from a national list. Of the respondents, 95 percent indicated that incidents had occurred within the past five years which warranted disciplinary action to professionals. Thirty-eight percent of the respondents reported an increase in the frequency of discipline of professionals in the past five years. Whatever the reasons for this increase in the discipline of the professional, several observations are appropriate: 1) The professional employee has increasingly become the subject of disciplinary action. This coupled with the trend toward professional unionization will cause the management's use of discipline to become more difficult. 2) Grievance of appeal procedures for non-union professionals can head off problems before they gain momentum. 3) As a means of reducing the likelihood of conflict in the first place, the professional employee should become more involved in decisions central to his welfare. 4) Management should remember that the proper administration of discipline is as important with professional employees as it is with nonprofessional employees. 5) Counseling and other "positive" techniques offer a productive alternative to the use of discipline with professional employees. The point to keep in mind is that effective planning can reduce not only the need for discipline but its impact when it becomes necessary.

EMPIRICAL

Horai, J. and Tedeschi, J. T., "Effects of Credibility and Magnitude of Punishment on Compliance to Threats," *Journal of Personality and Social Psychology*, June 1969, Vol. 12, No. 2, 164–169.

A modified Prisoner's Dilemma (PD) game allowed a simulated partner (SP) to threaten subjects with a loss of points if the subject non-complied to the SP's verbal demand. Independent variables included three threat-credibility levels (10 percent, 50 percent, and 90 percent), three punishment magnitude levels (5, 10, 20 points), and sex of subjects (45 males and 45 females). Compliance was a positive linear function of credibility. The highest punishment severity level elicited more compliance than either of the two nondiffering lower levels. There were no interaction effects. A punishment x sex interaction was found on delay of first testing the veracity of the threat. Males lied more than females when sending messages of intent. Subjects in the highest credibility condition defected more than did subjects in the other credibility conditions.

Schmitt, D. R., "Punitive Supervision and Productivity: An Experimental Analog," *Journal of Applied Psychology*, 1969, Vol. 53, No. 2, 118–123.

This research concerns one unexplored aspect of the relationship between supervision and worker productivity—the manner in which the supervisor's activities are scheduled. A laboratory setting provided an analog to the supervisor's use of one type of consequence, punishment, to maximize the amount of time a worker spends in task activity while minimizing various unauthorized behaviors. The setting involved two concurrent operants reinforced with money where work on the higher paying one was penalized at various intervals. The effects of variations in the schedule of these intervals and the size of the penalties were explored.

The results indicated that penalty magnitude significantly affected the allocation of work time when the penalties occurred at unequal intervals but not at equal ones. Under the unequal condition, the higher the penalties the less time spent on the punished task and the greater the time on the unpunished one. Low and moderate penalties, however, produced less work on the unpunished task than would be predicted on the basis of the possible losses through penalties.

INTEGRATIVE

Maier, N. R. F., "Discipline in the Industrial Setting," *Personnel Journal,* April 1965, Vol. 44, No. 4, 189–192.

The author looks at discipline in several different lights—from the point of view of the undesirable act that has already been committed; as a punishment provision, the person being made to pay a price; and as a prevention device to deal with recurrence of an undesirable act. A study was done with a simulated role-playing situation in which a foreman thinks he catches a man working on top of a telephone pole without a safety belt. What the different foremen did under these circumstances was studied. The author found that people don't execute decisions they don't like. Even when they think a man deserves punishment, they do not like to do things that hurt people's feelings, especially when they like a person. In industry there is a further complication because regulations are decided at the top. The people who make the regulations don't have to police them. Subordinates are obliged to do this. The very supervisors who are most effective are the ones who are the most considerate of people. Such considerate supervisors are the very ones who are least inclined to carry out the kind of disciplinary action that is established at the top.

Booker, G. S., "Behavioral Aspects of Disciplinary Action," *Personnel Journal,* July 1969, Vol. 48, No. 7, 525–529.

Any evaluation of the usefulness of disciplinary action should only be made according to the conditions of the situation. An examination of the traditional assumptions of management concerning the effectiveness of disciplinary action reveals that these assumptions lack sufficient support. Apparently disciplinary action is useful when the problem is simply to inform the individual of his mistake. However, as a solution to a more involved or a recurrent problem, disciplinary action is insufficient. Evidently, management must either avoid disciplinary problems by improving selection of techniques or eliminate the problem by establishing more efficient means of effecting the discharge of problem employees. Disciplinary action cannot be expected to provide an answer for all problems of deviant behavior within the organization.

Arvey, Richard D. and Ivancevich, John M., "Punishment in Organizations: A Review, Propositions and Research Suggestions," *Academy of Management Review*, January 1980, Vol. 5, No. 1, 123–132.

After defining punishment, the authors point out that there exists a lack of sufficient attention to the use of punishment in organizational settings. This is because punishment is viewed as having undesirable side effects. Numerous rebuttals to these notions are given. Six propositions that facilitate the effectiveness of punishment in reducing or eliminating undesirable behavior in an organizational setting involve: 1) the timing of punishment; 2) the intensity of punishment; 3) the relationship between the punisher and the worker being punished; 4) the schedule of punishment; 5) the provision of reasons for punishment; and 6) the availability of alternative desirable responses.

Guidelines about *how* to study punishment in organizational settings are suggested. Several dependent variables are provided. Tools of measurement include records of rule violations, unobtrusive observers, and ratings by managers, co-workers, and the employee. The authors suggest that after determining basic aversive stimuli, the "dimensions" of those stimuli should be measured. Various measurement strategies include: 1) the observing and recording of behaviors along certain dimensions; 2) the evaluating of case studies by employees; and 3) the rating by employees of the manager's punishment behavior on various rating dimensions. Based on this review, the authors emphasize that punishment, when used with caution and consideration, can be and is an effective aid in achieving changes in employee behavior.

Sims, Henry P. Jr., "Further Thoughts on Punishment in Organizations," *Academy of Management Review*, January 1980, Vol. 5, No. 1, 133–138.

The author briefly examines existing research on punishment in organizational settings. The studies are classified into three categories: 1) studies using cross-sectional psychometric designs; 2) studies using longitudinal psychometric designs; and 3) laboratory and field studies. Numerous investigations in each category are discussed briefly. From the cross-sectional studies group, two general conclusions are drawn: 1) a relatively strong positive correlation exists between reward behavior and employee performance; and 2) no consistent correlation is present between punitive behavior and performance. Two more general, yet tentative, conclusions are brought forth from the review of longitudinal studies: 1) a stronger relationship exists between reward behavior and employee performance than between punitive behavior and performance; and 2) low performance seems to cause punishment if performance and punishment are dominated by a causal direction. In the laboratory and field studies category, review of the existing research emphasizes further the different relationships between reward and punitive behaviors and employee performance.

When the findings from the three categories are combined, two tentative conclusions appear. First, most of the findings from the studies that contrast the effects of reward and punitive behaviors on employee performance suggest that reward behavior tends to have a stronger impact on performance than punitive behavior. Second, results from longitudinal and laboratory studies imply the notion that punishment tends not to be a cause, but a result of employee behavior. Of course, managerial implications arise from the research. It is suggested that reward behaviors and systems are the better ways of modifying employee behavior and that punitive behavior is *not* likely to be an effective overall means of influencing employees.

PRESCRIPTIVE

Bockley, P. W., "Effective Discipline--A Positive Profit Tool," *Personnel Journal*, October 1965, Vol. 44, No. 9, 475–479.

The basic objective of industrial discipline should be to make the company stronger. It should not and need not be disruptive in nature. It should be viewed as a positive "profit" tool. Employees are accustomed to rules and regulations; they are faced with them in every phase of their daily activity. Although none of us like to be controlled or regulated, the likelihood of a negative reaction to rules is greatly reduced if they are reasonable, realistic, and understood.

The author suggests how to design such a program with a view to its overall effect upon the ability of your supervisors to meet their production objectives--not for the sake of discipline solely: measure their effect upon productivity and profitability, and above all, anticipate in advance the impact they will have upon the employee group; design the program to minimize any negative impact; and make it a positive tool for improved employee relations and increased efficiency.

Luthans, F., "The Role of Punishment in Organizational Behavior Modification (OB MOD)," *Public Personnel Management*, May-June 1973, Vol. 2, No. 3, 156–161.

The role punishment plays in organizational behavior is currently clouded by doubt, emotion, and misunderstanding. A necessary starting point for clarifying the role of punishment is to establish an operational definition, which the author does. Armed with an operational definition, O.B. Mod can meet two major problems in assessing the role of punishment: 1) the difficulty of generalizing the results of animal experimentation to human application, and 2) the connotation that punishment is cruel and inhuman. These problems can be solved through socially acceptable human experimentation. Behaviorists see punishment as being capable of changing behavior but also stressed are the undesirable side effects such as anxiety, temporary suppression of behavior, and the generalization of the punishing stimulus to the punishing agent. These and other difficulties can be overcome by linking, on a contingency basis, the punishing stimulus with the undesirable response and concurrently providing and reinforcing a desirable alternative response. In this way punishment can play a valuable role in organizational behavior modification.

Behlohlav, James A. and Popp, Paul O., "Making Employee Discipline Work," *Personnel Administrator*, March 1978, Vol. 23, No. 3, 22–24.

Both private and public organizations encounter difficulties with the disciplinary structure they employ. The lack of uniform disciplinary policies and practices leads to dissatisfaction among subordinates. Questionnaires were sent to personnel directors in each of the 100 largest cities of the United States; 66 were useful (66 percent). Responses drawn from the questionnaires indicate that in order to be effective, an organization must: 1) control not only job specifications but actual individual worker selection also; 2) give new, inexperienced managers complete information on disciplinary policies and procedures; and 3) be consistent in disciplinary practices.

Kravetz, Dennis, J., "Counseling Strategies for Involuntary Terminations," *Personnel Administrator*, October 1978, Vol. 23, No. 10, 49–54.

One of the most difficult problems facing management is that of "involuntary termination" of an employee. In this article are detailed the various steps and emotional states that may surround the involuntary termination. These include what can be done by counselors before the actual firing; the psychological reactions that the employee goes through; and then what the effective counselor can do to aid the employee. Interestingly, it is noted that the psychological reactions of the terminated employee are nearly identical to reactions experienced by one who has just lost a spouse or close friend. The employee relations counselor then has a very important role in that, if done effectively, he may prevent psychological or even physiological complications from confronting the employee. Although involuntary termination counseling is not the most pleasant line of work, it is undoubtedly a necessity for all effective organizations.

Boncarosky, Leon D., "Guidelines to Corrective Discipline," *Personnel Journal*, October 1979, Vol. 58, No. 10, 698–702.

Results of applying discipline are serious and can be long-lasting for both employees who may be suspended or lose their jobs and supervisors whose position and/or authority may be threatened. Therefore, it is important to the individual and the organization that fair and proper avenues for discipline be established. Consideration must be given to why the misconduct occurs and how discipline can be administered so that employees will have an opportunity to change their behavior; how discipline can be imposed in a corrective rather than a punitive manner; and requirements for having a disciplinary decision sustained by an arbitrator. Basic causes of action that incurs disciplinary action are attributed to the employee, the supervisor, or the organization. An employee can be a disciplinary problem due to lack of knowledge, personal desires, unsuitability to the job, and emotional or external factors. Supervisors contribute to disciplinary problems due to using an inappropriate method of supervision or giving improper assignments or orders. Organizations contribute to the disciplinary problem because of unsound and unnecessarily restrictive policies and regulations and improper expectations. Alternative avenues for a discipline plan are outlined as well as a seven-point check list for a basic disciplinary procedure.

Sims, Henry, P., Jr., "Tips and Troubles with Employee Reprimand," *Personnel Administrator*, January 1979, Vol. 24, No. 1, 57–61.

Whether one is shocking white rats for refusing to cross a grid or giving an employee a two-day layoff for raising her voice to a customer, the notion of punishment or "aversive behavior management" has had a poor reputation among humanistic behavioralists and managers alike. However, if aversive behavior management is used widely, many believe that it can be of value in managing employee behavior. Traditionally, aversive behavior management has included such things as cuts in pay, layoffs and verbal reprimands. When used by themselves, these punishments have prompted the argument that reprimands have nasty side effects. If used effectively, though, these side effects need not appear. "Effective use" involves such courtesies as reprimanding in a private place, citing specific target behaviors that seem unnecessary, and always suggesting the appropriate replacement behavior for the one for which the employee was reprimanded. If one keeps these and other considerations in mind, perhaps aversive behavior management can be used to the advantage of everyone.

Commentary

PUNISHMENT

The role of punishment in an organization must be clarified and an operational definition must be established. Using punishment to change behavior is suggested as a legitimate route to follow (Luthans, 1973). However, applying a behavioral concept can produce undesirable side effects such as anxiety, temporary suppression of behavior, and generalization of the punishing stimulus to the punishing agent. But the author assures us that these difficulties can be overcome by linking the punishing stimulus with the undesirable response. Thus punishment can be used to change/modify behavior.

Another focus for the use of punishment is to improve the efficiency of the employee. If reasonable rules and regulations are established to assist supervisors in meeting their production goals and if they are designed to minimize any negative impact on the employees, these can be a positive tool for improved employee relations and increased efficiency (Bockley, 1965).

Looking at discipline from an individual point of view, one study (Booker, 1969) indicates that discipline as a solution to an involved or recurrent employee problem is simply not effective. Management must either avoid problems by improving selection techniques or eliminate the problem by discharging the employee. Disciplinary action cannot be expected to solve all behavioral problems in an organization.

In a study applying the use of punishment to worker productivity (Schmitt, 1969), it was found that penalty magnitude significantly affected time spent on a task when penalties occurred at unequal intervals but not at equal ones. Unequal interval penalty conditions resulted in less time being spent on the punished task and more time being spent on the unpunished task.

In looking at discipline in a industrial setting, one study found that people don't execute decisions they don't like; they don't like to do things that hurt people's feelings especially if they like a person. In addition, the supervisors who are the most effective are the ones who are most considerate of people and are least inclined to carry out the kind of disciplinary action established by others not in their immediate environment (1965).

Thus, present research indicates punishment may be used to change behavior or to improve efficiency. However, it is clear that only under specific conditions will punishment produce constructive behavioral change. Several general principles for the effective use of punishment can be prescribed:

1. Do not use punishment unless absolutely necessary.

2. Punish in private (and reward in public).

3. Couple the use of punishment with suggestions for correct or more desirable behavior.

4. Reinforce any trend toward the more desired behavior even though the present behavior may not achieve the ultimate goal immediately.

SCHEDULES AND EXPECTANCY

Type of Article	No. of Articles
Applied	3
Descriptive	4
Empirical	16
Integrative	5
Prescriptive	9
Theoretical	5

Applied

Schneier, C. E., "Behavior Modification: Training the Hard-Core Unemployed," *Personnel*, May-June 1973, Vol. 50, No. 3, 65–69.

Incorporation of behavior modification principles in a training program can especially benefit the hard-core unemployed (HCU). He may come from an environment sterile of proper work behavior. A supervisor/trainer can be used as a model of good work behavior. The HCU trainee is allowed to proceed at small, self-determined steps during training. Because tasks are broken into small components and precisely defined and the trainee is told exactly what is expected of him, the possibility of subjective and ambiguous evaluation of his performance is reduced. Management is benefited by such a behavior modification training program as it utilizes competent trainees and its supervisory talents effectively. A case example involving a manufacturer of metal bed frames who employed HCU workers and put them on a behavior modification training program was reported. Positive reinforcement was used in the form of points and praise. The procedure is currently working well.

Deslauries, Brian C. and Everett, Peter B., "Effects of Intermittent and Continuous Token Reinforcement of Bus Ridership," *Journal of Applied Psychology*, August 1977, Vol. 62, No. 4, 369–375.

The following conditions were successively instituted on the Experimental Bus (the 11:00 a.m. to 2:00 p.m. daily operation of a campus bus):

baseline, Variable Ratio 3 token reinforcement (every third passenger, on the average, received a token with about 10¢ for boarding the bus), continuous token reinforcement (every passenger received a token). Compared to the experimental controls, Experimental Bus ridership increased significantly during the token reinforcement manipulations. There was no difference in the effects of VR3 and continuous token reinforcement. The results suggest that compared to continuous token reinforcement, intermittent reinforcement may provide a viable and economical approach to increasing bus ridership.

Komaki, Judy; Waddell, William M. and Pearce, M. George, "The Applied Behavior Analysis Approach and Individual Employees: Improving Performance in Two Small Businesses," *Organizational Behavior and Human Performance*, August 1977, Vol. 19, No. 2, 337–352.

Strategies and techniques of the applied behavior analysis approach were used to improve the performance of individual employees in two small businesses, a neighborhood grocery store and a downtown game room. In Experiment I, several potentially reinforcing consequences (time off with pay, feedback, self-recording) were arranged for desired performance and desired tasks were clarified (i.e., being within proximity of counters, assisting customers, and restocking shelves). A multiple-baseline design across behaviors was employed. The mean performance level of the three behaviors improved from 53, 35 and 57 percent to 86, 87 and 86 percent respectively.

In Experiment II, a reversal design (ABAB) was used. Performance (i.e., being within proximity of the counter when a customer is present, fixing game machines, cleaning the premises) increased from baseline means of 62 and 63 percent to 93 and 97 percent, respectively, following the introduction of a goal-classification and contingent pay system (i.e., target cleaning behaviors were placed at the counter and take-home pay corresponded to the percentage of cleaning duties completed). The two studies indicate the potential of the behavior analysis approach for improving performance-providing consequences that have the effect of increasing specified work behaviors.

Descriptive

Komaki, Judy; Waddell, William M. and Pearce, M. George, "The Applied Behavior Analysis Approach and Individual Employees: Improving Performance in Two Small Businesses," *Organizational Behavior and Human Performance*, August 1977, Vol. 19, No. 2, 337–352.

Strategies and techniques of the applied behavior analysis approach were used to improve the performance of individual employees in two small businesses, a neighborhood grocery store and a downtown game room. In Experiment I, several potentially reinforcing consequences (time off with pay, feedback, self-recording) were arranged for desired performance and desired tasks were clarified (i.e., being within proximity of counters, assisting customers, and restocking shelves). A multiple-baseline design across behaviors was employed. The mean performance level of the three behaviors improved from 53, 35 and 57 percent to 86, 87 and 86 percent respectively. In Experiment II, a reversal design (ABAB) was used. Performance (i.e., being within proximity of the counter when a customer is present, fixing game machines, cleaning the premises) increased from baseline means of 62 and 63 percent to 93 and 97 percent, respectively, following the introduction of a goal-classification and contingent pay system (i.e., target cleaning behaviors were placed at the counter and take-home pay corresponded to the percentage of cleaning duties completed). The two studies indicate the potential of the behavior analysis approach for improving performance-providing consequences that have the effect of increasing specified work behaviors.

Rand, Thomas M., "Diagnosing the Valued Reward Orientations of Employees," *Personnel Journal*, September 1977, Vol. 56, No. 9, 451–464.

The author relates that reward systems, to increase levels of job effectiveness and employee satisfaction, must contain the following five elements: 1) the magnitude of rewards must satisfy the basic human need of survival and security; 2) organizations must choose relevant rewards over which they have the potential ability to provide and manipulate; 3) distribution of rewards must be perceived as being equitable; 4) members must perceive contingency between performance and reward; 5) and the reward must be valued by the individual.

Results taken on the JDI from 100 managers, drawn from widely diverse organizational settings, indicate an erroneous assumption concerning hourly employees' reward preferences. They emphasize extrinsic rewards such as pay and security while workers are more interested in growth opportunities, sense of accomplishment (intrinsic) instead (comparison with hourly workers reward preferences on JDI). The author believes that strategies to design work environments which provide individually valued rewards should be explored in addition to contingently granting extrinsic rewards for acceptable job performance to experience achievement.

Stephens, Tedd A. and Burroughs, Wayne A., "An Application of Operant Conditioning to Absenteeism in a Hospital Setting," *Journal of Applied Psychology*, 1978, Vol. 63, No. 4, 518–521.

Two financial reward systems were used in a hospital setting to reduce absenteeism among 92 nurses, ward clerks, and nursing assistants. Six nursing units were randomly assigned to one of the two reward systems. System A permitted subjects to become eligible for cash prize drawings of $20 if they evidenced no absenteeism during a three week period. System B allowed subjects to become eligible for $20 prize drawings if they were not absent on eight dates randomly selected from the three week period. An analysis of variance with a repeated measures design was used to assess differences between the two reward systems. Both reward systems resulted in significant decreases in absenteeism, and no significant differences were obtained between the two systems. Also, point-biserial correlations relating income level and absenteeism yielded nonsignificant results.

Petrock, Frank, "Analyzing the Balance of Consequences for Performance Improvement," *Journal of Organizational Behavior Management,* Spring 1978, Vol. 1, No. 3, 196–205.

This paper presents a systematic procedural and conceptual tool to aid the manager in analyzing the balance of consequences that affects performance. A model is outlined to assist in conceptualizing the balance of consequences for desired or undesired behavior (job performance). A procedure for analyzing the balance of consequence includes: 1) state clearly in measurable and observable terms the desired behavior and the undesired behavior; 2) identify and link all the current, potential reinforcing and punishing consequences contingent upon the desired behavior and list all potentially reinforcing and punishing consequences contingent upon the undesired behavior; 3) determine the characteristic and dimension combination of the reinforcing and punishing consequences listed for both desired and undesired behaviors. An action plan guide is presented to assist in developing action plans to balance the consequences most positively. The analysis and alteration of the balance of consequences represents one potentially effective management tool to effect performance improvement.

EMPIRICAL

Schwarz, J. C., "Contribution of Generalized Expectancy to Stated Expectancy Under Conditions of Success and Failure," *Journal of Personality and Social Psychology,* February 1969, Vol. 11, No. 2, 157–164.

The present study tests the generality of the proposition from Rotter's (1954) social learning theory that the influence of generalized expectancy (GE) upon expectancy (E) in a novel situation is a rapidly decreasing function of experience in that situation. An analysis was made of the change in correlation between GE (assessed by two methods) and successive E statements elicited after each trial under two sequences of reinforcement on a novel motor-skill task.

Under a reinforcement sequence beginning with three failures, GE remained significantly correlated with E over several trials. However, when the sequence of reinforcement began with three successes, the correlation between GE and E fell below statistically significant levels by the second successful trial. When reinforcements are dependent upon the skill of the subject and his skill is sufficient to determine success, a higher order expectancy may be evoked which terminates the influence upon E of expectancies generalized from closely related tasks. Evidence of the construct validity of the measure of E and GE is also present.

Schmitt, D. R., "Effects of Intermittent Reinforcing Consequences on Task Choice," *Psychological Reports*, 1971, Vol. 28, 771–776.

The study explored the effects of supplementary reinforcement on one of two tasks as an element determining task choice. In an experimental setting, work on the lower paying of two concurrent operants received additional reinforcement on either a fixed or variable interval schedule. A wide range of addition magnitudes was studied under each schedule. The results from eight Ss working for a number of hours on either a fixed or variable interval schedule indicated that addition magnitude significantly affected task choice only when additions were available at unequal intervals. Under this schedule, the higher the additions the greater the time spent on the lower paying task. The fixed interval schedule produced a small amount of time on the lower paying task regardless of addition magnitude. The results extend and replicate previous research on the effects of schedules of monetary penalties on task choice in a similar setting. Comparison of the results from the two studies suggest that additions and penalties when applied to opposing tasks in a concurrent setting have similar effects on patterns of task choice.

Pritchard, Robert D.; DeLeo, Philip J. and Von Berger, Jr., Clarence W., "A Field Experimental Test of Expectancy-Valence Incentive Motivation Techniques," *Organizational Behavior and Human Performance*, April 1976, Vol. 15, No. 2, 355–406.

Three types of incentive systems were developed in the context of expectancy-valence theory of work motivation. The first made valued outcomes contingent on performance; the second attempted to make these rewards contingent on effort; the third added additional, financially-based outcomes to the reward package. These three systems were run consecutively for eight months in an Air Force technical training environment utilizing subjects from two training courses. The results indicated that for one course, the first two systems resulted in slight, but meaningful increases in performance, and the third system was very powerful. No real performance effects were observed for the other course. Attitudes generally increased under the program. The results are discussed in terms of expectancy-valence theory and in terms of their practical implications.

Litrownik, Alan J.; Franzini, Louis R. and Skenderian, Daniel, "Effect of Locus of Reinforcement Control on a Concept-Identification Task," *Psychological Reports*, August 1976, Vol. 39, No. 1, 159–165.

One subject from each of 20 triads matched on age and sex was randomly assigned to yoked contingent external, noncontingent external, and self-reinforcement groups. Differential reinforcement was evaluated in terms of accuracy output of behavior during an acquisition, maintenance, and extinction on a concept-identification task. Performances of the contingent external and self-reinforcement groups were equivalent during acquisition and maintenance, which proved superior to the noncontingent control group. During maintenance the noncontingent group subjects continued at their same level of output and accuracy in contrast to both contingent groups which improved. Groups did not differ in accuracy during maintenance nor during the extinction phase when all subjects, as expected, were less accurate. Contrary to previous reports, the performances (output and accuracy) of subjects who administered their own reinforcers were not more resistant to withdrawal of an available external reinforcer than subjects who had received externally controlled consequences.

Pritchard, Robert D.; Leonard, Dale W.; Von Bergen Jr., Clarence W. and Kirk, Raymond J., "The Effects of Varying Schedules of Reinforcement on Human Task Performance," *Organizational Behavior and Human Performance*, August 1976, Vol. 16, No. 2, 205–230.

The present research utilized four schedules of financial reinforcement (Hourly, Fixed Ratio, Variable Ratio, and Variable Ratio-Variable Amount) in an organizational simulation setting. Subjects (teenage males who responded to a newspaper ad) were hired for what they perceived to be a real job of four weeks' duration, which required them to learn self-paced material about electronics (task). The schedules of reinforcement were operationalized through the process of scoring the subjects' tests over sections of the material. By means of a computer console, subjects either received a straight $2.00/hr (hourly), $3.00 for every three tests passed (FR), $3.00 at an intermittent rate (VR), or varying payoffs at an intermittent rate (VR-VA). Each subject worked for one week under each schedule of reinforcement. The dependent measures were performance, which was related to test-taking behavior (number of tests taken, number of tests passed, percent correct, time taken, and earnings) and job satisfaction as measured by the MSQ (short form) and a rating of the degree to which each pay system made the job more desirable.

Results indicate that performance quantity was lowest under the hourly schedule, the FR and VR and VR-VA (most tests passed) schedules produced higher performance, VR-VA was not significantly higher than FR or VR. Performance quality (percent correct) measures showed, however, that hourly schedules were just as high as the other three. Satisfaction tended, by the end of the week, to be highest under FR and lowest under hourly. The most important issue raised by this research is whether a VR-VA schedule will produce better performance than a classical FR schedule. The results show a large absolute difference, but the lack of a statistical difference argues against the reliability of the findings.

Shaw, Jerry I., "Response-Contingent Payoffs and Cooperative Behavior in the Prisoner's Dilemma Game," *Journal of Personality and Social Psychology*, November 1976, Vol. 34, No. 5, 1024–1033.

This study compares the effect on cooperative behavior of two response-contingent payoff structures with the invariant payoff structure of the Prisoner's Dilemma (PD) game. One hundred male dyads (students) played a 20-trial PD game that either rewarded joint cooperation by increased profits, punished joint competition, or left payoffs constant. Half of the pairs played for real money and half for points. Although punishment led to higher cooperation than either reward or constant payoffs, players perceived themselves as more cooperative under the reward contingency. A pattern of findings supported the interpretation that a predisposition to compete leads to earlier exposure to and superior learning of the punishment contingency. It is suggested that while this facilitates cooperative behavior, it may undermine cooperative motivation. Finally, real-money payoffs significantly increased both interdyad variability and interdyad uniformity in cooperative behavior. This effect of reward size on response variation is viewed as a threat to the external validity of conflict studies that have used only trivial rewards.

Yukl, G. A.; Latham, G. P. and Pursell, E. D., "The Effectiveness of Performance Incentives Under Continuous and Variable Schedules of Reinforcement," *Personnel Psychology*, Summer 1976, Vol. 29, No. 2, 221–231.

The present study attempted to compare the relative effectiveness of pay incentives on productivity using different reinforcement schedules and to investigate worker preferences for the different incentive plans. The subjects were male and female (N = 28) tree planters employed by a paper product company in North Carolina. The experimenters examined the effects of four incentive conditions ($2 continuous reinforcement, $8-VR4, $4-VR2 and no-incentive) on work performance. Manipulation of the incentive system was accomplished by making monetary bonuses contingent upon planting a specified number of trees and, in periods of variable reinforcement, correctly guessing the color of a marble. Productivity was defined as the number of trees planted by each worker per manhour.

Results showed that performance was higher in the CRF condition than in either the no-incentive preference for the different pay plans. Conclusions drawn from the results are limited to the group under study. However, it appears that a variable ratio schedule is less effective for improving performance than a continuous reinforcement schedule. Comparing these results with those on college students in Yukl et. al., (1972), the authors suggest that response rates under variable ratio schedules may in part be a function of education and cultural background.

Berger, Chris, J., "Reliability and Validity of Expectancy Theory Constructs," *Academy of Management Proceedings,* 1976, 74–78.

Fifteen female subjects were randomly assigned to three magnitude and schedule of reinforcement conditions (25¢ continuous; 25¢ VR-2; 50¢ VR-2) and worked on a data coding task for five days under these schedules. Five expectancy theory constructs were measured at several times during the experiment. Test-retest reliability estimates were generally significant and of moderate magnitude. Performance-reward probability estimates showed considerable convergence with the objective values prescribed by the particular schedule of reinforcement.

Deslauries, Brian C. and Everett, Peter **B.**, "Effects of Intermittent and Continuous Token Reinforcement of Bus Ridership," *Journal of Applied Psychology,* August 1977, Vol. 62, No. 4, 369–375.

The following conditions were successively instituted on the Experimental Bus (the 11:00 a.m. to 2:00 p.m. daily operation of a campus bus): baseline, Variable Ratio 3 token reinforcement (every third passenger, on the average, received a token with about 10¢ for boarding the bus), continuous token reinforcement (every passenger received a token). Compared to the experimental controls, Experimental Bus ridership increased significantly during the token reinforcement manipulations. There was no difference in the effects of VR3 and continuous token reinforcement. The results suggest that compared to continuous token reinforcement, intermittent reinforcement may provide a viable and economical approach to increasing bus ridership.

Komaki, Judy; Waddell, William M. and Pearce, M. George, "The Applied Behavior Analysis Approach and Individual Employees: Improving Performance in Two Small Businesses," *Organizational Behavior and Human Performance,* August 1977, Vol. 19, No. 2, 337–352.

Strategies and techniques of the applied behavior analysis approach were used to improve the performance of individual employees in two small businesses, a neighborhood grocery store and a downtown game room. In Experiment I, several potentially reinforcing consequences (time off with pay, feedback, self-recording) were arranged for desired performance and desired tasks were clarified (i.e., being within proximity of counters, assisting customers, and restocking shelves). A multiple-baseline design across behaviors was employed. The mean performance level of the three behaviors was employed. The mean performance level of the three behaviors improved from. 53, 35 and 57 percent to 86, 87 and 86 percent, respectively.

In Experiment II, a reversal design (ABAB) was used. Performance (i.e., being within proximity of the counter when a customer is present, fixing game machines, cleaning the premises) increased from baseline means of 62 and 63 percent to 93 and 97 percent, respectively, following the introduction of a goal-classification and contingent pay system (i.e., target cleaning behaviors were placed at the counter and take-home pay corresponded to the percentage of cleaning duties completed). The two studies indicate the potential of the behavior analysis approach for improving performance-providing consequences that have the effect of increasing specified work behaviors.

Behling, O. C. and McNaul, J., "A Functional Examination of Repetitive Choice Behavior Under Conditions of Non-Binary Positive Outcomes," Research project proposal, College of Administrative Science, Ohio State University, begun June 1974.

This study is a laboratory test of the effects of nonbinary positive outcomes on subject choice behavior in competitive and noncompetitive situations. The purpose of this study is to provide additional bases for the understanding of consumer brand choice and individual work motivation and performance as well as provide possible direction for more accurate and comprehensive models for repetitive decision making.

Scott, W. E., Jr. and Cherrington, D. J., "The Effects of Competitive, Cooperative, and Individualistic Reinforcement Contingencies," Graduate School of Business, Indiana University, Bloomington, Indiana, unpublished paper.

Ss who were told that they were in competitive contingency produced more and reported higher levels of arousal and less interpersonal attraction than Ss who were told they were in cooperative or individualistic contingencies. Those who were rewarded in the various conditions reported higher levels of interpersonal attraction and task attractiveness, but there was little evidence of a differential effect as postulated by Pettigrew. It was concluded that the behavioral effects of cooperative and competitive conditions will depend upon the reinforcement contingencies in effect.

Fisher, C. D., "The Effects of Personal Control, Competence, and Extrinsic Reward Systems on Intrinsic Motivation," *Organizational Behavior and Human Performance*, 1978, Vol. 21, No. 3, 273–288.

A review of the literature revealed that the effects of personal control on intrinsic motivation had not been directly investigated, that the interaction of competence and personal control had not been investigated, and that studies comparing the effects of contingent versus noncontingent reward systems on intrinsic motivation had produced conflicting results and conclusions. An experimental simulation was conducted using a 2 × 2 design in which levels of payment (contingent and noncontingent) were crossed with levels of personal control over performance (constrained and unconstrained). Cell sizes varied from 16 to 26. It was found that personal control over performance was a very important determinant of intrinsic motivation but that the type of reward system did not affect intrinsic motivation.

Latham, Gary P. and Dossett, Dennis L., "Designing Incentive Plans for Unionized Employees: A Comparison of Continuous and Variable Ratio Reinforcement Schedules," *Personnel Psychology*, 1978, Vol. 31, 47.

The relative effectiveness of incentive plans administered on continuous and VR-4 schedules of reinforcement was investigated with unionized employees using a within subjects design. Mountain beaver trappers working side by side were randomly assigned to one of two groups. In group A, the trappers received $1.00 for every rat they trapped. At the end of four weeks, they were switched to a VR-4 schedule in which they received $4.00 contingent upon trapping a rat and correctly guessing the color of one of four marbles prior to drawing it from a bag held by the supervisor. In group B, the order of the schedules was reversed. The results were analyzed in terms of cost-related, behavioral, and reaction criteria. The study increased employee productivity and decreased costs for the company. Inexperienced workers had higher productivity on the continuous reinforcement than on the VR-4 schedule; experienced workers had higher productivity on the VR-4 schedule than on the continuous schedule. Both the experienced and the inexperienced employees preferred the VR-4 schedule over the continuous schedule.

Runnion, Alex; Johnson, Twila and McWhorter, John, "The Effects of Feedback and Reinforcement on Truck Turnaround Time in Materials Transportation," *Journal of Organizational Behavior Management*, 1978, Vol. 1, 110–117.

The length of time which trucks spent at each mill while transporting goods between 58 plant locations of a textile company was reduced with the introduction of a feedback plus reinforcement system. The average truck turnaround time was reduced from a baseline average of 67 minutes to an average of 38.2 minutes. This level was maintained even though the frequency of feedback was reduced substantially. The project demonstrated the use of periodic feedback to improve and maintain improved performance of workers across many locations in a large textile company.

Stephens, Tedd A. and Burroughs, Wayne A., "An Application of Operant Conditioning to Absenteeism in a Hospital Setting," *Journal of Applied Psychology*, 1978, Vol. 63, No. 4, 518–521.

Two financial reward systems were used in a hospital setting to reduce absenteeism among 92 nurses, ward clerks, and nursing assistants. Six nursing units were randomly assigned to one of the two reward systems. System A permitted subjects to become eligible for cash prize drawings of $20 if they evidenced no absenteeism during a three-week period. System B allowed subjects to become eligible for $20 prize drawings if they were not absent on eight dates randomly selected from the three-week period. An analysis of variance with a repeated measures design was used to assess differences between the two reward systems. Both reward systems resulted in significant decreases in absenteeism, and no significant differences were obtained between the two systems. Also, point-biserial correlations relating income level and absenteeism yielded nonsignificant results.

INTEGRATIVE

Lefcourt, H. M., "Internal Versus External Control of Reinforcement," *Psychological Bulletin*, 1966, Vol. 65, No. 4, 206–220.

A summary of research concerning the internal vs. external control of reinforcement construct is presented. Investigations of this variable have utilized situational manipulations of locus of control or have involved differential predictions to given situations based on measures of the internal-external control dimension. In both types of investigation, locus of control is found predictive of different social behaviors, learning performances, and achievement-related activities. Suggestions for further areas of study are presented.

Locke, Edwin A., "The Myths of Behavior Modification in Organizations," *Academy of Management Review*, October 1977, Vol. 2, No. 4, 543–551.

The author asserts that the behavioristic model is not useful or valid as applied to industrial-organizational settings for improving employees' skills and motivation. In the process of examining the four categories where behavior modification principles have been represented in practice (programmed instruction, modeling, performance standards with feedback, and monetary incentives), the author provides alternative explanations and corroborative studies to support his contentions—"behavior mod" applications do not rest on behavioralist premises, but are interpretable through the employee's consciousness or mental processes and that the actual behavioral techniques used to "reinforce" are no different than the rewards and incentives used by nonbehavioralist practitioners.

Behling, O. C. and Starke, F., "Alternatives to Expectancy Theories of Work Motivation," Ohio State University, working paper.

The authors trace the development, elaboration, and modification of expectancy theory as an explanation of work effort, and examine the theory's underlying core and current arguments concerning its internal and external validity. They note that criticisms of the expectancy approach are sufficiently sound to warrant the examination of alternatives, and present and classify several possibilities found in the literature.

Nord, W., "The Fault Dear Brutus Lies Not in Ourselves but in Our Contingencies: The Application of Exchange Theory to Rehabilitation and the Disadvantaged," Graduate School of Business Administration, Washington University, St. Louis, Missouri, unpublished paper.

The purpose of this paper is to explore the potential of social-exchange theory as a conceptual framework for rehabilitation and training of the disadvantaged. The first part of the paper describes the social-exchange theory as a guide to rehabilitation policy, the purpose being to introduce the basic model, to suggest some of its limitations, and to discuss some of its general implications for rehabilitation. Part II discusses how the basis of the model, operant conditioning, has provided a basis for treatment of behavioral deficits and dysfunctional behavior. The final section attempts to extend the model to discover and highlight implications for dealing with the disadvantaged. It appears that social-exchange theory may provide the type of conceptual tool which facilitates simultaneous treatment of the micro and macro variables. A brief look at the model itself will reveal these possibilities.

Fisher, C. D., "The Effects of Personal Control, Competence, and Extrinsic Reward Systems on Intrinsic Motivation," *Organizational Behavior and Human Performance*, 1978, Vol. 21, No. 3, 273–288.

A review of the literature revealed that the effects of personal control on intrinsic motivation had not been directly investigated, that the interaction of competence and personal control had not been investigated, and that studies comparing the effects of contingent versus noncontingent reward systems on intrinsic motivation had produced conflicting results and conclusions. An experimental simulation was conducted using a 2×2 design in which levels of payment (contingent and noncontingent) were crossed with levels of personal control over performance (constrained and unconstrained). Cell sizes varied from 16 to 26. It was found that personal control over performance was a very important determinant of intrinsic motivation but that the type of reward system did not affect intrinsic motivation.

PRESCRIPTIVE

Grant, Philip C., "A Model for Employee Motivation and Satisfaction," *Personnel*, September–October 1969, 51–57.

The comprehensive model presented here suggests avenues management might pursue in its attempts to increase the efforts of employees toward achieving organizational goals. The author suggests that employees will be motivated to work harder to achieve organizational goals only as long as the rewards from the increased effort outweigh the costs. The conceptualization of the model captures the work of Maslow, Skinner, Barnard, and Vroom in an integrated theory and differentiates between effort and cost which other models of motivation have not done. Also, the model fuses motivation theory with decision theory and it establishes a link between motivation theory with the individual as the unit of analysis and organization theory with the group as the unit of analysis. The author illustrates results obtained (Figure 3) in considering multiple goal systems, suggesting that management needs to consider effects of competing off-the-job goal systems when motivating an employee toward company goals. Employees must perceive they will achieve higher satisfaction at a higher effort level, and at a cost (fatigue, stress, etc.) that is bearable to them. Therefore, rewards must clearly be contingent upon effort and the cost to an employee must be at a slower rate than the increase in reward.

Beatty, R. and Schneier, C. E., "Training the Hard Core Unemployed Through Positive Reinforcement," *Human Resource Management,* Winter 1972, Vol. 11, No. 4, 11–17.

Operant conditioning is particularly suited for training hard-core unemployed trainees for entry-level positions because these tasks can be broken into their component behaviors and isolated. Thus, trainees can learn component behaviors in the shaping process at their own pace. Trainees are not punished for educational or skill deficiencies, but positively reinforced for specific, observable, quantifiable behaviors and given good "models" of working behavior by supervisors, which is not always the case in the HCU (hard-core unemployed) environment. Operant conditioning principles suggest that positive behavior should be isolated, and rewarded when it is evidenced. Undesirable behavior should go unrewarded or unreinforced.

The model proposed here advances in three distinct stages. The first level is used for formal training off-the-job to "shape" the desired behavior that will be needed for a particular task. The second stage is used for on-the-job training to enable the trainee to experience positive reinforcement on a variable ratio schedule. The third stage consists of complete job performance in which the trainee generalizes the behavior learned to the actual job setting, reinforced by praise and regular wages per hour. Management can also use the operant techniques to reinforce behaviors other than the learning of job skills. These may include punctuality, speed, accuracy, initiative, and the learning of new skills other than the ones directly needed in a present job.

Luthans, Fred, "The Contingency Theory of Management," *Business Horizons,* June 1973, Vol. 16, No. 3, 67–72.

Management theory has taken divergent paths in recent years. The author discusses each of these as well as the movement to unify existing schools of thought. The process approach, traditional and classical, has been supplanted by the quantitative, the behavioral, and the systems approaches. The author defines these and explains their role in management theory and their function in actual practice. Certainly, none of these theories can be applied to every organization and management problem, and currently a theory is emerging that can be used to draw the disparate elements together. This new approach is the contingency theory of management, which can be applied situationally.

Kesselman, G. A.; Hagen, E. L. and Wherry, R. J. Sr., "A Factor Analytic Test of the Porter-Lawler Expectancy Model of Work Motivation," *Personnel Psychology*, Winter 1974, Vol. 27, 569–579.

This study attempts to measure a few key variables associated with the Porter-Lawler (1968) Expectancy model in order to determine its validity. Ss were 76 female telephone operators from a Midwestern telephone company. Ss completed a questionnaire which measured: job satisfaction, effort expended on the job, quality of job performance, productivity on the job, instrumental relationships between behavior and pay. The results of this study clearly support the general P-L Expectancy Model theory and the linkages predicted from the theory.

Beatty, R. W. and Schneier, C. E., "A Case for Positive Reinforcement," *Business Horizons*, April 1975, Vol. 18, No. 2, 57–66.

A case is presented for positive reinforcement as a remedy for poor job performance. Positive reinforcement places emphasis on the desired job behavior that leads to job outcomes or results, rather than results alone; on providing direct links between job behavior and rewards; and on the use of positive reinforcement, rather than punishment or the threat of punishment. The authors discuss the best known positive reinforcement model in an organization—Emery Air Freight—and its success with immediate feedback to employees. The motivational assumptions and problems of positive reinforcement are also discussed. It is concluded that the most advantageous aspect of the positive reinforcement system is its compatibility with other job performance remedies, job enrichment and management by objectives, as well as with present personnel practices.

Rand, Thomas M., "Diagnosing the Valued Reward Orientations of Employees," *Personnel Journal*, September 1977, Vol. 56, No. 9, 451–464.

The author relates that reward systems, to increase levels of job effectiveness and employee satisfaction, must contain the following five elements: 1) the magnitude of rewards must satisfy the basic human need of survival and security; 2) organizations must choose relevant rewards over which they have the potential ability to provide and manipulate; 3) distribution of rewards must be perceived as being equitable; 4) members must perceive contingency between performance and reward; and 5) the reward must be valued by the individual.

Results taken on the JDI from 100 managers, drawn from widely diverse organizational settings, indicate an erroneous assumption concerning hourly employees' reward preferences. They emphasize extrinsic rewards such as pay and security while workers are more interested in growth opportunities, sense of accomplishment (intrinsic) instead (comparison with hourly workers reward preferences on JDI). The author believes that strategies to design work environments which provide individually valued rewards should be explored in addition to contingently granting extrinsic rewards for acceptable job performance to experience achievement.

Nord, W., "The Fault Dear Brutus Lies Not in Ourselves but in Our Contingencies: The Application of Exchange Theory to Rehabilitation and the Disadvantaged," Graduate School of Business Administration, Washington University, St. Louis, Missouri, unpublished paper.

The purpose of this paper is to explore the potential of social-exchange theory as a conceptual framework for rehabilitation and training of the disadvantaged. The first part of the paper describes the social-exchange theory as a guide to rehabilitation policy, the purpose being to introduce the basic model, to suggest some of its limitations, and to discuss some of its general implications for rehabilitation. Part II discusses how the basis of the model, operant conditioning, has provided a basis for treatment of behavioral deficits and dysfunctional behavior. The final section attempts to extend the model to discover and highlight implications for dealing with the disadvantaged. It appears that social-exchange theory may provide the type of conceptual tool which facilitates simultaneous treatment of the micro and macro variables. A brief look at the model itself will reveal these possibilities.

Porter. L. W., "Role of the Organization in Motivation: Structuring Rewarding Environments," University of California, Graduate School of Business, Irvine, California, unpublished paper.

The theme of this paper is that, in the future, organizations can and should assume a more vigorous and imaginative role in contributing to employee motivation than they have in the past. It is expected that organizations can do this in such a way that will contribute to making the work situation both more rewarding and satisfying for individual employees as well as more of an aid in organizational goal attainment. The mechanism proposed is the active structuring of reward environments, and it is based on the twin assumptions that: 1) the behavior of individuals is modifiable, and 2) the work environment is modifiable. The possibilities and problems of utilizing rewards more creatively are illustrated in this paper by an intensive analysis of the motivational situation for marginal members of the work force, since this group currently represents complex motivational challenges for the organization. The analysis is then extended to "regular" or nonmarginal employees. The paper concludes with several speculations about possible long-range implications beyond the 1970s.

White, Donald D. and Davis, Bill, "Behavioral Contingency Management: A Bottom-Line Alternative for Management Development,"
Personnel Admistrator, April 1980, Vol. 25, No. 4, 67–75.

The main focus of management development involves holding down
costs and increasing productivity. Current methods of management development, however, often fail to reach this aim, but simply swamp the
manager with a barrage of "vague theories by the experts," rather than
specific programs and techniques. Behavior contingency management
(BCM) provides a new and effective way to achieve these main focuses.
Long used in various institutions, BCM is an outgrowth of operant conditioning, behavior modification and programs of positive reinforcement. BCM provides a results-oriented alternative to the motivation and
leadership orientations that characterize most management development programs. It emphasizes critical activities and behaviors that lead
directly to desired outputs. The five steps of BCM are: 1) identification
of performance-related events; 2) measurement of behavior; 3) functional analysis of the behavior; 4) development and implementation of
an appropriate strategy, and 5) measurement of the impact of BCM. The
actual workings of BCM are then evaluated through a study of a BCM
program at a 300-bed hospital. Use of this method of management resulted in both cost cuts and increases in productivity.

THEORETICAL

Luthans, Fred, "The Contingency Theory of Management," *Business Horizons*, June 1973, Vol. 16, No. 3, 67–72.

Management theory has taken divergent paths in recent years. The author discusses each of these as well as the movement to unify existing
schools of thought. The process approach, traditional and classical, has
been supplanted by the quantitative, the behavioral, and the systems
approaches. The author defines these and explains their role in management theory and their function in actual practice. Certainly, none of
these theories can be applied to every organization and management
problem, and currently a theory is emerging that can be used to draw
the disparate elements together. This new approach is the contingency
theory of management, which can be applied situationally.

Behling, O. C. and Frederick A. Starke, "The Postulates of Expectancy
Theory," *Academy of Management Journal*, 1973, Vol. 16, No. 3,
373–388.

This article reviews the basic expectancy formulation of work effort theory and touches briefly on some elaboration of it. The authors point out
that both the basic and elaborated versions rest on certain assumptions
which they state explicitly. Empirical evidence from general decision

theory literature is presented which indicates that these assumptions are not defensible. The implications for work effort theory are examined.

Mawhinney, Thomas C. and Behling, Orlando, "Differences in Predictions of Work Behavior from Expectancy and Operant Models of Individual Motivation," *Academy of Management Proceedings,* 1973, 383–389.

The cognitive expectancy model (Vroom) and acognitive operant model (Skinner) represent alternative explanations of motivations. While the models follow from polar opposite assumptions regarding cognition, the focus of this paper is upon the divergent predictions which logically follow from the models in equivalent circumstances. A review of the terms, concepts, and functional relationships between variables provides the foundation upon which to examine in detail the source of differing predictions from the models. One case of agreement in prediction provides a baseline against which divergences may be compared.

Divergences take the following forms: 1) lower and higher rates of behavior from baseline for the operant and expectancy models respectively in one case, 2) longer and shorter lasting effects in one case, 3) equal and different rates of adjustment in another, and 4) different and equal rates of choice (preference) in the final case. The requirements of research to determine the relative accuracy of each model for alternative cases of divergence are outlined and a comparative analysis recommended.

Berger, Chris J., "Reliability and Validity of Expectancy Theory Constructs," *Academy of Management Proceedings,* 1976, 74–78.

Fifteen female subjects were randomly assigned to three magnitude and schedule of reinforcement conditions (25¢ continuous; 25¢ VR-2; 50¢ VR-2) and worked on a data coding task for five days under these schedules. Five expectancy theory constructs were measured at several times during the experiment. Test-retest reliability estimates were generally significant and of moderate magnitude. Performance-reward probability estimates showed considerable convergence with the objective values prescribed by the particular schedule of reinforcement.

Locke, Edwin A., "The Myths of Behavior Modification in Organizations," *Academy of Management Review,* October 1977, Vol. 2, No. 4, 543–551.

The author asserts that the behavioristic model is not useful or valid as applied to industrial-organizational settings for improving employees' skills and motivation. In the process of examining the four categories where behavior modification principles have been represented in practice (programmed instruction, modeling, performance standards with feedback, and monetary incentives), the author provides alternative explanations and corroborative studies to support his contentions—"behavior mod" applications do not rest on behavioralist premises, but are interpretable through the employee's consciousness or mental processes and that the actual behavioral techniques used to "reinforce" are not different than the rewards and incentives used by nonbehavioralist practitioners.

Commentary

SCHEDULES AND EXPECTANCIES

Applied Behavior Analysis and Behavior Modification Approach

Several studies have demonstrated the application of behavioral modification principles utilizing positive reinforcement to attain top performance. For example, behavior modification has been used in a study of hard-core unemployed to provide a supervision-trainer model of good work behavior and positive reinforcement in the form of points and praise (Schneier, 1973). It was found this method was a workable solution to motivational problems in this difficult environment.

Management can also use operant techniques to reinforce a wide array of behaviors—e.g., punctuality, speed, accuracy, initiative, and learning of new skills. Social-exchange theory in conjunction with behavioral modification techniques has been used as a framework to rehabilitate and train the disadvantaged. Furthermore, the basis for the model—operant conditioning—provides a unique tool for the treatment of behavioral deficits and dysfunctional behavior (Nord, unpublished paper, Washington University).

In two illustrative experiments, the applied behavior analysis approach was found to have potentially reinforcing consequences and shows real promise for improving performance (Komaki, Waddell & Pearce, 1977). In these studies time off with pay, feedback, and self reporting were consequences used to obtain desired performance and complete desired tasks.

In another study (Rand, 1977), valued rewards of employees were found to be growth opportunities and a sense of accomplishment (intrinsic values). In this study it was found that a) valued rewards must fulfill basic survival and security needs, b) organizations must choose rewards they can provide and manipulate, c) equitable distribution is essential, d) employees must perceive a performance-reward relationship, and e) rewards offered must be valued by the individual.

A contrary perspective is provided by Locke (1977) who asserts that the behavioristic models are of limited usefulness in the industrial organizational setting for improving skills and motivation and that the behavior modification principles (programmed instruction, modeling, performance standards with feedback, and monetary incentives) are only interpretable through employees' consciousness or mental processes and are not fundamentally different than rewards and incentives used by nonbehavioralist practitioners.

Scheduling Strategies

In a study of factors affecting job choice and time spent on a task, it was found that only unequal intervals of reward magnitude affected task choice—the higher the rewards, the greater the time spent on the lower paying task. Fixed interval schedules produced a small amount of time on lower paying tasks regardless of reward magnitude. Results seem to indicate rewards and penalties when applied to opposing tasks in a concurrent setting have similar effects on patterns of task choice (Schmitt, 1970). An experiment relating performance and schedules shows that performance was lowest under a straight hourly schedule and highest under varying rates of pay and schedules. The lack of a statistically significant difference, however, questions the reliability of findings from this experiment (Pritchard, Leonard, Von Bergen & Kirk, 1976).

In further research on continuous versus variable schedules of reinforcement (Yukl, Latham, Pursell, 1976), results indicate a continuous schedule of reinforcement is more effective for improving performance. Similar findings obtained in a study by Berger (1976) and another study of bus ridership (Deslauries and Everett, 1977) tend to confirm this finding. It is important to note that both continuous and intermittent schedules tend to produce greater performance than noncontingent reinforcement.

The Need for Guiding Frameworks

Expectancy theory and operant conditioning principles appear to be the most fruitful frameworks for guiding the application of reinforcement schedules. While these two approaches differ in their emphasis on cognitive processes, they are essentially similar in recommending that any reinforcement approach to increasing productivity apply the following principles:

1. Identify those rewards that employees find most desirable.

2. Bring these rewards under the control of the organization.

3. Administer these rewards on the basis of performance differences among individuals or groups.

4. Attempt to remove all obstacles that would block the conversion of effort into productive outcomes.

There is ample evidence that the application of these principles will enhance performance.

TASK DESIGN

Type of Article	No. of Articles
Applied	5
Descriptive	6
Empirical	23
Integrative	10
Prescriptive	14
Theoretical	4

APPLIED

Sorcher, M. and Meyer, H. H., "Motivation and Job Performance," *Personnel Administration*, July-August 1968, Vol. 31, No. 4, 8–21.

This article deals with the dilemma of whether or not the direct labor employee can be motivated to become more involved in his work. The most common way of designing factory jobs has always been to simplify them. The object is to permit the hiring of minimally qualified employees at lower rates. However, simplification brought disadvantages along with its hoped-for advantages: it brought boredom, meaninglessness; it removed challenge and a sense of individual commitment. Simplification carried to its limits does damage to the worker's self-esteem and motivation, also increases rather than decreases poor work quality. It is now the point of view that the task of industry is to engage the employee in a more meaningful role. Some methods to achieve this end were presented: the use of goals, the encouragement of employee participation in goal-setting, and provision of more than minimum training for assembly line tasks. Productive motivation can be improved also by broadening the worker's responsibility, by reducing repetitiveness, and by introducing variety in the work. The author concludes by saying that, in the design of jobs, attention should be given not merely to the prescribed tasks to be performed, but also to those factors which enhance the self-esteem and thus heighten the motivation of the worker.

Gomez, L. R. and Mussio, S. J., "An Application of Job Enrichment in A Civil Service Setting: A Demonstration Study," *Public Personnel Management*, January-February 1975, Vol. 4, No. 1, 49–54.

This study took place in a civil service setting and was designed to empirically evaluate the effects of JE. Ss were eight females performing clerical tasks, ages ranging from 21 to 60, with average educational background of 12 years, three months. It was hypothesized that by reorganizing the clerks' tasks into a meaningful module of work, increasing their responsibility and recognition, and providing them with an opportunity for advancement, would have the following effects on these three dependent variables: increasing job satisfaction, improve work performance, and decrease absenteeism. Data was collected to measure these dependent variables by means of a questionnaire, a critical incident method, and personnel records, respectively. The next step was to lay out a series of changes in the clerk's job within a JE framework. Implementation of the changes was gradual and included training sessions. Measurement was taken periodically and records kept of progress.

Experimental results were obtained by comparing pretest-post test means scores. Both job satisfaction and work performance increased while the rate of absenteeism decreased. This study is important due to its empirical basis on which it evaluated the effects of JE. However, due to a small sample size, it cannot be known whether or not these findings can be generalized to other situations.

Peterson, Richard O., "Human Resources Development Through Work Design," *Training and Development Journal*, August 1976, Vol. 30, No. 8, 3–7.

A work design strategy is offered as a means of utilizing human resources more fully. The strategy has three fundamental phases: diagnosis of work and organizational design (obtaining data on work and organizational processes and individuals); redesigning work, organizational structure, and support systems (i.e., standards, administrative levels, and performance evaluation); and trying out, evaluating, implementing, and tracking. The efficacy of the work design strategy should be based on the achievement of all objectives of organizational performance: quality, efficiency, societal impact, and employee impact.

Gallegos, Robert C. and Phelan, Joseph G., "Effects on Productivity and Morale of a System-Designed Job-Enrichment Program in Pacific Telephone," *Psychological Reports*, February 1977, Vol. 40, No. 1, 283–290.

In the experiments over a 14-month period, 56 maintenance mechanics (framemen) served as experimental (N = 21) and control (N = 35) groups. Framemen carried work responsibilities on large "frames"—serving the larger business communities. Quantity aspect of the work consisted of 24-hour, day-to-day connection of wires to complete new, rearranged, or disconnected circuits. The quality aspect could be measured by number of customer complaints which could be directly traced to inefficient or careless work on the frames. For the experimental group only, all jobs were "systems analyzed". Analyses were carried out and job enlargement (horizontal leadings) and job enrichment (vertical leadings) were implemented. Feedback was provided on productivity of individuals. "Hawthorne effects" and fluctuations of effort due to subtle types of supervisor-employee interaction were controlled by alternating supervisors and other environmental controls. Job satisfaction of each group was measured by the JDI before and after each experiment.

Following introduction of job enrichment programs for experimental groups and measured before and after and during a 14-month period, significant improvement in quantity and quality occurred and was maintained after termination of experiments. Expressed job satisfaction was average or slightly below on the JDI for all workers. Despite improvements in productivity, there were no significant differences in expressed job satisfaction.

Gyllenhammar, Pehr G., "How Volvo Adapts Work to People," *Harvard Business Review*, July-August 1977, Vol. 55, No. 4, 102–113.

Work design changes in an automobile plant were reported to have positive effects for both employee satisfaction and productivity. Assembly-line production was transformed into an individual controlled carrier system. Subgroups, responsible for a particular portion of the car, were formed. Group members were given the opportunity to learn and perform various jobs (rotation), do their own group inspections and receive feedback information about quality. Also, incentive payments were shifted from an individual to a group basis.

The author emphasizes that technical changes should help improve worker satisfaction through greater opportunity for social contact and participation in the production process as well as enriched work conditions.

DESCRIPTIVE

Collins, D. C. and Raubolt, R. R., "A Study of Employee Resistance to Job Enrichment," *Personnel Journal*, April 1975, Vol. 54, No. 4, 232–248.

The association between employee background and occupational characteristics and degree of resistance to a job enrichment program was examined in a large-scale manufacturing firm. Education is the most important determinant of degree of resistance. Employees with a college degree were found to be less resistant to job enrichment than were employees without a degree. Other important determinants: age and kind of task performed revealed that more youthful employees are nonresistant than are older employees, and more employees performing similar tasks are nonresistant than are employees performing general tasks. The study also revealed other characteristics associated with resistance to job enrichment such as the number of years to retirement.

Umstot, Denis, D., "MBO and Job Enrichment: How to Have Your Cake and Eat it Too," *Management Review*, February 1977, Vol. 66, No. 2, 21–26.

The author attempted to test the effects of job enrichment and goal setting on satisfaction and productivity. An organization, composed of 42 temporary part-time employees, was created for research purposes. The employees performed zoning coding tasks for the county. The first phase of the experiment tested four conditions using four separate groups; a group with enriched job, a group with assigned specific goals, a group with both enrichment and goals and a group with neither enrichment nor goals. Employees' perceptions of whether their jobs were enriched or unenriched were verified by use of the JDS (Hackman and Oldham, 1975). Goals were established by supervisors alone and based on past productivity levels (the article did not provide information on how the variables were operationalized).

The results of this first phase confirmed the author's prediction that goal-setting increased productivity, but appeared, in addition, to enrich jobs and improve work satisfaction. Job enrichment, on the other hand, had no effect on productivity and only a weak effect on satisfaction. The author suggests that a job design combining both job enrichment and goal setting should improve both productivity and satisfaction.

Dunham, Randall, B., "Reactions to Job Characteristics: Moderating Effects of the Organization," *Academy of Management Journal*, March 1977, Vol. 20, No. 1, 42–65.

This study attempted to examine worker responses to task design from different functional speciality groups within an organization to determine if nontask environmental blocks are present and moderating task-design response relationships. There were 784 executives of a large retail merchandising corporation from eight functional specialty groups that were administered questionnaires. The questionnaire included 15 items from the JDS to measure perceived task variety, task identity, task significance, autonomy, and feedback from the job. A set of job satisfaction scales (IOR) were used to measure various aspects of satisfaction with the work, supervision, pay and company was included. Four subset scales were developed to measure different aspects of Perceived Environmental Characteristics: Climate scales, Managerial Style scales, a Work Assignment scale and a Career Description scale. Finally, demographic information was obtained through self-report. Canonical analysis established a significant relationship between task design and effective response measures. Functional specialty moderated the relationship. It was suggested that the moderating effect may be explained in terms of environmental elements which caused the worker to focus on or off task design.

Umstot, D. D., Mitchell, T. R. and Bell, C. H., "Goal-Setting and Job Enrichment: An Integrated Approach to Job Design," *Academy of Management Review*, 1978, Vol. 3, No. 4, 867–879.

This article reviews the empirical literature relating task goals and job enrichment to performance outcomes. The interaction of job characteristics, individual differences, and organizational characteristics is also reviewed and an integrated model presented that explains the relationships. The authors point out that available research suggests that most of the interactive effects of goal-setting and job enrichment are positive and job design should, therefore, integrate these techniques. Combining job enrichment and goal-setting should improve job satisfaction and productivity, two dominant concerns of managers which have often been viewed as incompatible.

Hackman, J. Richard; Pearce, Jone L. and Wolfe, Jane Caminis, "Effects of Changes in Job Characteristics on Work Attitudes and Behaviors: A Naturally Occurring Quasi-Experiment," *Organizational Behavior and Human Performance*, 1978, Vol. 21, 289–304.

The effects of changes in the motivational properties of jobs on work attitudes and behaviors were assessed in a quasi-experimental design. A number of clerical jobs in a metropolitan bank were redesigned because of a technological innovation. Changes were made without regard for the motivational characteristics of the jobs, and without cognizance by bank personnel that there might be motivational consequences of the changes. Some jobs were made more complex and challenging, some less so, and the motivational properties of still others were essentially unaffected. Measures of job characteristics, employee attitudes, and work behaviors were collected before and after the changes. Results showed that general satisfaction, growth satisfaction, and internal motivation were affected by changes in job characteristics. Satisfaction with the work context was not affected. Effects of the changes on absenteeism and performance depended on the strength of employee growth needs, which also tended to moderate attitudinal reactions to the changes. Contrary to expectation, employee growth needs themselves were not affected by the altered motivational characteristics of the jobs.

Kabanoff, Boris and O'Brien, Gordon E., "The Effects of Task Type and Cooperation Upon Group Products and Performance," *Organizational Behavior and Human Performance*, 1979, Vol. 23, 163–181.

Twenty-four three-person groups each performed three types of intellective tasks—production, discussion, and problem-solving—while employing one of four work organizations. Organizations differed in amount of two forms of cooperation—coordination and collaboration. Group products were rated on six descriptive dimensions (action orientation, optimism, length, issue involvement, originality, and quality of presentation) and on three performance dimensions (adequacy, quality, and creativity). Task type had the largest effect on the descriptive dimensions, accounting for up to 50 percent of the variance, but had little effect on the evaluative dimensions. Group structure accounted for 22 to 36 percent of the variance in both descriptive and evaluative measures. The major effect of the structural variables was on product length, but a MANOVA analysis showed that group structure affected the group performance measures even when product length was controlled for. There were a number of significant interactions between group structure and task type, though these accounted for little of the variance in group performance. Collaborative structures resulted in the lowest productivity, with discussion tasks the worst performed under collaborative structures. Coordinated and co-acting groups were not significantly different in productivity levels. The results were discussed in relation to the task typology employed and implications for research dealing with small group performance.

EMPIRICAL

Naylor, J.C.; Briggs, G. E. and Reed, W. G., "Task Coherence, Training Time, and Retention Interval Effects on Skill Retention," *Journal of Applied Psychology*, October 1968, Vol. 52, No. 5, 386–393.

Amount of training, secondary task coherence, and length of retention interval, each at two levels, were evaluated in terms of long-term skill retention effects. The criterion task was composed of a three-dimensional tracking task (primary task) and a nine-event monitoring task (secondary task). Retention loss varied inversely with the amount of training and with secondary task coherence (the latter only under the lesser amount of training) for both tasks. Absolute retention levels varied directly with the training and task coherence variables and inversely with retential interval. From these and previous data, task coherence emerges as an important variable in skill acquisition and retention.

Robey, D., "Task Design, Work Values, and Worker Response: An Experimental Test," *Organizational Behavior and Human Performance*, October 1974, Vol. 12, No. 2, 264–273.

Sixty subjects participated in an experiment to test the hypothesis that job satisfaction and performance are affected by the interaction of task design and work values, as suggested by Hulin and Blood (1968). Two routine decision tasks were performed by subjects classified as having either intrinsic work values or extrinsic work values. Findings support the hypothesis that the interaction between job content and work values affects job satisfaction. Performance data partially support the hypothesis. The job enlargement thesis is thus shown not to be generally valid but rather affected by individual differences of subjects.

Hackman, Richard J. and Oldham, Greg R., "Motivation Through the Design of Work: Test of a Theory," *Organizational Behavior and Human Performance*, August 1976, Vol. 16, No. 2, 250–279.

A model is proposed that specifies the conditions under which individuals will become internally motivated to perform effectively on their jobs. The model focuses on the interaction among three classes of variables: a) the psychological states of employees that must be present for internally motivated work behavior to develop; b) the characteristics of jobs that can create these psychological states; and c) the attributes of individuals that determine how positively a person will respond to a complex and challenging job. The model was tested for 658 employees who work on 62 different jobs in seven organizations, and results support its validity. A number of special features of the model are discussed (including its use as a basis for the diagnosis of jobs and the evaluation of job redesign projects), and the model is compared to other theories of job design.

Shiflett, Samuel, "Dyadic Performance on Two Tasks as a Function of Task Difficulty, Work Strategy, and Member Ability," *Journal of Applied Psychology*, August 1976, Vol. 61, No. 4, 455–462.

This study involves the manipulation of divided and shared labor strategies and the varying of task difficulty and member ability in order to examine their combined effects upon dyadic performance on two tasks: analogies and crossword puzzles. The subjects were 72 Army enlisted men assigned to dyads on the basis of relative homogeneity of ability on an analogies pretest. Labor strategy (i.e., either independent or interdependent task-solving) was manipulated by allowing each dyad to work together on a task (two of four tasks) and also separately, with each member working on half the task (two of four tasks). Task difficulty (i.e., the probability of an individual failing to perform adequately) was operationalized by providing two easy and two difficult crossword puzzle and analogy tasks. Ability levels were determined on the basis of pretest score and classified as either very high, high, low, and very low.

Dividing labor was found to be more efficient in terms of manhours to a performance criterion, but sharing labor was more effective—took less time to complete (performance). The efficiency effect (group productivity in terms of manhours to reach criterion) was more pronounced on the analogies tasks, while the effectiveness findings (maximum group performance without regard to time) were more pronounced on the crossword puzzles. These results occurred across task difficulty and group ability. The hypothesis that task difficulty would indicate the importance of ability redundancy on group performance was not supported. Differences in the performance curves for the two tasks were discussed in terms of the role of feedback regarding the adequacy of a response to the task.

Umstot, Denis D.; Bell, Cecil H. and Mitchell, Terence R., "Effects of Job Enrichment and Task Goals on Satisfaction and Productivity: Implications for Job Design," *Journal of Applied Psychology*, August 1976, Vol. 61, No. 4, 379–394.

A two-phase research project investigated the effects of job enrichment and goal-setting on employee productivity and satisfaction in a well controlled, simulated job environment. In the first phase, two conditions of goal-setting (assigned goals versus no goals) and two conditions of job enrichment (enriched versus unenriched) were established, producing four experimental conditions. The subjects were people who responded to a newspaper advertisement of a job offer. The task involved identifying and coding parcels of land with the appropriate zoning codes and filing the sets of account cards. In the assigned goal condition subjects were told they should be able to file 15 cards per hour above their baseline period. The no-goal group had no goal assigned. Job enrichment was operationalized through the manipulation of: skill variety (task strategy could be chosen); task identity (labeling their chosen area); task significance (told their codes would complete county's file); autonomy (able to obtain their own supplies); and feedback (were able to observe the day's production). The JDS (Hackman and Oldham, 1975) was used to measure enrichment, while the JDI (Smith, Kendall, and Hulin, 1969) measured job satisfaction and the average number of account cards filed served as the measure of productivity.

The results indicated that job enrichment had a substantial impact on job satisfaction but little effect on productivity. Goal-setting, on the other hand, had a major impact on productivity and a less substantial impact on satisfaction. In the second phase (after two day's work), people with unenriched jobs worked under enriched conditions and people originally without goals were assigned goals. Again, job enrichment had a positive effect on satisfaction, while goal-setting had a positive effect on performance. These results are discussed in terms of the current theoretical approaches for understanding employee motivation on the job.

Baird, Lloyd S., "Relationship of Performance to Satisfaction in Stimulating and Nonstimulating Jobs," *Journal of Applied Psychology*, December 1976, Vol. 61, No. 6, 721–727.

As suggested by Lawler and others, the theoretical reason for making jobs stimulating is to enable the job holders to experience satisfaction when they perform well. It was therefore, hypothesized that on stimulating jobs, satisfaction would be positively related to performance. To test the hypothesis, the Job Description Index was administered to 167 state-agency employees, and performance ratings were obtained from their supervisors. Job stimulation was determined by having three observers rate the jobs using the Job Diagnostic Survey. Analysis of variance and correlational analysis revealed that the relationships between performance and satisfaction were exactly opposite to those hypothesized. Satisfaction with work was correlated with performance only in nonstimulating jobs. It is suggested that the key variable in determining these relationships is the nature and use of feedback.

Sims, Henry P. and Szilagyi, Andrew D., "Job Characteristic Relationships: Individual and Structural Moderators," *Organizational Behavior and Human Performance*, December 1976, Vol. 17, No. 2, 211–230.

This research investigated the question of how characteristics of the individual moderated the relationships between perceptions of job characteristics and employee expectancies, satisfaction, and performance. The results generally confirmed the previous conclusions of Hackman and Lawler (1971) that individuals who have higher self-actualization need strength are potentially better candidates for job enrichment. In addition, this research found that locus of control (Rotter, 1966) generally did not moderate the job characteristic and satisfaction, performance relationships. Also, the influence of occupational level was investigated as a moderator of the job characteristic relationships. The lower occupational levels generally indicated lower levels of the job characteristic measures and a stronger relationship between variety and satisfaction. The highest occupational level indicated higher role ambiguity, and weaker relationships between variety and satisfaction, but stronger feedback and satisfaction. The nature of task requirements at different occupational levels and the influence on job characteristic relationships were discussed.

Gallegos, Robert C. and Phelan, Joseph G., "Effects on Productivity and Morale of a System-Designed Job-Enrichment Program in Pacific Telephone," *Psychological Reports*, February 1977, Vol. 40, No. 1, 283–290.

In the experiments over a 14-month period, 56 maintenance mechanics (framemen) served as experimental ($N=21$) and control ($N=35$) groups. Framemen carried work responsibilities on large "frames"—serving the larger business communities. Quantity aspect of the work consisted of 24-hour, day-to-day connection of wires to complete new, rearranged, or disconnected circuits. The quality aspect could be measured by number of customer complaints which could be directly traced to inefficient or careless work on the frames. For the experimental group only, all jobs were "systems analyzed". Analyses were carried out and job enlargement (horizontal leadings) and job enrichment (vertical leadings) were implemented. Feedback was provided on productivity of individuals. "Hawthorne effects" and fluctuations of effort due to subtle types of supervisor-employee interaction were controlled by alternating supervisors and other environmental controls. Job satisfaction of each group was measured by the JDI before and after each experiment.

Following introduction of job enrichment programs for experimental groups and measured before and after and during a 14-month period, significant improvement in quantity and quality occurred and was maintained after termination of experiments. Expressed job satisfaction was average or slightly below on the JDI for all workers. Despite improvements in productivity, there were no significant differences in expressed job satisfaction.

Umstot, Denis, D., "MBO and Job Enrichment: How to Have Your Cake and Eat it Too," *Management Review*, February 1977, Vol. 66, No. 2, 21–26.

The author attempted to test the effects of job enrichment and goal-setting on satisfaction and productivity. An organization, composed of 42 temporary part time employees, was created for research purposes. The employees performed zoning coding tasks for the county. The first phase of the experiment tested four conditions using four separate groups, a group with enriched job, a group with assigned specific goals, a group with both enrichment and goals and a group with neither enrichment nor goals. Employees' perceptions of whether their jobs were enriched or unenriched were verified by use of the JDS (Hackman and Oldham, 1975). Goals were established by supervisors alone and were based on past productivity levels (the article did not provide information on how the variables were operationalized).

The results of this first phase confirmed the author's prediction that goal-setting increases productivity, but appeared, in addition, to enrich jobs and improve work satisfaction. Job enrichment, on the other hand, had no effect on productivity and only a weak effect on satisfaction. The author suggests that a job design combining both job enrichment and goal setting should improve both productivity and satisfaction.

Dunham, Randall, B., "Reactions to Job Characteristics: Moderating Effects of the Organization," *Academy of Management Journal*, March 1977, Vol. 20, No. 1, 42–65.

This study attempted to examine worker responses to task design from different functional specialty groups within an organization to determine if nontask environmental blocks are present and moderating task-design response relationships. There were 784 executives of a large retail merchandising corporation from eight functional specialty groups that were administered questionnaires. The questionnaire included 15 items from the JDS to measure perceived task variety, task identity, task significance, autonomy, and feedback from the job. A set of job satisfaction scales (IOR) were used to measure various aspects of satisfaction with the work, supervision, pay and company was included. Four subset scales were developed to measure different aspects of Perceived Environmental Characteristics: Climate scales, Managerial Style scales, a Work Assignment scale and a Career Description scale. Finally, demographic information was obtained through self-report. Canonical analysis established a significant relationship between task design and effective response measures. Functional specialty moderated the relationship. It was suggested that the moderating effect may be explained in terms of environmental elements which caused the worker to focus on or off task design.

Rousseau, Denise M., "Technological Differences in Job Characteristics, Employee Satisfaction, and Motivation: A Synthesis of Job Design Research and Sociotechnical Systems Theory," *Organizational Behavior and Human Performance*, June 1977, Vol. 19, No. 1, 18–42.

Job characteristics suggested by sociotechnical systems theory and job design theory were examined in a survey of employee satisfaction and motivation in 19 production units. The job characteristics related to the variety of task performed and skill employed; the responsiblity for the control over work process; the completion of meaningful units of work; feedback; interpersonal interaction; and learning. The organizational units were classified into three technological categories (long-linked technology; mediating technology; and intensive technology) according to Thompson's (1967) scheme. A modified version of the JDS was used to measure perceived job characteristics. The Brayfield-Rothe Satisfaction Index and Miller's Alienation questionnaire were administered to measure global job satisfaction and intrinsic satisfaction, respectively. Questionnaires were distributed to employees on the job.

Results show a substantial positive relation between job characteristics, satisfaction, and motivation. Significant differences were also found between the job characteristics, satisfaction and motivation across technology. In addition, there was substantial positive relations between the job characteristics, satisfaction and motivation. The job characteristics Variety and Task Significance were found to be particularly important to employee satisfaction and motivation. In general, the results of this study support the view that characteristics of production jobs vary across technology as do levels of employee satisfaction and motivation. Satisfaction, alienation, and involvement are substantially and positively related to the job dimensions in this study.

Griffen, Ricky W., and Chonko, Lawrence B., "Employee Preferences for Job Characteristics," *Academy of Management Proceedings*, 1977, 57–61.

This study investigated worker preferences for different job characteristics. A sample of 65 managers and nonmanagers provided information concerning their preference for job variety (job requires a wide range of operations), autonomy (individual decides procedures to be followed on job), feedback (receiving information on performance), and identity (extent to which individual does a whole piece of work). Trade-off analysis, a multivariate technique that quantifies individual preferences for the attribute of a particular object, was used to show that workers in the present sample preferred feedback and autonomy more than variety and identity on their jobs as purported by questionnaires. Implications for the practicing manager and a tentative framework for a contingency approach to job design are presented.

Frederiksen, L. W., "Behavioral Reorganization of a Professional Service System," *Journal of Organizational Behavior Management*, 1978, Vol. 2, No. 1, 1–9.

The service delivery behavior of professional staff was altered with a systems level reorganization of an outpatient mental health clinic. Service delivery problems were specified and analyzed. Solutions were developed in the form of an intervention, which involved *rescheduling workloads*, increasing individual staff member's responsibility for specific patients, and installing a *feedback system*. Following this, patient drop-out rates decreased, average interval between appointments decreased, and lateness to first appointment was reduced. These improvements achieved organizational (service delivery) goals without observable negative side effects or major costs.

Hackman, J. Richard; Pearce, Jone L. and Wolfe, Jane Caminis, "Effects of Changes in Job Characteristics on Work Attitudes and Behaviors: A Naturally Occurring Quasi-Experiment," *Organizational Behavior and Human Performance*. 1978, Vol. 21, 289–304.

The effects of changes in the motivational properties of jobs on work attitudes and behaviors were assessed in a quasi-experimental design. A number of clerical jobs in a metropolitan bank were redesigned because of a technological innovation. Changes were made without regard for the motivational characteristics of the jobs, and without cognizance by bank personnel that there might be motivational consequences of the changes. Some jobs were made more complex and challenging, some less so, and the motivational properties of still others were essentially unaffected. Measures of job characteristics, employee attitudes, and work behaviors were collected before and after the changes. Results showed that general satisfaction, growth satisfaction, and internal motivation were affected by changes in job characteristics. Satisfaction with the work context was not affected. Effects of the changes on absenteeism and performance depend on the strength of employee growth needs, which also tended to moderate attitudinal reactions to the changes. Contrary to expectation, employee growth needs themselves were not affected by the altered motivational characteristics of the jobs.

Ivancevich, John M., "The Performance to Satisfaction Relationship: A Causal Analysis of Stimulating and Nonstimulating Jobs," *Organizational Behavior and Human Performance*, 1978, Vol. 22, 350–365.

This study investigated the source and direction of causal influence in the relationships among performance rating, performance output, intrinsic satisfaction, and extrinsic satisfaction. A cross-lag correlation design, corrected cross-lag procedures, dynamic correlations, and frequency-of-change-in-product-moment (FCP) techniques were used to analyze the data. Field data were collected from 108 experienced machinists and 62 machine repair technicians. Using a modified Job Diagnostic Survey (JDS), six qualified observers categorized the machinist and technician jobs as stimulating or nonstimulating. The data analysis and results indicate significant differences in the causal inferences made for the two categories of jobs. It was determined that it could be inferred that for stimulating jobs "performance rating causes intrinsic satisfaction," "performance output causes intrinsic satisfaction," and "extrinsic satisfaction causes performance output". In addition, the data for the nonstimulating jobs suggest that it can be inferred that "intrinsic and extrinsic satisfaction cause performance rating" and "intrinsic satisfaction causes performance output".

Kabanoff, Boris and O'Brien, Gordon E., "The Effects of Task Type and Cooperation Upon Group Products and Performance," *Organizational Behavior and Human Performance*, 1979, Vol. 23, 163–181.

Twenty-four three-person groups each performed three types of intellective tasks—production, discussion, and problem-solving—while employing one of four work organizations. Organizations differed in amount of two forms of cooperation—coordination and collaboration. Group products were rated on six descriptive dimensions (action orientation, optimism, length, issue involvement, originality, and quality of presentation) and on three performance dimensions (adequacy, quality, and creativity). Task type had the largest effect on the descriptive dimensions, accounting for up to 50 percent of the variance, but had little effect on the evaluative dimensions. Group structure accounted for 22 to 36 percent of the variance in both descriptive and evaluative measures. The major effect of the structural variables was on product length, but a MANOVA analysis showed that group structure affected the group performance measures even when product length was controlled for. There were a number of significant interactions between group structure and task type, though these accounted for little of the variance in group performance. Collaborative structures resulted in the lowest productivity, with discussion tasks the worst performed under collaborative structures. Coordinated and coacting groups were not significantly different in productivity levels. The results were discussed in relation to the task typology employed and implications for research dealing with small group performance.

Abdel-Halim, Ahmed A., "Individual and Interpersonal Moderators of Employee Reactions to Job Characteristics: A Reexamination," *Personnel Psychology*, Spring 1979, Vol. 32, No. 1, 121–137.

This study examines the moderating effects of employees' growth need strength (GNS) and their satisfaction with supervisors and coworkers on the relationship between the motivating potential of the job (as an over-all measure of job enrichment) and their intrinsic job satisfaction and job involvement. Data was collected from a sample of 89 managerial and professional personnel at middle-lower levels of a large midwest manu-facturing firm. The Hackman-Oldham model utilizing fine "core job di-mensions" was used to measure job enrichment and a Motivating Poten-tial Score (MPS) was obtained. The results tended to partially replicate and thus support previous research findings regarding the moderating effects of GNS but not on interpersonal satisfaction variables. A signifi-cant interaction was obtained between MPS and GNS in predicting in-trinsic satisfaction while no such interaction existed for job involvement. Implications of the findings for job design are discussed.

Champoux, Joseph E., "The World of Nonwork: Some Implications for Job Re-Design Efforts," *Personnel Psychology*, Spring 1979, Vol. 33, No. 1, 61–75.

The article illustrates the operation of the compensatory and spill-over models of adjustment to work. Data were acquired from employees of three firms by way of a questionnaire which each respondent used to describe his or her experiences at work and away from work. The ques-tionnaires incorporated 25 semantic differential scales and include five broad categories of employee types: 1) Scientists; 2) Office - Clerical; 3) White Collar; 4) Blue Collar; and 5) Sales People. Results indicate that White Collar groups are characterized mainly by the spillover model, while the Sales and Blue Collar groups are characterized mainly by the compensatory model. The results indicate that the Blue Collar employee finds nonwork experiences more exciting and creative than work expe-riences.

The author concludes that test results commend a more holistic view of people's reactions to their work as being beneficial to job redesign. Thus, he says the complexity of the relationship between work and non-work appears to bear important implications for approaches to job re-design and quality of working life.

Stone, Eugene F.; Ganster, Daniel C.; Woodman, Richard W. and Fusi-lier, Marcelline R., "Relationships between Growth Need Strength and Selected Individual Differences Measures Employed in Job Design Research," *Journal of Vocational Behavior*, June 1979, Vol. 14, No. 3, 329–340.

The present study examines the degree to which the Growth Need Strength scales of the Job Diagnostic Survey correlate with 1) other measures of needs and values employed in research as moderators of the job scope-job satisfaction relationship and 2) a measure of social desir-ability. Results showed only moderate correlations between the Growth

Need Strengths scales and the other measures of needs and values and a relatively high degree of correlation between social desirablity and the Would Like measure of the Growth Need Strength. On the basis of these results, it was recommended that additional research be carried out.

Evans, M. G.; Kiggundu, M. N. and House, R. J., "A Partial Test and Extension of the Job Characteristics Model of Motivation," *Organizational Behavior and Human Performance*, December 1979, Vol. 24, No. 3, 354–381.

This paper reports the results of a partial test and extension of the Hachman-Oldham job characteristics model which has been extended to include an expectancy theory type of outcome in addition to the those outcomes contained in the original model. A positive relation is hypothesized between each of the core dimensions of task significance, identity, variety, autonomy and expectances for both intrinsic and extrinsic rewards. The individual moderating effects of growth need strength and need for achievement are also investigated. Data was collected from 343 assembly line supervisors and managers of an automobile assembly plant using the TAT and Job Diagnostic Survey. The results provided partial support for the hypothesized relationships. Job characteristic relations with outcome measures were significant but low. The correlations with expectancy type outcomes were significant and consistent with the model's rationale. A weak relationship was shown for the moderator effects of growth need strength. Need for achievement showed no effects. The validity and superiority of the double multiplicative models was also tested but found unsupported. Future research directions are suggested.

Katerberg, Ralph Jr.; Hom, Peter W. and Hulin, Charles L., "The Effects of Job Complexity on the Reactions of Part-Time Employees," *Organizational Behavior and Human Performance*, December 1979, Vol. 24, No. 3, 317–332.

The literature on job complexity and job context indicates that full-time and part-time employees have significantly different job responses. This study examined several situational modifiers on the relationship between job scope and responses among part-time organizational members. Measures of job complexity, satisfaction with work context, reenlistment intentions, and decisions were obtained from 395 National Guardsmen. Moderating effects examined were satisfaction with pay, coworker relations and supervision. The moderating effects by job contextual factors on the relationship between job complexity and dependent measures were investigated. Job complexity was positively and strongly related to all dependent variables. Little evidence for moderators was found using subgroup analysis and moderated regression. The resulting implications are discussed in terms of recent research on moderator effects.

Cherrington, David J. and England, J. Lynn, "The Desire for an Enriched Job as a Moderator of the Enrichment-Satisfaction Relationship," *Organizational Behavior and Human Performance*, February 1980, Vol. 25, No. 1, 139–159.

The literature on job enrichment indicates that three kinds of moderators of the enrichment-satisfaction relationship have been examined: urban-rural influences, growth need strength, and work values. A recent review of 29 empirical investigations of individual differences concluded that there was no substantial evidence showing that individual differences moderated the effects of job enrichment. The present study argued that the evidence was not so pessimistic and showed that the individual's desire for an enriched job was a significant moderator of the enrichment-satisfaction relationship. A survey was taken of 3,053 workers in 53 companies throughout the United States regarding attitudes toward one's specific job, company, and work in general plus demographic information. Direct assessments of the person's desire for job enrichment was postulated and found to be much better moderators than indirect estimates inferred from work values or urban-rural influences. Implications for new employee placement and job re-design are discussed.

Dreher, George H., "Individual Needs or Correlates of Satisfaction and Involvement with a Modified Scanlon Plan Company," *Journal of Vocational Behavior*, August 1980, Vol. 17, No. 1, 89–94.

The purpose of this study was to examine individual need strengths as they relate to job satisfaction and job involvement with a company using a modified Scanlon Plan. The individual needs focused on in this study were achievement, affiliation, autonomy and dominance. Prior research has indicated that these needs are related to important work attitudes and behavior. The study was carried out in a manufacturing company with 80 employees in the midwest. Work teams met with the author to describe various aspects of the management system. After the group interviews, questionnaires which assessed job satisfaction, job involvement and need strength scales were individually distributed. It was found that job satisfaction and involvement were positively related to achievement and dominance, but negatively related to autonomy. The affiliation results could not be interpreted. Systematic research on the conditions which influence Scanlon Plan success seem worthy of additional effort since the Scanlon Plan continues to represent a promising alternative to traditional production jobs. These results suggested that individual differences may play an important role in understanding the Scanlon Plan process.

INTEGRATIVE

Porter, L. W., "Effects of Task Factors on Job Attitudes and Behavior," *Personnel Psychology*, 1969, Vol. 22, 415–444.

Symposium of the motivational effects of the task itself on job attitudes and behaviors. Four authors attack the problem from differing levels of analysis, but central themes revolve around the use of valued skills and abilities as affecting intrinsic motivation, and the identification of organizational and task dimensions involved.

Rush, H. M. F., "Motivation Through Job Design," *Conference Board Record*, January 1971, Vol. 8, No. 1, 52–56.

In past years it had been a widespread assumption that production requirements and individual needs are at variance. However, as of recently, research into motivation and job satisfaction indicates that this may not be so and that greater productivity is best achieved through increased employee motivation. As a basis for understanding motivation, the author discusses what factors serve as intrinsic and extrinsic rewards for people. From the experience of the organizations studied, several job design techniques which included motivational factors were being used with varying degrees of success. These include job rotation, job enrichment, job enlargement, and work simplification. Generally companies tend to subscribe to one of the job design philosophies, to the exclusion of others. However, there's an emerging kind of organizational work unit which combines all of the foregoing job designs as components of a day-to-day mode of functioning and is known as the autonomous work group. Within the framework of the organization's objectives, the work group as a whole is accountable for a predetermined quantity and quality of output and, beyond this, can operate independently. The group sets work objectives and prepares a schedule of periods with production goals. The group is accountable to management; individual members are accountable to the group. The group brainstorms and uses work simplification methods to analyze what must be done. In an autonomous work group, usually each member is capable of performing each step of the operation, thus making job rotation, enlargement, and enrichment possible. The incentive for this kind of flexibility and willingness to assume increased work loads is the key factor that identifies the autonomous work group: members are accountable as a group.

Sirota, D. and Wolfson, A. D., "Job Enrichment: What are the Obstacles?", *Personnel*, May-June 1972, Vol. 49, No. 3, 8–17.

The authors deal with the gap between principle and practice in job enrichment. The reasons why JE plans have not been more widely adopted, as the authors see them, fall into 11 basic categories: 1) Educational: it's easier to preach JE principles than it is to make the specific called for changes in work content; 2) Ideological: the belief that job fragmentation and rigid content controls over workers are necessary for productive efficiency still prevails in many companies; 3) Organizational: there are three aspects to this category. First, job enrichment is an investment. Second, that workers and managers generally change jobs often in a dynamic organization, and thirdly, tampering with the functional form of the organization is required—taking work from one function of the company and giving it to another; 4) Managerial: JE can rob a manager of some sense of secureness; 5) Technological: JE is seen by most managements as being too risky to warrant large-scale technology expenditures: 6) The employee: JE does not compensate for employee incompetence; 7) The enricher: when the JE practitioner fails, the employee gets labeled "scared" or "backward looking" instead of putting any blame on the manager or JE plan; 8) Diagnosis: all job ails tend to be diagnosed as needing JE; 9) "Prove it here": before a manager will accept a JE plan, they want proof that it will work in their organization; 10) "Nothing new here": the manager who believes that there is nothing that needs changing/enriching in their company; 11) Time: managers find their enthusiasm slowly leaving with realization of how time consuming JE becomes.

Shepard, J. M., "Job Enrichment: Some Problems With Contingency Models," *Personnel Journal*, December 1974, Vol. 53, No. 12, 886–889.

Although employee response to job enrichment varies, it has been found that a large percentage of people in various social categories are receptive to the idea and would welcome the chance to assume responsibility, add to their skills, and perform more meaningful work. The researchers who contend that job enrichment is not suitable for all types of workers feel that the applicability of JE is contingent upon various factors. Several contingency models have been developed by Hulin and Blood, among others, based upon that insight.

Shepard discussed the problems associated with the contingency model: 1) when we conclude on a statistical basis that certain segments of the labor force abhor responsibility, autonomy, freedom and control, and therefore, should not be given such, we are closing the door on a sizeable proportion of persons within these segments who may respond well to JE; 2) contingency models may provide a blanket rationalization against the institution of JE programs even in situations where they would be appropriate; 3) the contention that employees in highly specialized jobs resist responsibility may be specious. Even, if on the surface this may appear to be the case, analysis of the matter cannot stop at this point, or one leaves out the possibility of change; 4) a final problem with contingency models touches on the important matter of whether or not alienated and unresponsive employees are retrievable. Cross-sectional data which has been collected over time has not been able to provide any indication of whether attitudes toward JE can change over time. The author concludes by expressing our need for further research in work settings that would help to determine the advisability of providing job enriching opportunities as opposed to routinized work.

Chung, Kae H. and Ross, Monica F., "Differences in Motivational Properties Between Job Enlargement and Job Enrichment," *The Academy of Management Review*, January 1977, Vol. 2, No. 1, 113–121.

Differences in motivational properties between job enlargement (adding more elements to the existing job) and job enrichment (allowing workers to perform managerial functions) are investigated. Task attributes of enlarged jobs include: variety, meaningful work modules, feedback on performance, ability utilization and control over work-pace. Task attributes of job enrichment include: participation, goal internalizations, autonomy, and group management. In determining an appropriate type of job design, the authors advise focusing on differences in employees' motivation and ability. Strategies in designing work systems should take into account that enrichment may only have motivational value to those employees in the organization who prefer demanding and challenging jobs, have the ability to perform, and have high higher-order need strength. Enlargement is suggested for those workers at the lower levels of the organization who are primarily motivated by lower-order needs.

Steers, Richard M. and Mowday, Richard T., "The Motivational Properties of Tasks," *Academy of Management Review*, October 1977, Vol. 2, No. 4, 645–657.

An integrative review of the task design literature is undertaken. Seven conceptual models are examined in terms of their efficacy in explaining the motivational properties of tasks (effort and performance). The author presents criticisms for each of the models. One criticism is the failure of the model to account for the process through which task characteristics influence attitude and behavior (i.e., Requisite Task Attributes Model; Socio-Technical Systems Model: Jobs Characteristics Model). A second criticism appears to be the absence of an explanation concerning individual or situational differences (i.e., Two-Factor Theory; Socio-Technical Systems Model; Expectancy Theory). A third criticism seems to stem from a lack of supporting empirical evidence or limited utility (i.e., Requisite Task Attribute Model; Activation Theory; Need Achievement Theory; Expectancy Theory). Finally, the need for an unambiguous statement concerning the "how and when" of job enrichment and also stable measurement is noted (i.e., Two-Factor Theory; Activation Theory; Achievement Motivation Theory; Job Characteristic Model and Expectancy Theory).

Rosenbach, William E.; Zawacki, Robert A. and Morgon, Cyril P., "Research Round-Up," *Personnel Administrator*, October 1977, Vol. 22, No. 8, 51–61.

The growing dissatisfaction of the American worker has led to research into the quality of work life. The theory of "work redesign" seems to offer a hopeful alternative to the current trend through changing the work itself thus leading to improved worker attitudes. This article examines some of the available research which both supports and contradicts the effectiveness of work redesign as a method promoting job satisfaction and better work behavior. The studies cited include research at IBM, Texas Instruments and a state employment center.

The authors' conclusions are: 1) research techniques used must be more clearly defined; 2) the studies which attempt to contradict positive results of work redesign do so poorly and some actually lend support to the work redesign concept; 3) any study must include a discussion of job characteristics and individual employee differences; and 4) overgeneralized statements about the application of work redesign must be examined carefully.

Unstot, D. D.; Mitchell, T. R. and Bell, C. H., "Goal-Setting and Job Enrichment: An Integrated Approach to Job Design," *Academy of Management Review*, 1978, Vol. 3, No. 4, 867–879.

This article reviews the empirical literature relating to task goals and job enrichment to performance outcomes. The interaction of job characteristics, individual differences, and organizational characteristics is also reviewed, and an integrated model presented that explains the relationships. The authors point out that available research suggests that most of the interactive effects of goal-setting and job enrichment are positive and job design should, therefore, integrate these techniques. Combining job enrichment and goal-setting should improve job satisfaction and productivity, two dominant concerns of managers which have often been viewed as incompatible.

Macy, Barry A., "A Progress Report on the Bolivar Quality of Work Life Project," *Personnel Journal*, August 1979, Vol. 58, No. 8, 527–530 and 557–559.

This article reviews the Bolivar Quality of Work Life Project which came into being through the persistence and beliefs of Dr. Sidney Harmon, former Undersecretary of the United States Department of Commerce and Chairman/CEO of Harmon International Industries, Inc. The objectives of the project were to improve employees' quality of work life and to enhance organizational effectiveness. Changing the system required a cooperative effort beginning at the top with Harmon and Irving Bluestone (UAW) and the creation of new in-plant social structures, processes and relationships with the assistance of the project's Harvard consulting group. This group facilitated the change process with regard to leadership style, (i.e., learning how to analyze problems cooperatively and to stimulate participation) and union leaders needed to learn how to work cooperatively. As the goals of the program developed, they were gradually identified as 1) security, 2) equity, 3) individuation (i.e., each person to be treated as a unique human being and the job being designed to maximize control at the person's own best pace and style), 4) democracy (a say in decisions affecting them—their own jobs and rights of free speech and due process as part of the industrial experience). Besides some of the positive behavioral and financial changes experienced through the Bolivar program has been the general commitment to the project by both top and local management and union officials. Some believe such cooperation may be a portent of the future. At any rate the changes brought about at Bolivar present an interesting and meaningful outcome to a project whose initial goal was to improve employees' quality of work life.

Cooper, Cary L., "Humanizing the Work Place in Europe: An Overview of Six Countries," *Personnel Journal*, June 1980, Vol. 59, No. 6, 488–491.

Mechanization and computerization were the First and Second Industrial Revolutions and were concerned with "products" and "things" as opposed to people. It is said we are now entering the Third Revolution in which the needs and aspirations of employees will be uppermost in the design and implementation of production and other work systems. Companies within the European Economic Community have begun to experiment with employee participation and "quality of working life" programs and many governments within this Community have set up governmental agencies to encourage this development. The author provides a thumbnail sketch of the better documented examples in a sample of Community countries to give some flavor of their approach and some assessment of their effect. Examples include Denmark, France, The Netherlands, Italy, West Germany and the United Kingdom. The author contends that introduction of autonomous work groups, greater worker participation, and quality of working life improvements are not a panacea for all industrial ills, but rather a step in the right direction. In the long term, they hold out prospects for improving industrial relations, solving some of the problems of technological change, and meeting the "non-hygiene" needs—a la Herzberg—of people at work.

PRESCRIPTIVE

Nissley, H. R., "Incentives and Job Design," *Industrial Management*, March 1972, Vol. 14, No. 3, 8–14.

This article is divided into three areas: a) Proving the Validity of Your Work Standard; b) Disadvantages of Incentive Systems; and c) Improving the Efficiency of the Efficiency Department. In discussing these topics, several case studies are examined which are within the framework of conventional stop-watch time-study techniques. In concluding, the author suggests that most industrial engineering departments which have come under the scrutiny of the author could greatly improve their operations by: a) using two watches for stop watch time studies, one for snap-back readings and one for continuous or batch reading; b) using the parenthesis-median technique for arriving at an average and for testing the sample size on the production floor; and c) integrating job improvements into the final time study report for cost-reduction purposes.

Sirota, D. and Wolfsman, A. D., "Job Enrichment: Surmounting the Obstacles," *Personnel*, July-August 1972, Vol. 49, No. 4, 8–19.

This article describes an approach that was developed in Company X to help overcome the major JE obstacles and the results of its application, in terms of both actual job changes and the effects of those changes on workers' productivity and attitudes. The steps taken can be grouped into four categories or phases. Phase One: Diagnosis. By pinpointing the location, causes, and consequences of low employee morale, an action strategy was designed to improve organization, with JE the component recommended to correct job content problems. Phase Two: Top Management Exposure. The analyses were organized into an easel chart presentation that had manpower utilization as its central theme and concluded with recommendations for alleviation of problems in this area. Phase Three: Training Program. The basic objective of the program is to give the key men sufficient theoretical and technique background as consultants to managers interested in initiating and carrying through JE projects in their departments. Phase Four: Job Enrichment. The trained key men are ready to market their new skills and explain and implement steps towards JE. More than 30 JE projects are now under way at Company X. A few case histories are disclosed and a discussion follows of which aspects of the procedure were most important in overcoming the obstacles to Job Enrichment: 1) the first step was diagnosis; 2) managers were given guidance about what to do; 3) a multiple resource was provided (a training program for five to 12 persons from a single facility); 4) JE practitioners were fully aware of their limitations in power and knowledge; 5) JE was not enforced on line management; 6) flexibility was emphasized; 7) internal resources were used; and 8) evidence was collected and disseminated.

Greenblatt, A. D., "Maximizing Productivity Through Job Enrichment," *Personnel*, March-April 1973, Vol. 51, No. 1, 31–39.

The redesigning of an existing job must cover five overall structural concepts: 1) natural work units meaning the grouping of random work components according to any logical system to carve out of them a single responsibility in a consistent unit; 2) "client identification" is the development of continuing accountability for a specific unit of work; 3) vertical and horizontal job leading is the process of putting into the job new responsibilities that are of a higher order and more difficult and challenging; 4) feedback systems refer to both supervisory feedback of information about performance and also feedback which the employee receives directly from the job process itself; 5) task advancement includes both establishing career paths for advancement through promotion to higher level jobs and establishing proficiency levels within the job itself.

The strategies used in implementing job enrichment are crucial. The first and probably most important is the style of supervision involved. Job enrichment must be viewed as an ongoing philosophy of managing people. A formal meeting of management including all first-line supervisors should be called for the purpose of introducing job enrichment concepts. The supervisory workshop should follow where innovative thinking and brainstorming should take place. When proposed JE plans are decided upon, team participation is required for their implementation.

Carroll, A. B., "Conceptual Foundations of Job Enrichment," *Public Personnel Management*, January-February 1974, Vol. 3, No. 1, 35–38.

Job enrichment describes the strategy which has evolved from Herzberg's findings, and may be defined as a program aimed at injecting into a job situation opportunities for those "motivator" factors revealed through his study and analysis. The author prescribes a five-step plan for job enrichment. Step One: Experimentation. It is probably wise to conduct a brief experiment involving one or several jobs in which the enrichment strategy could prove valuable. In the experiment, determine job satisfaction and productivity results and learn intricacies of implementation. Step Two: Supervisory Coaching. It will be necessary to train supervisory personnel in job enrichment concepts. Step Three: Identification of Jobs. Realization that some jobs are more conducive to enrichment than others. In introducing enrichment strategy, it is necessary to be able to select those jobs in which the opportunity for success appears to be maximal. Step Four: Implementation. Begin by brainstorming job changes which might conceivably have a favorable impact on employee performance, then screen out meaningless suggestions. Once enrichment suggestions are implemented, the manager should expect a temporary drop in performance as the employee adjusts to a new situation. Step Five: Feedback Follow-Up. This manadatory step involved continual appraisal of attitudes and performance.

Tregoe, B. B., "Job Enrichment: How to Avoid the Pitfalls," *Personnel Journal*, June 1974, Vol. 53, No. 6, 445–449.

The author speculates as to why so many JE programs fail and links these failures with the number of misconceptions which are currently held in the field of management relations. Some of these misconceptions include: 1) if you increase the employee's responsibility, you will automatically enrich the job; 2) bringing people together to exchange freely their ideas will solve their problems; 3) JE must focus on the individual, as an entity, and his job; 4) JE is concerned only with the worker; 5) the restructuring of jobs is a necessary element of JE. The author describes his experiences with JE when his organization developed a problem-solving program—Analytical Trouble Shooting (ATS). ATS is based on the principle that the best source of information about any production problem is the production worker himself. The worker is given practical techniques and skills for applying logic to problems and for putting his own experiences and intelligence to the most effective use. The most important benefits that were noticed of workers who were enrolled in a trouble-shooting course are: 1) the nature of the worker's job changes, he moves from being a mere routine worker to being a trained trouble-shooter; and 2) the worker is given a language and a process that he shares with other people in other parts of the plant.

Yorks, L., "Determining Job Enrichment Feasibility," *Personnel*, November-December 1974, Vol. 51, No. 6, 18–25.

This article discusses the basic categories of diagnostic data important in assessing feasibility of implementing job enrichment and the basic methods for collecting such data. There are three categories of data to tap in the process of determining JE feasibility: symptomatic, attitudinal, and structural. Symptomatic data: this type of data includes turnover rates, absenteeism figures, and customer complaints. They serve as a red flag, a warning of emerging people-related problems. Secondly, should these statistics become linked with job design upon further investigation, they point to excess cost to the organization. Attitudinal data: includes data obtained from personal interviews and formal questionnaires. This type of data is valuable because they relate to a number of feasibility factors measuring employee reactions and possible impacts on the work organization. Structural data: Provides information about the technical feasibility of JE. In determining structural opportunities for JE, there is an attempt made to determine the possibilities for assigning work on a user basis or task combination, or building more decision-making and control into the job. Five basic data collection techniques are available to the JE specialist for tapping the foregoing categories of data: 1) department records, 2) questionnaires, 3) interviews, 4) direct observation, and 5) charting.

Whitsett, D. A., "Where are Your Unenriched Jobs?" *Harvard Business Review*, January-February 1975, Vol. 53, No. 1, 74–80.

The growing popularity of JE as a problem-solving technique has led some organizations to believe that it can be applied anywhere, anytime. Not so, when the organization is beset by certain severe difficulties—such as widespread dissatisfaction over pay levels—job enrichment naturally has little chance to flower. But more to the point, the procedure can be incorporated only where poorly designed positions exist. The author lists and describes 11 structural clues for spotting opportunities to improve the shape of the job and productivity and satisfaction of the person filling it. 1) Communications units: allow workers to have some contact with the flow of information and communication. 2) Checking functions or jobs: let the worker be responsible for quality control. 3) Trouble-shooting jobs: reference is made here to work positions which are poorly designed and have incomplete responsibilities for decision-making. 4) The super-gurus: identify persons who hold special positions on the merit of their long service or technical knowledge. 5) Job title elephantiasis: overspecialization of functions can create an excess of position titles. 6) One-to-one reporting relationships. 7) Dual reporting relationships. 8) Unclear division of responsibility. 9) Overcomplicated work flow. 10) Duplication of functions. 11) Labor pools.

Peterson, Richard O., "Human Resources Development Through Work Design," *Training and Development Journal*, August 1976, Vol. 30, No. 8, 3–7.

A work design strategy is offered as a means of utilizing human resources more fully. The strategy has three fundamental phases: diagnosis of work and organizational design (obtaining data on work and organizational processes and individuals); redesigning work, organizational structure, and support systems (i.e., standards, administrative levels, and performance evaluation); and trying out, evaluating, implementing, and tracking. The efficacy of the work design strategy should be based on the achievement of all objectives of organizational performance: quality, efficiency, societal impact, and employee impact.

Chung, Kae H. and Ross, Monica F., "Differences in Motivational Properties Between Job Enlargement and Job Enrichment," *The Academy of Management Review*, January 1977, Vol. 2, No. 1, 113–121.

Differences in motivational properties between job enlargement (adding more elements to the existing job) and job enrichment (allowing workers to perform managerial functions) are investigated. Task attributes of enlarged jobs include: variety, meaningful work modules, feedback on performance, ability utilization and control over work-pace. Task attributes of job enrichment include: participation, goal internalizations, autonomy, and group management. In determining an appropriate type of job design, the authors advise focusing on differences in employees' motivation and ability. Strategies in designing work systems should take into account that enrichment may only have motivational value to those employees in the organization who prefer demanding and challenging jobs, have the ability to perform, and have high higher-order need strength. Enlargement is suggested for those workers at the lower levels of the organization who are primarily motivated by lower-order needs.

Bagadia, Krishan S., "An Update on Job Enrichment," *Administrative Management*, February 1977, Vol. 38, No. 2, 52–58.

The success of job enrichment programs is seen as contingent upon managerial strategy for implementation. The author prescribes the following approach for successful implementation: diagnostics of the job (nature of work, technology, worker attributes and managerial commitment), training supervisory personnel in enrichment concepts, providing employees with additional authority to handle enriched tasks and job assignments, and monitoring employee performance (feedback). Improved productivity and satisfaction is suggested as a result of successful job-intent enrichment programs.

Rousseau, Denise M., "Technological Differences in Job Characteristics, Employee Satisfaction, and Motivation: A Synthesis of Job Design Research and Sociotechnical Systems Theory," *Organizational Behavior and Human Performance*, June 1977, Vol. 19, No. 1, 18–42.

Job characteristics suggested by sociotechnical systems theory and job design theory were examined in a survey of employee satisfaction and motivation in 19 production units. The job characteristics related to the variety of tasks performed and skill employed; the responsibility for and control over work process; the completion of meaningful units of work; feedback; interpersonal interaction; and learning. The organizational units were classified into three technological categories (long-linked technology; mediating technology; and intensive technology) according to Thompson's (1967) scheme. A modified version of the JDS was used to measure perceived job characteristics. The Brayfield-Rothe Satisfaction Index and Miller's Alienation questionnaire were administered to measure global job satisfaction and intrinsic satisfaction, respectively. Questionnaires were distributed to employees on the job.

Results show a substantial positive relation between job characteristics, satisfaction, and motivation. Significant differences were also found between the job characteristics, satisfaction and motivation across technology. In addition, there were substantial positive relations between the job characteristics, satisfaction, and motivation. The job characteristics Variety and Task Significance were found to be particularly important to employee satisfaction and motivation. In general, the results of this study support the view that characteristics of production jobs vary across technology as do levels of employee satisfaction and motivation. Satisfaction, alienation, and involvement are substantially and positively related to the job dimensions in this study.

Lawler III, Edward E., "Developing a Motivating Work Climate," *Management Review*, July 1977, Vol. 66, No. 7, 25–38.

The author recommends the adoption of various job design and reward system measures to create a more motivating work climate. Seven societal trends are identified with the attendant proposals for increasing performance in the organization and satisfaction for the worker: 1) educational level increases; 2) greater diversity of the work force; 3) constant technological change; 4) restrictive union contracts; 5) restrictive government regulation; 6) organizational growth; 7) greater attractiveness of nonwork (leisure). Prescribed approaches for improving the work environment include establishing cooperative labor-management projects; styling individualized reward systems; providing realistic job previews; involving workers in analyzing new technologies; designing jobs to fit the values and needs of the individual; and designing smaller autonomous subunits within the large organization.

Frederiksen, L. W., "Behavioral Reorganization of a Professional Service System," *Journal of Organizational Behavior Management*, 1978, Vol. 2, No. 1, 1–9.

The service delivery behavior of professional staff was altered with a systems level reorganization of an outpatient mental health clinic. Service delivery problems were specified and analyzed. Solutions were developed in the form of an intervention, which involved *rescheduling workloads,* increasing individual staff member's responsibility for specific patients, and installing a feedback system. Following this, patient dropout rates decreased, average interval between appointments decreased, and latency to first appointment was reduced. These improvements achieved organizational (service delivery) goals without observable negative side effects or major costs.

Fuller, Stephen H. and Jönsson, Berth, "Corporate Approaches to the Quality of Work Life," *Personnel Journal,* August 1980, Vol. 59, No. 8, 645–648.

A Conference Report including Stephen H. Fuller, Vice President-Personnel, GM, and Berth Jönsson, Corporate Planning Executive at AB Volvo in Sweden, discusses the concept of the approach to Quality of Working Life programs from a corporate viewpoint. Fuller outlines the key elements of the philosophy as being: 1) more employee involvement, 2) improving relationships, 3) better cooperation, 4) innovative and more effective design of jobs and organizations, and 5) improved-integration (of people and technology). He emphasized the concept is a *process;* it is utilizing all of our human resources—better today than yesterday and even better tomorrow; it is developing among all employees an awareness and understanding of the concerns and needs of others; it is improving the way things get done to assure long-term effectiveness and success of the organization. Jönsson covers the development of this concept as it is used at Volvo and outlines in detail the concept, the criteria, and the stages of development at Volvo. In summary, Jönsson indicates the development of this program is a pragmatic approach to problem-solving and an appreciation of the potential energy only man can mobilize. Fuller states GM management believes improvements have to be initiated at the local level and that the responsibility of management is to help create a climate that supports and encourages improvement and innovation.

THEORETICAL

Ross, J. E. and Murdick, R. G., "People, Productivity, and Organizational Structure," *Personnel,* September-October 1973, Vol. 50, No. 5, 8–18.

For the large part, people in managing positions have underemphasized two major sources of increased productivity. First is the broad area known as white collar and middle management. Few who fall into this population work to any standard of performance or under any productivity measurement system. The second source of increased productivity is the organizational structure, the framework that facilitates organizational dynamics and guides company operations. The various choices that exist today in organizational structure are presented here.

The classical organization (pyramid) is the most common corporate structure and includes such basic components as specialization of work, span of management, and unity of command. The most persistent critics of the classical organizational structure are those supporters of the behavioral model of organization. In this model, an attempt is made to overcome some of the mechanistic objections to the classical organization. The model assumes that objective of economic productivity but adds a new dimension of employee satisfaction. Another approach to organizational structure is the organic model of organization. Also behavioral in nature, the organic approach goes one step further and addresses itself to the fundamentals of structure and specialization of tasks. Several emerging concepts have recently come into light. The team approach seems to combine the essentials of the organic model, namely, temporary, flexible, and accommodating to change, within the traditional pyramidal structure. Versions of the team approach include project management, matrix management, and venture teams.

A rather new concept, the contingency model, attempts to pool all of the above approaches to come up with a workable systems approach to organization. This model examines which factors, forces, or variables are important in designing an organizational structure. Among these are: the manager, the work, the environment, the individual contributors. The implications of studying these types of organizational structures suggest that the right structure is a function of the interaction of the variables, each balanced against effects of others and against the desired output of the organization. In practice, no one style of organizational design is universally appropriate.

Chung, Kae H. and Ross, Monica F., "Differences in Motivational Properties Between Job Enlargement and Job Enrichment," *The Academy of Management Review,* January 1977, Vol. 2, No. 1, 113–121.

Differences in motivational properties between job enlargement (adding more elements to the existing job) and job enrichment (allowing workers to perform managerial functions) are investigated. Task attributes of enlarged jobs include: variety, meaningful work modules, feedback on performance, ability utilization and control over work-pace. Task attributes of job enrichment include: participation, goal internalizations, autonomy, and group management. In determining an appropriate type of job design, the authors advise focusing on differences in employees' motivation and ability. Strategies in designing work systems should take into account that enrichment may only have motivational value to those employees in the organization who prefer demanding and challenging jobs, have the ability to perform, and have high higher-order need strength. Enlargement is suggested for those workers at the lower levels of the organization who are primarily motivated by lower-order needs.

Steers, Richard M. and Mowday, Richard T., "The Motivational Properties of Tasks," *Academy of Management Review,* October 1977, Vol. 2, No. 4, 645–657.

An integrative review of the task design literature is undertaken. Seven conceptual models are examined in terms of their efficacy in explaining the motivational properties of tasks (effort and performance). The author presents criticisms for each of the models. One criticism is the failure of the model to account for the process through which task characteristics influence attitude and behavior (i.e., Requisite Task Attributes Model; Socio-Technical Systems Model; Jobs Characteristics Model). A second criticism appears to be the absence of an explanation concerning individual or situational differences (i.e., Two-Factor Theory; Socio-Technical Systems Model; Expectancy Theory). A third criticism seems to stem from a lack of supporting empirical evidence or limited utility (i.e., Requisite Task Attribute Model; Activation Theory; Need Achievement Theory; Expectancy Theory). Finally the need for an unambiguous statement concerning the "how and when" of job enrichment and also stable measurement is noted (i.e., Two-Factor Theory; Activation Theory; Achievement Motivation Theory; Job Characteristic Model and Expectancy Theory).

Shaw, James B., "An Information-Processing Approach to the Study of Job Design," *Academy of Management Review*, January 1980, Vol. 5, No. 1, 41–48.

An information-processing/judgmental framework is proposed in the study of job design. The author emphasizes the perceptual processes which occur when the worker has a redesigned job. The author notes that most job design theories view the job as a perceptual event. However, existing job design research has paid little attention to the perceptual processes. First, ambiguity exists in the exact number and character of relevant job dimensions. Second, studies have not been able to demonstrate convergence of job characteristic ratings between supervisors, employees, observers, and other kinds of raters. The author argues that these are shortcomings with the current "moderator" approach to job design. In the proposed framework of this study, the author attempts to combine various current research, and to guide new research toward specific processes included in employee perceptions of the job and its environment. At the core of this framework is Anderson's Information Integration Theory of Judgment which claims that the combination of information creates a judgment about any entity. A particular emphasis is given to the distinction between the "scale value" and "weights" of information.

The author argues that the information-processing/judgment approach has several benefits for current and future job design research. First, it offers a way to distinguish moderators affecting the perception of a task, and second, the approach stimulates further study of external sources of task information that may influence a worker's perception and evaluation of, and reaction to, a task. Finally, this information-processing approach presents a way of relating job dimensions, moderators, external task environment, and other areas of job design research.

Commentary

TASK DESIGN

Factory jobs traditionally have been simplified—supposedly to accommodate a large, readily available, low-skilled, and low-cost job market. With the development of technology, an increasingly well educated population, and elevating aspirations for human development at work, this approach is becoming less viable. Job fragmentation and simplification have resulted in employee boredom, lack of challenge, and meaninglessness which, some argue, may have resulted in a significant adverse effect on productivity. So with industrial growth and development, a trend began to more deeply involve the employee in his/her job and to design tasks that would motivate him/her to greater performance and at the same time hold a degree of satisfaction for the employee. In some cases, industrial programs have developed to educate employees in such areas as task responsibility and challenge, participation in decision-making, and quality and production control. Work design strategies, particularly job enrichment programs, have developed as a result of an awareness of the possibilities for increased productivity as well as a desire to develop a more capable labor force.

Applications of Work Design/Job Enrichment Programs

Application of job enrichment programs in a variety of work environments has generated an improvement in quantity and quality of work, and improvement of worker satisfaction with the job.

One experiment applied job enrichment to a clerk's job in a small civil service group via a series of job changes. Results indicated an increase in job satisfaction and performance with an accompanying decrease in absenteeism (Gomez & Mussio, 1975). A job enrichment program in a large telephone company showed significant improvement in quantity and quality of work and maintenance crews. In this instance, no changes were found in expressed job satisfaction, but this may have been due to a lack of communication and feedback as a part of the enrichment program rather than to dissatisfaction with the enriched job itself (Gallegos & Phelan, 1977).

Another study of the effects of job enrichment and goal-setting on employee productivity and satisfaction indicated that job enrichment had a substantial positive impact on job satisfaction but little effect on productivity. Goal-setting, however, had a major impact on productivity and a less substantial impact on satisfaction. These results seem significant for an understanding of employee motivation (Umstot, Bell &

Mitchell, 1976). That is, to enhance motivation for productivity both job expansion and goal-setting may be necessary. Without both, productivity gains may not be as large as otherwise possible.

Work design changes in an automobile assembly plant involved making subgroups responsible for a complete work unit, rotation of persons across jobs within the unit, group self-inspection, feedback, and group incentive payments. Results appear to have been improved worker satisfaction through greater opportunity for social contact and participation in the production process as well as enriched and more motivating work conditions (Gyllenhammar, 1977).

Impact of Specific Job Characteristics

Individual preferences for job characteristics moderate the relationship between type of satisfaction or productivity measure and work design strategies. In a study investigating how characteristics of individuals moderated the relationships between perceptions of job characteristics and employee expectancies, satisfaction, and performance, previous research (Hackman & Lawler, 1971) was confirmed that individuals with higher self-actualization need strength are potentially better candidates for job enrichment. Influence of occupational level as a moderator of the job characteristic relationships was investigated and it was found that lower occupational levels indicated lower levels of job characteristic measures and a stronger relationship between variety and satisfaction. Highest occupational levels indicated higher role ambiguity and weaker relationships between variety and satisfaction (Sims & Szilagyi, 1976).

In a study of technological differences, there was a substantial positive relationship between job characteristics, indexing job enrichment, employee satisfaction, and motivation. This study also found that characteristics of production jobs vary across types of technology as do levels of employee satisfaction and motivation, and that satisfaction, alienation, and involvement were substantially and positively related to job dimensions. The job characteristics "variety" and "task significance" also were found to be substantially related to employee satisfaction and motivation (Rousseau, 1977). In another study, worker preferences for different job characteristics indicated that workers preferred feedback and autonomy more than variety and identity on their jobs. This finding, along with others abstracted in this section, suggest significant implications for the design of jobs by practicing managers (Griffen & Chonko, 1977).

Job design techniques which consider motivational factors have been applied in several organizations with varying degrees of success. These techniques have included job rotation, job enrichment, job enlargement, and work simplification. All of these have been combined in the autonomous work group. Each member of such a group is capable of performing each part of the group's operation, thus making job rotation, enlargement, and enrichment possible. The group is accountable as a whole and thus has the incentive for flexibility and willingness to assume increased work loads (Rush, 1971).

However, such work design strategies have recognized that job enrichment factors may have motivational values only to those employees who prefer demanding and challenging jobs, have the ability to perform, and have high higher-order need strength. Job enlargement (adding more elements to the existing job) may be most suitable for those workers who are motivated primarily by lower-order needs (Chung & Ross, 1977).

It would seem, then, that in considering job design or redesign, management should look at techniques that would include natural work units and/or an autonomous work group. Key components to be identified are responsibility for decision-making, a quality control method, or a production standard (goal-setting). Adding more difficult and challenging responsibilities, an open communication and feedback system, and opportunities for advancement outside the work group may enhance the effects produced by enrichment of the immediate job of the performer.

Obstacles to Job Enrichment

Obstacles to a more widely accepted use of job enrichment by managements are many. Some of those noted in the literature reviewed are:

1. The educational efforts necessary to establish job enrichment principles;

2. The belief that job fragmentation and rigid control by management is necessary for productive efficiency;

3. Need to make substantial organizational changes that may accompany job design changes;

4. The feeling of insecurity of some managers, created by changes in responsibilities;

5. The belief that applying the concept is "too risky"—that it will not "pay off" and will require large-scale technological expenditures;

6. Such changes will not compensate for employee incompetence;

7. The unrealistic assumption that job enrichment can solve all performance ailments;

8. Management's premature demand for "proof of success" before complete implementation of a job enrichment plan;

9. Management's belief that nothing in their organization needs changing or enriching—i.e., a comfortable sense of "all is well,"; and

10. Management's naive disenchantment with the realization of how time-consuming job enrichment programs become.

Some researchers contend that job enrichment is not suitable for all and that applicability is contingent upon various factors. But the contingent nature of job enrichment has been argued to be an excuse for incomplete attempts at application on the following grounds:

1. Incorrect assumptions have been made in restricting application of job enrichment to certain segments of the labor force.

2. Blanket rationalizations have been made against the application of job enrichment programs. These prevent applications where they would be appropriate.

3. That the highly specialized employee resists responsibility, where, in actuality, such employees would welcome additional challenge.

4. That alienated and unresponsive employees are retrievable but, unfortunately, such assertions are made in the absence of information on whether attitudes toward job enrichment can change over time.

Strategies for Implementing a Job Enrichment Program

It should be emphasized that a job enrichment program is not a panacea despite its apparent popularity as a productivity-enhancing technique. Job enrichment may be successful only where poorly designed jobs exist initially. The following "structural clues" are offered to improve the shape of the job and the productivity and satisfaction of the person filling it:

1. Communication system—link the performer to the outcomes achieved via feedback.

2. Quality control—build responsibility for quality into the job.

3. Avoid fragmented responsibility for decision making.

4. Identify people for special training positions due to long service or technological knowledge.

5. Avoid overspecialization of jobs/titles.

6. Avoid unclear division of responsibilities.

7. Avoid overcomplicated work flows.

8. Avoid duplications of functions except where needed to create autonomous work groups.

9. Build labor pools which allow flexible allocation of human resources to expanded jobs (Whitsett, 1975).

In one company a four-phase program was developed to implement a job enrichment program. It included: 1) diagnosis, 2) top management exposure, 3) training key personnel, and 4) implementing the program. This program was reinforced, flexibility was emphasized, and the resources for implementation were made available. There are now 30 ongoing programs using this approach (Sirota & Wolfson, 1972).

Another five-step plan prescribed for job enrichment implementation included:

1. Experiment with one or two applications to learn intricacies of implementation and the associated job satisfaction and productivity results, if any;

2. Supervisory training;

3. Selection of jobs where job enrichment success appears to be most likely;

4. Brainstorm to select job changes (enrichment suggestions) that may impact on employee productivity/performance; and

5. Feedback—continual appraisal of attitudes and performance changes resulting from job changes (Carroll, 1974).

Yet another approach to implementation included gathering three sets of data to determine feasibility: 1) symptomatic (including turnover, absenteeism, and customer complaints) data which serves as a warning of impending human resource problems; 2) attitudinal data (measures of employee reactions foretelling possible impacts on the organization); and 3) structural data (including information on the technical feasibility of implementing job enrichment) (Yorks, 1974).

Above all, success of job enrichment programs is contingent upon the managerial strategies used for implementation. Important factors to incorporate are: 1) a participative style of supervision, 2) the introduction of management to job enrichment concepts, 3) supervisory workshops for brainstorming, and 4) team participation (Greenblatt, 1973). Other considerations crucial to success are: 1) pre-intervention diagnosis, 2) training supervisory personnel, 3) providing employees with additional authority to handle enriched tasks and job assignments, and 4) monitoring employee performance (feedback).

Improved employee productivity and satisfaction can be the result of a successful job enrichment/task design program. Clearly, a successful job enrichment program is related to the type of climate and management style characteristic of an organization. In reviewing organizational models, i.e., classical (pyramidal), behavioral, organic, or contingency, it is important to note that:

> . . . the right structure of organization is a function of the interaction of the variables, each balanced against effects of others and against the desired output of the organization. Thus, no one style of organization design is universally appropriate. (Ross & Murdick, 1973).

While this quote relates most directly to organizational design, it is clear that the same prescriptions can be made at the level of task design.

However, there is need for further research in actual work settings to determine the advisability of providing job enriching opportunities. In addition to further empirical research, a need is evident for generalizable frameworks to guide the "how" and "when" of applications as well as accurate measurements in assessing job enrichment programs.

Independent Variable

TIME OFF WORK

Type of Article	No. of Articles
Descriptive	1
Prescriptive	1

DESCRIPTIVE

Nealey, S. M. and Goodale, J. G., "Worker Preferences Among Time-Off Benefits and Pay," *Journal of Applied Psychology*, 1967, Vol. 51, No. 4, 357–361.

Industrial workers (N = 197) expressed their preferences among six proposals for additional paid time off the job. Preference for a comparable pay raise was also measured. Extra vacation was most preferred while a proposal to shorten the work day was least preferred. The pay raise was fifth in preference. Differences in preference were related to sex, age, marital status, and job satisfaction. Foremen were able to predict overall worker preferences with high accuracy.

PRESCRIPTIVE

Howell, M. A., "Time Off as a Reward for Productivity," *Personnel Administration*, November-December 1971, Vol. 34, No. 6, 48–51.

Maslow's Hierarchy of Needs theory is discussed as one way of viewing the pyschological factors involved in motivating employees. This article examines the use of time off as an incentive which affords the possibility of restoring the dignity of the individual and rescuing him from the anonymity associated with industrialization and domination by the corporation. It would allow a reorientation of societal values from the materialistic preoccupation with money and what it can buy, to time, and how it can be utilized.

Commentary

TIME OFF WORK

Most of the literature on time-off work as a reward is prescriptive and without empirical foundation. The use of time off as an incentive has been examined and viewed from a simplistic interpretation of the psychological aspects of Maslow's theory of a need hierarchy. It is suggested that time off would rescue workers from the anonymity associated with industrialization and domination by the corporation. Further, time off has been prescribed as encouraging a change from materialistic values to the more creative use of free time (Howell, 1971).

In one of the few empirical studies available (Nealey & Goodale, 1967), it was found that workers preferred extra vacation to extra pay. Differences in preferences were related to sex, age, marital status, and job satisfaction. In addition, in this sample at least, foremen were fairly accurate in predicting worker preferences.

Little research has been done to systematically investigate the impact of time off work on performance or job satisfaction or as an important reinforcement tool. Given the limited evidence available, prescriptions for managerial action are inappropriate.

Independent Variable

WORK SCHEDULES

Type of Article	No. of Articles
Applied	6
Descriptive	8
Empirical	2
Integrative	1
Prescriptive	3

APPLIED

Gannon, M. J., Poole, B. A. and Prangley, R. E., "Involuntary Job Rotation and Work Behavior," *Personnel Journal*, June 1972, Vol. 31, No. 6, 446–448.

While job rotation has usually been shown to be related to favorable outcomes, it is possible that this technique may result in negative consequences if it is enforced upon the employees involuntarily. The present study is an analysis of the relationship between involuntary job rotation (as the independent variable) and several measures of work behavior, i.e., absenteeism, turnover, overtime, lateness, changes in job assignment, number of accidents (dependent variables). The study was conducted in a municipal works department in a small suburban city. The department consisted of three divisions: streets, sanitation, and warehouse. Workers did not know of their assignments until the morning briefing each day.

Results indicated that the number of accidents and absences were significantly and positively associated with involuntary job rotation. Although overtime and lateness were not significantly correlated with involuntary job rotation, the relationships were in the predicted direction. The research suggests that involuntary job rotation minimizes participative decision making and heightens role ambiguity.

Fields, C. J., "Variable Work Hours—The MONY Experience," *Personnel Journal*, September 1974, Vol. 53, No. 9, 675–678.

An experiment was conducted with variable work hours in one department of a large New York insurance company, Mutual of New York's Group Insurance Company. The experiment was set up to allow a pilot group of 22 clerical employees to choose daily arrival times without advance notice. A seven and one quarter hour work day was required. Each individual maintained a daily record of hours worked. The pilot study, when evaluated at the end of six months, was found to be an unqualified success both in productivity figures (measured by average number of transactions processed per day) and by employee response. Supervisors, as well as staff, have responded favorably to the concept of variable work hours.

Zawacki, Robert A. and Johnson, Lason S., "Alternative Workweek Schedules: One Company's Experience with Flextime," *Supervisory Management*, 1976, Vol. 21, No. 6, 15–19.

This study reports the findings of a survey of a flextime program adopted by one large U.S. firm. The work schedule allowed for employees to come into work anytime between 6:30 and 8:30 a.m., and go home eight and one-half hours later. Questionnaires were distributed to 390 employees (supervisory and nonsupervisory). The results of the survey indicated that employees, in general, felt that flextime had a positive effect on such areas as productivity, tardiness, absenteeism, and morale. The authors conclude that these findings show that flextime has favorable consequences with regard to employee satisfaction, increased commitment to organizational goals and greater productivity.

Golembiewski, Robert T. and Hilles, Richard J., "Drug Company Workers Like New Schedules," *Monthly Labor Review*, February 1977, Vol. 100, No. 2, 65–69.

A flexible work hours policy was instituted in a large drug corporation. The new schedules allowed employees to start work anytime between 7:00 and 9:15 a.m., and stop work anytime between 3:00 and 6:00 p.m. of a five-day work week. All employees were required to be present for the hours between 9:15 a.m. and 3:00 p.m. Four programs with varying degrees of flexibility (amount of time an employee may "bank" in one day to shorten another work day in the same week) were used, dependent on the particular work group (i.e., manufacturing office employees [least flexible] and research and development [most flexible]). An evaluation of the attitudes of both supervisors and employees about their work, as well as information about absenteeism was done by the survey. Employee reaction, as taken from the survey, was favorable toward retaining flexible work hours. Most employees reported no perceived reduction in productivity. In addition, supervisors were also positive about flexible work hours. They reported improved employee morale and productivity. Single-day sick absences decreased although total sick days increased substantially.

Morgan, Frank T., "Your (Flex) Time May Come," *Personnel Journal*, February 1977, Vol. 56, No. 2, 82–96.

A case study involving a large business organization investigated the effects of flextime work schedules on employee absenteeism, tardiness, satisfaction level, and job performance. Schedules were comprised of the two "core time" periods: when mandatory attendance was required (9:30 a.m. to 12:00 noon and 1:30 p.m. to 4:00 p.m. [25 hours per week]) and flex hours: when people were permitted to establish their own schedule to complete the other 15 hours in a week (40 hours).

Results after a two-month (prior to flextime and two months after implementation) period showed a decrease in rate of absenteeism by 50 percent, virtual elimination of tardiness, a high level of satisfaction with the flextime schedule (as reported by survey) and about the same level of job performance. Differences between the flextime and nonflextime group with regard to satisfaction, work performance and personal life were statistically significant (ANOVA) and stable over an extended period of time. The author concludes that flextime schedules provide benefits for both the company and the employees. However, he recommends the use of research in the social psychology field relating to attitude and opinion change in overcoming any managerial resistance to flextime schedule changes.

Gomez-Mejia, Luis R.; Hopp, Michael A. and Sommerstad, C. Richard, "Implementation and Evaluation of Flexible Work Hours: A Case Study," *Personnel Administrator*, January 1978, Vol. 23, No. 1, 39–41.

This article examines a pilot study of flexitime which began in 1972 in the Microcircuit and Aerospace operations of Control Data Corporation. Guidelines were given to managers to aid implementation of the program (i.e., initial restriction of flexibility, maintenance of controls at all times, etc.). Different types of flexibility were made available such as individual or group flexibility, varying hours weekly or on a seasonal basis. After three years of operation, a questionnaire administered to a random sample of management and nonmanagement personnel yielded overall positive results. The authors conclude that the program was well received by both levels of employees who felt that they experienced an improved quality of life.

DESCRIPTIVE

Golembiewski, Robert T. and Hilles, Richard J., "Drug Company Workers Like New Schedules," *Monthly Labor Review*, February 1977, Vol. 100, No. 2, 65–69.

A flexible work hours policy was instituted in a large drug corporation. The new schedule allowed employees to start work any time between 7:00 and 9:15 a.m., and stop work any time between 3:00 and 6:00 p.m. of a five-day work week. All employees were required to be present for the five hours between 9:15 a.m. and 3:00 p.m. Four programs with varying degrees of flexibility (amount of time an employee may "bank" in one day to shorten another work day in the same week) were used, dependent on the particular work group (i.e., manufacturing office employees [least flexible] and research and development [most flexible]). An evaluation of the attitudes of both supervisors and employees about their work, as well as information about absenteeism was done by the survey. Employee reaction, as taken from the survey was favorable toward retaining flexible work hours. Most employees reported no perceived reduction in productivity. In addition, supervisors were also positive about flexible work hours. They reported improved employee morale and productivity. Single-day sick absences decreased although total sick days increased substantially.

Ivancevich, John M. and Lyon, Herbert L., "The Shortened Workweek: A Field Experience," *Journal of Applied Psychology*, February 1977, Vol. 62, No. 1, 34–37.

Effects of the four-day, 40-hour workweek were examined in the present field study by comparing two experimental groups (N = 97, N = 111) and a comparison group (N = 94) of operating employees in a medium-sized manufacturing company. Comparisons were made on dimensions of self-actualization, autonomy, personal worth, social affiliation, job security, pay and overall job satisfaction, anxiety-stress, absenteeism, and performance over a 13-month and 25-month period. The analysis of 13-month data indicated that the workers in four-day, 40-hour groups were: a) more satisfied with autonomy, personal worth, job security, and pay; b) experienced less anxiety-stress; and c) performed better with regard to productivity than did the comparison group. However, these improvements were not found with the 25-month data.

Morgan, Frank T., "Your (Flex) Time May Come," *Personnel Journal*, February 1977, Vol. 56, No. 2, 82–96.

A case study involving a large business organization investigated the effects of flextime work schedules on employee absenteeism, tardiness, satisfaction level and job performance. Schedules were comprised of the two "core time" periods: when mandatory attendance was required (9:30 a.m. to 12:00 noon and 1:30 p.m. to 4:00 p.m. [25 hours per week]) and flex hours: when people were permitted to establish their own schedule to complete the other 15 hours in a week (40 hours).

Results after a two-month (prior to flextime and two months after implementation) period showed a decrease in rate of absenteeism by 50 percent, virtual elimination of tardiness, a high level of satisfaction with the flextime schedule (as reported by survey) and about the same level of job performance. Differences between the flextime and nonflextime group with regard to satisfaction, work performance and personal life were statistically significant (ANOVA) and stable over an extended period of time. The author concludes that flextime schedules provide benefits for both the company and the employees. However, he recommends the use of research in the social psychology field relating to attitude and opinion change in overcoming any managerial resistance to flextime schedule changes.

Glueck, William F., "Changing Hours of Work: A Review and Analysis of the Research," *Personnel Administrator*, March 1979, Vol. 24, No. 3, 44–62.

As the majority of our conscious lives is affected by work and work hours, much energy has understandably been devoted to the formulation of alternative work schedules. This article summarizes the work on two approaches to changing hours of work. The first approach is called the "compressed work week". A compressed work week is the scheduling of the "normal" 40 hours in less than five days, usually in four 10-hour days. After listing the pros and cons of the compressed work week, it was concluded that this work schedule would most likely be accepted by employees with jobs that do not require heavy physical or taxing mental work. Also indicating a preference for the compressed work week were employees whose businesses do not require full-week service and who do not have capital intensive technology.

Originally implemented to help avoid traffic congestion in Europe, the second alternative work schedule is called "flexitime". A typical flexitime schedule is to work a "core time" of midmorning through midafternoon with the employee receiving the discretion of when to work the other hours. It is basically the scheduling of "normal" 40 hours a week, but only in more than one set of hours for the employees. Again, the pros and cons of this type of work schedule were listed. While these alternative work schedules have been well formulated, research on the issue is by no means complete. This article reported on what is known now and what needs to be done to improve the understanding of the impact of working hours on employees and interprice effectiveness.

Copperman, Lois F., "Alternative Work Policies in Private Firms," *Personnel Administrator*, October 1979, Vol. 24, No. 10, 40–44.

Although there have been many articles examining the pros and cons of alternative work policies, there have been few large scale surveys to determine the actual incidence of implementation. This is one such survey whose purpose was to examine employer policies which affect the labor force participation of older workers, policies which can and are generalized to all interested groups. The survey found implementation of alternative work patterns by 1,900 firms. The study involved a mail survey of 5,500 private firms with 20 or more employees randomly selected from the files of Dun & Bradstreet. A telephone survey of 250 private firms with 500+ employees was also used. Together the two surveys included 1,982,652 workers. The mail survey asked firms to indicate company position on alternative work policies by choosing one of five answers ranging from "implemented" to "not considered". They found that

14 percent have implemented "flexitime;" a small percentage uses "part-time options," although many are considering it; 7 percent have shared retirement programs; 6 percent have increased vacation time, and 79 percent have not considered these last two programs. The telephone survey indicated that 19 percent of the firms in this group employ one of these programs. It was also shown that there was no significant relationship between size of firms and alternative work policies.

Frease, Michael and Zawacki, Robert A., "Job Sharing: An Answer to Productivity Problems," *Personnel Administrator*, October 1979, Vol. 24, No. 10, 35–38.

A question addressed in many industries is "Does increased productivity outweigh increased expenses?" Job sharing, many feel, could be an answer to productivity problems. The term "job sharing" really implies three slightly different employment situations—job sharing, job pairing and job splitting. Thus far, three groups have benefitted most from job sharing, namely, women, students and retired teachers. Like any new innovation, job sharing has its share of advantages and disadvantages. Foremost on the advantage list are increased productivity, a wider pool of applicants and reduced costs. Research in one southeastern firm has shown that job sharing resulted in a seven percent higher output and a 12 percent lower scrap ratio. Heading the disadvantage list are difficulties with job sharers' continuity, supervision and accountability, and increased expenses, found mainly in the form of benefits packages (insurance, retirement, etc). Research here has shown that employers are still somewhat negative toward these programs, though both Maryland and Wisconsin are implementing statewide programs to help job sharers. Despite the disadvantages, proponents still underline the benefit of increased productivity that results from the job sharer's ability to work harder for shorter periods.

Petersen, Donald J., "Flexitime in the United States: The Lessons of Experience," *Personnel*, January-February 1980, 21–31.

The practice of flexitime was introduced in the United States about 1972 via Europe and it has proved to be a viable and mutually beneficial arrangement for both organizations and employees. The underlying principal of flexitime is to replace traditionally fixed times at which an employee begins and ends work by allowing him or her a limited choice in selecting work hours for each work day. A "core" period of hours is set up when all employees must be on the job and a flexible band of hours at the beginning and/or end of the work day is added on at the discretion of the employee to make up the required daily total. In a 1978 survey of American organizations using flexitime, it was found that it: 1) almost always raised employee morale, 2) reduced tardiness in 84 percent of the cases, 3) reduced absenteeism in more than 75 percent of the organizations, 4) reduced turnover 50 percent, 5) cut employee commuting time 75 percent of the time, and 6) increased productivity in almost 50 percent of the companies using flexitime. Some limitations of such a program are pointed out, indicating that the crucial consideration is to make sure that any program adopted will meet an organization's particular needs and characteristics. The article summarizes 11 reported case histories of American firms in which empirical studies have been undertaken and extracts from them some guidelines on the conditions under which flexitime is most likely to succeed. Results of available data and analyses indicate that, properly administered, flexitime offers benefits to employers in the form of a more satisfied and more highly motivated workforce, and it gives workers a sense of greater responsibility and autonomy in their working lives.

Barad, Cary B., "Flexitime Under Scrutiny: Research On Work Adjustment and Organizational Performance," *Personnel Administrator,* May 1980, Vol. 25, No. 5, 69–74.

The Social Security Administration implemented a pilot program in selected headquarters and field components to determine the effects of flexible working hours on employee work adjustment and organizational effectiveness. Employees could choose starting and quitting times on a daily basis but must be present for a five-and-a-half hour core period. Employees' reaction to introducing flexitime was overwhelmingly favorable while supervisors, though positive, were less enthusiastic than subordinates. Employee satisfaction with the system grew over time. The impact on morale and job satisfaction was generally more pronounced in operational settings than in those dealing with administrative or staff kinds of functions. Flexitime substantially curtailed employee tardiness. Short-term leave usage was reduced in three out of four cases. A sizeable proportion of the flexitime employees perceived an increase in the amount and accuracy of their work product which was attributed to flexitime. Supervisory perceptions and substantive output measures, however, were more temperate. Little evidence suggested that flexitime adversely affected job performance. In four of the five settings having objective data, the system was associated with varying degrees of improvement. As a result of this pilot project, flexitime was implemented throughout the SSA wherever feasible so that 47 percent of their total workforce now works on flexitime.

EMPIRICAL

Ivancevich, John M. and Lyon, Herbert L., "The Shortened Workweek: A Field Experience," *Journal of Applied Psychology,* February 1977, Vol. 62, No. 1, 34–37.

Effects of the four-day, 40-hour workweek were examined in the present field study by comparing two experimental groups ($N = 97$, $N = 111$) and a comparison group ($N = 94$) of operating employees in a medium-sized manufacturing company. Comparisons were made on dimensions of self-actualization, autonomy, personal worth, social affiliation, job security, pay and overall job satisfaction, anxiety-stress, absenteeism, and performance over a 13-month and 25-month period. The analysis of 13-month data indicated that the workers in a four-day, 40-hour group were: a) more satisfied with autonomy, personal worth, job security, and pay; b) experienced less anxiety-stress; and c) performed better with regard to productivity than did the comparison group. However, these improvements were not found with the 25-month data.

Schein, Virginia E.; Maurer, Elizabeth H. and Jovak, Jan F., "Impact of Flexible Working Hours on Productivity," *Journal of Applied Psychology*, August 1977, Vol. 62, No. 4, 463–465.

Using a sample of 246 clerical-level employees, the impact of a four-month flexible working hours experimental program on productivity for five production units within a large financial institution was investigated. The results of the study were mixed, but overall they indicated that the introduction of flexible working hours had no adverse impact on productivity. Based upon comparisons with productivity outcomes during the same time period the previous year, the results for one group indicated significant positive effects, based on pre-post comparisons, although other organizational changes may have produced this effect. The results for the other three groups indicated neither positive nor negative effects of flexible working hours on productivity.

INTEGRATIVE

Newstrom, John W. and Pierce, Jon L., "Alternative Work Schedules: The State of the Art," *Personnel Administrator*, October 1979, Vol. 24, No. 10, 19–23.

It has long been considered American to work hard and to work long, without any complaints. Thus, work scheduling alternatives have been virtually ignored. Recently, however, accompanying the increase in the standard of living, and the resultant increased interest in leisure time activities, the trend has been a slow and quiet evolution toward a shorter work week. This article reviews the state of the art, focusing on three objectives: the alternative work schedules themselves, research results, and implementation of the programs. Three related and unique themes can be found in the types of alternatives mentioned. They are the "compressed work week" (four 10-hour days instead of five eight-hour days); "discretionary working time" which consists of staggered start, staggered week and flexitime systems; and part-time employment, divided into job sharing and job splitting.

Initial research results are somewhat discouraging because of the questionable validity of the data, e.g., "we tried it" or "we liked it". The only real strong conclusion is that employee satisfaction increases (while absenteeism decreases) in conjunction with the implementation of these work schedules. However, the effects on productivity are less clear. Several suggestions are made for implementing these programs. They include: surveying work force values, closely examining many alternative forms, early research, employee acceptance, a pilot test, and constant evaluation. If these measures are taken, then it seems that alternative schedules of work hours can indeed improve the quality of work life.

PRESCRIPTIVE

Zeira, Y., "Job Rotation for Management Development," *Personnel*, July-August 1974, Vol. 51, No. 4, 25–35.

Of the many on-the-job training methods, job rotation is being advocated as one of the most effective management tools. Job rotation is defined and its advantages, limitations, and necessary requirements for application are looked at.

Swart, J. C., "What Time Shall I Go to Work Today?", *Business Horizons*, October 1974, Vol. 17, No. 5, 19–26.

This article focuses on flexible working hours—an arrangement that provided for a "gliding" workday that can vary from day to day in its length as well as in the time that it begins and ends. Also, some feedback information is provided in the form of initial experiences of some organizations in the United States with the new workweek format. Applications of flexi-time so far indicate that it will be used widely and that it will improve both job satisfaction and morale levels. Its effects in terms of productivity are less clear. The advantages of flexi-time are not based on solid research. A list of drawbacks and advantages has been drawn up and was included in the article to aid managers in putting flexible working hours into proper perspective.

Atwood, Caleb S., "A Work Schedule to Increase Productivity," *Personnel Administrator*, October 1979, Vol. 24, No. 10, 29–33.

There have been many attempts at reorganizing the work week. One successful technique is the American Productivity Center scheduling technique. Based on the assumption that Americans now actually work a 33.6 hour week (taking into account vacations, holidays, lunch hours, etc.), it is a way to increase employment, leisure time and profits while using a 35-hour work week. Basically, this technique involves the division of the employees into two groups which then alternate in the days that they work. The system has three- and four-day weekends and is set up in such a way that 10 days of vacation can result in 24 consecutive days off. This plan obviously has many advantages, one being the utilization of additional capacity. This article examines the detailed workings of this innovative system in a manufacturing operation, but can be easily adapted to other types of industries.

Commentary

WORK SCHEDULES

The literature on work scheduling abounds with such terms as job rotation, variable work hours, alternative work week, flextime, gliding work day, and core period. The common theme seems to be the assumed productivity improvements resulting from work schedules other than the traditional five-day, 40-hour week. Recently, variable work scheduling has begun to be perceived as a possibility and a definite asset to an organization. In applying variable scheduling to the work place, the literature reviewed is generally favorable concerning its impact. Most results have been positive. The benefits that appear to accrue to an organization through its use may include improved employee morale and productivity, a decrease in tardiness and absenteeism, and increased employee satisfaction. In addition, some advocates argue that these benefits are due to an employee's increased sense of autonomy—of directing his or her own life—and of personal worth.

In one study (Morgan, 1977), the impact of flextime work schedules on employee absenteeism, tardiness, satisfaction level, and job performance was investigated and results showed a decrease in rate of absenteeism by 50 percent, elimination of tardiness, and a high level of satisfaction along with an unchanged level of job performance. Conclusions were drawn that flextime schedules provide benefits for both employees and the company. In a survey (Golembiewski & Hilles, 1977) of employee and supervisor attitudes, it was found that both were positive about flextime scheduling and that it improved morale and productivity.

However, involuntary job rotation, which frequently accompanies nontraditional work schedules, showed some negative results in a study by Gannon, Poole & Prangley (1972). They found it to be associated with an increased number of accidents and absences and suggested that it also minimized participative decision-making and heightened role ambiguity. More research is needed here before we should make all-inclusive decisions about the use of job rotation (voluntary or involuntary) as a component of work scheduling and where it may be applicable. The literature is scarce and more evidence is needed as to its advantages/disadvantages, its impact on employee satisfaction, and on productivity.

While none of the changes in work scheduling surveyed has produced adverse effects on productivity, further evidence is needed to support its unequivocal prescription. For example, it is important to know whether positive effects dissipate over time and how to choose the best type of scheduling to match a specific organization's needs.

So far, applications indicate variable work scheduling will be widely used and will improve both job satisfaction and morale and present no adverse effects on productivity. However, it needs to be more widely researched to discover its full potential as a management tool—its advantages and disadvantages in different organizations should be defined. If a certain type of work scheduling fits an organization's technology and product or service markets, it may be a managerial controllable that may pay off in increased benefits to employees—and at little cost to the organization.

Dependent Variable

Absenteeism
Drugs/Drinking
Performance Quality
Safety
Satisfaction
Turnover

Dependent Variable

ABSENTEEISM

Type of Article	No. of Articles
Applied	10
Descriptive	9
Empirical	8
Integrative	2
Prescriptive	13

APPLIED

Grove, B. A., "Attendance Reward Plan Pays," *Personnel Journal*, February 1968, Vol. 47, No. 2, 119–120.

Two attendance incentive periods per year were established beginning January 1 and July 1. One-hundred dollars or 40 hours straight time pay (whichever is greater) was offered for *perfect attendance;* $50 or 20 hours straight time pay (whichever is greater) for perfect attendance, except for up to three occurrences of either tardiness or leaving early or a combination of these two, totalling no more than three occurrences; or perfect attendance except for one day's absence—no tardiness or leaving early. There was a 34 percent decrease in absenteeism.

Lawler, E. E., III and Hackman, J. R., "Impact of Employee Participation in the Development of Pay Incentive Plans," *Journal of Applied Psychology*, 1969, Vol. 53, No. 6, 467–471.

This article reports on a study of effects of employee participation in the development of pay incentive plans. The Ss were part-time workers who clean buildings in the evenings. Three autonomous work groups developed their own pay incentive plans to reward good attendance on the job (Condition A). These plans were then imposed by the company on other work groups (Condition B). There were two groups of control Ss: one talked with Ss about job attendance problems but received no additional experimental treatment, and the other received no treatment. A significant increase in attendance followed on Condition A. Possible reasons cited: a) participation caused Ss to be more committed to the plan, b) Ss who participated in the development of their plan were more knowledgeable about it, and c) participation increased the employees' trust of the good intentions of management with respect to the plan.

Gary, A. L., "Industrial Absenteeism: An Evaluation of Three Models of Treatment," *Personnel Journal*, May 1971, Vol. 50, No. 5, 352–353.

This study, conducted in a manufacturing plant employing 4600 people, was designed to evaluate the effectiveness of preventive and corrective measures for unexcused absences. The rule enforced begins with a written reprimand and progresses to an extended time of suspension from work, and finally, to dismissal. After careful examination of the disciplinary files, it was discovered that absentee employees could be subdivided into one of three groups: those designated as "disciplined permanently," those "disciplined indiscriminantly," and those who received "no discipline". Based on experimental evidence, it was hypothesized that there would be no significant differences in the three treatment methods. The first two categories, N = 50 in each, were drawn from absentee records. All personal data were gathered from personnel records. Ss were then assigned to one of the three categories. At this time causal absences for the previous 20 months were recorded for each subject. Analysis of variance technique was applied.

The hypothesis was rejected offering support for the "permanent discipline" method. Results also indicate that well-intentioned discipline removals may tend to serve as rewards for undesirable behavior. Subjects for all categories were then sorted into two groups: production jobs and nonproduction jobs. Unexcused absences over an identical 20-month period were used as a criterion. Results were contrary to those expected by management. For some time, members of management had believed that the assembly-type work characteristic of production jobs resulted in a higher absentee rate. The means indicate that this is not the case. Finally, age and years of service were correlated with absences and little association was found. Since the factors of age, years of service, and racial category apparently are insignificantly related to absenteeism, the type of job an individual holds and the interaction between the supervisor and the disciplined employee become crucial. Permanent discipline, when used in conjunction with the other two methods, proved to be most effective.

Pocock, S. J.; Sergean, R. and Taylor, P. J., "Absence of Continuous Three-Shift Workers: A Comparison of Traditional and Rapidly Rotating Systems," *Occupational Psychology*, 1972, Vol. 46, 7–13.

Complete absence records of 782 shift workers in one factory have been studied before and after a change from a continuous seven day "traditional" rota to a rapidly rotating "continental" rota. A comparion between a 12-month period before the change and similar period afterwards show a rise in certified sickness absence of 36 percent, in uncertified sickness absence of 29 percent, and a fall in absence for reasons other than sickness of two percent. Certified sickness of the insured population in that part of England rose by only eight percent. Sickness absence commences most frequently on the night shift under both systems but this became even more marked for uncertified sickness after the change. These results suggest that social acceptability should not be the only factor considered when a change of system is contemplated.

Pedalino, E. and Gamboa, V. U., "Behavior Modification and Absenteeism: Intervention in One Industrial Setting," *Journal of Applied Psychology*, 1974, Vol. 59, No. 6, 694–698.

Behavior modification was used in an attempt to decrease absenteeism in a sample of 215 hourly employees at a manufacturing/distribution facility. Employees in four adjoining plants served as comparison groups. An ABA (baseline, intervention, return to baseline) intervention using a lottery incentive system constituted the experimental design. Absenteeism decreased significantly following the experimental group intervention but did not decrease in any of the four comparison groups. Further, stretching the schedule of reinforcement did not increase the rate of absenteeism. Findings are discussed in light of Lawler and Hackman's 1969 study which indicated participation, not the incentive system, decreased absenteeism. Caution should be taken in interpreting these results, as "significance" is probably due solely to nonindependent observations. At the least, results are likely to be positively inflated to a high degree because of this problem.

Rotondi, Thomas, Jr., "Behavior Modification on the Job," *Supervisory Management*, February 1976, Vol. 21, No. 2, 22–28.

The author advocates the use of operant conditioning (behavior modification techniques) in the organizational context by means of a seven-step procedure: creating a consistent work environment (defining policies and procedures consistently); determining the desired behaviors of subordinates (i.e., high level of output produced); determining the type of rewards to use (i.e., money, promotion, praise, etc.); clearly communicating desired behaviors and rewards to subordinate (employee knows what is expected of him); providing immediate rewards for desired behaviors; providing rewards on a variable-ratio schedule; and minimizing the use of punishment. The author relates that behavior modification can be used to decrease tardiness and absenteeism.

Wallin, Jerry A. and Johnson, Ronald D., "The Positive Reinforcement Approach to Controlling Employee Absenteeism," *Personnel Journal*, August 1976, Vol. 55, No. 8, 390–392.

The authors advocate the application of operant conditioning principles, a Positive Reinforcement System (PRS), to improve worker attendance and reduce sick leave costs. A pilot study was conducted in an electronics firm where absenteeism was high. A program was implemented in which production and office personnel could participate in a monthly lottery drawing contingent upon perfect monthly attendance and punctuality records. A $10 cash prize was awarded to the winner of each monthly draw selected from a basket containing the names of eligible employees. In addition to the monetary reward, all qualifying employees also had their names listed on the plant bulletin board (social reinforcement). In comparing the sick leave costs for the 11 months prior to initiating the lottery reward system with the 11 post-lottery months, the authors cite an average monthly decrease of 30.6 percent ($3,100 total savings).

The authors conclude from this pilot study that a lottery-base work attendance reward system can be a powerful supplement to an organizations compensation system. Moreover, they suggest possible applications to other areas such as safety and production rates.

Luthans, Fred and Martinko, Mark, "An Organizational Behavior Modification Analysis of Absenteeism," *Human Resource Management*, Fall 1976, Vol. 15, No. 3, 11–18.

The authors present a problem-solving model based on organizational behavior modification (operant conditioning paradigm) for analyzing and remedying absenteeism in work organizations. Predicated on the knowledge that positive consequences will increase the behavior's frequency of occurrence (reinforcement) and that negative and neutral consequences decrease the behavior's frequency of occurrence (punishment and extinction), the authors approach that problem of absenteeism as a process characterized by the following steps: identifying and measuring (baseline) the exact behavior which is to be changed, analyzing the antecedent cues and consequences influencing past and present behavior (attendance/absenteeism), developing an intervention strategy to control target behaviors through environmental consequences either by a program for reinforcing attendance (i.e., credit towards personal time, supervisor recognition, social reinforcers, feedback), a punishment strategy (i.e., verbal warnings) or extinction (i.e., ignoring absenteeism) or by combinations (i.e., ignoring absenteeism and praising attendance). Finally, the frequency of the resulting behavior is monitored and performance is evaluated.

The authors cite two salient features of successful programs—rewards must be meaningful and the criterion for achieving the reward is realistic and contingently applied to the majority in the organization. Moreover, they suggest that consequences can be dispensed on either a continuous or intermittent scheduling basis, depending on the intended results.

Orphen, C., "Effects of Bonuses for Attendance on the Absenteeism of Industrial Workers," *Journal of Organizational Behavior Management*, 1978, Vol. 1, No. 2, 110–117.

Pedalino and Gamboa (1974) found that a lottery incentive system reduced absenteeism significantly. Herman, Montez, Dominquez, Montez, and Hopkins (1973) found that a bonus for punctuality decreased tardiness markedly. The success of these studies provided the impetus for the present study, which was an attempt to improve attendance among industrial workers by giving bonuses for regular attendance. The subjects, a sample of 46 female factory workers in South Africa, were randomly assigned to either a treatment or nontreatment group. The treatment group received a small bonus (50¢) for each week they attended work every day, while the nontreatment group received no extra money for attendance. An ABAB design was used in which baseline measures were taken (A), the intervention (small bonus) was applied (B), removed (A), and then reapplied (B). The bonus payment decreased the rate of absenteeism in the treatment group significantly compared to its own baseline rates and to those of the nontreatment group over the same time periods. These results suggest that tying a small weekly bonus to attendance is a practical procedure for decreasing absenteeism among certain workers.

Kent, Harry M; Malotl, Richard W. and Greening, Marie, "Improving Attendance at Work in a Volunteer Food Cooperative with a Token Economy," *Journal of Organizational Behavior Management*, Summer 1977, Vol. 1, No. 1, 89–98.

The present study sought to evaluate the effects of an added conditioned reinforcer on previously voluntary behavior in a business setting. The behavior was attendance at work and the setting included 196 workers at a food cooperative. Response techniques included a sign-up sheet for committed workers, a $.50 token to be exchanged for food for each committed hour actively worked. For the last 15 weeks of the study, a posted notice of the food credit was added to the food credit condition. Study results indicated that dependability with which workers attended showed an increase, the introduction of the food credit condition and the increase was maintained throughout the study. In analyzing the results of this study, it is suggested that data of this sort should help reduce the many failures of cooperative ventures caused by over-emphasis on "inner causes" of behavior. Other volunteer organizations may also profit and obtain increased participation through the use of small extrinsic consequences.

DESCRIPTIVE

Vaid, K. N., "Work Behavior and Work Attitude—A Study of Absentees," *Indian Journal of Industrial Relations*, January 1967, Vol. 2, No. 3, 378–392.

This paper reports an investigation conducted to study perceptions of "work" of chronic absentee workers, and to compare them with those of the extremely regulars. The perceptions sought to be studied included such aspects of work as company, task, working conditions and wages, work group, supervisors, and communication. The study involved interviews with 75 chronic absentees and 75 extremely regular workers, which were conducted with the help of a specially designed questionnaire. The author found that workers' attitudes towards statutorily regulated aspects of work were not relevant to their work behavior. Chronic absenteeism was related to the extent of workers' identification with the company, integration with work group, satisfaction with supervisors, and the belief in the fair play and justice of the company. The workers' image of the company was not dependent on their attitude towards work because they valued the "job".

Fegley, R. K., "Bonus Plan Rewards Good Attendance," *Administrative Management*, January 1968, Vol. 29, No. 1, 43–44.

Two goals were sought (reward good attendance and reduce absenteeism) and achieved. Two hours bonus pay was given for each full month of perfect attendance; for each three-month period an extra three hours of pay was earned; a full year was worth 36 hours. Absence for death in immediate family is an exception. Tardiness within reasonable limits was not considered a loss of bonus hours. The program was considered an excellent morale booster.

Gerstenfeld, A., "Employee Absenteeism: New Insights," *Business Horizons*, October 1969, Vol. 12, No. 5, 51–57.

The purpose of this study is twofold: to disentangle several of the elements of satisfaction and try to relate them to absenteeism; to examine other factors such as age, and relate these factors to absenteeism. Research presented was conducted in two major companies. One hundred forty-eight female employees completed questionnaires.

In investigating correlates with absenteeism, the author found that some factors were strongly related to absenteeism, while others showed little or no relationship. An employee's satisfaction with the company in general shows no relation to his absentee record. There is also no relation found between the employee's attitude toward his work load or his pay and absenteeism. There is, however, a strong relation between the worker's attitude toward his immediate supervisor and his absences. Those workers who feel that their boss is frequently unfair are generally the same workers with poor records of attendance. The employee's attitude toward working conditions (such as heat, light, ventilation, etc.) is related to his attendance record. Employees who rate their working conditions as generally bad are the same employees who are high on absences. Those employees who rate the working conditions as very good and good, are the same employees who show a low record of absences. The implications of this study seem to indicate management should be urged to reexamine the physical working conditions as a major contributor to absences. Management also should be urged to consider the problem of child care as a major contributor to absences where working mothers are employed.

Burke, R. J. and Wilcox, D. S., "Absenteeism and Turnover Among Female Telephone Operators," *Personnel Psychology*, Winter 1972, Vol. 25, No. 4, 639–647.

The investigation considered in this article considers the following questions: 1) Are absenteeism (AB) and turnover (TO) related? 2) Is there a progression of alienation or withdrawal indicated by AB followed by eventual TO? The investigation examines the nature of the relationship between AB and TO at 1) both group and individual levels of analysis, using 2) objective and control procedures, for 3) individuals with the same relative length of tenure with the organization.

Method:
Group level: 14 operator offices were used as subject groups. Two measures of AB were used. First was total unexcused absence hours divided by total hours worked. The second was similar to the first, but excluded any absence time beyond the seventh calendar day after the last day worked.

Individual level: 127 telephone operators, who were divided into four experimental groups based on the amount of time they stayed with the organization. The measure of TO used was voluntary resignation. Two measures of AB were used: annualized days of absence and annualized number of times absent.

Results:
Group level: Results of this investigation show that TO correlates positively and significantly with incidental absence rates, but not with total absence rates, across the 14 telephone operator groups. The author examined some possible explanations for the variations in results, among those being the definitions and measures of AB and TO; the age and seniority level characteristics of the individual involved; the presence or absence of effective attendance control procedures in the organization.

Individual level: Results indicated a positive and significant relationship between AB and TO for female telephone operators. In each tenure period, the "leavers" had higher AB than the "stayers"—even though some of the "stayers" left shortly thereafter. The data strongly supports the progression of withdrawal hypothesis—that of progressively worsening AB culminating in TO.

Morgan, Lillie Guinell and Herman, Jeanne Brett, "Perceived Consequences of Absenteeism," *Journal of Applied Psychology*, December 1976, Vol. 61, No. 6, 738–742.

The present study was designed to investigate whether organizational policies and practices can be effective deterrents to absenteeism. Hypotheses about the relationships between consequences of absenteeism and past and future absenteeism were based on an expectancy model of behavior. Data was collected (individual structured interviews) from 60 blue-collar employees in one department of a unionized automobile-parts foundry. Consequences of absenteeism were measured by a three-point Likert-type scale, grouped by whether or not they were likely to motivate or deter absenteeism.

The results indicate that for some employees absenteeism provides an opportunity to experience consequences that tend to encourage absenteeism and that are not offset by organizationally controlled consequences that would tend to deter absenteeism. An absenteeism policy that both rewards attendance with consequences that usually motivate absenteeism and one that penalizes absenteeism is proposed.

Pate, Larry E.; Nielsen, Warren R. and Mowday, Richard T., "A Longitudinal Assessment of the Impact of Organization Development on Absenteeism, Grievance Rates and Product Quality," *Academy of Management Proceedings*, 1977, 353–357.

Archival data (160 weeks) were collected before, during, and after a major OD effort in an automotive manufacturing plant. The present study attempted to determine the efficacy of OD (team skill training and planning, etc.) in reducing absenteeism, grievances, and quality of work in approximately 2,600 hourly employees. The results suggest that the OD intervention may have resulted in decreased absenteeism. However, increases in quality of production (i.e., percentage of cars produced that met quality standards) were slight.

Stephens, Tedd A. and Burroughs, Wayne A., "An Application of Operant Conditioning to Absenteeism in a Hospital Setting," *Journal of Applied Psychology*, 1978, Vol. 63, No. 4, 518–521.

Two financial reward systems were used in a hospital setting to reduce absenteeism among 92 nurses, ward clerks, and nursing assistants. Six nursing units were randomly assigned to one of the two reward systems. System A permitted subjects to become eligible for case prize drawings of $20 if they evidenced no absenteeism during a three-week period. System B allowed subjects to become eligible for $20 prize drawings if they were not absent on eight dates randomly selected from the three-week period. An analysis of variance with a repeated measures design was used to assess differences between the two reward systems. Both reward systems resulted in significant decreases in absenteeism, and no significant differences were obtained between the two systems. Also, point-biserial correlations relating income level and absenteeism yielded nonsignificant results.

Kempen, Robert W. and Hall, R. Vance, "Reduction of Industrial Absenteeism: Results of a Behavioral Approach," *Journal of Organizational Behavior Management*, Summer 1977, Vol. 1, No. 1, 1–21.

This study was undertaken to extend the meager data base on the effects of behavioral interventions on absence rates. Specifically, the study was designed to investigate the long-term effects of non-monetary incentives, coupled with disciplinary procedures for excessive absenteeism on the attendance of workers who are representative of the bulk of employees in American industry. Detailed descriptions of the method used in the study covered subjects and setting (groups of hourly-rate workers in tool factories of a large manufacturing company), measurement, reliability (of data obtained), and procedure. Experimental procedures and conditions were described. Results of the study using the Attendance Management Systems intervention produced socially significant improvements in attendance among hourly employees at the two experimental plants. Within the limits of this quasi-experimental study, the results strongly suggest that the procedures for AMS design provide a practical framework to resolve the widespread and growing problem of industrial absenteeism.

Kuzmits, Frank E., "How Much Is Absenteeism Costing Your Organization?" *Personnel Administrator*, June 1979, Vol. 24, No. 6, 29–33.

Kuzmits' report says that traditional accounting and personnel information systems simply do not generate data which reflects the estimated dollars-and-cents costs of absenteeism. Kuzmits details the data that management must gather to make such cost estimates and, using a hypothetical steel manufacturer with 1,200 employees, attempts to realistically portray the problems and costs related to employee absenteeism and to explore the mechanics of computing costs.

EMPIRICAL

Gerstenfeld, A., "Employee Absenteeism: New Insights," *Business Horizons*, October 1969, Vol. 12, No. 5, 51–57.

The purpose of this study is twofold: to disentangle several of the elements of satisfaction and try to relate them to absenteeism; to examine other factors such as age, and relate these factors to absenteeism. Research presented was conducted in two major companies. One hundred forty-eight female employees completed questionnaires.

In investigating correlates with absenteeism, we found that some factors were strongly related to absenteeism, while others showed little or no relationship. An employee's satisfaction with the company in general show no relation to his absentee record. There is also no relation found between the employee's attitude toward his work load or his pay and absenteeism. There is, however, a strong relation between the worker's attitude toward his immediate supervisor and his absences. Those workers who feel that their boss is frequently unfair are generally the same workers with poor records of attendance. The employee's attitude toward working conditions (such as heat, light, ventilation, etc.) is related to his attendance record. Employees who rate their working conditions as generally bad are the same employees who are high on absences. Those employees who rate the working conditions as very good and good are the same employees who show a low record of absences. The implications of this study seem to indicate management should be urged to reexamine the physical working conditions as a major contributor to absences. Management also should be urged to consider the problem of child care as a major contributor to absences where working mothers are employed.

Wallin, J. A. and Johnson, R. D., "The Use of Positive Reinforcement to Reduce the Costs Associated With Employee Absenteeism," *Proceedings of the 28th Annual Winter Meeting*, Industrial Relations Research Association, December 1975, Dallas, Texas, 41–46.

This study reports the results of applying a monetary lottery for regular attendance and zero tardiness. The sample consisted of 80 nonexempt employees of an electronics manufacturing firm. The lottery combined elements of fixed interval and variable-ratio schedules of reinforcement. A before/after design yielded a 28.8 percent decrease in sick-leave expenses incurred by the company and a 41 percent drop in absenteeism. Implications are drawn for applications of reinforcement principles to other problem areas: safety, production quantity, and quality.

Wallin, Jerry A. and Johnson, Ronald D., "The Positive Reinforcement Approach to Controlling Employee Absenteeism," *Personnel Journal*, August 1976, Vol. 55, No. 8, 390–392.

The authors advocate the application of operant conditioning principles, a Positive Reinforcement System (PRS), to improve worker attendance and reduce sick leave costs. A pilot study was conducted in an electronics firm where absenteeism was high. A program was implemented in which production and office personnel could participate in a monthly lottery drawing contingent upon perfect monthly attendance and punctuality records. A $10 cash prize was awarded to the winner of each monthly draw selected from a basket containing the names of eligible employees. In addition to the monetary reward, all qualifying employees also had their names listed on the plant bulletin board (social reinforcement). In comparing the sick leave costs for the 11 months prior to initiating the lottery reward system with the 11 post-lottery months, the authors cite an average monthly decrease of 30.6 percent ($3,100 total savings).

The authors conclude from this pilot study that a lottery-base work attendance reward system can be a powerful supplement to an organizations compensation system. Moreover, they suggest possible applications to other areas such as safety and production rates.

Ilgen, Daniel R. and Hollenback, John H., "The Role of Job Satisfaction in Absence Behavior," *Organizational Behavior and Human Performance*, June 1977, Vol. 19, No. 1, 148–161.

Two models of absence behavior were compared for a sample of 166 clerical workers in a university setting. The first considered absence behavior (sick leave and personal level) as a function of job satisfaction (as measured by the MSQ). Additional pressures toward attendance, both internal (the individual's value system) and external (co-workers and job structure) as well as four demographic variables (age, husband a student, number of children, children under seven years old) were considered as moderators of the absenteeism/job satisfaction relationship. The role pressure variables (internal and external) were measured with a 5-point Likert scale (strongly disagree to strongly agree). The second model considered absenteeism as a function of role pressures and job satisfaction in an additive rather than a moderate faction. Only the additive model was supported. The conclusion reached was that job satisfaction was unrelated to absenteeism. This was also true when the possibility of moderated relationship was explored.

Stephens, Tedd A. and Burroughs, Wayne A., "An Application of Operant Conditioning to Absenteeism in a Hospital Setting," *Journal of Applied Psychology*, 1978, Vol. 63, No. 4, 518–521.

Two financial reward systems were used in a hospital setting to reduce absenteeism among 92 nurses, ward clerks, and nursing assistants. Six nursing units were randomly assigned to one of the two reward systems. System A permitted subjects to become eligible for cash prize drawings of $20 if they evidenced no absenteeism during a three-week period. System B allowed subjects to become eligible for $20 prize drawings if they were not absent on eight dates randomly selected from the three-week period. An analysis of variance with a repeated measures design was used to assess differences between the two reward systems. Both reward systems resulted in significant decreases in absenteeism, and no significant differences were obtained between the two systems. Also, point-biserial correlations relating income level and absenteeism yielded nonsignificant results.

Orphen, C., "Effects of Bonuses for Attendance on the Absenteeism of Industrial Workers," *Journal of Organizational Behavior Management*, 1978, Vol. 1, No. 2, 110–117.

Pedalino and Gamboa (1974) found that a lottery incentive system reduced absenteeism significantly. Herman, Montez, Dominquez, Montez, and Hopkins (1973) found that a bonus for punctuality decreased tardiness markedly. The success of these studies provided the impetus for the present study, which was an attempt to improve attendance among industrial workers by giving bonuses for regular attendance. The subjects, a sample of 46 female factory workers in South Africa, were randomly assigned to either a treatment or nontreatment group. The treatment group received a small bonus (50¢) for each week they attended work every day, while the nontreatment group received no extra money for attendance. An ABAB design was used in which baseline measures were taken (A), the intervention (small bonus) was applied (B), removed (A), and then reapplied (B). The bonus payment decreased the rate of absenteeism in the treatment group significantly compared to its own baseline rates and to those of the nontreatment group over the same time periods. These results suggest that tying a small weekly bonus to attendance is a practical procedure for decreasing absenteeism among certain workers.

Dittrich, John E. and Carrell, Michael R., "Organizational Equity Perceptions, Employee Job Satisfaction, and Departmental Absence and Turnover Rates," *Organizational Behavior and Human Performance*, August 1979, Vol. 24, No. 1, 29–40.

Employee job satisfaction and perceptions of equitable treatment and their relationship to employee absence and or turnover are examined longitudinally in a field setting. The sample consists of 158 clerical employees, mostly female, more than 40 percent of whom are 25 years of age or younger. Individual questionnaires were used to obtain perceptions of equity and feeling of job satisfaction. The response rate was more than 90 percent. The authors conclude that dimensionalized perceptions of equity displayed several predictive relationships. Their effects seem more important in organizational behavior than had been suspected. Internally oriented equity perception dimensions were stongly related to job satisfaction. But, perceptions of equitable treatment were found to be stronger predictors of absence and turnover than were job satisfaction variables.

Cheloha, Randall S. and Farr, James L., "Absenteeism, Job Investment and Job Satisfaction in an Organizational Setting," *Journal of Applied Psychology*, August 1980, Vol. 65, No. 4, 467–473.

Measures of job satisfaction, job involvement and absenteeism were gathered for a sample of state government employees. The results include the finding that job involvement does relate to absenteeism, though job satisfaction does not. It is possible, the authors conclude, that job satisfaction functions as one element of a broader field of variables that influence job involvement. Further conceptual and empirical work delineating the constructs of job involvement and intrinsic job satisfaction appear warranted, the study says. Conclusions of the study should be treated cautiously since the number of statistical tests performed on the data was relatively large given the sample size and that could increase the likelihood of spurious findings.

INTEGRATIVE

Lyons, T. F., "Turnover and Absenteeism: A Review of Relationships and Shared Correlates," *Personnel Psychology*, Summer 1972, Vol. 25, No. 2, 271–281.

There has been little attention in the past to the interrelationship of absenteeism and turnover. Three points of view reflect some assumptions that have been made about the relationships of these two behaviors. First, there is a continuum of withdrawal behaviors, progressing from absenteeism to turnover. A second view sees absences, along with accidents, as being forms of withdrawal behavior that are alternatives to turnover. A third view is that the two behaviors, related or not, share common causes. Therefore, the questions being asked are: 1) Are absenteeism and turnover associated? 2) Is there a progression of alienation indicated by absenteeism and followed by turnover? 3) Are these two forms of behavior influenced, determined, or related to the same factors? The author reviews the literature of individual-level studies and group-level studies in this area and arrives at some conclusions.

Pertaining to the first question of whether AB and TO are related, 16 of 29 independent tests of this relationship were significant and positive; one was significant and negative. On the individual level there was unanimous support of the relationship. In regard to the second question, whether or not AB and TO were influenced by common factors, it was found that in 11 samples examining 92 variables, both AB and TO were related significantly to only eight, pointing to little support for the notion of common correlates.

Schmitz, Loretta M. and Heneman, Herbert G. III, "Do Positive Reinforcement Programs Reduce Employee Absenteeism?" *Personnel Administrator*, September 1980, Vol. 25, No. 9, 87–93.

This article reviews the accumulated evidence on the effectiveness of continuous or partial reinforcement schedules to bring about positive desired attendance behavior in organizations. Ten studies were reviewed as having investigated the effectiveness of positive reinforcement programs in reducing employee absenteeism, and a discussion of the results followed. Several limitations of the studies were pointed out, since it was not at all certain as to which components of the reinforcement programs were responsible for the results obtained, or if additional behaviors (i.e., supervisory awareness reflected in new behaviors that function as reinforcers such as praise or posting absenteeism records) also contributed to results. The evidence from the studies suggest that implementation of a positive reinforcement program is accompanied by some reduction in employee absenteeism. Rigorous experimental designs are necessary so that the effects of the programs in general can be gauged, as well as the relative effects of their specific components, with greater concern for and measurement of the cost effectiveness of these reinforcement programs over the long run.

PRESCRIPTIVE

Ruchti, W. N., "Is There an Answer for Lateness and Absenteeism?", *Supervisory Management*, November 1967, Vol. 12, No. 11, 20–23.

The article summarizes a number of aspects uncovered about tardiness and absenteeism. The author gives a long list of factors which have been thought to influence tardiness and absenteeism. Whether or not these problems are accidental or controllable is also discussed and how a supervisor can determine this. A workable plan for handling the chronically late is identified: 1) Identify the steady offender by means of up-to-date attendance records. 2) Investigate the underlying causes of lateness, by means of a quiet, confidential talk with the employee. 3) Ask the employee what he is planning to do to correct his tardiness. 4) If the tardiness continues, feel free to resort to appropriate discipline. 5) Dismissal, as a last resort.

Alexander, A. M., "Controlling Absenteeism: What Can Be Done," *Public Personnel Management,* April 1969, Vol. 30, No. 2, 93–96.

This article tells of the experience of one agency that implemented aggressive, yet fair and equitable uniform attendance standards as an aid in controlling absenteeism. The attendance standards are outlined and the benefits to be gained are: 1) Employees are treated equitably and objectively throughout the organization. 2) Employees know what is expected of them and can take positive action when their performance starts to falter. 3) Management can plan and control workload more efficiently through better utilization of staff. 4) Management can produce the best possible product at the least cost. 5) Employees and management can utilize available fringe benefits to their advantage.

Vaid, K. N., "Discussion and Communication on Containing Absenteeism," *Indian Journal of Industrial Relations,* July 1970, Vol. 6, No. 1, 69–74.

The purpose of this article is to suggest measures to contain both the rates of and fluctuations in absenteeism in industrial enterprises. Suggestions were formulated on the basis of some analytical studies on the subject conducted in Indian industrial enterprises. Absenteeism is one of the major labor problems in Indian enterprises. Traditionally, it has been understood as a form of worker behavior caused by various socio-personal factors. However, it has been noticed during recent years that workers resort to absenteeism as a part of their industrial relations strategy for securing specific gains which are not otherwise available to them.

To contain the problem of absenteeism, a number of measures are suggested which a company might follow: 1) Companies should distinguish between "absence" (authorized) and absenteeism (unauthorized). 2) Companies should distinguish between the forms of absenteeism, one which is resorted to by workers as a strategy in industrial relations and the other which represents a form of workers' behavior. 3) The companies should adopt manning standards, keeping in mind the rates of absence as well as absenteeism. 4) A company will do well in keeping a watch over those workers who take medical leaves of short durations too frequently, and take up such cases with specified doctors. 5) A company should analyze the structure of workers' absence. The peripheral cases could be disregarded as those of unavoidable absenteeism. The core groups should be located and given counseling. 6) In between the peripheral and core groups of absentees, there rests a large number of absentee workers who could be expected to become more regular in their attendance as a result of administrative action. 7) Frequently leaves are given liberally at a time when the men are needed most. The companies should operate counter-seasonal leave policies.

Wilkinson, R., "How to Help Control Absenteeism," *Supervision*, August 1970, Vol. 32, No. 8, 3–4.

Absenteeism is a business problem and can be solved only in a business-like way. First, find out as much as possible about the reality of the situation, by asking questions such as how many were absent, from which shifts, what age groups, a relation between this and that, etc. The next thing to do is to draw up a good work picture of the situation that will show *where* the problem lies *when* the problem occurs; *why* it seems to happen most of the time. The next step is to plan a series of training meetings among the managers or supervisors where most of the problems lie. Implement training sessions placing emphasis on: stating the absenteeism facts, establish what exactly can be controlled in absenteeism, and organize a discussion as how this it to be done.

Nord, W., "Improving Attendance Through Rewards," *Personnel Administration*, November-December 1970, Vol. 33, No. 6, 37–41.

The intent of this article is to show how reward systems may be modified to increase the rate of one type of behavior, work attendance, which is necessary to realize organizational goals. Case histories of two organizations are discussed in terms of the reward programs that were used at the companies. One organization implemented a "lottery" method to improve attendance, in which those eligible for the prize drawings would be those who had perfect attendance and punctuality records for the preceding month. The second organization chose to use an interval reward program, a program which rewards everyone who has met the specified criterion with a fixed reward after a certain time interval. Results from both programs have been successful; however, in comparing the two, the lottery method seems to be more consistent with knowledge about the control of human behavior.

The author concludes by saying that many personnel practices reward people for behavior which leads away from organizational goals. By defining what behavior is desired, and rewarding it, future personnel policies can contribute to an organization's ends more than they do now.

Clark, W., "How to Cut Absenteeism and Turnover," *Administrative Management*, March 1971, Vol. 32, No. 3, 64–65.

This article prescribes steps to be taken to substantially reduce absenteeism and turnover: 1) Understand your absenteeism/turnover problem by studying its past and present effects on your organization. 2) Compile statistical data on your experience with absenteeism and turnover. 3) Make a detailed study of present company policies and practices to determine if any of them might unwittingly contribute to absenteeism and/or turnover. 4) Study the information gathered previously to determine what specific actions must be initiated to reduce absenteeism and turnover. 5) Establish standards (maximum acceptable level of absenteeism/turnover). Base the standards on the departmental experience learned during initial compilation of data. 6) Implement a "caretaker" policy in which the firm's absenteeism and turnover activity are monitored at regular intervals by your personnel department.

Hartman, R. E. and Gibson, J. J., "The Persistent Problem of Employee Absenteeism," *Personnel Journal*, July 1971, Vol. 50, No. 7, 535–539.

Causes of absenteeism are examined: poor leadership or supervision; job dissatisfaction; sickness or injury, job or nonjob-related; lack of group cohesiveness; poor working conditions; absence-prone individuals. There are a number of other minor contributing factors. Designing an absentee control program involves: 1) defining what you mean by absenteeism, 2) developing adequate means of measuring absenteeism, 3) careful employee selection process, 4) employee orientation program, 5) supervisory training, 6) union management relations, 7) provide a good working environment, and 8) encourage group cohesiveness.

Gemmell, A. J., "Personnel and Line Management: Partners in Absentee Control," *Personnel Journal*, February 1973, Vol. 52, No. 2, 113–115.

To alleviate absenteeism, personnel managers should make sure that line management is fully aware of the consequences of absenteeism. The personnel manager can easily illustrate the cost factors of absenteeism—the actual dollars and cents impact. One approach used with success has been to portray the industrial life of a chronically absent employee and cost out the various stages developing and subsequently terminating the employee. Recruiting individuals who replace terminated employees costs money. The proper procedure then is to analyze the absentee problem and to come up with a concrete, usable, and immediate policy. Once the policy is understood by all, the line managers must be given the tools to put it into action. Line management should be counseled regarding performance appraisals, with emphasis on how such appraisals can be effective in controlling absenteeism. How to spot potential absentee problems is another area in which line managers should develop expertise. The personnel executive as well as the line manager has obligations to analyze his hiring standards and audit his organization.

Scherba, J. and Smith, L., "Computerization of Absentee Control Programs," *Personnel Journal*, May 1973, Vol. 52, No. 5, 367–372.

The mechanics of an absentee control program are often cumbersome and involve lengthy and tedious clerical operations whereas, computerization of absence records can be a logical solution to the problem of identifying employees with absenteeism problems and providing accurate records of attendance. This article describes a computerized program in a plant of approximately 2,000 employees. The two main program objectives were: 1) to accurately and efficiently record absence information through data processing, and 2) to establish a method of identifying problem absentees so that individual counseling or necessary disciplinary action can be taken. The program provided absence information daily on record sheets. Absence information is later extracted by the data processing section. Output from the computer consists of two major sections. The first section covers basic reporting and permits a fast and efficient method of recording and reviewing an employee's attendance record. The second section involves a special chronic report which identifies employees with poor attendance records and provides detailed information as to their attendance. The computer program also has been designed so that on special request, a record of a particular department or man for a specific time period, can be run any time during the year.

Wallin, J. A. and Johnson, R. D., "The Use of Positive Reinforcement to Reduce the Costs Associated with Employee Absenteeism," *Proceedings of the 28th Annual Winter Meeting*, Industrial Relations Research Association, December 1975, Dallas, Texas, 41–46.

This study reports the results of applying a monetary lottery for regular attendance and zero tardiness. The sample consisted of 80 nonexempt employees of an electronics manufacturing firm. The lottery combined elements of fixed-interval and variable-ratio schedules of reinforcement. A before and after design yielded a 28.8 percent decrease in sick-leave expenses incurred by the company and a 41 percent drop in absenteeism. Implications are drawn for applications of reinforcement principles to other problem areas: safety, production quantity, and quality.

Rotondi, Thomas, Jr., "Behavior Modification on the Job," *Supervisory Management*, February 1976, Vol. 21, No. 2, 22–28.

The author advocates the use of operant conditioning (behavior modification techniques) in the organizational context by means of a seven-step procedure: creating a consistent work environment (defining policies and procedures consistently); determining the desired behaviors of subordinates (i.e., high level of output produced); determining the type of rewards to use (i.e., money, promotion, praise, etc.); clearly communicating desired behaviors and rewards to subordinate (employee knows what is expected of him); providing immediate rewards for desired behaviors; providing rewards on a variable-ratio schedule; and minimizing the use of punishment. The author relates that behavior modification can be used to decrease tardiness and absenteeism.

Luthans, Fred and Martinko, Mark, "An Organizational Behavior Modification Analysis of Absenteeism," *Human Resource Management*, Fall 1976, Vol. 15, No. 3, 11–18.

The authors present a problem-solving model based on organizational behavior modification (operant conditioning paradigm) for analyzing and remedying absenteeism in work organizations. Predicated on the knowledge that positive consequences will increase the behavior's frequency of occurrence (reinforcement) and that negative and neutral consequences decrease the behavior's frequency of occurrence (punishment and extinction), the authors approach the problem of absenteeism as a process characterized by the following steps: identifying and measuring (baseline) the exact behavior which is to be changed, analyzing the antecedent cues and consequences influencing past and present behavior (attendance/absenteeism); developing an intervention strategy to control target behaviors through environmental consequences either by a program for reinforcing attendance (i.e., credit towards personal time, supervisor recognition, social reinforcers, feedback), a punishment strategy (i.e., verbal warnings) or extinction (i.e., ignoring absenteeism) or by combinations (i.e., ignoring absenteeism and praising attendance). Finally the frequency of the resulting behavior is monitored and performance is evaluated.

The authors cite two salient features of successful programs—rewards must be meaningful and the criterion for achieving the reward is realistic and contingently applied to the majority in the organization. Moreover, they suggest that consequences can be dispensed on either a continuous or intermittent scheduling basis, depending on the intended results.

Stone, Thomas J., "Absence Control: Is Your Company a Candidate?" *Personnel Administrator*, September 1980, Vol. 25, No. 9, 77–84.

The author intends his article to serve as a guide through the stages necessary to measure employee absenteeism, its cost to the company, its possible causes, and careful consideration of control options. Stone says any increase in absenteeism should first be regarded as a sign to investigate employee satisfaction as well as organizational factors, rather than as a call for the last fad in absence control. He further says combinations of both reward and disciplinary systems should be considered, but in the last analysis any control system adopted must be tailored to treat the causes disclosed from the company's own research.

Commentary

ABSENTEEISM

Considerable research has been done on the causes of and cures for absenteeism in organizations. It is a practice frequently abused and costing companies thousands of dollars in production time. Chronic absenteeism is often used by employees as a strategy to obtain benefits not otherwise available to them or it is a signal that something is wrong with the person/organization relationship. It is frequently related to job satisfaction per se and to the several elements of the work environment.

In a study investigating the perceptions of work held by chronic absentee workers, absenteeism was found to be negatively related to the extent of the workers' identification with the company, integration with the work group, satisfaction with supervisors, and the belief in the fair play and justice of the company (Vaid, 1967). Another study relating several factors to absenteeism found that an employee's satisfaction with the company in general showed no relation to his absentee record. However, there was a strong relation indicated between the worker's attitude toward his immediate supervisor and his absences. Workers who felt their boss was frequently unfair were generally those with poor attendance records. Attitude toward working conditions was related to attendance record. Thus, employees who rate their working conditions as bad generally are those who show a high absentee record. And those employees who rate working conditions as very good show a low record of absences.

The impact of organizational policies and practices on absenteeism and whether these are effective deterrents to absenteeism has been investigated. Interestingly, results indicate that for some employees absenteeism provides an opportunity to experience consequences that tend to encourage absenteeism and that are not offset by organizationally controlled consequences that would tend to deter absenteeism. A revision of policy is prescribed toward motivating regular attendance and penalizing absenteeism (Morgan and Herman, 1976).

Attempts at preventing and controlling absenteeism vary widely. Most absentee-control programs include some combination of the following steps (Hartmand and Gibson, 1971):

1. Define absenteeism.

2. Measure absenteeism.

3. Careful employee selection.

4. Provide an orientation program.

5. Improve supervisory training.

6. Improve union management relations.

7. Provide a good working environment.

8. Encourage group cohesiveness.

Several approaches to correcting problems of absenteeism have been investigated. Employee participation in incentive pay plans and operant conditioning or behavior modification are two that are noteworthy and have produced a measure of success. One study, in particular, reported the development of a participative incentive pay plan which proved to be effective in significantly increasing attendance. Reasons for success were suggested as: a) more commitment by employees to the plan due to their participation in its development, b) employees were knowledgeable about their plan because of participation, and c) participation increased employees' trust of the good intentions of management regarding the plan (Lawler and Hackman, 1969).

In applying the concepts of behavioral modification to the problem of absenteeism, the following procedure is advocated:

1. Identify and measure the exact behavior to be changed.

2. Analyze the cues and consequences influencing past and present behavior (attendance/absenteeism).

3. Develop an intervention strategy to control target behaviors.

4. Monitor frequency of resulting behavior and evaluate performance (Luthans and Martinko, 1976).

Other studies reporting use of a behavioral modification approach via a lottery system indicate considerable success in decreasing absenteeism. Participation in the lottery for eligible employees (those with perfect attendance for a one-month period), the possibility of a $10.00 cash award for the lottery, and the social recognition (of being eligible to participate and of having their name posted on the bulletin board) seemed to stimulate employees toward success for the program (Wallin and Johnson, 1976; Pedalino and Gamboa, 1974).

Rewarding good attendance seems to be one of the most effective means to reduce absenteeism and various plans have been advocated to achieve this goal. In reviewing several plans that have a history of success, some important elements are emphasized as being crucial for a workable plan.

These include:

1. *Analyze* the organization's absenteeism pattern—overall and individually—and its production and dollar impact on the company.

2. *Review company policies* to ensure they do not encourage absenteeism.

3. *Adopt standards* based on historical statistics.

4. *Communicate problems/programs* to employees so they know policies, standards, and what is expected of them.

5. *Reward attendance* through an incentive bonus plan or other recognition of the desired behavior (Fegley, 1968; Grove, 1968; Nord, 1970).

The research on absenteeism seems to be largely prescriptive but there now exists an ample base of empirical research sufficient to provide assurance to success in adopting policies and procedures necessary to establish an effective program to cope with undesired absenteeism in many organizations.

DRUG USE AND ALCOHOLISM

Type of Article	No. of Articles
Applied	1
Descriptive	6
Integrative	2
Prescriptive	3

Applied

Lavino, John J., Jr. "Personal Assistance Program," *Personnel Administrator*, November 1978, Vol. 23, No. 11, 35–42.

Growing concern has been devoted to the issue of alcoholism and its effects on employees. Although alcoholism is oftentimes more common and more serious than other diseases, it is frequently slighted by large sections of the business community. The Kemper Insurance Co., however, has a far-reaching and comprehensive Personal Assistance Program. This article, based on the Kemper Personal Assistance Program, contains several helpful suggestions in the implementation and maintenance of similar programs in other organizations.

DESCRIPTIVE

Trice, H. M., "New Light on Identifying the Alcoholic Employee," *Personnel*, September-October 1964, Vol. 41, No. 5, 18–25.

This article attempts to arrive at a new focus for identifying alcoholic employees through a study in a large Eastern company. There the immediate superiors of 72 employees who had been diagnosed as alcoholics by the medical department were given a list of 44 on-the-job signs of alcoholism. The supervisors were asked to write from this list the first five signs of alcoholism they recalled noticing in their alcoholic subordinates. Of the 44 items on the list, 17 were most often checked by the supervisors as being among the first few signs of alcoholism they had become aware of. A group of alcoholics were given the same list of on-the-job signs of alcoholism to rate. Considerable divergence was discovered between how supervisors and alcoholics ranked the signs of developing alcoholism.

Findings of the study indicate that alcoholics are aware much sooner than their bosses of a variety of easy-to-camouflage and subjective clues to their problems. It was discovered that the supervisors of alcoholic employees in one large company not only picked out early and recurrent signs of developing alcoholism; they also agreed in general terms with alcoholics themselves when the subjective, private signs that the boss cannot see were discounted. Since response to therapy seems to require work with the early-to-middle symptoms, the supervisors' observations of such clues as poorer work and various kinds of absenteeism probably coincides with the time when the alcoholic best responds to therapy.

Habbe, S., "The Drinking Employee—Management's Problem?", *Conference Board Record*, February 1969, Vol. 6, No. 2, 27–32.

A series of questions concerning the seriousness of the alcohol problem in industry today were asked of executives in 160 companies. A look at questionnaire results indicate a number of findings: 1) Almost half of the respondents feel that certain management attitudes and practices may be contributing factors in the development of alcoholism. 2) Forty-two percent of the respondents have taken at least beginning steps to control the alcohol problem within their organizations. 3) Sixty-nine percent had already established an alcohol program policy. The components of a desirable alcohol control program are outlined. 4) Forty-two companies were involved in alcohol prevention programs. 5) Companies with well established control programs testify that they need and use all the resources available to them. Alcoholics Anonymous was widely acclaimed and used as a prime source by 90 percent of the respondents.

Kelley, J. W., "Case of the Alcoholic Absentee," *Harvard Business Review*, May-June 1969, Vol. 47, No. 3, 14–18.

This case presents a situation at the ABC Electronics Company but the problem exists in almost any plant and office. This is an actual case with the names changed. It concerns the alcoholic, the effect he has on those with whom he works, and the posture of his employer toward his problem. After presentation of the case, the author asks the readers to put themselves into the situation of what they would do about this employee. *Harvard Business Review* conducted a panel of three men with considerable expertise in the area of dealing with situations similar to the one discussed here. Excerpts from this panel are included in this article and provide a framework from which the reader can evaluate this case study and come upon some conclusions.

Parker, P. H., "Washington State's Employee Alcoholism Program," *Public Personnel Management*, May-June 1973, Vol. 2, No. 3, 212–215.

In January 1973, the state of Washington embarked upon a program which has two primary objectives: 1) to help supervisors identify problem drinkers, and 2) to assist employees with alcohol problems to obtain appropriate treatment. The rights and responsibilities of employer, employee, and employee representatives are all spelled out in the approved policy statement. Washington's alcoholism program is keyed to job performance. The training goals and objectives of the state's alcoholism program are closely tied with those of the Training Division of the State Department of Personnel and to the supervisory training plans of the various agencies which it serves. Once the alcoholic problem has been identified, it is a simple matter for supervisors to contact the alcoholism program staff in the Department of Personnel for evaluation of the degree of the illness, and in arranging for the appropriate treatment. This type of program has resulted in recovery for 60 to 80 percent of the alcoholic employees in private industry and is expected to do that well in the public service.

Ralston, August, "Employee Alcoholism: Response of the Largest Industrials," *Personnel Administrator*, August 1977, Vol. 22, No. 6, 50–56.

Employee alcoholism (EA) is a widespread and costly problem. The National Council on Alcoholism (NCA) estimates that EA costs industry $10 billion annually. The purpose of this article is to review and update the status of and the response to the EA problem within the largest U.S. industrial corporations. A questionnaire was sent to the nation's 50 largest industrials (according to asset size) to try and assess how they dealt with this problem. Of the 35 respondents to the survey, 25 companies indicated that they have formal alcoholic employee rehabilitation programs (AERPs), regarded as integral parts of the personnel administration structure. Eight companies have informal AERPs where some services are offered to alcoholic employees but with no written policy. Two companies indicated that they had no AERPs and offered no reason for not having them. The presence of these AERPs suggests that many companies are discovering that the initial response to an alcoholic employee need not be termination. If firms with AERPs intensify their efforts and if those without AERPs create them, it would seem that the problem of EA could soon be managed.

Perone, Michael; De Waard, Richard J. and Baron, Alan, "Satisfaction with Real and Simulated Jobs in Relation to Personality Variables and Drug Use," *Journal of Applied Psychology*, December 1979, Vol. 64, No. 6, 660–668.

The authors state that only rarely has laboratory research been undertaken to answer questions about work-related behaviors, due in large part to the assumption that industrial research is best conducted in the kind of setting in which the findings eventually will be applied. The authors tested young adult male industrial workers, selected in terms of reported drug use. The participants were given a battery of job satisfaction and personality questionnaires. Some of the subjects were hired to work individually at a repetitive task in a laboratory simulation for two-to-five weeks, and questionnaires were given to assess reactions to the simulated job. Satisfaction with real jobs and satisfaction with the simulated job showed similar correlations with several personality variables and were positively related to each other. The comparison of drug users and nonusers revealed no major differences with regard to either real or simulated job satisfaction. The authors conclude that the results provide empirical support for the validity of a laboratory approach, in that the general pattern of relationships observed in the field data also was observed in the laboratory data.

INTEGRATIVE

Buchanan, H. W., "How Companies are Dealing with Alcoholism," *Personnel*, November-December 1966, Vol. 43, No. 6, 20–27.

Not until recently have people come to the realization that alcoholism is a serious health problem which this country faces. The vast majority of companies still have no programs for dealing with problem drinkers in their organizations, leaving the handling of any problems that arise to the alcoholic's supervisor. In the past, dismissal of the affected employee offered an easy solution. The impracticality of this action is being realized by more and more companies. Industry is becoming increasingly concerned with the costs that are involved with the alcoholic's problems. Company programs that deal with alcoholic problems are greatly increasing in number. The requisites for what the author feels would make for a successful alcohol control program are outlined. But in the final analysis, the immediate supervisor is the keystone of any rehabilitative effort, concludes the author.

Rogers, R. E. and Colbert, J. T. C., "Drug Abuse and Organizational Response: A Review and Evaluation," *Personnel Journal*, May 1975, Vol. 54, No. 5, 266–271, 281.

This paper attempts to present a review of the effects that the present day drug culture has on modern organizations. The authors discuss the type of drugs used, the impact of drugs on employee work efficiency, how management can deal with the problem, and recommendations on how organizations can approach drug abuse among their employees. Previously centered in high schools and colleges, the use of drugs has now expanded into the organization as young drug users leave school and begin a working career. Companies are forced to screen for drug use as part of their selection program, educate their employees on the effects of drugs, and deal with those found using them while at work.

PRESCRIPTIVE

Carding, A. D. K., "Enlightened Treatment for the Alcoholic Employee," *Management Review*, March 1970, Vol. 59, No. 3, 39–43.

A policy of terminating any employee or executive who reveals himself as an alcoholic is wasteful and uneconomic. Any company stands only to gain by implementing a straightforward policy toward alcoholism, with the aim of correcting behavior problems in employees before they become unemployable. The article includes an interesting chart which delineates the various behavioral phases of alcoholism, the percentage efficiency of the worker at each phase, and the visible signs of alcoholism at each phase (variables being attendance, general behavior, and job performance). What form should a company's policy on alcoholism take? The responsibility for detecting a problem lies with the employee's supervisor. He should not attempt to diagnose the problem but rather discuss with the employee his poor performance on the job. A counselor should be retained by the company to deal with alcoholics and their problems. Employers then have a greater chance than almost anybody else to help the alcoholic before he progresses to the later stages of the disease. His job performance provides a yardstick of behavior that is denied other people.

Presnall, L. F., "What's Wrong With Alcoholism Control Programs?", *Personnel*, March-April 1970, Vol. 47, No. 2, 38–43.

In recent years management has made considerable progress toward a more enlightened attitude about the alcoholic employee, but there is still a "mystique" surrounding the subject that distorts not only the fact-gathering and opinions about it, but also judgments about how to deal with the problem. This article presents a number of observations supporting this opinion which were drawn from confidential personnel record studies done for companies and governmental employers in plants ranging from 700–17,000 employees. If a company is concerned about alcoholism, management should first probe for the facts as they are now recognized and obtain qualified expert advice in the fact-gathering process. Getting the facts and dispelling the mystique of alcoholism are essential before organizational changes in personnel procedures and alcoholism control programs are instituted.

Wijting, Jan P., "Employing the Recovered Drug Abuser—Viable?" *Personnel*, May-June, 1979, 56–63.

In a study by the National Association on Drug Abuse Problems, Inc. (NADAP) to assess the employment capabilities of former drug addicts, it was found that 1) ex-addicts perform on a par with employees in comparable jobs who are not former drug abusers and prove to be satisfactory employees; 2) the most common reasons for termination—tardiness, absenteeism, and productivity—are not directly related to their past drug involvement but are problems caused by a former life style and can be eliminated by proper counseling and a degree of patience and tolerance on the part of employers; and 3) the problem of retention is often due to the kind of positions offered NADAP's clients which are typically entry level with low rates of compensation. If recovered drug abusers are to be successful employees, they must be placed in jobs that provide them with a living wage and at least a moderate chance for development. Conclusions of the study suggest that for programs such as NADAP to be successful in their rehabilitating efforts, we need to know more about societal reassimilation of former drug abusers, employment experiences and their effect on the lives of former drug abusers, and expectations of the impact of gainful employment on their lives. It also would be helpful to know about the kinds of interpersonal experiences ex-addicts have in work settings and how steady employment affects them socially. Such information would facilitate the design of more effective employment programs for the recovered drug abuser.

Commentary

DRUG USAGE AND ALCOHOLISM

Recently, the American population has embarked on a "health kick." Special programs and many books abound with how to enjoy total health—and how to obtain it. Yet alcoholism seems to be one of the by-products of our affluent society and remains one of the most serious health problems in our country today.

Although alcoholism is now widely recognized as a disease and should be treated as such, and in spite of its prevalence in industry today, the prevalent solution has always been the dismissal of the alcoholic employee. But realization of the impracticality of this action—of the wasteful and adverse economic impact on the company—has forced industry to take a second look. Thus programs of rehabilitation of alcoholic employees are beginning to be accepted and endorsed as a legitimate part of a company personnel program.

Yet, the majority of companies have no programs for problem drinkers and leave the handling of this problem up to the supervisor. Even with a systematic rehabilitation effort, the supervisor remains the keystone to a good program. Frequently, the responsibility and likelihood of detection lies with the immediate supervisor. In addition, knowledge and use of proper referral procedures is becoming an accepted part of the supervisor's job. Changes in job performance provide an early behavioral yardstick of emerging problems and, thus, employers have a greater opportunity to help alcoholics before the disease progresses to the chronic stages.

Response to therapy for alcoholism requires work with early to middle stage symptoms and the first clues noticed by the supervisor probably coincide with the time that an alcoholic best responds to therapy. Recently, management has made progress toward a more enlightened attitude about the alcoholic employee, and qualified fact-gathering processes and expert counseling programs have aided in disspelling some of the mystique surrounding the alcoholic employee (Presnall, 1970).

One study of a 160-industry sample indicates that certain management attitudes and practices may contribute to the alcoholism problem. However, 42 percent were taking steps to control alcoholism in their organizations, 69 percent had established an alcohol program policy with 42 companies involved in an alcohol prevention program. Those companies with well established control programs say they need and use all the resources available to them and that Alcoholics Anonymous is acclaimed and used as a prime resource (Habbe, 1969).

Another study of the alcoholism prevention program in the state of

Washington outlines the procedures and policies they are following to assure success for the program. Their primary objectives were to help supervisors identify problem drinkers and assist employees with alcohol problems in obtaining appropriate treatment. With policies and procedures set up for identification, referral, and treatment, they expect their program to lead to 60 to 80 percent recovery (Parker, 1973).

A study on drug abuse (Rogers and Colbert, 1975) reviews the effects of the present-day drug culture on modern organizations. The authors deal with types of drugs used, their impact on employee efficiency, and how management can deal with the problem. The drug culture, originally centered in high schools and colleges, has now been moving out into the industrial and business world as young drug users leave school and begin a working career. Thus companies are now inheriting a new cultural problem and are forced to deal with drug use/abuse in their selection programs as well as educating their employees on the effects of drug use and learning how to discipline or deal with those found using drugs while at work.

Little systematic evidence exists suggesting the optimal preventive or remedial program for alcohol and/or drug abuse. There are probably several reasons for this disappointing fact. First, the exact behaviors that index abuse are not well defined and are a source of uncertainty for most in management. Second, in the face of such ambiguity, many managers are reluctant to identify, diagnose, and label the causes of low performance or excessive absenteeism as abuse of drugs and/or alcohol. Third, the application of many of the most effective remedial techniques requires skills and knowledge that many managers do not possess. This makes systematic intervention a risky, even unethical, managerial policy. The development of diagnostic and referral skills by increasing numbers of managers would seem to be the most effective and cost efficient prescription.

Dependent Variable

PERFORMANCE QUALITY

Type of Article	No. of Articles
Descriptive	1
Empirical	5

DESCRIPTIVE

McCarthy, M., "Decreasing the Incidence of High Bobbins in a Textile Spinning Department Through a Group Feedback Procedure," *Journal of Organizational Behavior Management*, 1978, Vol. 1, No. 2, 150–154.

This case study reports the management of employees' behavior in a textile operation that resulted in improved performance quality. A "high bobbin" is the consequence of a doffer not pushing all the way down on a spindle. This causes tangles, resulting in waste, lower wind efficiency, and lost man-hours clearing tangles. Baseline data on the incidence of high bobbins were collected and then the ABAB reversal design was employed. In phase one, a feedback graph of the baseline data was posted in the spinning department showing the number of high bobbins on each of four shifts. Revised data were posted daily. Also, supervisors were instructed to reinforce their doffers verbally whenever an improvement was made. In phase two, feedback and reinforcement were removed, while in phase three they were restored. High bobbins decreased dramatically during phase one. Removal of feedback and reinforcement resulted in an increase in high bobbins. When feedback and reinforcement were restored there was again a decrease in the number of high bobbins.

EMPIRICAL

Lawler, E. E., III, "Effects of Hourly Overpayment on Productivity and Work Quality," *Journal of Personality and Social Psychology*, November 1968, Vol. 10, No. 3, 306–313.

This study focuses upon several predictions of Adams' equity theory that appear to be in disagreement with the assumption that people try to maximize their economic gain and minimize their job inputs. The effects of hourly overpayment on productivity and work quality are considered. Adams' finding that overpayment leads to high productivity was replicated. However, in contrast to the predictions of equity theory, there was a general tendency for the overpaid Ss to do lower quality work, particularly during the last two of three sessions they worked. An additional group of overpaid Ss was included in the study and, in contrast to the Ss used in Adams' work, they were made to feel overpaid by virtue of circumstance rather than by their own low qualifications. The data from this group suggested that just feeling overpaid is not enough to cause Ss to produce large quantities of work. The significance of this finding for equity and expectancy theory was considered, and it was concluded that much of the data from the overpaid hourly equity studies can be explained without recourse to equity theory.

Adam, E. E. and Scott, W. E., "The Application of Behavioral Conditioning Procedures to the Problems of Quality Control," *Academy of Management Journal*, June 1971, Vol. 14, No. 2, 175–193.

Rather than only emphasizing statistical techniques to control performance quality, it is suggested that modification of performance quality may be readily understood as the behavioral consequences of psychological conditioning procedures. Operant conditioning principles are reviewed and implications are related to the industrial quality control problem. An experimental investigation provides an example of the quality control problem phenomenon, where the agent for change is the use of conditioning procedures.

Adam E. E., "An Analysis of Changes in Performance Quality With Operant Conditioning Procedures," *Journal of Applied Psychology*, 1972, Vol. 56, No. 6, 480–486.

Operant conditioning procedures were applied to 160 Ss performing a routine repetitive task to investigate the effectiveness of these procedures in obtaining changes in performance quality (and quantity) over time. Results of the study indicate that a) when the response-reinforcement contingency was shifted from emphasis on quantity to emphasis on quality, behavior was not changed significantly by either verbal or monetary reinforcers; b) during contingency shifts from quality to quantity, overt performance changed significantly using either reinforcer quality falling from high levels to low levels and quantity mounting from low levels to high levels; c) as an effective behavioral change agent, the verbal reinforcer was either equal to or greater than the monetary reinforcer; d) shifting the contingency from quality to quantity yielded greater performance changes than did shifting from quantity to quality, and e) conditioning procedures, when compared to an absence of conditioning, facilitated higher levels of performance and maintenance of these higher levels over time.

Adam, Everett E., Jr., "Behavior Modification in Quality Control," *Academy of Management Journal*, December 1975, Vol. 18, No. 4, 659–679.

Combined attitude change and operant conditioning procedures to improve operative worker performance were investigated. Results indicate no attitude change, no quality change, quantity improvement, and cost reduction. Based on this study, it is concluded that operant conditioning procedures did not provide an alternative to Zero Defects type quality motivation programs.

Runnion, Alex; Johnson, Twila and McWhorter, John, "The Effects of Feedback and Reinforcement on Truck Turnaround Time in Materials Transportation," *Journal of Organizational Behavior Management*, 1978, Vol. 1, 110–117.

The length of time which trucks spent at each mill while transporting goods between 58 plant locations of a textile company was reduced with the introduction of a feedback plus reinforcement system. The average truck turnaround time was reduced from a baseline average of 67 minutes to an average of 38.2 minutes. This level was maintained even though the frequency of feedback was reduced substantially. The project demonstrated the use of periodic feedback to improve and maintain improved performance of workers across many locations in a large textile company.

Commentary

PERFORMANCE QUALITY

Behavioral techniques are useful in many ways to create a more effective and forceful organization but it seems that the requirements of a good quality control program are not always met by this approach. Based on the research reviewed, it does not seem appropriate to strongly advocate behavioral/operant conditioning techniques to reduce quality control problems. In the studies reviewed, using behavioral conditioning as a change strategy was not consistently effective in producing either better quality work or more quantity. One study has reported that quantity improved at the expense of quality when using an operant conditioning approach. When quantity of performance was consistently reinforced, quantity did increase and was maintained over time.

Research investigating effects of overpayment have found that this practice can result in lower quality work. Employees were made to feel overpaid due to their own low qualifications or due to circumstances. Apparently feeling inequitably overpaid is not enough to cause employees to produce large quantities of work. So both quality and quantity of work can be affected by overpayment.

Since it is apparently evident that overpayment results in no increase in quality and in even lower quality of work, one may assume that employees feel they can take advantage of a company that uses poor judgment in its pay system, and, therefore, do not put forth their best effort to reduce the apparent inequity produced by overpayment.

Dependent Variable

SAFETY

Type of Article	No. of Articles
Descriptive	2
Empirical	1
Prescriptive	1

DESCRIPTIVE

Sulzer-Azaroff, Beth, "Behavioral Ecology and Accident Prevention," *Journal of Organizational Behavior Management*, Fall 1978, Vol. 2, No. 1, 11–44.

The literature on industrial accidents in business and industry indicates that by applying aversive consequences unsafe practices can be reduced. However, in university laboratories, some of the degrees of freedom to implement aversive events contingent on unsafe practices are missing. As a result, while major OSHA regulated safety practices are met, less obvious daily safety precautions may be overlooked or treated casually. Many laboratory accidents could be readily avoided by carefully arranging the physical environment to reduce potential hazards by utilizing effective, non-intrusive economical safety strategies. This study was designed to identify and analyze the ecological impact of a simple, non-intrusive, cost-efficient system to reduce hazards in a university laboratory. The system involved periodic inspections by safety officers who provided written feedback about and suggestions for ameliorating hazards. An across-subjects-multiple-baseline experimental design was used with 30 laboratories assigned to either an early, middle or late feedback condition. The results showed a substantial reduction in safety hazards following the delivery of feedback. The ecological assessment indicated a general increase in safety consciousness and safety related activities by Institute members. These qualitative changes, combined with the hazard reduction data, support the author's conclusion that it is possible to design a simple, non-intrusive feedback system that will reduce safety hazards in an economically and ecologically sound manner.

Komaki, Judi; Heinzmann, Arlene T. and Lawson, Loralie, "Effect of Training and Feedback: Component Analysis of a Behavioral

Safety Program," *Journal of Applied Psychology*, June 1980, Vol. 65, No. 3, 261–270.

This article reports the findings of 165 observations conducted over a 45-week period in a city's vehicle maintenance division where time lost due to accidents was considered to be high. Whereas employees showed only slight improvement in safety practices during the Training Only period, performance improved substantially when feedback was combined with training in the Training and Feedback phase. In this phase feedback was provided three to four times per week. During the eight month program, the number of lost time accidents declined from 3.0 accidents per month during the previous year to 0.4 accidents per month.

The authors conclude that only a slight improvement can be expected when training includes only written, verbal and visually-aided sessions. With feedback added, however, performance can be substantially improved and maintained.

EMPIRICAL AND PRESCRIPTIVE

Komaki, Judi; Barwick, Kenneth, D. and Scott, Lawrence R. "A Behavioral Approach to Occupational Safety: Pinpointing and Reinforcing Safe Performance in a Food Manufacturing Plant," *Journal of Applied Psychology*, 1978, Vol. 63, No. 4, 434–445.

The behavior analysis approach was used to improve worker safety in two departments in a food manufacturing plant. Desired safety practices were identified, permitting construction of observational codes suitable for observing workers' on-the-job performance over a 25-week period of time. The intervention consisted of an explanation and visual presentation of the desired behaviors (with a goal being set) as well as frequent, low-cost reinforcement in the form of feedback. A within-subject (multiple baseline) design was used. Employees in the two departments substantially improved their safety performance from 70 percent and 78 percent to 96 percent and 99 percent, respectively, after the staggered introduction of the program. During the reversal phase, performance returned to baseline (71 percent and 72 percent). It was concluded that the intervention, particularly the frequent feedback, was effective in improving safety performance. Not only did employees react favorably to the program, but the company was later able to maintain the program with a continuing decline in the injury frequency rate. The results suggest that behaviorally defining and positively reinforcing safe practices is a viable approach to occupational accident reduction.

Commentary

SAFETY

A viable approach to effective worker safety practices in manufacturing plants has been achieved through visual presentation of desired behaviors and reinforcement through frequent feedback. Employees react favorably to such a program, resulting in a substantial improvement of safety performance and a continuing decline in the injury rate (Komaki, et al., 1978).

Dependent Variable

SATISFACTION

Type of Article	No. of Articles
Descriptive	8
Empirical	10
Integrative	1
Prescriptive	2
Theoretical	3

DESCRIPTIVE

Weaver, C. N., "Sex Differences in Job Satisfaction," *Business Horizons,* June 1974, Vol. 17, No. 3, 43–49.

It is the intent of this article to add to the knowledge about the job satisfaction of blacks with special attention on this attitude as reported by black females. The measurement of job satisfaction is based on responses to a survey. The survey deals with a variety of areas of interest such as social stratification, the family, race relations, social control, civil liberties, and morale. When the data was cross-tabulated to expose comparative levels of job satisfaction between blacks and whites, the results agree with previous findings that blacks are generally less satisfied. The same pattern of dissatisfaction is applicable to black women. The following variables were analyzed: financial circumstances, number in household, occupation, reported happiness, age, frequency of church attendance, and marital status.

Perhaps the most significant result of this research is the disclosure that the well-documented tendency of black males to report lower job satisfaction apparently extends to black female employees. Also unearthed was an overall pattern of similarity in the reports of job satisfaction by males and females of both races. There appears to be sufficient evidence in the data to suggest that the job-related attitudes of each group should be the main focus of separate studies.

Costello, J. M. and Lee, S.M., "Needs Fulfillment and Job Satisfaction of Professionals," *Public Personnel Management*, September-October 1974, Vol. 3, No. 5, 454–461

The purpose of this study is to analyze the relationship between needs fulfillment and job satisfaction among professional employees in a publicly owned utility firm. Subjects were 164 professional personnel at the City Public Service Board of San Antonio. The study employed Porter's questionnaire which measured the needs satisfaction, perceived equitable needs, and the importance of needs on seven-point scales. From the questionnaire each individual's level of need satisfaction (NS); perceived equity level of need satisfaction (ENS); and perceived importance of the need (IN) were measured for 14 need-items. From these data, various need deficiency data were calculated. An analysis of the relationship of job satisfaction to level of needs satisfaction and needs deficiency was made.

Important findings of this study can be summarized as: 1) most professional employees are fairly well satisfied; 2) most employees in the sample are striving for high order needs, mainly self-esteem, autonomy, and self-actualization; 3) the employee sample indicates that among all aspects of the job, that of being informed about their company is quite deficient; 4) the overall job satisfaction level of the sample is about 80 percent, lower than that for managerial personnel in general as reported by other studies; 5) the employee sample indicates that higher order needs are important for their job satisfaction and also demonstrates that the greatest deficiency exists among these needs; and 6) the study presents two effective models to predict the employee job satisfaction.

Pritchard, R. D. and Peters, L. H., "Job Duties and Job Interests as Predictors of Intrinsic and Extrinsic Satisfaction," *Organizational Behavior and Human Performance*, December 1974, Vol. 12, No. 3, 315–330.

The present research develops the argument that actual job duties are a significant determinant of job satisfaction, especially intrinsic satisfaction. It is further argued that the degree of fit between job duties and interests in these job duties should be related to satisfaction. To test these hypotheses, data were collected on job duties, job interests, and job satisfaction from 629 enlisted naval personnel on three aircraft carriers and associated air squadrons. The results indicated that satisfaction could be predicted from job duties and that intrinsic satisfaction was better predicted than was extrinsic satisfaction. Only partial support was given to the hypothesis that discrepancy between interests and job duties could predict satisfaction.

Dimarco, N. and Norton, S., "Life Style, Organization Structure, Congruity and Job Satisfaction," *Personnel Psychology*, Winter 1974, Vol. 27, 581–591.

It is hypothesized that if tension results from life style-organization structure incongruity, such tension could affect the individual's satisfaction with the job itself. This study tests the hypothesis that life style-organization structure congruity explains variance in job satisfaction. Subjects were 78 staff employees from six large manufacturing organizations. Three measures were used in the study: Life Style Questionnaire (LSQ) which instructs subjects to indicate to what extent each of 78 statements represents their attitudes; the Organization Structure Questionnaire (OSQ) which instructed Ss to indicate to what extent each of 63 statements reflects the structures and processes characterising their organizational work unit; the Job Reaction Survey (JRS) which measures the Ss perception of the extent to which his job contains Herzberg's motivators. Ss were given the LSQ, OSQ, and JRS at work and asked to complete it during nonwork hours.

Study findings indicate that job satisfaction decreases as the bureaucracy of the organization increases. This can be explained by the lack of individual responsibility and control characterizing bureaucratic structures. Job satisfaction was also found to be positively related to personalistic-coordinative congruence. This suggests that job satisfaction is maximized when the individual places a high value on individuality, inner-directedness, freedom and independence, and is in an environment characterized by placing a great deal of control and responsibility in the hands of the individual. In conclusion, it appears that organizations pursuing the goal of job satisfaction should focus on developing environments with a low bureaucratic organization.

Grupp, F. W. and Richards, A. R., "Job Satisfaction Among State Executive in the U.S.," *Public Personnel Management*, March-April 1975, Vol. 4, No. 2, 104–109.

American state executives are more satisfied with their jobs than either federal or business executives among the 10 states used in this study and they look forward to a promising future. The state executive's job satisfaction is associated with age, years of state employment, hierarchial level, salary, and career speed. The values most appealing to state executives are job security, an opportunity to serve the public, and the challenge that they find in their work. They find least appealing political interference with their work, their lack of self-determination, and their salary levels.

LaFollette, W. R. and Sims, H. P., Jr., "Is Satisfaction Redundant With Organizational Climate?", *Organizational Behavior and Human Performance*, April 1975, Vol. 13, No. 2, 257–278.

This research investigated the question raised by Johannesson (*Organizational Behavior and Human Performance*, 1973, 10, 118–144) as to whether organizational climate is redundant with job satisfaction. For a sample of employees in a major medical center, organization climate

(G. G. Litwin and R. A. Stringer, Jr., *Motivation and Organizational Climate*, Boston: Harvard University, 1968) and organization practices (R. J. House and J. R. Rizzo, *Journal of Applied Psychology*, 1972, 56, 388–396) were found to be related to performance in a different manner than the satisfaction/performance relationship, which did not tend to support the redundancy hypothesis. Johannesson's research methodology was evaluated, and the redundancy hypothesis was found to rest on judgmental assumptions, rather than causal or longitudinal analysis. In addition, other research was evaluated which tended to support the climate-causes-satisfaction hypothesis as opposed to the redundancy hypothesis. The need for further longitudinal research to evaluate causality was emphasized.

Ronen, S., "Personal Values: A Basis for Work Motivational Set and Work Attitudes," *Organizational Behavior and Human Performance*," 1978, Vol. 21, 80–107.

This paper investigates the interrelationship among the employee's personal value system, job attitude, and organizational reward system. It was assumed that individual values are part of the set with which employees approach their work environment and evaluate the organizational reward system. Two separate and distinct Israeli employment communities were compared. One consisted of industrial workers from 11 kibbutzim (n = 135) and the other of employees working in privately owned factories (n = 187). Workers from the kibbutz industry where differential financial remuneration does not exist, reported a higher level of self-realization values and more satisfaction. In contrast, employees in the private sector, who receive differential extrinsic rewards, reported a higher level of both aggrandizement values and job satisfaction.

Moch, Michael K., "Racial Differences in Job Satisfaction: Testing Four Common Explanations," *Journal of Applied Psychology*, June 1980, Vol. 65, No. 3, 299–306.

This study attempts to identify and assess structural, cultural, social and social psychological explanations for differential employee satisfaction by race. Data were collected from 466 employees in an assembly and packaging plant, consisting of white Americans, black Americans and Mexican Americans. Race variables accounted for 21 percent of the variance in satisfaction beyond that accounted for by all other factors considered in the test. These other factors, in contrast, are determined to account for only four percent of the variance in satisfaction beyond that accounted for by race.

The author concludes that supervisors seeking to erase racial differences in job satisfaction may have an impact by manipulating work group assignments so that groups have proportional representation by race. Yet more research is needed, Moch concludes, to account for the finding that the Mexican Americans were more job satisfied than were blacks.

EMPIRICAL

Kuhn, D. G., Slocum, J. W., and Chase, R. B., "Does Job Performance Affect Employee Satisfaction?", *Personnel Journal*, June 1971, Vol. 50, No. 6, 455–459.

The purpose of this study is to examine Maslow's theory of motivation as it applies to nonmanagerial employees' performance. Do higher order needs motivate operative employees? Specifically, what is the relationship between performance and job satisfaction for these employees? Data for the operative employees were obtained by means of the Porter need satisfaction questionnaire distributed to 184 nonsupervisory employees in a steel mill in central Pennsylvania. The questionnaire contained 12 need items derived from Maslow's theory of motivation. For each item, two questions were asked: a) How much of the characteristic is there now? and b) How much should be connected with the job? Need satisfaction was defined as the difference between (a) and (b). All employees were on an incentive wage payment system.

Study results show that the greatest need satisfaction appears in the social need category. The security need was least satisfied in this study, whereas in other studies in the literature dealing with managerial personnel, this need was the most satisfied. Only two need items were found to be significantly associated with productivity. Security and social needs were significantly and positively related to job productivity. The data in this study suggest that incentive pay strengthens the relationship between "extrinsic" rewards and performance. The data further suggests that workers' orientations towards their jobs are primarily aimed at satisfying lower order needs.

Cherrington, D. J.; Reitz, H. J. and Scott, Jr., W. E., "Effects of Contingent and Noncontingent Reward on the Relationship Between Satisfaction and Task Performance," *Journal of Applied Psychology*, 1971, Vol. 55, No. 6, 531–536.

It was proposed that there is no inherent relationship between satisfaction and productivity, and that relationships between the two variables are highly dependent upon performance-reward contingencies. Ninety (90) Ss performed a task for one hour. A monetary reward was then delivered to 21 of 42 high performers and 21 of 42 low performers. The Ss next completed self-report measures of satisfaction and attitudes and performed the same task for another hour. Correlations between self-reports and satisfaction and second-hour productivity over all Ss was .00. Significant positive correlations, however, were found between satisfaction and productivity of appropriately reinforced Ss (rewarded high performers and nonrewarded low performers) while significant negative correlations were found for inappropriately reinforced Ss (rewarded low performers and nonrewarded high performers).

Weaver, C. N., "Sex Differences in Job Satisfaction," *Business Horizons*, June 1974, Vol. 17, No. 3, 43–49.

It is the intent of this article to add to the knowledge about the job satisfaction of blacks with special attention on this attitude as reported by black females. The measurement of job satisfaction is based on responses to a survey. The survey deals with a variety of areas of interest such as social stratification, the family, race relations, social control, civil liberties, and morale. When the data was cross-tabulated to expose comparative levels of job satisfaction between blacks and whites, the results agree with previous findings that blacks are generally less satisfied. The same pattern of dissatisfaction is applicable to black women. The following variables were analyzed: financial circumstances, number in household, occupation, reported happiness, age, frequency of church attendance, and marital status. Perhaps the most significant result of this research is the disclosure that the well-documented tendency of black males to report lower job satisfaction apparently extends to black female employees. Also unearthed was an overall pattern of similarity in the reports of job satisfaction by males and females of both races. There appears to be sufficient evidence in the data to suggest that the job-related attitudes of each group should be the main focus of separate studies.

Costello, J. M. and Lee, S. M., "Needs Fulfillment and Job Satisfaction of Professionals," *Public Personnel Management*, September-October 1974, Vol. 3, No. 5, 454–461.

The purpose of this study is to analyze the relationship between needs fulfillment and job satisfaction among professional employees in a publicly owned utility firm. Subjects were 164 professional personnel at the City Public Service Board of San Antonio. The study employed Porter's questionnaire which measured the needs satisfaction, perceived equitable needs, and the importance of needs on seven-point scales. From the questionnaire each individual's level of need satisfaction (NS); perceived equity level of need satisfaction (ENS); and perceived importance of the need (IN) were measured for 14 need-items. From these data, various need deficiency data were calculated. An analysis of the relationship of job satisfaction to level of needs satisfaction and needs deficiency was made.

Important findings of this study can be summarized as: 1) most professional employees are fairly well satisfied; 2) most employees in the sample are striving for high order needs, mainly self-esteem, autonomy, and self-actualization; 3) the employee sample indicates that among all aspects of the job, that of being informed about their company is quite deficient; 4) the overall job satisfaction level of the sample is about 80 percent, lower than that for managerial personnel in general as reported by other studies; 5) the employee sample indicates that higher order needs are important for their job satisfaction and also demonstrates that the greatest deficiency exists among these needs; and 6) the study presents two effective models to predict the employee job satisfaction.

Pritchard, R. D. and Peters, L. H., "Job Duties and Job Interests as Predictors of Intrinsic and Extrinsic Satisfaction," *Organizational Behavior and Human Performance*, December 1974, Vol. 12, No. 3, 315–330.

The present research develops the argument that actual job duties are a significant determinant of job satisfaction, especially intrinsic satisfaction. It is further argued that the degree of fit between job duties and interests in these job duties should be related to satisfaction. To test these hypotheses, data were collected on job duties, job interests, and job satisfaction from 629 enlisted naval personnel on three aircraft carriers and associated air squadrons. The results indicated that satisfaction could be predicted from job duties and that intrinsic satisfaction was better predicted than was extrinsic satisfaction. Only partial support was given to the hypothesis that discrepancy between interests and job duties could predict satisfaction.

Dimarco, N. and Norton, S., "Life Style, Organization Structure, Congruity and Job Satisfaction," *Personnel Psychology*, Winter 1974, Vol. 27, 581–591

It is hypothesized that if tension results from life style-organization structure incongruity, such tension could affect the individual's satisfaction with the job itself. This study tests the hypothesis that life style-organization structure congruity explains variance in job satisfaction. Subjects were 78 staff employees from six large manufacturing organizations. Three measures were used in the study: Life Style Questionnaire (LSQ) which instructs subjects to indicate to what extent each of 78 statements represented their attitudes; the Organization Structure Questionnaire (OSQ) which instructs Ss to indicate to what extent each of 63 statements reflects the structures and processes characterizing their organizational work unit; the Job Reaction Survey (JRS) which measures the Ss perception of the extent to which his job contains Herzberg's motivators. Ss were given the LSQ, OSQ, and JRS at work and asked to complete it during nonwork hours.

Study findings indicate that job satisfaction decreases as the bureaucracy of the organization increases. This can be explained by the lack of individual responsibility and control characterizing bureaucratic structures. Job satisfaction was also found to be positively related to personalistic-coordinative congruence. This suggests that job satisfaction is maximized when the individual places a high value on individuality, inner-directedness, freedom and independence, and is in an environment characterized by placing a great deal of control and responsibility in the hands of the individual. In conclusion, it appears that organizations pursuing the goal of job satisfaction should focus on developing environments with a low bureaucratic organization.

Grupp, F. W. and Richards, A. R., "Job Satisfaction Among State Executives in the U.S.," *Public Personnel Management*, March-April 1975, Vol. 4, No. 2, 104–109.

American state executives are more satisfied with their jobs than either federal or business executives among the 10 states used in this study and they look forward to a promising future. The state executive's job satisfaction is associated with age, years of state employment, hierarchial level, salary, and career speed. The values most appealing to state executives are job security, an opportunity to serve the public, and the challenge that they find in their work. They find least appealing political interference with their work, their lack of self-determination, and their salary levels.

LaFollette, W. R. and Sims, H. P., Jr., "Is Satisfaction Redundant With Organizational Climate?", *Organizational Behavior and Human Performance*, April 1975, Vol. 13, No. 2, 257–278.

This research investigated the question raised by Johannesson (*Organizational Behavior and Human Performance*, 1973, 10, 118–144) as to whether organizational climate is redundant with job satisfaction. For a sample of employees in a major medical center, organization climate (G. H. Litwin and R. A. Stringer, Jr., *Motivation and Organizational Climate*, Boston: Harvard University, 1968) and organization practices (R. J. House and J. R. Rizzo, *Journal of Applied Psychology*, 1972, 56, 388–396) were found to be related to performance in a different manner than the satisfaction/performance relationship, which did not tend to support the redundancy hypothesis. Johannesson's research methodology was evaluated, and the redundancy hypothesis was found to rest on judgmental assumptions, rather than causal or longitudinal analysis. In addition, other research was evaluated which tended to support the climate-causes-satisfaction hypothesis as opposed to the redundancy hypothesis. The need for further longitudinal research to evaluate causality was emphasized.

Ivancevich, John M., "The Performance to Satisfaction Relationship: A Causal Analysis of Stimulating and Nonstimulating Jobs," *Organizational Behavior and Human Performance*, 1978, Vol. 22, 350–365.

This study investigated the source and direction of causal influence in the relationships among performance rating, performance output, intrinsic satisfaction, and extrinsic satisfaction. A cross-lag correlation design, corrected cross-lag procedures, dynamic correlations, and frequency-of-change-in-product-moment (FCP) techniques were used to analyze the data. Field data were collected from 108 experienced machinists and 62 machine repair technicians. Using a modified Job Diagnostic Survey (JDS), six qualified observers categorized the machinist and technician jobs as stimulating or nonstimulating. The data analysis and results indicate significant differences in the causal inferences made for the two categories of jobs. It was determined that it could be inferred that for stimulating jobs "performance rating causes intrinsic satisfaction," "performance output causes intrinsic satisfaction," and "extrinsic satisfaction causes performance output". In addition, the data for the nonstimulating jobs suggest that it can be inferred that "intrinsic and extrinsic satisfaction cause performance rating" and "intrinsic satisfaction causes performance output".

Schmitt, Neal and Mellon, Phyllis M., "Life and Job Satisfaction: Is the Job Central?" *Journal of Vocational Behavior*, February 1980, Vol. 16, No. 1, 51–58.

Recently there has been an increased interest in the quality of work life on the part of management and researchers. Past literature suggests two models dealing with worker satisfaction; the "spillover" model, which postulates a positive relationship between job and life satisfaction, having an implicit causality link, and the "compensation model" which says that people with boring jobs will have exciting and interesting non-work activities. The purpose of this study, then, was to examine the relationship between work and life situations and to ascertain whether the work satisfaction—life satisfaction causal pattern was more plausible than the life—work satisfaction one. To prove this 158 female and 96 male workers filled out questionnaires for $3.00. The assessment of the source and direction of causality was examined by computing cross-logged correlations using corrections for changes in reliability and the Pearson-Filon test and by computing the dynamic correlations holding initial scores of the variable constant. It was tentatively concluded that life satisfaction leads to job satisfaction and not the reverse. If being satisfied with ones life has impact on ones job attitudes, efforts at counseling should have economic implications for employers. A happy worker is a productive worker and it is therein that the economic consequences lie.

INTEGRATIVE

Weaver, Charles N., "Job Satisfaction in the United States in the 1970s," *Journal of Applied Psychology*, June 1980, Vol. 65, No. 3, 364–367.

The article reviews data from 1972 through 1978 as compiled by General Social Surveys cross-sectional nationwide surveys conducted in face-to-face interviews by interviewers of the National Opinion Research Center at the University of Chicago. Each survey was designed to be representative of the entire non-institutionalized civilian population age 18 and older and employed.

Weaver concludes there were no substantial changes in overall levels of job satisfaction during the 1972-78 period. Blacks were considerably less satisfied than whites, there were no sex distinctions in job satisfaction, and there was a positive association between job satisfaction and education, age, income and occupation. It appears, Weaver says, that the global measure of job satisfaction has been very stable and may be somewhat unresponsive to changes in society.

PRESCRIPTIVE

Bowles, W. J., "The Management of Motivation: A Company-Wide Program," *Personnel*, July-August 1966, Vol. 43, No. 4, 16–26.

It has become the basic responsibility of corporate management to utilize human resources and to develop ways of measuring specific results of utilization of human resources. These fundamental responsibilities require that a company establish systematic means by which it can avail itself of new knowledge and insights arrived at through the behavioral sciences and also benefit from internal experience. For this purpose, a Corporate Personnel Research and Development team has been organized at Texas Instruments with its primary aims the translation of significant personnel and behavioral research into terms and forms applicable within the company. The Personnel R & D process as it operates at TI usually originates with research which is broadly defined as the uncovering of data of information from both internal and external sources. These inputs, which may be in the form of raw data, are reviewed in terms of relevance and potential contribution to organizational needs, and those that qualify are then developed, or translated, into a usable form. The next step is to bring about new or changed practices and procedures. Finally, in the measurement phase, the impact of these changes is tested; then new data are generated to begin inputs to the research phase, and the cycle is repeated. This process was followed in TI's effort to give direction and cohesiveness to the management of motivation of work.

Ash, P., "Job Satisfaction and the Productive Employee," *Personnel Management*, December 1971, Vol. 13, No. 12, 13–14.

The author, a staff member of MANPLAN Consultants of Chicago, has studied employee attitude surveys and sheds some light on beneficial areas to assess: job demands, pay, relationships with supervision, evaluation of managerial technical competence, human relation skills. Problem areas may be pinpointed by organizational unit, age, sex, ethnic group, skill level, and other classifications. The availability of data on previous studies permits comparisons with other companies in the industry, other industries and broad occupational groups in addition to intra-company comparisons.

Ash's experience with employee attitude surveys indicates that they will be useful and productive only if four important ground rules are observed: 1) the anonymity of the individual employee replying to the survey be clearly and explicitly guaranteed and protected; 2) results of the survey be fed back to employees in language they can understand; 3) in undertaking the survey, management publicly commits itself to constructive action in the main problems that are revealed, within the limits of their resources and capabilities; 4) management should act promptly upon completion of the survey in response to the problems that are identified.

THEORETICAL

Freud, E., "Toward a Quantitative Approach to Organizational Morale," *Public Personnel Review*, April 1969, Vol. 30, No. 2, 102–106.

The purpose of this article is to analyze not only what the elements of morale are but how they combine to produce morale. The author attempted to uncover the elements of job satisfaction and isolate those elements that are open to influence by management. Second, the article attempts to bring the explored phenomenon of morale closer to being measurable. Difficulties in the quantification can be overcome by appropriate Guttman scaling or other quantifiable methods. Third, the author's observation that equal increases or rewards are differentially efficient in producing satisfaction, and his conclusions about conditions under which that efficiency might be increased, hopefully have paved the way toward practical application by the administrator. They may enable him to review the profile of intrinsic and extrinsic job satisfaction prevailing in his organization to locate significant discrepancies and correct them, and to use his resources more efficiently with a view toward improving performance by minimizing resentment and maximizing approval.

Sutermeister, R. A., "Employee Performance and Employee Need Satisfaction—Which Comes First?", *California Management Review*, Summer 1971, Vol. 13, No. 4, 43–47.

The author investigates whether or not there is a cause-and-effect relationship between employee performance and need satisfaction or whether there is a circular relationship, each contributing to the other and each being affected by the other. The studies of Herzberg, Sorcher, and Meyer are reviewed as evidence to imply that satisfaction contributes to improved performance and productivity. Authors implying a different point of view (Miles, Porter and Lawler, Craft) state that outstanding performance leads to greater satisfaction of needs. The author suggests it to be useful to think of the performance-satisfaction relationship in terms of a series of cycles. An analysis was also made of "life cycles" through which each person passes, involving changes in individual aspiration levels.

In concluding, the author predicts that the degree of satisfaction at the end of one performance-satisfaction cycle and the individual's position in his life cycle will affect his level of aspiration in the new performance-satisfaction cycle. It is then theorized that effort and performance affect satisfaction, and the satisfaction by its influence on level of aspiration affects subsequent effort and performance.

Wofford, J. C., "The Motivational Bases of Job Satisfaction and Job Performance," *Personnel Psychology*, Autumn 1971, Vol. 24, No. 3, 501–518.

A motivational model of job satisfaction and job performance is presented in cognitive terms. Eight specific hypotheses are tested in a survey of four organizations. Need strength and need fulfillment are found to be related to satisfaction and performance. Herzberg's model and a Maslowian model were not supported by the data. Results were interpreted as supporting an expectancy theory approach, although the complete expectancy theory model was not tested.

Commentary

SATISFACTION

Satisfaction—or need fulfillment—is derived from different sources and for different reasons for different people. With the world of work changing rapidly in both its social and functional aspects and with more leisure time being available to people than ever before, it is crucial for business to design jobs and motivate employees to maintain and increase the productivity and efficiency of the organization and to encourage employees to give their best efforts toward achieving organizational goals along with their personal goals. An important element in achieving this end is the overall satisfaction of the employees in the organization. Thus, the relationship of job satisfaction to other aspects of the organization as well as to individual needs has been researched. Much effort has been devoted to finding methods and means of retaining employees who will find their work interesting, challenging, and supportive of their needs while contributing to the needs/requirements of the organization.

A review of some studies indicates that conditions can be generated wherein improved performance and productivity can contribute to increased satisfaction. Frequently, however, there is a circular relationship between satisfaction/productivity—i.e., one's life cycle correlates with a performance/satisfaction cycle at different levels of aspiration (Sutermeister, 1971).

In a study attempting to isolate the elements of job satisfaction open to influence by management and in an attempt to make it measureable, it was found that equal increases of rewards are differentially efficient in producing satisfaction. It was suggested that by using a profile of specific conditions of intrinsic and extrinsic job satisfaction prevailing in an organization, an administrator may be able to locate and correct discrepancies and thus improve performance by minimizing resentment and maximizing approval (Freud, 1969).

Research relating job duties and job interests to degree of satisfaction has found that satisfaction could be predicted from job duties. In addition, intrinsic satisfaction has been found to be better predicted than extrinsic satisfaction. There was little support given to the hypothesis that discrepancy between job interest and job duties could predict satisfaction (Pritchard and Peters, 1974). This finding is clearly contradictory to one of the major prescriptions of the job design literature. If confirmed across several job types, this finding will cast doubt on the convergence theories of job satisfaction.

In a study across employee groups, job satisfaction was found to be more prevalent among state executives than either federal or business executives. Job satisfaction was associated with age, years of state employment, hierarchial level, salary, and career speed. The values these executives held most appealing were job security, opportunity to serve the public, and the challenge they find in their work. Least appealing were political interference with their work, their lack of self-determination, and their salary levels (Grupp and Richards, 1975).

Data on employees has been gathered on a number of nonmanagerial samples to seek the relationship between performance and job satisfaction. In one typical study, security and social needs were significantly and positively related to job productivity. Data from this study also suggest that incentive pay strengthens the relationship between extrinsic rewards and performance. In this study, workers' orientations toward their jobs were primarily directed toward satisfying lower order needs (Kuhn, Slocum, and Chase, 1971).

Several studies analyzing the characteristics of an organization that impact upon satisfaction have found that job satisfaction decreases as the bureaucracy of an organization increases. This is explained because of the lack of individual responsibility and control which characterizes bureaucratic structures. It also suggests that satisfaction can be maximized when an individual places high value on individuality, innerdirectedness, freedom, and independence, and is in an environment which places a great deal of control and responsibility in the hands of the individual. Some have prescribed that organizations pursuing the goal of job satisfaction should focus on developing environments with a minimum of bureaucratic features (Dimarco and Norton, 1974).

Since it has become the responsibility of corporate management to utilize human resources and develop ways of measuring specific results of this use, it is necessary for management, therefore, to avail itself of new knowledge and experience. One study of a company describes the procedure used for effective and continued maximum use of their human resources as follows:

1. Gather data from both internal and external sources.

2. Review data in terms of relevant and potential contribution to the organization's needs.

3. Develop qualified data and translate into usable forms.

4. Apply form to bring about changes.

5. Measure impact of changes specified.

6. Develop new data from measurement of changes and repeat cycle.

This process is followed in an effort to give direction and cohesiveness to the management of motivation of work (Bowles, 1966).

The attitude survey has been used to assess satisfaction with job demands, pay, supervision, managerial technical competence, and supervisory human relations skills. Such surveys can point to problem areas in an organization unit and assist in relating satisfaction to age, sex, ethnic group, skill level, and organizational function. However, experience indicates that attitude surveys will be useful and productive only if the following ground rules are observed:

1. Anonymity of the individual respondent is explicitly guaranteed and protected.

2. Results of the survey are given to the employees in terms they can understand.

3. Management commits itself to constructive action on the main problems that are revealed.

4. Management should act promptly on completion of the survey in response to the problems identified.

Several models relating job satisfaction to performance have been presented. While there is no consistent relation between job satisfaction and job performance, one feature of the reinforcing environment has been found to produce predictable relations. For example, one study suggests that while there is no *inherent* relationship, this relation does consistently depend upon performance-reward contingencies. Data have consistently revealed significant positive correlations between satisfaction and productivity of appropriately reinforced employees and negative correlations for inappropriately reinforced employees (Cherrington, Reitz, and Scott, 1971). That is when high performing employees receive greater rewards than low performers, a positive relation between performance and satisfaction is generated. This also means that the high performers are likely to be most satisfied. This is, of course, the desired outcome in a productive organization.

TURNOVER

Type of Article	No. of Articles
Descriptive	5
Empirical	7
Integrative	3
Prescriptive	10
Theoretical	6

DESCRIPTIVE

Saleh, S. D., Lee, R. J., and Prien, E. P., "Why Nurses Leave Their Jobs—An Analysis of Female Turnover," *Personnel Administration*, January-February 1965, Vol. 28, No. 1, 25–28.

A group of 415 nurses was studied to analyze female turnover. It was hypothesized that job characteristics such as odd working hours and rotating shifts as well as the traditional conflict between career/family may have an impact on turnover. Exit questionnaires were given to all resigning employees. Questions dealt with reasons for leaving the hospital, i.e., family reasons, intentions to leave city, work situation. The results of the study point to the existent career/family conflict that most women experience. Usually, the conflict is resolved by preferring the traditional role and quitting the job. It was concluded that some job-related factors could be changed to reduce turnover and allow combining career with home interests. Factors mentioned were part-time hours, training male nurses for night shifts, structuring the work to make it more challenging and satisfying, having supervisors appreciate nurses achievements and providing chances for growth.

Stark, M. J., "Turnover: Pay Does Make a Difference," *Conference Board Record*, 1970, Vol. 7, No. 4, 48–50.

A standard list of reasons for turnover would likely include: 1) better position elsewhere, 2) dissatisfaction with pay and benefits, 3) job content dissatisfaction, 4) dissatisfaction with supervisor, 5) dissatisfaction with promotion policies, and 6) military service or illness. The majority of these reasons seem to signal something amiss in the man/job relationship. The job (organization) side of the man/job relationship is what executives can manipulate if interested in reducing turnover. A survey of 419 companies in the United States and Canada was made to determine reasons for turnover. Among U.S. firms it was found that turnover rates in the early years of a person's career is related to the relative starting salaries earned. It was further hypothesized that the apparent relationship found between compensation and turnover may be nothing more than a reflection of the influence of job content on turnover. To test this, three different types of selling jobs were studied, each widely different in content. Again, results showed the effect of compensation remained significant.

York, C. M., "As Your Were Saying–", *Personnel Journal*, June 1972, Vol. 51, No. 6, 449–450.

An analysis of long-haul truck drivers' personnel records was made. Dependent variables studied were termed nonterminators and terminators. Independent variables included two psychological indices of ability, an interest measure, two personality inventories and biodata including age, education, marital status, etc. The sample consisted of 313 termination cases and 132 long-term driver files that were drawn, coded, and submitted to statistical tests. Results of the study showed significant differences found for age, education, number of children, and two personality dimensions (self-sufficiency and dominance) for the group terminator versus nonterminator. No significant predictive relationship was obtained for the ability and interest measures. The turnover profile for long-haul drivers employed by one large company was found to be young, more intelligent, dominant, and self-sufficient. Because of high costs of associations with selection, training, and equipment use, a substantial savings might be realized by means of this aid in personnel decision-making.

Kraut, A. I., "Predicting Turnover of Employees From Measured Job Attitudes," *Organizational Behavior and Human Performance*, 1975, Vol. 13, No. 2, 233–243.

The study looks at the prediction of turnover among 911 salesmen by employee job attitudes and intent to remain with the company. Intent to remain was highly correlated with actual turnover, both short term and long term. During the 18 months after attitudes were surveyed, turnover for men who stated they intended to remain was nine percent versus 30 percent of those who were less committed. Employees' expressed intent was a better predictor of turnover than were other job attitudes. An examination of static and dynamic correlations showed that employees' intent to remain is most closely tied to feelings about the work itself and about the company as a place to work.

Embrey, Wanda R.; Mondy, Wayne and Noe, Robert M., "Exit Interview:
A Tool for Personnel Management," *The Personnel Manager*, May
1979, Vol. 24, No. 5, 43–48.

Whatever reason departing employees may offer, there is a strong possibility that there are more deep-seated motives which are being con-
cealed, the authors say. A company may never learn the truth unless it
takes the time to identify underlying causes of terminations. The article
develops two suggested approaches for management use in discovering
the truth behind voluntary departures during the exit interview. The
"patterned exit interview" method detailed was tested with a large company in the Southwest. The company had experienced unusually high
turnover of qualified personnel. The exit interview proved to be beneficial in identifying the real reasons for termination.

EMPIRICAL

York, C. M., "As You Were Saying–", *Personnel Journal*, June 1972, Vol.
51, No. 6, 449–450.

An analysis of long-haul truck drivers' personnel records was made. Dependent variables studied were termed nonterminators and terminators.
Independent variables included two psychological indices of ability, an
interest measure, two personality inventories and biodata including age,
education, marital status, etc. The sample consisted of 313 termination
cases and 132 long-term driver files that were drawn, coded, and submitted to statistical tests. Results of the study showed significant differences found for age, education, number of children, and two personality
dimensions (self-sufficiency and dominance) for the group terminator
versus nonterminator. No significant predictive relationship was obtained for the ability and interest measures. The turnover profile for
long-haul drivers employed by one large company was found to be
young, more intelligent, dominant, and self-sufficient. Because of high
costs of associations with selection, training, and equipment use, a substantial savings might be realized by means of this aid in personnel decision-making.

Burke, R. J. and Wilcox D. S., "Absenteeism and Turnover Among Female Telephone Operators," *Personnel Psychology*, Winter 1972,
Vol. 25, No. 4, 639–647.

The investigation considered in this article considers the following questions: 1) Are absenteeism (AB) and turnover (TO) related? 2) Is there a
progression of alienation or withdrawal indicated by AB followed by
eventual TO? The investigation examines the nature of the relationship
between AB and TO at 1) both group and individual levels of analysis,
using 2) objective measures collected by the organization as part of its
regular monitoring and control procedures, for 3) individuals with the
same relative length of tenure with the organization.

Method:

Group level: 14 operator offices were used as subject groups. Two measures of AB were used. First was total unexcused absence hours
   divided by total hours worked. The second was similar to the first,
   but excluded any absence time beyond the seventh calendar day
   after the last day worked.

Individual level: 127 telephone operators, who were divided into four
   experimental groups based on the amount of time they stayed
   with the organization. The measure of TO used was voluntary resignation. Two measures of AB were used: annualized days of absence and annualized number of times absent.

Results:

Group level: Results of this investigation show that TO correlates positively and significantly with incidental absence rates, but not with
   total absence rates across the 14 telephone operator groups. The
   author examined some possible explanations for the variations in
   results, among those being the definitions and measures of AB and
   TO; the age and seniority level characteristics of the individual
   involved; the presence or absence of effective attendance control
   procedures in the organization.

Individual level: Results indicated a positive and significant relationship
   between AB and TO for female telephone operators. In each tenure
   period, the "leavers" had higher AB than the "stayers"—even
   though some of the "stayers" left shortly thereafter. The data
   strongly supports the progression of withdrawal hypothesis—that
   of progressively worsening AB culminating in TO.

Waters, L. K. and Roach, Darrell, "Job Satisfaction, Behavioral Intention
   and Absenteeism on Predicators of Turnover," *Personnel Psychology*, Summer 1979, Vol. 32, No. 2, 393–397.

This study focuses on three correlates of employee turnover: job satisfaction, intention about remaining with the company and absenteeism.
These factors were correlated with turnover for a sample of 132 female
clerical employees over two one-year periods. When the three potential
turnover predicators were considered individually, the results were consistent with previous research relating job satisfaction, intention and absenteeism to termination decisions. A step-wise multiple regression indicated that both intent to remain with the company and frequency of
absences added to the prediction of turnover during both one-year periods whereas job satisfaction did not.

Hom, Peter W.; Katerbert, Ralph Jr. and Hulin, Charles L., "Comparative Examination of Three Approaches to the Prediction of Turnover," *Journal of Applied Psychology*, June 1979, Vol. 64, No. 3,
   280–290.

Three approaches to the prediction of turnover in a sample of National
Guard members were compared. All three predicted enlistment behaviors during the six months following attitude assessments occurred with

a high degree of accuracy. Implications of these results for organizational attitude-behavior relations are discussed. The authors also declare that this study fits in well with others that suggest that attitudes toward aspects of work can be expected to be changed by unionization, indeed predict at the group level the occurrence of unionization activity and predict individual pro- or anti-union votes.

Mowday, Richard R.; Stone, Eugene F. and Porter, Lyman W., "The Interaction of Personality and Job Scope in Predicting Turnover," *Journal of Vocational Behavior*, August 1979, Vol. 15, No. 1, 78–89.

Recent research on job design has shown the importance of considering interactions between employee personality characteristics and the nature of the job. The purpose of this article, then, was to extend both the turnover and job design literature by examining the extent to which interactions between employee personality characteristics and the nature of the job are related to turnover. Three needs were considered relative to job and work setting-achievement autonomy and affiliation. With these needs in mind, it was predicted that needs for achievement and autonomy would be negatively related to turnover for low scope jobs and positively related to turnover for employees on high scope jobs. On the other hand, needs for affiliation would be positively related to turnover for employees on high scope jobs and negatively related to turnover for employees on low scope jobs. This study took place in a large west coast firm where employees took questionnaires to determine their personality characteristics (Jackson's Personality Research Form), perceived job scope and demographic variables. Two jobs were looked at, one high scope and one low scope, and the turnover data was acquired from the company records. No direct relationships were found between personality characteristics and turnover for the combined sample of employees on high and low scope jobs. A correlational analysis indicated that personality and job scope interacted in predicting turnover. Employees on high scope jobs showed a turnover rate negatively related to the need for achievement and positively related to the need for affiliation. Turnover was negatively related to the need for affiliation among employees on low scope jobs.

Bartol, Kathryn M., "Individual vs. Organizational Predictions of Job Satisfaction and Turnover Among Professionals," *Journal of Vocational Behavior*, August 1979, Vol. 15, No. 1, 55–67.

In a constructive replication and extension of previous research, the relative importance of individual (personality and professional attitudes) versus organizational (professional reward system and tenure) variables in predicting job satisfaction and turnover was investigated for the case of professionals. Predictions, based on prior research, suggested that both individual and organizational variables are related to turnover among professionals. It has also been indicated that need for achievement and autonomy are positively related while organizational tenure is negatively related to professional turnover. In this study 250 members of a division of a large national association of computer specialists were mailed questionnaires and a letter explaining that the survey was a study of various aspects of working in the computer and related fields. The needs for autonomy and achievement were measured using the 20 item manifest needs questionnaire. Professional attitudes were measured using the 20 item a-priori measure, consisting of five subscales. Subjects rated items on a seven point scale ranging from strongly agree to strongly disagree. It was found that, among professionals, individual variables are more important than organizational ones in predicting satisfaction with the work itself; but individual variables often played a major role in satisfaction with contextual aspects of the job as well. Organizational factors were found to be significantly predictive of satisfaction with all aspects of the job, but were the only significant predicators of turnover. So, in summary, the notion that organizational factors were more important than individual ones was supported.

Spencer, Daniel G. and Steers, Richard M., "The Influence of Personal Factors and Perceived Work Experiences on Employee Turnover and Absenteeism," *Academy of Management Journal*, September 1980, Vol. 23, No. 3, 567–572.

The study examines the relative influence of two major antecedents—personal factors and work experiences—on employee turnover and absenteeism. The study used a sample of 200 clerical and service workers of a major midwestern hospital, average age 37 and average tenure seven years. Turnover data were collected for one year after questionnaire administration, and absenteeism was measured over a nine month period. The study finds that personal characteristics exhibited a higher correlation with absenteeism than turnover, and work experiences had correlations of similar magnitude with absenteeism and turnover. The authors conclude that the results point to the importance of using multivariate and comparative analyses in the study of withdrawal behavior.

INTEGRATIVE

Palmer, W. W. and Dean, C. C., "Increasing Employee Productivity and Reducing Turnover," *Training and Development Journal*, March 1973, Vol. 27, No. 3, 52–54.

This article reviews the components of responsible management: recruiting, maintaining, and training; hygiene factors and motivators; goal and objective setting; and performance measurement. Through utilization of such a responsible system of management, the accomplishment of three things is enhanced. These are: 1) the company personnel will more likely achieve the goals adopted by the board of directors, 2) the problem of employee turnover probably will be reduced, and 3) productivity will probably be increased.

Flowers, V. S. and Hughes, C. L., "Why Employees Stay," *Harvard Business Review*, July-August 1973, Vol. 51, No. 4, 49–60.

This article describes a research project designed to find out why employees stay—motivational reasons, hygiene reasons, and environmental reasons. The authors present some correlations between job satisfaction in various employee groups and hygiene and environmental factors. While the results of the study have a definite scope, the thinking represented here will be of use to companies that want to take a more positive approach to the management of retention and turnover.

Forrest, C. R.; Cummings, L. L. and Johnson, A. C., "Organizational Participation: A Critique and Model," *Academy of Management Review*, October 1977, Vol. 2, No. 4, 586–600.

A critique of the current state of theory and research on employee tardiness, absenteeism, turnover and job choice is presented. Research and theory reviewed illustrated problems and unresolved issues underlying current knowledge of the determinants of organizational participation. An expanded valence-instrumentality-expectancy model provides the basis for integrating psychological and economic perspectives on organizational participation. Guidelines for future research and conceptual development are provided.

PRESCRIPTIVE

Kahl, K. L., "What's Behind Employee Turnover?", *Personnel*, September-Obtober 1968, Vol. 45, No. 5, 53–58.

Reasons for labor turnover are discussed including salary dissatisfaction, problems with selection and placement, defects in training, poor supervision, faulty communication, and poorly handled compensation systems. The author speculates that managers often fail to recognize that behind all of these reasons are two basic problems: 1) the average employee is frustrated at least to some degree because he really does not know what his boss expects of him—he works and produces according to his view of what he is supposed to do but his work may be evaluated according to an entirely different set of standards; 2) related to the first problem are compensation "inaccuracies," but competition also has produced glaring compensation inequities.

Marion, B. W. and Trieb, S. E., "Job Orientation—A Factor in Employee Performance and Turnover," *Personnel Journal*, October 1969, Vol. 48, No. 10, 799–804.

Problems in a competitive labor market include shortages of both competent employees and management and a high rate of employee turnover. Part of the turnover problem may be due to inadequate efforts by firms to orient their employees. The research presented here was conducted among the employees of two supermarkets. It is suggested that the new employee is confronted with a great many unknown situations when he first begins a job. The research hypothesis of this study is that the manager and the immediate supervisor can help remove these unknowns by carefully orienting the employee to his new job. A five-question schedule designed to measure favorable and unfavorable initial experiences was used. Results of this research inquiry isolated employee job orientation as an important influence on work group performance and employee satisfaction.

Clark, W., "How to Cut Absenteeism and Turnover," *Administrative Management*," March 1971, Vol. 32, No. 3, 64–65.

This article prescribes steps to be taken to substantially reduce absenteeism and turnover:

1) Understand your absenteeism/turnover problem by studying its past and present effects on your organization.

2) Compile statistical data on your experience with absenteeism and turnover.

3) Make a detailed study of present company policies and practices to determine if any of them might unwittingly contribute to absenteeism and/or turnover.

4) Study the information gathered previously to determine what specific actions must be initiated to reduce absenteeism and turnover.

5) Establish standards (maximum acceptable level of absenteeism/TO). Base the standards on the departmental experience learned during initial compilation of data.

6) Implement a "caretaker" policy in which the firm's absenteeism and turnover activity are monitored at regular intervals by your personnel department.

Scott, R. D., "Job Expectancy—An Important Factor in Labor Turnover," *Personnel Journal*, May 1972, Vol. 51, No. 5, 360–363.

Research suggests that employees often terminate their jobs because they lack the opportunity to achieve what they expected when they were hired. Failure to correct unrealistic expectations, due to the inadequacy of a company's orientation program, results in unnecessary expenditure of training time and money on new hires whose jobs do not provide the anticipated satisfaction.

Kotter, J. P., "The Psychological Contract: Managing the Joining-Up Process," *California Management Review*, Spring 1973, Vol. 15, No. 3, 91–99.

This article is concerned with the process of assimilating new employees into an organization, which we call the "joining-up" process. It is the purpose of this article to present research that argues the following points:

1) Early experiences (the joining-up period) have a major effect on an individual's later career in an organization.

2) Efficient management of the joining-up process can save an organization a great deal of money by making employees more efficient faster, by increasing job satisfaction, morale and productivity, by decreasing turnover, by increasing the amount of creativity, by decreasing counterproductive conflict and tension, and by increasing the number of effective members within an organization.

3) Due to a complex set of forces, most organizations do a poor job of managing the joining-up process.

This article outlines some recent research and presents the results. To clarify the implications of the research, two case studies are presented and followed by a summary. It is concluded that the quality of the management of the joining-up process will effect two major outcomes: 1) the cost of getting more people on board and keeping them in the firm, and 2) the level of productivity.

Hiller, W. F., "Case Study of a Plan to Reduce Turnover," *Personnel Journal*, September 1974, Vol. 53, No. 9, 702.

Walter F. Hiller, manager of Howard Johnson's restaurant in Wollaston, Massachusetts, in 1973, authorized his personnel department to test a program designed to reduce turnover. Basic program ingredients were proper selection and controlled training. The program was tested in the Boston and New York areas using the AVA (Activity Vector Analysis) program in their selection process and the JAR (Job Activity Rating) designed to produce a hiring standard. Hiring was followed by a seven-week training on the job. At the end of 1973, turnover rate was 46 percent lower than other divisions of Howard Johnson restaurants not following this program.

Raphael, M. A., "Work Previews Can Reduce Turnover and Improve Performance," *Personnel Journal*, February 1975, Vol. 54, No. 2, 97–98.

This article focuses on an available method of providing realistic job expectations which has not been investigated often—a work preview or job sample. A work sample test consists of a task that is representative of work actually done on the job. In addition to being a potential means of providing job expectancy, the work preview seems to serve as an excellent bridge between the selection process and the early training of the new employee. An application of the Career Orientation Program (COP), a job sample-oriented precontract program, was cited. A life insurance company was using the COP with effective results. Reduced turnover and improved performance were statistically supported.

Hawk, Donald L., "Absenteeism & Turnover," *Personnel Journal*, June 1976, Vol. 55, No. 6, 293–303.

This article presents a model illustrating the causes for and the relationships between absenteeism and turnover for the purpose of developing a reduction strategy. The author advocates careful diagnosis of the company's absenteeism/turnover position before formulating any strategy. Where withdrawal is on a continuum ranging from absenteeism to turnover, job dissatisfaction plays a critical role and is influenced by the various factors, i.e., supervisory style (in regard to providing reinforcement and feedback), salary (wage rate and equitable structure) and job design (variety, task identity, autonomy, feedback, significance). Insofar as the most significant causal variables are identified, implementation of the most appropriate and direct solution is facilitated.

Szilagyi, Andrew D., "Keeping Employee Turnover Under Control," *Personnel*, November-December 1979, 42–52.

This article examines several aspects of turnover, reviews results of a study of turnover in six large companies, and presents implications that can help managers control turnover rates in their organizations. Only voluntary turnover for organizational reasons (compensation, promotion/advancement opportunities, supervisory relations, job challenge, etc.) was considered. A managerial framework/model is presented for studying turnover consisting of three basic parts: 1) Job satisfaction (relates to job characteristics, interpersonal relations, organizational practices, and reward systems); 2) individual characteristics (age, education, and personal needs); and 3) turnover intention (level of satisfaction/dissatisfaction influenced by external job opportunities). Results of a study of over 3,000 employees in six large companies is then presented and implications of these results for managers were indicated. The author calls attention to two important factors to note in studying turnover: 1) inappropriate ways of measuring turnover may be giving a false reading on the actual situation, and 2) a cost/benefit analysis of any program designed to reduce turnover should be made. Consideration must be given also to the impact of the changes necessary to accomplish reduced turnover and if they're paying off.

Dalton, Dan R. and Todor, William D., "Turnover Turned Over: An Expanded and Positive Perspective," *Academy of Management Review*, April 1979, Vol. 4, No. 2, 225–235.

In this article turnover is examined from the viewpoint of a positive phenomenon and is investigated from four perspectives: 1) organizational; 2) economic; 3) sociological; and 4) psychological/social psychological. 1) Organizational—There is evidence that turnover *increases,* not decreases, organizational effectiveness. It is suggested that mobility is a force by which innovation is moved from firm to firm and that immobility is "trained incapacity" or the inability to conceive of or utilize new ideas. Thus it is dysfunctional and reduces organizational effectiveness. 2) Economic—The existence of opportunity knowledge suggests an important implication of turnover for the economy. Given that mobility results in net positive income to migraters, it may be concluded that mobility increases net national product and contributes to long-term growth rate of the economy. Nonmobility in the labor market will result in short-run cost increases to employers in wages and benefits and long-run costs for the community for unemployment compensation and other support programs. 3) Sociological—Society has a stake in both the social and economic advancement of its citizens. One way this growth can be accomplished is through vertical mobility within the organization. 4) Psychological/Social Psychological—Organizations should not deter turnover by employees inflicted with physical manifestations of stress. The health of the individual and the organization are clearly enhanced by withdrawal in these cases. There is evidence that turnover increases organizational effectiveness and innovation, assists development of institutional management and interfirm cooperation, and augments technological change. Also, the costs of reducing turnover may exceed the actual costs of turnover. To view turnover as a strictly positive or negative phenomenon seems somewhat short-sighted. Clearly turnover has both positive and negative aspects for the organization. Several factors to be considered in achieving an appropriate level of turnover are suggested.

THEORETICAL

Lyons, T. F., "Turnover and Absenteeism: A Review of Relationships and Shared Correlates," *Personnel Psychology,* Summer 1972, Vol. 25, No. 2, 271–281.

There has been little attention in the past to the interrelationship of absenteeism and turnover. Three points of view reflect some assumptions that have been made about the relationships of these two behaviors: first, there is a continuum of withdrawal behaviors, progressing from absenteeism to turnover. A second view sees absences, along with accidents, as being forms of withdrawal behavior that are alternatives to turnover. A third view is that the two behaviors, related or not, share common causes. Therefore, the questions being asked are: 1) Are absenteeism and turnover associated? 2) Is there a progression of alienation indicated by absenteeism and followed by turnover? 3) Are these two forms of behavior influenced, determined, or related to the same factors? The author reviews the literature of individual-level studies and group-level studies in this area and arrives at some conclusions.

Pertaining to the first question of whether AB and TO are related, 16 of 29 independent tests of this relationship were significant and positive; one was significant and negative. On the individual level there was unanimous support of the relationship. In reference to the second question: In all 10 samples of individuals the people who eventually left had had significantly higher absenteeism than those who stayed. The last question, whether or not AB and TO were influenced by common factors, found that in 11 samples, 92 variables were related significantly to either TO or AB. Of these 92 variables, both AB and TO were related significantly to only eight, pointing to little support for the notion of common correlates.

Porter, L. W. and Steers, R. M., "Organizational, Work and Personal Factors in Employee Turnover and Absenteeism," *Psychological Bulletin*, 1973, Vol. 80, 151–176.

This article reviews the research on turnover and absenteeism conducted during the 1960's and early 1970's. The authors draw several conclusions from their analysis. First, both forms of withdrawal from an organization seem to be negatively associated with overall satisfaction with the job and the organization. Several facets of an organization and its management are reported to be differentially related to withdrawal; e.g., facets dealing with the total organization, those dealing with the immediate work group, those focusing on the content of the employee's job, and those centered in the employee her/himself. An underlying theme is used to integrate a diverse literature. That theme centers on the importance of whether an organization meets the expectations that employees have for their work experience. Unmet expectations, rather than the absolute level of wages or other rewards, are argued to be the major, general cause of employee withdrawal.

Hawk, Donald L., "Absenteeism and Turnover," *Personnel Journal*, June 1976, Vol. 55, No. 6, 293–303.

This article presents a model illustrating the causes for and the relationships between absenteeism and turnover for the purpose of developing a reduction strategy. The author advocates careful diagnosis of the company's absenteeism/turnover position before formulating any strategy. Where withdrawal is on a continuum ranging from absenteeism to turnover, job dissatisfaction plays a critical role and is influenced by the various factors; i.e., supervisory style (in regard to providing reinforcement and feedback), salary (wage rate and equitable structure) and job design (variety, task identity, autonomy, feedback, significance). Insofar as the most significant causal variables are identified, implementation of the most appropriate and direct solution is facilitated.

Forrest, C. R.; Cummings, L. L. and Johnson, A. C., "Organizational Participation: A Critique and Model," *Academy of Management Review*, October 1977, Vol. 2, No. 4, 586–600.

A critique of the current state of theory and research on employee tardiness, absenteeism, turnover, and job choice is presented. Research and theory reviewed illustrate problems and unresolved issues underlying current knowledge of the determinants of organizational participation. An expanded valence-instrumentality-expectancy model provides the basis for integrating psychological and economic perspectives on organizational participation. Guidelines for future research and conceptual development are provided.

Miller, Howard E.; Katerberg, Ralph and Hulin, Charles L., "Evaluation of the Mobley, Horner, and Hollingsworth Model of Employee Turnover," *Journal of Applied Psychology*, October 1979, Vol. 64, No. 5, 509–517.

The validity of the Mobley, Horner, and Hollingsworth simplified turnover model was investigated in a predictive design with data gathered from two independent military samples. Measures of job satisfaction, intention to search for an alternate job, intention to quit, thoughts of quitting, tenure, age and perceptions of job opportunities were related to reenlistment decisions made within six months of attitude assessment. Data was provided by samples of 235 and 225 National Guard members. Cross-validated results supported a four-construct model. Job satisfaction and career mobility (age, tenure, job opportunities) influenced turnover only through withdrawal cognitions (intentions to quit and to search for a job, thoughts of quitting). Relations among the specific measures fit moderately well with links hypothesized by Mobley, Horner, and Hollingsworth. Overall, the results indicate high predictive validity, moderate internal consistency, and a need for extending the range of variables assessed.

Staw, Barry M., "The Consequences of Turnover," *Journal of Occupational Behavior*, 1980, 1, 253–273.

The goal of this paper is to make the case for a redirection of turnover research, illustrating the reasons for this change and showing the possible shape of new research. Costs and benefits of turnover in organizations are outlined and an attempt is made to specify the conditions under which benefits are likely to be greatest and the costs lowest. Considering costs of turnover, the author covered selection and recruitment costs, training and development costs, operational disruption costs, and costs of demoralization of organizational membership. The author points out that the statement that turnover is costly to an organization should really be translated to an inquiry into the extent to which turnover will prove burdensome to the organization. Positive consequences of turnover covered increased performance, reduction of entrenched conflict, increased mobility and morale, and innovation and adaptation. The author covers research on managerial succession, states the necessity of restoring the balance to the treatment of turnover, and indicates avenues of further research. In proposing an intensive study of turnover's consequences, the author states the study of turnover must stand on its own as more basic research has the potential to illuminate central aspects of organizational functioning and may accomplish this with a rather unified and delimited focus.

Commentary

TURNOVER

Turnover in most organizations is of real concern because of the attending problems it causes—the high cost of training, and its effect on the productivity and efficiency of the organization. It is a consequence which affects the total "health" of an organization.

Absenteeism and turnover are usually considered as the same or similar problem. This is true both in the available research evidence and in actual practice as indicated by the way it is treated in many firms. However, in reviewing the empirical literature, we find that the underlying causes are not always identical.

Frequently found reasons for turnover are dissatisfaction with salary, selection and placement mistakes, defects in training, poor supervision, faulty communication, and poorly handled compensation systems. All these criticisms are focused on problems with the organization or management of the organization. The implication is that in order to solve the turnover problem, one must "look to the organization" to change policies, to modify and adapt to needs as problems arise. Relatively little attention has been given to the self-selection mistakes that many job candidates make as they consider and accept job offers. The reciprocal nature of influences causing turnover has only recently received attention.

Some research suggests that early experiences in an organization affect an individual's later career in that organization. Thus, effective management of the "joining up" process or of initial training is a critical element when new employees come on board. The quality of management's orientation program will affect the cost of obtaining and keeping new personnel and the level of productivity of the organization. Many employees leave an organization because of lack of opportunity to achieve what they expected—and management failed to correct unrealistic expectations due to inadequacy of the company's orientation program. A survey of 419 U.S. and Canadian companies revealed that early career turnover rates are negatively related to starting salaries earned (Stark, 1970). This finding certainly points to a need for more honest recruiting programs so that employee expectations will be understood and an attempt made to meet them. Management can help remove the many "unknowns" for a new employee by careful orientation. Alternatively, candidates considering a job can more accurately assess the fit between their expectations and the rewards likely in a job.

Some studies have been done on specific jobs which emphasize the need for flexibility and matching human needs to job requirements. In a study of high turnover of nurses, it was found that career/family conflicts caused much of the turnover and that job related factors could be changed to accommodate career/home interests—i.e., part-time hours, training male nurses for night shifts, restructuring work to make it more challenging and satisfying, showing appreciation for achievements, and providing opportunity for growth (Saleh, Lee, and Prien, 1965).

A study of turnover in the trucking industry developed a profile for terminators versus nonterminators. The turnover profile was found to be young, more intelligent, dominant, and self-sufficient (York, 1972). A significant relationship between absenteeism and turnover was found in a study of telephone operators. In each period tested, the "leavers" had higher absenteeism records than the "stayers". This data strongly supports the "progression of withdrawal" hypothesis—progressively worsening absenteeism culminating in leaving the organization (Burke & Wilcox, 1972). In a study of salesmen, employees' expressed intent to leave was a more accurate predictor of subsequent turnover than were other job attitudes. Intent, in turn, was closely tied to feelings about the work itself and about the company as a place to work (Kraut, 1975).

Several methods have been presented in the literature as means of reducing turnover. One study advocated taking the following steps:

1. Study past and present effects of turnover on your organization.

2. Compile statistical data on company experience.

3. Outline in detail the company's policies and practices—determine if they unknowingly contribute to absenteeism/turnover.

4. Determine corrective action to be taken.

5. Establish standards.

6. Implement corrective action—to be monitored at regular intervals by personnel department (Clark, 1971).

In a Career Orientation Program consisting of a work preview or job sample of a task representative of the work actually done on the job, it was found that the program can provide accurate information for the formation of employee expectations and was an excellent bridge between the selection process and early training of new employees (Raphael, 1975). Another model was presented illustrating the causes for and relationships between absenteeism and turnover. The purpose of such a causal analysis is the development of a reduction strategy. Careful diagnosis of a company's absenteeism/turnover position was recommended before formulating a strategy. It was found that job dissatisfaction was the main cause of withdrawal and this dissatifaction was attributed to supervisory style, salary, and job design (Hawk, 1976). When causal variables can be identified, implementation of an appropriate solution is made easier.

What conclusions seem to be warranted based on the literature to date? While many of the findings and prescriptions are organizationally specific:

1. There is strong support for the assumption that absenteeism and turnover are related on an individual level.

2. There is considerable support for the progression hypothesis— i.e., the "leavers" have a record of higher absenteeism than the "stayers".

3. There is little support for common correlates of absenteeism and turnover—in a sample test, 92 variables were related to either and only eight to both (Lyons, 1972).

Few models of employee recruitment and turnover have been developed. There are, however, two significant papers which review the research and present integrating and expanded models of various aspects of organization participation (Lyons, 1972; Forrest, Cummings and Johnson, 1977). These papers offer guidelines for future research and conceptual development. One excellent review of the literature covers the current state of theory and research on tardiness, absenteeism, and turnover as well as job choice (Porter and Steers, 1973). These models form an excellent base for further research to help pinpoint the reasons for turnover, the cause and effect relationships involved, and how withdrawal impacts on various systems within the organization.

REFERENCES

Type of Reference	No. of References
Applied	7
Descriptive	10
Integrative	11
Prescriptive	4
Theoretical	6

APPLIED

Williams, J. L., *Operant Learning: Procedures for Changing Behavior*, Monterey, CA: Brooks/Cole Publishing Company, 1973.

In the author's words, . . . "This book gives a concise but detailed account of the theory, experimental research, and recent applications of operant learning. . . . The concepts of operant learning are presented in a logical order. Numerous everyday examples are given of behavioral phenomena and control procedures. . . . A critical review is presented of the recent applications of operant procedures to the fields of mental health and education" (Preface, 1973).

Luthans, F. and Kreitner, R., *Organizational Behavior Modification*, Glenview, IL: Scott, Foresman & Company, 1975.

This and the book by Connellan (also abstracted in this section) are the most applicable, overall references for those seeking step-by-step procedures for applying reinforcement techniques. After reviewing the basic principles of human learning, Luthans and Kreitner develop an applications strategy which they label "Organizational Behavior Modification". This strategy consists of a step-by-step procedure for identifying and solving behavioral problems in organizations. Examples of applications of this strategy are offered in several contexts; e.g., a manufacturing problem, a customer service problem, an overall application in an organizational development program in a food processing company and a military application at the battalion level.

Miller, L. K., *Principles of Everyday Behavior Analysis*, Monterey, CA: Brooks/Cole Publishing Company, 1975.

This is a very practical description of how to conduct and implement a behavior analysis program. The material is learner oriented and is presented in easy-to-follow steps. The book provides ample coverage of most of the typical techniques used in behavior analysis including graphing of behaviors, differential reinforcement, extinction, use of various schedules of reinforcement, stimulus discrimination, use of conditional reinforcers, and the effective use of punishment.

Thompson, T. and Dockens, W. W., III, *Applications of Behavior Modification*, New York: Academic Press, Inc., 1975.

This book is an excellent collection of essays written by experts in the application of behavioral modification techniques to a wide variety of behavioral problems. Included among the problems dealt with are: anxiety, sexual malfunctions, marital dysfunctions, academic performance weaknesses, and alcoholism. Two helpful chapters present guidelines for training nonprofessionals to apply behavioral modification techniques.

Hamner, W. C. and Hamner, E. P., "Behavior Modification on the Bottom Line," *Organizational Dynamics*, Spring 1976, 3–10.

This article is especially valuable because it presents descriptions of several successful implementations of reinforcement concepts and theories in solving human resource problems. The article also includes several "rules" for applying behavioral modification to enhance performance.

Hamner, W. C., "Using Reinforcement Theory in Organizational Settings," in Tosi, H. L. and Hamner, W. C., *Organizational Behavior and Management: A Contingency Approach* (revised edition), Chicago, IL: St. Clair Press, 1977, 388–395.

This selection provides the manager with six rules for use when attempting to enhance performance via the reinforcement approach. The rules are:

1. Don't reward all people the same.

2. Failure to respond has reinforcing consequences.

3. Be sure to tell a person what s/he can do to get reinforced.

4. Be sure to tell a person what s/he is doing wrong.

5. Don't punish in front of others.

6. Make the consequences equal to the behavior.

The article also contains a useful discussion of the ethical dilemmas created by the application of behavioral modification techniques in organizations.

Connellan, T. K., *How to Improve Human Performance: Behaviorism in Business and Industry*, New York: Harper & Row Publishers, 1978.

This and the book by Luthans and Kreitner (also abstracted in this section) are the most applicable, overall references for those interested in direct application of reinforcement techniques to management problems in business. After reviewing basic techniques of performance planning, feedback, and reinforcement, Connellan presents several excellent illustrations of applied behavioral analysis to improve performance in typical business areas (e.g., quality control, sales improvement, warehouse management).

DESCRIPTIVE

Nord, W. R., "Beyond the Teaching Machine: The Neglected Area of Operant Conditioning in the Theory and Practice of Management," *Organizational Behavior and Human Performance*, 1969, Vol. 4, No. 4, 375–401.

This article was one of the first to appear in the organizational behavior literature relating a reinforcement approach to several managerial techniques; e.g., training, job design, compensation, and organizational design. The article describes the Skinnerian approach to the management of human behavior and contrasts that with the position advocated by Douglas McGregor in the now famous Theory Y approach to managerial assumptions and actions. The article represents an excellent early review and a good introduction to the reinforcement in management literature.

Rachlin, H., *Introduction to Modern Behaviorism*, San Francisco: W. H. Freeman & Company, 1970.

This book presents the basic models underlying behaviorism as an approach to understanding and changing behavior. It contrasts operant and classical conditioning as behavior change strategies. Reinforcement and punishment are discussed in terms of the appropriate principles for their application. The book presents an excellent historical perspective on the development of modern behavior analysis.

MacMillan, D. L., *Behavior Modification in Education*, New York: The MacMillan Company, 1973.

This book describes and integrates the principles underlying behavioral modification. It also describes several application of these principles within the educational sector. The highlights of the book are the excellent description of various schedules of reinforcement (Chapter 4) and the material in Chapter 6 on the design, implementation, and evaluation of token economies.

Sherman, A. R., *Behavior Modification: Theory and Practice*, Monterey, CA: Brooks/Cole Publishing Company, 1973.

This book provides a readable, short overview of behavior modification principles and practices. The primary application focus is on psychotherapeutic uses in clinical settings. The second section of the book (Chapters 4 through 11) presents one of the best available descriptions of the techniques used in behavior modification, including operant conditioning and extinction, systematic desensitization, social modeling, expressive training, aversion therapy, and a variety of methods of self control.

Williams, J. L., *Operant Learning: Procedures for Changing Behavior*, Monterey, CA: Brooks/Cole Publishing Company, 1973.

In the authors words, "This book gives a concise but detailed account of the theory, experimental research, and recent applications of operant learning. . . . The concepts of operant learning are presented in a logical order. Numerous everyday examples are given of behavioral phenomena and control procedures. . . . A critical review is presented of the recent applications of operant procedures to the fields of mental health and education" (Preface, 1973).

Reynolds, G. S., *A Primer of Operant Conditioning*, revised edition, Glenview, IL: Scott, Foresman & Company, 1975.

This book presents an account of the theory and principles of operant conditioning. It is particularly useful for those desiring an understanding of the research designs and methodologies used in operant analysis of behavior. Chapter 7 provides one of the most thorough, yet readable, accounts of complex schedules of reinforcement that apply to most complex, everyday behaviors. The book does offer a few guides for application. Its primary focus, however, it on the basic understanding of operant conditioning as a fundamental learning process.

Thompson, T. and Dockens, W. S., III., *Applications of Behavior Modification*, New York: Academic Press, Inc. 1975.

This book is an excellent collection of essays written by experts in the application of behavioral modification techniques to a wide variety of behavioral problems. Included among the problems dealt with are: anxiety, sexual malfunctions, marital dysfunctions, acedemic performance weaknesses, and alcoholism. Two helpful chapters present guidelines for training nonprofessionals to apply behavioral modification techniques.

Hamner, W. C., "Reinforcement Theory" in Tosi, H. L. and Hamner, W. C. (Eds.), *Organizational Behavior and Management: A Contingency Approach*, Chicago, IL: St. Clair Press, 1977, 93–112.

This is an excellent, though brief, summary of the definitions and principles underlying a reinforcement approach to managing human resources. Basic definitions of classical and operant conditioning are offered. Emphasis is given to the importance of arranging the contingencies of reinforcement in designing behavioral change efforts. A useful description of various schedules of reinforcement is provided along with an analysis of the effects usually produced by each of the schedules.

McGhee, W. and Tullar, W., "A Note on Evaluating Behavioral Modification and Behavior Modeling as Industrial Training Techniques," *Personnel Psychology*, 1978, Vol. 31.

The training literature (1967-1976) was searched for reports of scientific evaluations of behavior modification and behavior modeling used in industrial training. No reported scientific evaluations of behavior modification were found. Four reports (1976) of scientific evaluation of behavior modeling used in training managers were found. The reserach designs used in these studies were analyzed for possible threats to internal validity. While the authors note the difficulty of field research in training, enough threats to internal validity were discovered in the designs used to question the reported results of behavior modeling training of managers.

Murphy, G. L. and Remnyi, A. G., "Behavioral Analysis and Organizational Reality: The Need for a Technology of Program Implementation," *Journal of Organizational Behavior Management*, Winter 1979, Vol. 2, No. 2, 121–131.

Behavioral programs have been effectively implemented in numerous individual cases as well as in a number of academic, clinical and research settings where considerable program control was possible. Effective behavioral programs have also been implemented in institutions committed to or organized along lines compatible with the principles of behavioral psychology such as token economies in educational and correctional settings. However, an analysis of the contents of behavioral publications reveals that little systematic attention has been paid to identifying and solving the difficulties experienced by behavioral change agents operating in institutions or organizations which are not organized along behavioral lines. The authors suggest that a lack of organizational support for behavioral programs may be due to the following

problems: unfamiliar language, a lack of support for data-based programming of behavior analysis, and ideological nit-picking about "un-
answerable" philosophical questions, The authors suggest restricting the
use of behavioral jargon, training in effectively overcoming staff objections, controlling staff reinforcers, adopting realistic time perspectives,
choosing target behaviors that avoid an immediate win-lose situation,
and attending to the literature on effective leadership behavior as methods for dealing with implementation problems. The authors also suggest
that need for extensive research by behavior analysis in this area of program implementation.

INTEGRATIVE

Nord, W. R., "Beyond the Teaching Machine: The Neglected Area of Op-
    erant Conditioning in the Theory and Practice of Management,"
    Organizational Behavior and Human Performance, 1969, Vol. 4,
    No. 4, 375–401.

This article was one of the first to appear in the organizational behavior
literature relating a reinforcement approach to several managerial techniques; e.g., training, job design, compensation, and organizational design. The article describes the Skinnerian approach to the management
of human behavior and contrasts that with the position advocated by
Douglas MacGregor in the now famous Theory Y approach to managerial assumptions and actions. The article represents an excellent early
review and a good introduction to the reinforcement in management literature.

Jablonsky, S. F. and DeVries, D. L., "Operant Conditioning Principles
    Extrapolated to the Theory of Management," *Organizational Be-
    havior and Human Performance*, 1972, Vol. 7, 340–358.

This is a theoretical article extending the Nord (1969) paper also abstracted in this section. These authors describe the implications of viewing the behavior of an employee as determined by the reinforcement
contingencies applied to that individual and by that individual's cognitive assessment of these contingencies. Three primary characteristics of
these contingencies are given emphasis: the effects of positive versus
negative reinforcement, schedules of reinforcement, and the immediacy
of reinforcement.

MacMillan, D. L., *Behavior Modification in Education*, New York: The
    MacMillan Company, 1973.

This book describes and integrates the principles underlying behavior
modification. It also describes several applications of these principles
within the educational sector. The highlights of the book are the excel-

lent descriptions of various schedules of reinforcement (Chapter 4) and the material in Chapter 6 on the design, implementation and evaluation of token economies.

Cummings, L. L.; Behling, O. C.; Luthans, F.; Nord, W. R. and Mitchell, T. R., "Reinforcement Analysis in Management: Concepts, Issues and Controversies: A Symposium," *Organization and Administrative Sciences*, Winter (1975-76), Vol. 6, No. 4, 41–72.

This is a report of a symposium within which the papers covered a broad range of issues relevant to reinforcement in management. These issues include:

1. A review of the types of theoretical orientations presently guiding reinforcement analyses and applications (the Behling and Mitchell papers).

2. Keys to successful attempts at employee and organizational development using a reinforcement perspective (the Luthans paper).

3. Diagnosis and discussion of methodological, epistemological, and ethical issues involved in adopting a reinforcement analysis (the Nord and Mitchell papers).

Luthans, F. and Kreitner, R., *Organizational Behavior Modification*, Glenview, IL: Scott, Foresman & Company, 1975.

This and the book by Connellan (also abstracted in this section) are the most applicable, overall references for those seeking step-by-step procedures for applying reinforcement techniques. After reviewing the basic principles of human learning, Luthans and Kreitner develop an applications strategy which they label "Organizational Behavior Modification". This strategy consists of a step-by-step procedure for identifying and solving behavioral problems in organizations. Examples of applications of this strategy are offered in several contexts; e.g., a manufacturing problem, a customer service problem, an overall application in an organizational development program in a food-processing company, and a military application at the battalion level.

Mawhinney, T. C., "Operant Terms and Concepts in the Description of Individual Work Behavior: Some Problems of Interpretation, Application, and Evaluation," *Journal of Applied Psychology*, 1975, Vol. 60, 704–712.

This will be of use to those concerned with the conduct and utilization of research utilizing the operant paradigm. It presents key issues and problems in conducting and interpreting such research. For those not familiar with the operant paradigm, it presents an excellent discussion of the conditions necessary for the proper interpretation and application of results produced by behavior analysts of the operant persuasion.

Hamner, W. C. and Hamner, E. P., "Behavior Modification on the Bottom Line," *Organizational Dynamics*, Spring 1976, 3–10.

This article is especially valuable because it presents descriptions of several successful implementations of reinforcement concepts and theories in solving human resource problems. The article also includes several "rules" for applying behavioral modification to enhance performance.

Hamner, W. C., "Reinforcement Theory," in Tosi, H. L. and Hamner, W. C. (Eds.), *Organizational Behavior and Management: A Contingency Approach*, Chicago, IL: St. Clair Press, 1977, 93–112.

This is an excellent, though brief, summary of the definitions and principles underlying a reinforcement approach to managing human resources. Basic definitions of classical and operant conditioning are offered. Emphasis is given to the importance of arranging the contingencies of reinforcement in designing behavioral change efforts. A useful description of various schedules of reinforcement is provided along with an analysis of the effects usually produced by each of the schedules.

Babb, H. W. and Kopp, D. G., "Applications of Behavior Modification in Organizations: A Review and Critique," *Academy of Management Review*, 1978, Vol. 3, No. 2, 281–292.

The authors assert that behavior modification has many implications for organizations and note the common application of programmed instruction techniques (which are based on a learning strategy using operant principles). Yet, they argue, the recent surge of suggestions for possible applications (e.g., quality control, improving attendance) may go untested. In their review and critique of past applications, the authors emphasize critical comments in the areas of metaphysics, ethics, theory building and generalization to industrial settings. Areas for extension of behavior modification are then suggested.

Connellan, T. K., *How to Improve Human Performance: Behaviorism in Business and Industry*, New York: Harper & Row Publishers, 1978.

This and the book by Luthans and Kreitner (also abstracted in this section) are the most applicable, overall references for those interested in direct application of reinforcement techniques to management problems in business. After reviewing basic techniques of performance planning, feedback, and reinforcement, Connellan presents several excellent illustrations of applied behavioral analysis to improve performance in typical business areas (e.g., quality control, sales improvement, warehouse management).

Prue, Donald M.; Frederiksen, Lee W. and Bacon, Ansley, "Organizational Behavior Management: An Annotated Bibliography," *Jour-*

nal of Organizational Behavior Management, Summer 1978, Vol. 1, No. 4, 216–257.

The purposes of this bibliography are to take an initial step toward integrating the divergent literature relevant to OBM and to provide a reference source that may prompt continued development of the field. The articles in the bibliography are categorized by general topic areas for ease of reference as follows: 1) *General Discussion*—This section includes articles and books that describe the principles of behavior analysis and how the principles can be applied in organizations 2) *Task Completion*—The literature in this section substantiates both the internal and external validity of OBM and begins to delineate the rudimentary OBM technology for large-scale change 3) *Absenteeism and Tardiness*—This section includes discussion papers, reviews, case studies and experimental investigations of both traditional and OBM research in the area 4) *Management Information Systems/Management By Objectives/Systems Analysis*—This section includes topics appearing more often in the behavioral literature and a number of these articles attempt to clarify the critical issues of management information systems, systems analysis and management-by-objectives by defining the relationships between them 5) *Pay and Incentive Systems*—This topic has received surprisingly little attention in OBM literature, but a number of excellent discussion articles are included here 6) *Performance Assessment*—Issue oriented articles are included covering traditional work on performance assessment/appraisal in business and industrial settings 7) *Training*—Excellent reviews of traditional organizational training as well as training in behavior analysis are included here 8) *Miscellaneous*—This last section collects a group of articles that does not fit easily into a category. Articles here range from theoretical discussions to experimental interventions.

PRESCRIPTIVE

Luthans, F. and Kreitner, R., *Organizational Behavior Modification,* Glenview, IL: Scott, Foresman & Company, 1975.

This and the book by Connellan (also abstracted in this section) are the most applicable, overall references for those seeking step-by-step procedures for applying reinforcement techniques. After reviewing the basic principles of human learning, Luthans and Kreitner develop an applications strategy which they label "Organizational Behavior Modification". This strategy consists of a step-by-step procedure for identifying and solving behavioral problems in organizations. Examples of application of this strategy are offered in several contexts; e.g., a manufacturing problem, a customer service problem, an overall application in an organizational development program in a food-processing company, and a military application at the battalion level.

Miller, L. K., *Principles of Everyday Behavior Analysis*, Monterey, CA: Brooks/Cole Publishing Company, 1975.

This is a very practical description of how to conduct and implement a behavior analysis program. The material is learner oriented and is presented in easy-to-follow steps. The book provides ample coverage of most of the typical techniques used in behavior analysis including graphing of behaviors, differential reinforcement, extinction, use of various schedules of reinforcement, stimulus discrimination, use of conditioned reinforcers, and the effective use of punishment.

Connellan, T. K., *How to Improve Human Performance: Behaviorism in Business and Industry*, New York: Harper & Row Publishers, 1978.

This and the book by Luthans and Kreitner (also abstracted in this section) are the most applicable, overall references for those interested in direct application of reinforcement techniques to management problems in business. After reviewing basic techniques of performance planning, feedback, and reinforcement, Connellan presents several excellent illustrations of applied behavioral analysis to improve performance in typical business areas (e.g., quality control, sales improvement, warehouse management).

Babb, H. W. and Kopp, D. G., "Applications of Behavior Modification in Organizations: A Review and Critique," *Academy of Management Review*, 1978, Vol. 3, No. 2, 281–292.

The authors assert that behavior modification has many implications for organizations and note the common application of programmed instruction techniques (which are based on a learning strategy using operant principles). Yet, they argue, the recent surge of suggestions for possible applications (e.g., quality control, improving attendance) may go untested. In their review and critique of past applications, the authors emphasize critical comments in the areas of metaphysics, ethics, theory building and generalization to industrial settings. Areas for extension of behavior modification are then suggested.

THEORETICAL

Rachlin, H., *Introduction to Modern Behaviorism*, San Francisco: W. H. Freeman & Company, 1970.

This book presents the basic models underlying behaviorism as an approach to understanding and changing behavior. It contrasts operant and classical conditioning as behavior change strategies. Reinforcement and punishment are discussed in terms of the appropriate principles for their application. The book presents an excellent historical perspective on the development of modern behavior analysis.

Jablonsky, S. F. and DeVries, D. L., "Operant Conditioning Principles Extrapolated to the Theory of Management," *Organizational Behavior and Human Performance*, 1972, Vol. 7, 340–358.

This is a theoretical article extending the Nord (1969) paper also abstracted in this section. These authors describe the implications of viewing the behavior of an employee as determined by the reinforcement contingencies applied to that individual and by that individual's cognitive assessment of these contingencies. Three primary characteristics of these contingencies are given emphasis: the effects of positive versus negative reinforcement, schedules of reinforcement, and the immediacy of reinforcement.

Sherman, A. R., *Behavior Modification: Theory and Practice*, Monterey, CA: Brooks/Cole Publishing Company, 1973.

This book provides a readable, short overview of behavior modification principles and practices. The primary application focus is on psychotherapeutic uses in clinical settings. The second section of the book (Chapters 4 through 11) presents one of the best available descriptions of the techniques used in behavior modification including operant conditioning and extinction, systematic desensitization, social modeling, expressive training, aversion therapy, and a variety of methods of self control.

Williams, J. L., *Operant Learning: Procedures for Changing Behavior*, Monterey, CA: Brooks/Cole Publishing Company, 1973.

In the author's words, "This book gives a concise but detailed account of the theory, experimental research, and recent applications of operant learning. . . . The concepts of operant learning are presented in a logical order. Numerous everyday examples are given of behavioral phenomena and control procedures. . . . A critical review is presented of the recent applications of operant procedures to the fields of mental health and education" (Preface, 1973).

Reynolds, G. S., *A Primer of Operant Conditioning*, revised edition, Glenview, IL: Scott, Foresman & Company, 1975.

This book presents an account of the theory and principles of operant conditioning. It is particularly useful for those desiring an understanding of the research designs and methodologies used in operant analysis of behavior. Chapter 7 provides one of the most thorough, yet readable, accounts of complex schedules of reinforcement that apply to most complex, everyday behaviors. The book does offer a few guides for application. Its primary focus, however, is on the basic understanding of operant conditioning as a fundamental learning process.

Cummings, L. L.; Behling, O. C.; Luthans, F.; Nord, W. R. and Mitchell, T. R., "Reinforcement Analysis in Management: Concepts, Issues and Controversies: A Symposium," *Organization and Administrative Sciences*, Winter (1975-76), Vol. 6, No, 4, 41–72.

This is a report of a symposium within which the papers covered a broad range of issues relevant to reinforcement in management. These issues include:

1. A review of the types of theoretical orientations presently guiding reinforcement analyses and applications (the Behling and Mitchell papers).

2. Keys to successful attempts at employee and organizational development using a reinforcement perspective (the Luthans paper).

3. Diagnosis and discussion of methodological, epistemological, and ethical issues involved in adopting a reinforcement analysis (the Nord and Mitchell papers).

Commentary

OVERVIEW ARTICLES

This section does not contain a commentary since each of the sources abstracted within this section are, in themselves, summaries and commentaries on the literature of the field.

SUMMARY

Independent Variables

A major part of the research abstracted in this book covering the independent variables is either empirical or prescriptive in nature. However, in many of the topical areas the prescriptions offered are not systematically or even directly drawn from the evidence available. In some cases, this is due to the absence of adequate evidence; in others it is due to the lack of professionalism and careful scholarship by those prescribing. Notably lacking, relative to empirical and prescriptive papers, are those offering theoretical and, to a lesser extent, careful integrative contributions. Thus, management's role of administering the independent variables to achieve organizational productivity and human satisfaction becomes a risky venture. Clearly, the literature is not yet developed sufficiently to warrant a proven collection of technologies for management. Yet, in the case of most of the independent variables, the available knowledge presented in this book can (and has in some cases) lead to more effective human resource management.

There is an interrelatedness among these variables which reflects the general organizational climate of a specific organization and each has been applied with varying degrees of managerial skill and knowledge and with varied success. The research here offers assistance to management in solving some of its most crucial problems but, admittedly, with a certain amount of uncertainty in areas that have not been fully investigated.

We will now summarize the findings by indicating what types of themes have appeared most and least frequently in the literature on each independent variable. What variables do we know the most about? The least? Are there trends toward practicality and empirically based prescriptions in any of the areas? Are there movements toward emphasizing some areas and away from attention to others? What are the most fruitful variables, all things considered, for managerial action?

It is clear that the amount of literature available is unevenly distributed across the 17 topics reviewed (11 independent variables and six dependent variables). This is evident from Tables 1 and 2 which follow.

TABLE 1 **Numbers of Articles and Total Citations Across Independent Variables**

Topic	No. of Articles	No. of Citations
Feedback	49	89
Goals	45	68
Interaction	30	39
Money	77	93
Praise	6	6
Productivity:		
Concepts and Measurement	26	29
Punishment	14	14
Schedules and Expectancy	28	42
Task Design	45	62
Time Off Work	2	2
Work Scheduling	18	20
TOTALS	340	464

It is clear from the matrix entitled *Overview of References Abstracted by Topic, Category and Source* that the literature available on each topic is unevenly distributed across the themes. This matrix is presented on the following pages.

FEEDBACK

APPLIED

1. *MPQ,* '70, 9, 2, 26–32
2. *BH,* '77, 20, 3, 36–45
3. *JAP,* '77, 62, 4, 363–68
4. *PJ,* '77, 56, 10, 512–15
5. *JOBM,* '78, 1, 125–33
6. *JOBM,* '78, 1, 134–41
7. *JOBM,* '78, 2, 11–44
8. *JOBM,* '78, 1, 4, 258–66
9. *JOBM,* '79, 2, 2, 113–19
10. *JOBM,* '80, 2, 2, 183–91

DESCRIPTIVE

1. *JAP,* '66, 50, 2, 118–20
2. *PP,* '68, 21, 4, 441–55
3. *OBHP,* '72, 8, 217–29
4. *JOP,* '76, 49, 2, 75–84
5. *AMP,* '76, 70–73
6. *PMS,* '76, 43, 1339–45
7. *JAP,* '77, 62, 4, 363–68
8. *JOBM,* '78, 1, 2, 150–54
9. *JOBM,* '78, 1, 155–63
10. *JOBM,* '78, 1, 2, 142–49
11. *AMJ,* '79, 22, 1, 157–62

EMPIRICAL

1. *JAP,* '64, 48, 4, 263–67
2. *JAP,* '66, 50, 1, 33–34
3. *JAP,* '67, 51, 4, 324–29
4. *PP,* '69, 22, 291–305

5. *JP & SP,* '69, 11, 2, 148–56
6. *JP & SP,* '69, 11, 4, 363–73
7. *JAP,* '69, 53, 3, 224–26
8. *OBHP,* '72, 8, 44–57
9. *JAP,* '72, 56, 6, 514–16
10. *OBHP,* '72, 8, 340–46
11. *PPM,* '74, 3, 4, 325–31
12. *OBHP,* '75, 13, 2, 244–56
13. Navy Study, '75
14. *PMS,* '76, 42, 2, 487–90
15. *OBHP,* '76, 16, 2, 388–402
16. *PR,* '76, 39, 2, 568–70
17. *JP & SP,* '76, 34, 5, 809–20
18. *OBHP,* '76, 17, 2, 275–88
19. *PMS,* '76, 43, 1339–45
20. *AMP,* '76, 70–73
21. *OBHP,* '77, 18, 2, 316–28
22. *JOP,* '76, 49, 2, 75–84
23. *JOBM,* '78, 1, 125–33
24. *JAP,* '78, 63, 4, 428–33
25. *JOBM,* '78, 1, 134–41
26. *JOBM,* '78, 2, 1, 1–9
27. *JAP,* '78, 63, 4, 434–45
28. *JOBM,* '78, 1, 110–17
29. *JAP,* '78, 63, 4, 446–50
30. *JOBM,* '78, 2, 11–44
31. *JOBM,* '78, 1, 155–63
32. *AMJ,* '79, 22, 1, 157–62
33. *JAP,* '79, 64, 5, 533–40
34. *AMJ,* '80, 23, 2, 267–86

INTEGRATIVE

1. Univ. of Mich, diss., '73
2. *PPM,* '74, 3, 6, 524–30
3. *OBHP,* '79, 23, 1, 309–38
4. *JAP,* '79, 64, 4, 349–71

PRESCRIPTIVE

1. *PA,* '68, 31, 2, 21–27
2. *P,* '69, 46, 4, 34–43
3. *JMS,* '70, 7, 3, 335–46
4. *HRM,* '72, 11, 4, 2–10
5. *PJ,* '76, 55, 12, 613–15
6. *P,* '76, 53, 3, 10–20
7. *BH,* '77, 20, 3, 36–45
8. *PJ,* '77, 56, 10, 512–15
9. *BH,* '77, 20, 6, 54–58
10. *JOBM,* '78, 1, 125–33
11. *JAP,* '78, 63, 4, 428–33
12. *JOBM,* '78, 1, 134–41
13. *JOBM,* '78, 2, 1, 1–9
14. *JAP,* '78, 63, 4, 434–45
15. *JOBM,* '78, 1, 110–17
16. *JAP,* '78, 63, 4, 446–50
17. *JOBM,* '78, 2, 11–44
18. *JOBM,* '78, 1, 155–63
19. *TPA,* '80, 25, 1, 49–54
20. *PJ,* '80, 59, 3, 216–21

THEORETICAL

1. *S,* '73, 179, 351–56

GOALS

APPLIED

1. *JAP,* '74, 59, 2, 187–91
2. *JAP,* '75, 60, 3, 299–302
3. *JAP,* '76, 61, 3, 319–24

DESCRIPTIVE

1. Univ. of Akron, Wkg Paper, 1–16
2. *JMS,* '73, 10, 2, 141–61
3. *JAP,* '73, 58, 3, 302–7
4. *P,* '73, 50, 1, 21–25
5. *HBR,* '73, 51, 2, 65–74
6. *PJ,* '74, 53, 10, 767–69

7. *OBHP,* '75, 13, 3, 392–403
8. *AMJ,* '76, 19, 1, 6–16
9. *JAP,* '76, 61, 5, 605–12
10. *AMJ,* '77, 20, 2, 282–90
11. *AMJ,* '77, 20, 3, 406–19
12. *AMJ,* '77, 20, 4, 552–63
13. *AMR,* '78, 3, 4, 867–79

EMPIRICAL

1. *JAP,* '66, 50, 1, 60–66
2. *JAP,* '66, 50, 4, 289–91
3. *JAP,* '67, 51, 2, 120–30
4. *JAP,* '67, 51, 3, 274–77

5. *JAP,* '68, 52, 2, 104–21
6. *OBHP,* '69, 4, 35–42
7. *OBHP,* '70, 5, 135–58
8. *OBHP,* '73, 10, 175–83
9. *OBHP,* '74, 12, 2, 217–29
10. *PJ,* '74, 53, 6, 423–27
11. *JAP,* '76, 61, 1, 48–57
12. *AMJ,* '76, 19, 1, 6–16
13. *JAP,* '76, 61, 2, 166–71
14. *OBHP,* '76, 15, 2, 268–77
15. *JAP,* '76, 61, 3, 319–24
16. *JAP,* '76, 61, 5, 605–12
17. *JAP,* '76, 61, 5, 613–21
18. *OBHP,* '76, 17, 2, 328–50
19. *AMJ,* '77, 20, 3, 406–19
20. *JAP,* '77, 62, 5, 624–27

GOALS (continued)

21. *JAP*, '77, 62, 6, 665–73
22. *AMJ*, '77, 20, 4, 552–63
23. *JAP*, '78, 63, 4, 428–33
24. *JAP*, '78, 63, 2, 163–71
25. *JAP*, '78, 63, 4, 446–50
26. *JAP*, '78, 63, 1, 29–39
27. *PP*, '78, 31, 2, 305–323
28. *AMJ*, '79, 22, 1, 163–68
29. *JAP*, 79, 64, 2, 151–56
30. *JAP*, '79, 64, 3, 291–98
31. *AMJ*, '80, 23, 3, 561–66

INTEGRATIVE

1. *T & DJ*, '68, 22, 11, 2–9

2. *AMR*, '78, 3, 3, 594–601
3. *AMR*, '78, 3, 3, 505–14
4. *AMR*, '78, 3, 4, 867–79
5. *AMR*, '79, 4, 1, 75–86

PRESCRIPTIVE

1. *PJ*, '70, 15, 3, 29–33
2. *IM*, '73, 15, 1, 1–3
3. *BH*, '75, 18, 1, 45–52
4. *JAP*, '78, 63, 4, 428–33
5. *AMR*, '78, 3, 3, 594–601
6. *JAP*, '78, 63, 4, 446–50
7. *JAP*, '78, 63, 1, 29–39
8. *TPA*, '79, 24, 5, 51–61
9. *PJ*, '80, 59, 5, 368–72, 402

THEORETICAL

1. *CMR*, '69, 11, 3, 81–88
2. *AMJ*, '77, 20, 2, 282–90
3. *AMR*, '78, 3, 3, 505–14
4. *AMR*, '79, 4, 1, 75–86
5. *AMR*, '79, 4, 2, 193–201
6. *TPA*, '79, 24, 5, 65–68
7. *AMR*, '79, 4, 3, 433–38

INTERACTION

APPLIED

1. *PP*, '76, 24, 2, 329–35
2. *PP*, '76, 29, 2, 337–43
3. *PP*, '76, 29, 2, 345–49
4. *PP*, '76, 29, 2, 351–59

DESCRIPTIVE

1. *OBHP*, '69, 4, 284–98
2. *JAP*, '69, 53, 6, 460–66
3. *CMR*, '71, 13, 4, 37–42
4. *JAP*, '74, 59, 2, 172–78
5. *OBHP*, '74, 11, 355–67
6. *OBHP*, '75, 13, 17–30
7. *PP*, '76, 24, 2, 329–35
8. *PP*, '76, 29, 2, 337–43
9. *PP*, '76, 29, 2, 345–49
10. *PP*, '76, 29, 2, 351–59
11. *AMP*, '77, 363–67

EMPIRICAL

1. *OBHP*, '70, 5, 33–67
2. *OBHP*, '76, 15, 1, 66–68
3. *OBHP*, '76, 16, 2, 350–65
4. *PP*, '76, 24, 2, 329–35
5. *PP*, '76, 29, 2, 337–43
6. *PP*, '76, 29, 2, 351–59
7. *AMJ*, '76, 19, 4, 619–27
8. *AMP*, '76, 114–17
9. *JAP*, '77, 61, 4, 433–40
10. *AMP*, '77, 91–96
11. *OBHP*, '79, 23, 2, 163–81
12. *JAP*, '79, 64, 5, 526–32
13. *OBHP*, '80, 25, 1, 123–38

INTEGRATIVE

1. *PP*, '67, 20, 4, 461–95
2. *AMR*, '78, 3, 2, 338–47

PRESCRIPTIVE

1. *T & DJ*, '70, 24, 1, 36–38
2. *MR*, '72, 61, 10, 28–32, 41–42
3. *PA*, '73, 2, 2, 113–17
4. *PPM*, '74, 3, 1, 70–82
5. *TPA*, '78, 23, 7, 27–28

THEORETICAL

1. *OBHP*, '70, 5, 277–98
2. *OBHP*, '74, 12, 1, 62–82
3. *AMR*, '77, 2, 3, 398–411
4. *AMR*, '78, 3, 2, 338–47

Independent Variables

MONEY

APPLIED

1. *JAP*, '59, 43, 6, 417–20
2. *PJ*, '68, 47, 2, 119–20
3. *JAP*, '70, 54, 6, 549–51
4. *JAP*, '71, 55, 3, 182–86
5. *PPR*, '72, 33, 1, 21–24
6. *PJ*, '73, 52, 5, 387–92
7. *HBR*, '74, 52, 4, 30–48
8. *PJ*, '76, 55, 9, 460–63

DESCRIPTIVE

1. *JAP*, '64, 48, 1, 7–12
2. *JAP*, '68, 52, 5, 343–47
3. *IM*, '69, 11, 5, 13–15
4. *PJ*, '70, 49, 9, 726–31
5. *HBR*, '72, 50, 3, 58–66
6. *PPM*, '74, 3, 1, 4–9
7. *BH*, '74, 17, 2, 79–86
8. *P*, '74, 51, 6, 45–49
9. *JAP*, '77, 62, 1, 9–15
10. *TPA*, '77, 22, 7, 26–29
11. *TPA*, '79, 24, 5, 37–40
12. *TPA*, '80, 25, 5, 45–57

EMPIRICAL

1. *JAP*, '59, 43, 6, 417–20
2. *JAP*, '64, 48, 1, 7–12
3. *JAP*, '64, 48, 4, 201–10
4. *PMS*, '65, 20, 1193–99
5. *PMS*, '65, 20, 259–69
6. *PMS*, '65, 21, 907–13
7. *JAPM*, '67, 51, 4
   Whole No. 636, 1–24
8. *JAP*, '67, 51, 5, 411–16
9. *JP&SP*, '68, 10, 3, 306–13

10. *JAP*, '70, 54, 6, 549–51
11. *OBHP*, '72, 8, 217–20
12. *OBHP*, '76, 16, 1, 114–42
13. *JP&SP*, '76, 34, 6, 1235–44
14. *OBHP*, '76, 16, 2, 294–307
15. *AMJ*, '76, 19, 3, 482–88
16. *OBHP*, '76, 17, 1, 159–70
17. *JAP*, '76, 61, 6, 693–700
18. *JP&SP*, '76, 34, 2, 179–90
19. *AMJ*, '76, 19, 4, 537–46
20. *AMP*, '76, 270–72
21. *AMJ*, '77, 20, 1, 34–41
22. *OBHP*, '77, 20, 1, 31–53
23. *JAP*, '78, 63, 1, 29–39

INTEGRATIVE

1. *P*, '60, 37, 4, 20–27
2. *P*, '64, 41, 1, 8–21
3. *P*, '65, 42, 2, 57–65
4. *CMR*, '66, 8, 4, 11–20
5. *OBHP*, '67, 2, 175–216
6. *PA*, '67, 30, 2, 23–39
7. *MLR*, '69, 92, 7, 49–53
8. *JMS*, '70, 7, 3, 310–34
9. *IM*, '71, 13, 6, 7–10
10. *PA*, '72, 35, 1, 31–41
11. *HBR*, '72, 50, 3, 58–66
12. *HRM*, '73, 12, 2, 28–32
13. *PPM*, '74, 3, 1, 29–34
14. *TPA*, '78, 23, 1, 51–57
15. *AMR*, '78, 3, 3, 505–14
16. *AMR*, '79, 4, 1, 75–86
17. *TPA*, '80, 25, 5, 59–64
18. *AMR*, '80, 5, 3, 455–67

PRESCRIPTIVE

1. *P*, '64, 41, 2, 45–50
2. *HBR*, '69, 47, 5, 109–18
3. *MPQ*, '69, 8, 3, 35–38
4. *PJ*, '70, 49, 11, 907–17
5. *CBR*, '70, 7, 1, 35–89
6. *PA*, '70, 33, 1, 52–57
7. *MPQ*, '71, 10, 1, 2–5
8. *BH*, '72, 15, 2, 15–23
9. *PJ*, '72, 51, 5, 313–16
10. *HBR*, '72, 50, 4, 117–24
11. *CBR*, '72, 9, 11, 17–21
12. *BH*, '73, 16, 2, 37–42
13. *PPM*, '74, 3, 1, 4–9
14. *PJ*, '74, 53, 7, 513–17
15. *P*, '74, 51, 6, 45–49
16. *PJ*, '74, 53, 12, 890–93
17. *HBR*, '75, 53, 2, 104–12
18. *PJ*, '75, 54, 5, 275–81
19. *PJ*, '76, 55, 9, 460–63
20. *JAP*, '78, 63, 1, 29–39
21. *TPA*, '78, 23, 5, 32–36
22. *TPA*, '78, 23, 5, 42–48
23. *P*, 'July–Aug '79, 59–63
24. *PJ*, '79, 58, 9, 597–99
25. *P*, Sept–Oct '79, 23–31
26. *P*, Jan–Feb '80, 32–37

THEORETICAL

1. *JAP*, '64, 48, 4, 201–10
2. *JAPM*, '67, 51, 4, Whole No. 636, 1–24
3. *BJIR*, '69, 7, 385–97
4. *OBHP*, '72, 8, 217–20
5. *AMR*, '78, 3, 3, 505–14
6. *AMR*, '79, 4, 1, 75–86

Independent Variables

PRAISE

APPLIED

1. *JOBM*, '80, 2, 3, 213–27

EMPIRICAL

1. *PMS*, '76, 42, 1283–86

PRESCRIPTIVE

1. *P*, '66, 43, 5, 40–49
2. *IM*, '73, 32–35
3. *BH*, '76, 19, 5, 76–81
4. *SM*, '76, 21, 10, 2–9

PRODUCTIVITY: CONCEPTS AND MEASUREMENT

DESCRIPTIVE

1. *JAP*, '46, 30, 3, 199–211
2. *JAP*, '47, 31, 5, 484–89
3. *JAP*, '58, 42, 3, 182–86
4. *JAP*, '61, 45, 1, 50–54
5. *HRM*, '72, 11, 2, 22–26
6. *PP*, '74, 27, 245–55
7. *P*, '74, 51, 2, 38–41
8. *JOBM*, '78, 1, 3, 164–78
9. *TPA*, '79, 24, 7, 65–76
10. *TPA*, '79, 24, 8, 59–68

EMPIRICAL

1. *JAP*, '61, 45, 1, 50–54
2. *ES*, Fall '68, 96–104
3. *BH*, '74, 17, 6, 35–44

INTEGRATIVE

1. *PPM*, '74, 3, 5, 425–30
2. *PJ*, '76, 55, 10, 513–25
3. *VNR*, '78, 1–192

PRESCRIPTIVE

1. *P*, '67, 44, 4, 68–75
2. *P*, '71, 48, 2, 8–16

3. *BH*, '72, 15, 4, 43–48
4. *SMR*, '73, 15, 1, 1–9
5. *PJ*, '74, 53, 7, 498–506
6. *HBR*, '74, 52, 6, 91–98
7. *HBR*, '74, 52, 6, 99–104
8. *PPM*, '74, 3, 5, 425–30
9. *HBR*, '75, 53, 3, 74–80
10. *PJ*, '76, 55, 10, 513–25
11. *TPA*, '79, 24, 6, 55–62
12. *TPA*, '79, 24, 9, 51–60

THEORETICAL

1. *PJ*, '75, 54, 2, 114–17

PUNISHMENT

DESCRIPTIVE

1. *TPA*, '79, 24, 3, 35–38
2. *JOBM*, '79, 2, 103–11

EMPIRICAL

1. *JP&SP*, '69, 12, 2, 164–69
2. *JAP*, '69, 53, 2, 118–23

INTEGRATIVE

1. *PJ*, '65, 44, 4, 189–92
2. *PJ*, '69, 48, 7, 525–29
3. *AMR*, '80, 5, 1, 123–32
4. *AMR*, '80, 5, 1, 133–38

PRESCRIPTIVE

1. *PJ*, '65, 44, 9, 475–79
2. *PPM*, '73, 2, 3, 156–61
3. *TPA*, '78, 23, 3, 22–24
4. *TPA*, '78, 23, 10, 49–54
5. *TPA*, '79, 24, 1, 57–61
6. *PJ*, '79, 58, 10, 698–702

SCHEDULES AND EXPECTANCY

APPLIED

1. *P*, '73, 50, 3, 65–69
2. *OBHP*, '77, 19, 2, 337–52
3. *JAP*, '77, 62, 4, 369–75

DESCRIPTIVE

1. *OBHP*, '77, 19, 2, 337–52
2. *PJ*, '77, 56, 9, 451–64
3. *JAP*, '78, 63, 4, 518–21
4. *JOBM*, '78, 1, 3, 196–205

EMPIRICAL

1. *JP&SP*, '69, 11, 2, 157–64
2. *PR*, '71, 28, 771–76
3. Ohio State Univ, '74
4. *OBHP*, '76, 15, 2, 355–406
5. *OBHP*, '76, 16, 2, 205–30
6. *PR*, '76, 39, 1, 159–65
7. *JP&SP*, '76, 34, 5, 1024–33
8. *AMP*, '76, 74–78
9. *PP*, '76, 29, 2, 221–31

10. *JAP*, '77, 62, 4, 369–75
11. *OBHP*, '77, 19, 2, 337–52
12. Ind. Univ. unpub paper
13. *OBHP*, '78, 21, 3, 273–88
14. *PP*, '78, 31, 47
15. *JOBM*, '78, 1, 110–17
16. *JAP*, '78, 63, 4, 518–21

INTEGRATIVE

1. *PB*, '66, 65, 4, 206–20
2. *AMR*, '77, 2, 4, 543–51

SCHEDULES AND EXPECTANCY (continued)

3. Ohio State Univ, wkg paper
4. Wash Univ, unpub paper
5. *OBHP*, '78, 21, 3, 273–88

PRESCRIPTIVE

1. *P*, Sept-Oct '69, 51–57

2. *HRM*, '72, 11, 4, 11–17
3. *BH*, '73, 16, 3, 67–72
4. *PP*, '74, 27, 569–79
5. *BH*, '75, 18, 2, 57–66
6. Univ of CA, unpub paper
7. Wash Univ, unpub paper
8. *PJ*, '77, 56, 9, 451–64
9. *TPA*, '80, 25, 4, 67–75

THEORETICAL

1. *BH*, '73, 16, 3, 67–72
2. *AMJ*, '73, 16, 3, 373–88
3. *AMP*, '73, 383–89
4. *AMP*, '76, 74–78
5. *AMR*, '77, 2, 4, 543–51

TASK DESIGN

APPLIED

1. *PA*, '68, 31, 4, 8–21
2. *PPM*, '75, 4, 1, 49–54
3. *T&DJ*, '76, 30, 8, 3–7
4. *HBR*, '77, 55, 4, 102–13
5. *PR*, '77, 40, 1 283–90

DESCRIPTIVE

1. *PJ*, '75, 54, 4, 232–48
2. *MR*, '77, 66, 2, 21–26
3. *AMJ*, '77, 20, 1, 42–65
4. *AMR*, '78, 3, 4, 867–79
5. *OBHP*, '78, 21, 289–304
6. *OBHP*, '79, 23, 163–81

EMPIRICAL

1. *JAP*, '68, 52, 5, 386–93
2. *OBHP*, '74, 12, 2, 264–73
3. *AMJ*, '76, 61, 4, 455–62
4. *OBHP*, '76, 16, 2, 250–79
5. *JAP*, '76, 61, 6, 721–27
6. *OBHP*, '76, 17, 2, 211–30
7. *AMJ*, '77, 20, 1, 42–65
8. *OBHP*, '77, 19, 1, 18–42

9. *AMP*, '77, 57–61
10. *PR*, '77, 40, 1, 283–90
11. *MR*, '77, 66, 2, 21–26
12. *OBHP*, '78, 21, 289–304
13. *OBHP*, '78, 22, 350–65
14. *JOBM*, '78, 2, 1, 1–9
15. *OBHP*, '79, 23, 163–81
16. *JAP*, '76, 61, 4, 379–94
17. *PP*, '79, 32, 1, 121–37
18. *PP*, '79, 33, 1, 61–75
19. *JVB*, '79, 14, 3, 329–40
20. *OBHP*, '79, 24, 3, 317–32
21. *OBHP*, '79, 24, 3, 354–81
22. *OBHP*, '80, 25, 1, 139–59
23. *JVB*, '80, 17, 1, 89–94

INTEGRATIVE

1. *PP*, '69, 22, 415–44
2. *CBR*, '71, 8, 1, 52–56
3. *P*, '72, 49, 3, 8–17
4. *PJ*, '74, 53, 12, 886–89
5. *AMR*, '77, 2, 1, 113–21
6. *AMR*, '77, 2, 4, 645–57
7. *TPA*, '77, 22, 8, 51–61
8. *AMR*, '78, 3, 4, 867–79
9. *PJ*, '79, 58, 8, 527–30, 57–59
10. *PJ*, '80, 59, 6, 488–91

PRESCRIPTIVE

1. *IM*, '72, 14, 3, 8–14
2. *P*, '72, 49, 4, 8–19
3. *P*, '73, 51, 1, 31–39
4. *P*, '74, 51, 6, 18–25
5. *PJ*, '74, 53, 6, 445–49
6. *PPM*, '74, 3, 1, 35–38
7. *HBR*, '75, 53, 1, 74–80
8. *T&DJ*, '76, 30, 8, 3–7
9. *AMR*, '77, 2, 1, 113–21
10. *AM*, '77, 38, 2, 52–58
11. *MR*, '77, 66, 7, 25–38
12. *OBHP*, '77, 19, 1, 18–42
13. *JOBM*, '78, 2, 1, 1–9
14. *PJ*, '80, 59, 8, 645–48

THEORETICAL

1. *P*, '73, 50, 5, 8–18
2. *AMR*, '77, 2, 1, 113–21
3. *AMR*, '77, 2, 4, 645–57
4. *AMR*, '80, 5, 1, 41–48

TIME OFF WORK

DESCRIPTIVE

1. *JAP*, '67, 51, 4, 357–61

PRESCRIPTIVE

1. *PA*, '71, 34, 6, 48–51

Independent Variables

WORK SCHEDULES

APPLIED

1. *PJ*, '72, 31, 6, 446–48
2. *PJ*, '74, 53, 9, 675–78
3. *SM*, '76, 21, 6, 15–19
4. *MLR*, '77, 100, 2, 65–69
5. *PJ*, '77, 56, 2, 82–96
6. *TPA*, '78, 23, 1, 39–41

DESCRIPTIVE

1. *MLR*, '77, 100, 2, 65–69

2. *JAP*, '77, 62, 1, 34–37
3. *PJ*, '77, 56, 2, 82–96
4. *TPA*, '79, 24, 3, 44–62
5. *TPA*, '79, 24, 10, 40–44
6. *TPA*, '79, 24, 10, 35–38
7. *P*, Jan–Feb '80, 21–31
8. *TPA*, '80, 25, 5, 69–74

EMPIRICAL

1. *JAP*, '77, 62, 1, 34–37
2. *JAP*, '77, 62, 4, 463–65

INTEGRATIVE

1. *TPA*, '79, 24, 10, 19–23

PRESCRIPTIVE

1. *P*, '74, 51, 4, 25–35
2. *BH*, '74, 17, 5, 19–26
3. *TPA*, '79, 24, 10, 29–33

Dependent Variables

ABSENTEEISM

APPLIED

1. *PJ*, '68, 47, 2, 119–20
2. *JAP*, '69, 53, 6, 467–71
3. *PJ*, '71, 50, 5, 352–53
4. *OP*, '72, 46, 7–13
5. *JAP*, '74, 59, 6, 694–98
6. *SM*, '76, 21, 2, 22–28
7. *PJ*, '76, 55, 8, 390–92
8. *HRM*, '76, 15, 3, 11–18
9. *JOBM*, '77, 1, 1, 89–98
10. *JOBM*, '78, 1, 2, 110–17

DESCRIPTIVE

1. *IJIR*, '67, 2, 3, 378–92
2. *AM*, '68, 29, 1, 43–44
3. *BH*, '69, 12, 5, 51–57
4. *PP*, '72, 25, 4, 639–47
5. *JAP*, '76, 61, 6, 738–42

6. *AMP*, '77, 353–57
7. *JOBM*, '77, 1, 1, 1–21
8. *JAP*, '78, 63, 4, 518–21
9. *TPA*, '79, 24, 6, 29–33

EMPIRICAL

1. *BH*, '69, 12, 5, 51–57
2. *PAWM-IRRA*, '75, 41–46
3. *PJ*, '76, 55, 8, 390–92
4. *OBHP*, '77, 19, 1, 148–61
5. *JAP*, '78, 63, 4, 518–21
6. *JOBM*, '78, 1, 2, 110–17
7. *OBHP*, '79, 24, 1, 29–40
8. *JAP*, '80, 65, 4, 467–73

INTEGRATIVE

1. *PP*, '72, 25, 2, 271–81
2. *TPA*, '80, 25, 9, 87–93

PRESCRIPTIVE

1. *SM*, '67, 12, 11, 20–23
2. *PPM*, '69, 30, 2, 93–96
3. *IJIR*, '70, 6, 1, 69–74
4. *SU*, '70, 32, 8, 3–4
5. *PA*, '70, 33, 6, 37–41
6. *AM*, '71, 32, 3, 64–65
7. *PJ*, '71, 50, 7, 535–39
8. *PJ*, '73, 52, 2, 113–15
9. *PJ*, '73, 52, 5, 367–72
10. *PAWM-IRRA*, '75, 41–46
11. *SM*, '76, 21, 2, 22–28
12. *HRM*, '76, 15, 3, 11–18
13. *TPA*, '80, 25, 9, 77–84

Dependent Variables

DRUGS AND DRINKING

APPLIED

1. *TPA*, '78, 23, 11, 35–42

DESCRIPTIVE

1. *P*, '64, 41, 5, 18–25
2. *CBR*, '69, 6, 2, 27–32

3. *HBR*, '69, 47, 3, 14–18
4. *PPM*, '73, 2, 3, 212–15
5. *PJ*, '77, 22, 6, 50–56
6. *JAP*, '79, 64, 6, 660–68

INTEGRATIVE

1. *P*, '66, 43, 6, 20–27
2. *PJ*, '75, 54, 5, 266–71, 281

PRESCRIPTIVE

1. *MR*, '70, 59, 3, 39–43
2. *P*, '70, 47, 2, 38–43
3. *P*, May-June '79, 56–63

Dependent Variables

PERFORMANCE QUALITY

DESCRIPTIVE

1. Univ of MO, unpub paper
2. *JOBM*, '78, 1, 2, 150–54

EMPIRICAL

1. Univ of MO, unpub paper
2. *JP&SP*, '68, 10, 3, 306–13⁼
3. *AMJ*, '71, 14, 2, 175–93

4. *JAP*, '72, 56, 6, 480–86
5. *AMJ*, '75, 18, 4, 659–79
6. *JOBM*, '78, 1, 110–17

Dependent Variables

SAFETY

DESCRIPTIVE

1. *JOMB*, '78, 2, 1, 11–44
2. *JAP*, '80, 65, 3, 261–70

EMPIRICAL

1. *JAP*, '78, 63, 4, 434–45

PRESCRIPTIVE

1. *JAP*, '78, 63, 4, 434–45

Dependent Variables

SATISFACTION

DESCRIPTIVE

1. *BH*, '74, 17, 3, 43–49
2. *PPM*, '74, 3, 5, 454–61
3. *OBHP*, '74, 12, 3, 315–30
4. *PP*, '74, 27, 581–91
5. *PPM*, '75, 4, 2, 104–9
6. *OBHP*, '75, 13, 2, 257–78

7. *OBHP*, '78, 21, 80–107
8. *JAP*, '80, 65, 3, 299–306

EMPIRICAL

1. *PJ*, '71, 50, 6, 455–59
2. *JAP*, '71, 55, 6, 531–36

3. *BH*, '74, 17, 3, 43–49
4. *PPM*, '74, 3, 5, 454–61
5. *OBHP*, '74, 12, 3, 315–30
6. *PP*, '74, 27, 581–91
7. *OBHP*, '75, 13, 2, 257–78
8. *PPM*, '75, 4, 2, 104–9
9. *OBHP*, '78, 22, 350–65
10. *JVB*, '80, 16, 1, 51–58

Dependent Variables

SATISFACTION (continued)

INTEGRATIVE

1. *JAP*, '80, 65, 3, 364–67

PRESCRIPTIVE

1. *P*, '66, 43, 4, 16–26
2. *PM*, '71, 13, 12, 13–14

THEORETICAL

1. *PPR*, '69, 30, 2, 102–6
2. *CMR*, '71, 13, 4, 43–47
3. *PP*, '71, 24, 3, 501–18

Dependent Variables

TURNOVER

DESCRIPTIVE

1. *PA*, '65, 28, 1, 25–28
2. *CBR*, '70, 7, 4, 48–50
3. *PJ*, '72, 51, 6, 449–50
4. *OBHP*, '75, 13, 2, 233–43
5. *TPM*, '79, 24, 5, 43–48

EMPIRICAL

1. *PJ*, '72, 51, 6, 449–50
2. *PP*, '72, 25, 4, 639–47
3. *PP*, '79, 32, 2, 393–97
4. *JAP*, '79, 64, 3, 280–90
5. *JVB*, '79, 15, 1, 78–89

6. *JVB*, '79, 15, 1, 55–67
7. *AMJ*, '80, 23, 3, 567–72

INTEGRATIVE

1. *T&DJ*, '73, 27, 3, 52–54
2. *HBR*, '73, 51, 4, 49–60
3. *AMR*, '77, 2, 4, 586–600

PRESCRIPTIVE

1. *P*, '68, 45, 5, 53–58
2. *PJ*, '69, 48, 10, 799–804
3. *AM*, '71, 32, 3, 64–65
4. *PJ*, '72, 51, 5, 360–63

5. *CMR*, '73, 15, 3, 91–99
6. *PJ*, '74, 53, 9, 702
7. *PJ*, '75, 54, 2, 97–98
8. *PJ*, '76, 55, 6, 293–303
9. *P*, Nov-Dec '79, 42–52
10. *AMR*, '79, 4, 2, 225–35

THEORETICAL

1. *PP*, '72, 25, 2, 271–81
2. *PB*, '73, 80, 151–76
3. *PJ*, '76, 55, 6, 293–303
4. *AMR*, '77, 2, 4, 586–600
5. *JAP*, '79, 64, 5, 509–517
6. *JOB*, '80, 1, 253–273

OVERVIEW ARTICLES

APPLIED

1. *BC*, '73
2. *SF*, '75
3. *BC*, '75
4. *AP*, '75
5. *OD*, '76, 3–10
6. *SCP*, '77, 388–95
7. *H&R*, '78

DESCRIPTIVE

1. *OBHP*, '69, 4, 4, 375–401
2. *WHF*, '70
3. *MC*, '73
4. *BC*, '73
5. *BC*, '73
6. *SF*, '75

7. *AP*, '75
8. *SCP*, '77, 93–112
9. *PP*, '78, 31
10. *JOBM*, '79, 22, 121–31

INTEGRATIVE

1. *OBHP*, '69, 4, 4, 375–401
2. *OBHP*, '72, 7, 340–58
3. *MC*, '73
4. *OAS*, '75–76, 6, 4, 41–72
5. *SF*, '75
6. *JAP*, '75, 60, 704–12
7. *OD*, '76, 3–10
8. *SCP*, '77, 93–112
9. *AMR*, '78, 3, 2, 281–92
10. *H&R*, '78
11. *JOBM*, '78, 1, 4, 216–57

PRESCRIPTIVE

1. *SF*, '75
2. *BC*, '75
3. *H&R*, '78
4. *AMR*, '78, 3, 2, 281–92

THEORETICAL

1. *WHF*, '70
2. *OBHP*, '72, 7, 340–58
3. *BC*, '73
4. *BC*, '74
5. *SF*, '75
6. *OAS*, '75–76, 6, 4, 41–72

GLOSSARY

JOURNALS

AM-Administrative Management
AMJ-Academy of Management Journal
AMP-Academy of Management Proceedings
AMR-Academy of Management Review
BH-Business Horizons
BJIR-British Journal of Industrial Relations
BS-Business Studies
CBR-Conference Board Record
CMR-California Management Review
diss-Dissertation
HBR-Harvard Business Review
HRM-Human Resources Management
IJIR-Indian Journal of Industrial Relations
IM-Industrial Management
JAP-Journal of Applied Psychology
JAPM-Journal of Applied Psychology Monograph
JMS-Journal of Management Studies
JOB-Journal of Occupational Behavior
JOBM-Journal of Organizational Behavior Management
JOP-Journal of Occupational Psychology
JP&SP-Journal of Personality and Social Psychology
JVB-Journal of Vocational Behavior
MLR-Monthly Labor Review
MPQ-Management of Personnel Quarterly
MR-Management Review
OAS-Organization and Administrative Sciences
OBHP-Organizational Behavior and Human Performance
OD-Organizational Dynamics
OP-Occupational Psychology
P-Personnel
PA-Personnel Administration
PAWM-IRRA-Proceedings of the 28th Annual Winter Meeting-Industrial
      Relations Research Association
PB-Psychological Bulletin
PJ-Personnel Journal
PMS-Perceptual and Motor Skills
PP-Personnel Psychology
PPM-Public Personnel Management

PPR-Public Personnel Review
PR-Psychological Reports
S-Science
SM-Supervisory Management
SMR-Sloan Management Review
SU-Supervision
T&DJ-Training and Development Journal
TPA-Personnel Administrator
TPM-The Personnel Manager
UP-Unpublished Paper

PUBLISHERS

AP-Academic Press, Inc.
BC-Brooks/Cole Publishing Company
H&R-Harper & Row Publishers
MC-MacMillan Company
SCP-St. Clair Press
SF-Scott, Foresman and Company
VNR-Van Nostrand Reinhold Company
WHF-W. H. Freeman and Company

From a prescriptive perspective it is clear that the most information is available on the use of feedback and money as reinforcement tools for management. In addition, the area of task design is rapidly developing a prescriptive literature with a particularly strong surge of prescriptions emerging in 1977. The rate of appearance of prescriptive articles on feedback also seems to have accelerated in the latter half of the 1970s. On the other hand, prescriptions for the use of money as a reinforcer seem to have slowed down from the early and mid-1970s.

It is also clear that we know the most (combining empirical and theoretical references) about the use of money as a reinforcement technique. However, the most striking recent growth in our knowledge has and continues to occur in the subjects of feedback, goal-setting, and task design. These are the topics to watch most closely for emerging managerial implications and techniques for application. As our knowledge base in these areas continues to expand, we can expect the development and application of even more practical strategies for managerial use.

It is disheartening to note that relatively little attention has been given to developing systematic knowledge as a basis for managerial use of techniques such as time-off-work, work scheduling, praise, and punishment. However, there is currently considerable research being conducted on the first two of these topics and we can expect the development of more descriptive and prescriptive literature.

Also glaring by their absence are theoretical works which serve as a stimulus to extend our research and understanding. This is true for all of our independent variables. If "nothing is so practical as a good theory," then extensive theoretical contributions should be welcomed by executives, as well as scholars, in each of the areas reviewed. It is important to note, however, that the positive benefits of having theory available to guide our work are evident in two areas. First, much of the empirical research on goal-setting (and some on feedback) and some applications for goal-setting techniques have been guided by Locke's theory of the effects of goals on behavior. Second, some of the research on the effects of money on behavior and the associated prescriptions for action have been influenced by theoretical development in expectancy theory and operant conditioning. So, there is reason to hope that *if* additional theoretical contributions were to appear, then research on implementation and actual applications would increase.

The matrix highlights the fact that little attention has been given to the effects on performance (or on other dependent variables) generated by the actual definitions and measurements of productivity used by organizations. It would be valuable to know what effects the assessment of productivity, per se, has on human performance. Can management shift the attention of employees toward more productive outcomes by assessing those outcomes? Can particular components of jobs be emphasized through merely measuring the degree of productivity achieved on those components without changing the reward or feedback systems? Behavioral scientists have only begun to direct their attention toward providing practical answers to such questions.

Dependent Variables

Table 2 presents a summary of the number of articles and citations across the dependent variables reviewed.

TABLE 2   Number of Articles and Total Citations Across Dependent Variables

Topic	No. of Articles	No. of Citations
Absenteeism	33	42
Drug Usage and Alcoholism	12	12
Performance Quality	5	8
Safety	3	4
Satisfaction	17	24
Turnover	29	31
TOTALS	99	121

The matrix entitled *Overview of References Abstracted by Topic, Category and Source* provides an overview of the distribution of the dependent variable literature by theme. It is very clear that absenteeism, turnover, and employee satisfaction have received the most attention in the literature. Very little attention has been given to safety and, interestingly, performance quality utilizing a reinforcement paradigm. Of course, a great deal of literature has appeared on the general topics of performance quantity and quality but extremely little of that has been presented within a reinforcement framework. Clearly, this is an area warranting and deserving our attention. It may well be that considerable advances in applying reinforcement techniques toward performance improvements have been made in practice. However, few have been reported in the literature.

It also seems evident that the once popular question of the relations between dependent variables is beginning to dissipate. Over the last decade, the proportion of studies examining the relationship between satisfaction and performance, absenteeism and turnover has declined. In their place, studies that identify the determinants of the dependent variables are on the increase. In many ways this is a trend to be welcomed. Theoreticians are arguing that the relationship between dependent variables (e.g., performance and satisfaction) are complex, dynamic, and moderated by numerous other constructs. Many scholars have recently argued that a more fruitful route for understanding is to focus upon the nature of the independent variables causing variations in performance, satisfaction, etc. and on the underlying processes. It is also true that practitioners find studies relating specific managerial controllables to one or more dependent variables to be of great value. Even if satisfaction and turnover/absenteeism were simply and consistently related, and they are not, this knowledge would be of little value unless managers understood the determinants of satisfaction and could consistently influence them.

So, several needs and themes for the future can be predicted. First, increasing attention will be given to analyzing performance outcomes through the use of reinforcement models. Second, advances are likely in our understanding of the determinants of employee commitment, attendance, satisfaction, and on-the-job productivity. Third, it is likely that less attention will continue to be given to general, robust theories of the relationships among dependent variables. Fourth, we are likely to witness the gradual development of models and assessments of organizational effectiveness that incorporate multiple dependent variables. This seems to be particularly likely in evaluating our efforts at effective utilization of human resources.